Japanese/Korean Linguistics

Volume 22

Japanese/Korean Linguistics

Volume 22

edited by

Mikio Giriko, Naonori Nagaya,

Akiko Takemura, & Timothy J. Vance

Published for the Stanford Linguistics Association by

CSLI PUBLICATIONS

Center for the Study of Language and Information

Stanford, California

Center for the Study of Language and Information
Leland Stanford Junior University
Printed in the United States
18 17 16 15 14 1 2 3 4 5

Library of Congress Cataloging-in-Publication Data

Conference on Japanese/Korean Linguistics (1st : 1989 : University of Southern California)

Japanese/Korean Linguistics / edited by Hajime Hoji.

Volume 22 / edited by Mikio Griko, Naonori Nagaya, Akikio, Takemura, and Timothy Vance

p. cm.

Includes bibliographical references and index.
ISBN-13: 978-1-57586-751-9(pbk.)

1. Japanese language—Congresses. 2. Korean language—Congresses. 3. Japanese language—Grammar, Comparative—Korean—Congresses. 4. Korean language—Grammar, Comparative—Japanese—Congresses. 5. Linguistics—Congresses. I. Hoji, Hajime. II. Stanford Linguistics Association. III. Center for the Study of Language and Information (U.S.) IV. Title.
PL503.C6 1989
495.6–dc20 90-2550
CIP

∞ The acid-free paper used in this book meets the minimum requirements of the American National Standard for Information Sciences—Permanence of Paper for Printed Library Materials, ANSI Z39.48-1984.

For a list of volumes in this series, along with a cumulative table of contents, please visit

http://cslipublications.stanford.edu/site/JAKO.shtml

CSLI was founded in 1983 by researchers from Stanford University, SRI International, and Xerox PARC to further the research and development of integrated theories of language, information, and computation. CSLI headquarters and CSLI Publications are located on the campus of Stanford University.

CSLI Publications reports new developments in the study of language, information, and computation. Please visit our web site at
http://cslipublications.stanford.edu/
for comments on this and other titles, as well as for changes and corrections by the author and publisher.

Contents

Part IV
Discourse

Part V
Syntax and Semantics

Acknowledgments

The 22nd Japanese/Korean Linguistics Conference was held at the National Institute for Japanese Language and Linguistics (NINJAL) in Tokyo on October 12–14, 2012. The principal organizers were Haruo Kubozono, Prashant Pardeshi, Tim Vance, and John Whitman, and the Director General of NINJAL, Taro Kageyama, was also centrally involved in the planning.

We would also like to express our appreciation the Standing Organizing Committee (Pat Clancy, Hajime Hoji, Shoichi Iwasaki, and Sung-Ock Sohn) for their encouragement and for their enduring commitment to the annual J/K conference.

We received nearly 150 abstracts in response to the call for papers, and we are very much indebted to the many busy scholars around the globe who so generously agreed to serve as reviewers. Their input made it possible to put together an excellent three-day program with twenty-nine oral presentations and nearly forty poster presentations.

We would like to thank all the presenters, especially the invited speakers: Agnes Kang (University of Hong Kong), Michael Kenstowicz (MIT), Satoshi Kinsui (Osaka University), SeungJae Lee (Seoul National University), Masayoshi Shibatani (Rice University), and Akira Watanabe (University of Tokyo). Twenty-three of the papers presented orally are included in this volume.

We are grateful to NINJAL not only for generous financial support but also for the time and energy that many staff members put into ensuring that the conference would run smoothly. In particular, we would like to thank Michiko Hirai, Kyoko Kanzaki, and Junko Yoneda.

Mikio Giriko
Naonori Nagaya
Akiko Takemura
Timothy J. Vance

Part I

Phonology

The Adaptation of Contemporary Japanese Loanwords in Korean

CHIYUKI ITO
Tokyo University of Foreign Studies
MICHAEL KENSTOWICZ
Massachusetts Institute of Technology

In this paper we report some of the results of a study of the adaptation of Japanese loanwords into Korean by Korean speakers living in Japan, focusing on the treatment of the laryngeal features in stops and affricates. Our goal is to first document and then explain the differences between the contemporary adaptation patterns and those found in loans that entered the language in the first half of the last century, a period we refer to as Classical Loans.

Japanese has a binary contrast of voiced vs. voiceless obstruents in both word-initial and intervocalic position. It also distinguishes between an alveolar and alveo-palatal affricate. Korean has the ternary lax–tense–aspirated contrast in its stops and affricates in both initial and medial inter-sonorant positions and a single affricate series whose place of articulation as alveolar vs. alveo-palatal has been a matter of some controversy (H-S. Kim 1999; Kang 2006). Finally, Japanese has a medial singleton–geminate opposition, which Korean lacks. Our discussion proceeds as follows. We first review the laryngeal adaptations in the Classical period and then provide an overview of the correspondences we have found in our Contemporary speakers. Section 3 examines the phonetic basis of the laryngeal adaptations in both

Japanese/Korean Linguistics 22.
Edited by Mikio Giriko, Naonori Nagaya, Akiko Takemura, and Timothy J. Vance.

periods. Section 4 treats the behavior of affricates. Section 5 looks at the correspondences for word-medial position for singletons and section 6 for geminates. Section 7 summarizes our findings.

1. Classical Adaptations

Ito et al. (2006) discuss the correspondences between Japanese and Korean in c. 1,300 loans found in an etymological dictionary (M-S. Kim 1997). (1) illustrates the onset adaptation patterns for obstruents in Classical loanwords.

(1) Word-initial

Japanese	Korean	example			gloss
b	p	baketsu	→	pak*es*ɨ	'bucket'
d	t	daNgo	→	taŋko	'dumpling'
g	k	gaku	→	kak*u	'frame'
t	t	tamago	→	tamako	'egg'
k	k	kagami	→	kakami	'mirror'

Word-medial

Japanese	Korean	example			gloss
b	p	nabe udoN	→	nape utoŋ	'udon type'
d	t	sodenasi	→	sotenasi	'sleeveless shirt'
g	k	maguro	→	makuro	'tuna'
t	t	sita	→	sita	'subordinate'
k	k*	mikaN	→	mik*an	'tangerine'

Transcription: p, t, k = lax, p^h, t^h, k^h = aspirated, p*, t*, k* = tense

Several puzzling asymmetries were identified in how the Japanese binary voiced vs. voiceless contrast in stops and affricates aligns with the Korean ternary lax–tense–aspirated distinction. The finding that is most relevant here was that Japanese voiced and voiceless plosives were both adapted as Korean lax consonants in word-initial position but were distinguished word-medially. Ito et al. (2006) speculated as to the phonetic bases responsible for this difference. The word-initial merger of voiced and voiceless plosives is particularly puzzling since English and French loans into Korean do distinguish these laryngeal categories, albeit differently as primarily lax vs. aspirated and lax vs. tense, respectively.

Shinohara et al. (2011) investigated the Japanese–Korean correspondences experimentally and showed that young Seoul speakers readily distinguish word-initial Japanese voiced vs. voiceless plosives in stimuli of the form [data] vs. [tata], [gata] vs. [kata], etc., as lax vs. aspirated. They also collected a set of c. 150 loanwords taken from restaurant menus, fashion magazines, and tourist maps in which the word-initial voiced and voiceless

> lax correspondences persist. Given the discrepancy between the experimental results and the loanword correspondences, Shinohara et al. (2011) conclude that loanword adaptations, at least in this case, are not based on acoustic/perceptual similarity but rather have been "phonologized" or "conventionalized."

These conflicting results raise a number of questions. Granted that the classical correspondence is no longer based on perception and has become conventionalized, what was it based on originally? Why is there a difference among Japanese, English, and French, which phonologically all have a voiced vs. voiceless contrast? It is now well known that for contemporary younger Seoul speakers F0 in the following vowel is the primary cue for the lax vs. aspirated distinction in word-initial position, while for earlier generations VOT was the major discriminant (M-R. Kim et al. 2002, Silva 2006). Also, Japanese voiceless stops now occupy an intermediate position on the VOT dimension between the short-lag stops of French and Spanish and the longer-lag stops of English and Korean (Riney et al. 2007). Moreover, Japanese initial voiced stops with closure voicing (negative VOT) now have alternative realizations with a short voicing lag for many speakers (Kong et al. 2012, Takada 2012). What role, if any, do these diachronic changes in the phonetic implementation of the voicing contrast in both languages play in the loanword adaptations?

In order to address these (and other) questions, we collected a corpus of data from Korean speakers residing in Japan who use Korean in their daily lives with family and friends but are also fluent in Japanese. For these speakers there is thus extensive Japanese–Korean language contact, which may better replicate the kind of contact situation found in the Classical period (1890–1945), when Japanese words first entered Korean in significant numbers, compared to present-day Korea, where the language contact is more remote, sporadic, and conventionalized.

2. Contemporary Japanese > Korean Loans

We assembled a corpus of 628 Japanese words that we knew to be frequently used by Korean people living in Japan and polled 23 native speakers for the form of these words in their everyday Korean. Our speakers include 8 from Yanbian in China, while the remaining 15 come from South Korea: Seoul (5), Kyungsang (8), Ceolla (1), and Ceju (1). They range in age from their 20s to 40s with most 20–35. Some speakers are recently arrived students studying in Japan, while others are married to Japanese spouses and/or work in Japan and hence reside permanently (although most make periodic visits back to their Korean homeland).

The loanwords in our corpus include 178 Western-origin words (primarily from English) as well as 450 native Japanese items: e.g., /koNbini/ >

/k^h^ompini/ 'convenience store' vs. /koNbu/ > /k^h^ompu/ 'sea tangle'. In many cases a Japanese word is adapted into Korean in multiple ways, resulting in considerable variation. For example, Japanese /ikebukuro/ 'Ikebukuro' is adapted variously as /ik^{h}epuk^{h}uro/, /ik^{h}epuk*uro/, /ik^{h}epuk*ɨro/, /ik*epuk*uro/, and /ik*epuk*ɨro/. Thus, the total number of distinct loanword forms in our data are 2,140 items. The words (almost all nouns) comprise a variety of lexical fields that reflect contemporary culture: cuisine, place-names, personal names, transportation, fashion, technology/products, health, commerce/trends.

In word-initial position, Japanese voiced stops and affricates continue to be mapped to the Korean lax category. However, voiceless stops are now split between lax and aspirated, with a bias in favor of aspirated. Moreover, Japanese voiceless affricates have a substantial number of Korean tense adaptations, while this mapping is essentially never found for stops. The overall proportions for initial position are shown below in (3) along with some examples in (2).

(2) Word-initial

Japanese	Korean	example			gloss
b	p	bjooiN	→	pjo:in	'hospital'
d	t	deNsja	→	tensja	'train'
g	k	gomi	→	komi	'garbage'
p	p^h	pasokoN	→	p^hasok^{h}on	'p.c.'
t	t^h, t	tako	→	t^hak*o, tak*o	'octopus'
k	k^h, k	kinoko	→	k^hinok*o, kinok*o	'mushroom'
ts	c*, c^h	tsubaki	→	c*ɨpak*i, c^hɨpak*i	'Tsubaki'
tʃ	c*, c^h	tʃiNtai	→	c*int*ai, c^hint*ai	'rental'

Word-medial

Japanese	Korean	example			gloss
b	p	waribiki	→	waribik*i	'discount'
d	t	Noda	→	nota	personal name
g	k	onigiri	→	onikiri	'riceball'
p	p*, p^h	suupaa	→	sɨ:p*a:, sɨ:p^ha:	'supermarket'
t	t*, t^h	keetai	→	k^he:t*ai, k^he:t^hai	'cell phone'
k	k*, k^h	eki	→	ek*i, ek^{h}i	'station'
ts	c*, c^h	netsu	→	nec*ɨ, nec^{h}ɨ	'fever'
tʃ	c*, c^h	yatʃiN	→	jac*iŋ, jac^{h}iŋ	'rent'

(3)

Korean/Japanese	Voiceless stop (t, k)	Voiceless affricate
Lax	813 (.27)	25 (.04)
Aspirate	2,174 (.73)	380 (.62)
Tense	11 (.00)	209 (.34)
Totals	2,998	614

There are some refinements we can make in the data for voiceless adaptations. First, there is a statistically significant ($p < .0001$) difference between native Japanese and Western loans. The aspiration adaptation rate for the latter is 90% and approaches the 100% found for loans transmitted directly from English to Korean. This contrasting behavior implies that speakers can distinguish the source of the loan.

(4)

	Native	Western
Lax	745 (.32)	68 (.10)
Aspirate	1,555 (.68)	619 (.90)

Second, in native Japanese words the aspiration rate is higher for /t/ than for /k/ ($p<.0001$).

(5)

	Native	Western
t > Lax	244 (.27)	15 (.09)
t > Aspirate	649 (.73)	156 (.91)
k > Lax	501 (.36)	53 (.10)
k > Aspirate	906 (.64)	463 (.90)

Third, Japanese /ts/ is adapted primarily as Korean tense /c*/ while /tʃ/ is adapted primarily as aspirated /c^h/ in native loans.

(6)

	Native	Western
ts > Lax	2 (.00)	0 (.00)
ts > Aspirate	95 (.38)	37 (.63)
ts > Tense	151 (.62)	22 (.37)
tʃ > Lax	22 (.12)	1 (.01)
tʃ > Aspirate	128 (.69)	120 (.99)
tʃ > Tense	36 (.19)	0 (.00)

Finally, there is a fairly good correlation between the aspiration rate and the age (year of birth) of the speakers, with a higher rate for younger speakers.

(7)

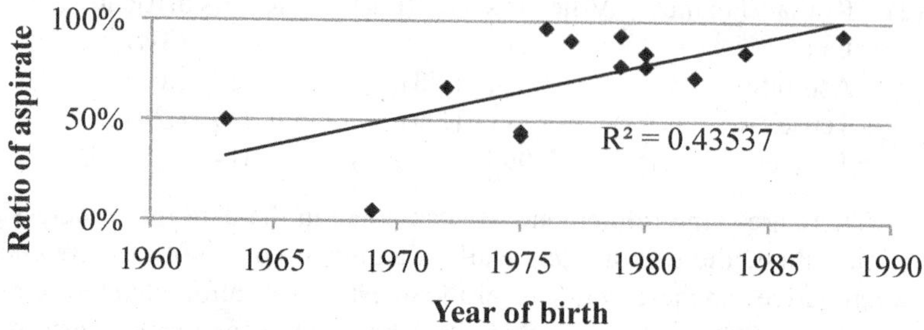

3. Phonetic Correlates: Stops

We believe that the different adaptation strategies for voiceless plosives between the Classical and Contemporary loans are elucidated by taking into account the phonetic correlates of the laryngeal contrasts that are likely to be/have been in play in the two periods. There is good reason to believe that VOT was the primary correlate distinguishing the Korean lax vs. aspirated stops in the Classical period. A survey of publications dated until c. 1980 consistently finds long voicing lags for the aspirated stops, while more recent studies, particularly with Seoul speakers, report substantial overlap between these two categories, with an increase in the VOT values for lax stops and a decrease for aspirated ones, as compared to the earlier period. This diachronic trend has also been noted by Nagato (2003), Utsugi (2009), and M-R. Kim (2012).

(8)

VOT (ms)	Lax	Aspirate	Tense
Lisker and Abramson (1964)	30	103	12
C-W. Kim (1965)	35	93	12
Han and Weitzman (1970)	30	107	7
Hardcastle (1973)	37	113	10
Kagaya (1974)	60	160	15
H-S. Park (1982) (k only)	58	116	26
Lee (2000)	53	64	15
Silva (2006) Seoul	70	75	10
Kang and Guion (2008) young	68	72	17
Kang and Guion (2008) older	70	90	16

Particularly relevant here is Kang and Han's (2012) analysis of a 1935 recording of a teacher and his students from an elite Seoul elementary school reciting short passages from a school reader. They find that VOT is the primary discriminant; and while small F0 differences exist, they are confined to the vocalic region adjacent to the stop release, unlike in contemporary Seoul speech, where F0 differences persist well into the vowel (Jun 1996).

(9)

	VOT (ms)	F0 (Hz, V onset)	F0 (Hz, V mid)
Lax	37	128	123
Aspirate	84	134	126

In sum, the available evidence indicates that during the Classical period the Korean lax vs. aspirated stops were distinguished primarily by VOT and that F0 played a minimal role.

What were the correlates of the Japanese voiced vs. voiceless distinction in the Classical period? The table below shows our measures of a recording made prior to 1938 of speakers reading the syllabary and some elementary vocabulary from a Japanese textbook for foreigners (The Society for Teaching Japanese as a Foreign Language 2003). The data indicate a closure voicing (negative VOT) vs. short lag contrast comparable to Spanish or Dutch. There is also an F0 difference at vowel onset as well as breathy voice after voiceless stops.

(10) Mean and Standard Deviation

Stop	VOT (ms)	F0 (Hz, V onset)	H1−H2 (dB, V onset)
Voiced	−93 (17.6)	162 (2.7)	
Voiceless	17 (5.2)	184 (3.9)	3.3 (2.4)

In the Contemporary period the Japanese voicing contrast in stops has shifted along the VOT dimension, with an increased lag for voiceless stops, while the closure voicing of voiced stops has either decreased in magnitude or developed a short-lag variant.

(11)

VOT (ms)	Voiced	Voiceless
Homma (1981)	−35	25
Sugito (1996)	−58	45
Shimizu (1996)	−80	46
Lee (2000)	−20	38
Riney et al. (2007)		38 (t=20, p=30, k=55)
Takada (2012)	−90 ≈ −60; 0 ≈ 20	
Ogasawara (2011)	−70 ≈ 20	30 ≈ 40
Kong et al. (2012)	10 ≈ 20	10 ≈ 90

We conclude from this survey that during the Classical period the Japanese short-lag voiceless stop was too distant from the Korean long-lag aspirated category to make an aspirated stop an appropriate adaptation. But in the Contemporary period, the Japanese intermediate-lag voiceless stop now approaches the overlapping (Seoul dialect) lax and aspirated categories allowing for a dual adaptation. Viewed in this light, the correlation between speaker age and aspiration rate noted in (7) above now makes sense. The higher aspiration rate reflects the decreased VOT value for /p^h, t^h, k^h/ in younger speakers. This diachronic perspective also sheds light on the sample of adaptations of Japanese /k/ seen in (12) below. Words higher in the table are ones that are more likely to have come into common usage more recently and tend to show a higher aspiration rate, while loans such as *kimono* and *kabuki* presumably entered Korean in the Classical period (if not earlier) and hence are more likely to retain the original lax adaptation.

(12) Aspiration adaptation rate

彼氏 karesi 'boyfriend'	.87
婚活 koNkatsu 'activity to get married'	.79
クロネコ kuroneko 'delivery service'	.73
携帯 keetai 'cell phone'	.71
神戸 Kobe	.58
キリン kiriN 'Kirin beer'	.46
着物 kimono	.40
歌舞伎 kabuki	.28

Another point worth making is that the nature of the Korean speaker's initial contact with Japanese seems to influence their adaptation strategy. The table below shows the treatment of initial voiceless stops for words in our corpus for two Yanbian speakers.

(13)

Native	YB1	YB2	Western	YB1	YB2
Lax	54	11	Lax	8	5
Tense	0	0	Tense	1	0
Aspirate	4	81	Aspirate	17	45

YB1 received formal classroom instruction in Japanese before coming to Japan, while YB2 acquired her Japanese via immersion in Japan. The first speaker follows the conventionalized Classical adaptation style that largely merges voiceless stops as lax, while the second speaker has a strong preference for the aspirated adaptation that more likely indicates a phonetically based mapping. It is notable that both speakers adapt voiceless stops in Western loans primarily as aspirated.

In the Classical period the Japanese short-lag voiceless stops would have matched the Korean tense series in VOT, which has consistently maintained a low value throughout both periods. Why wasn't a Japanese voiceless stop adapted as tense? Here we must be more speculative. Voice quality data such as spectral tilt are not provided in the earliest studies of Korean. To try to get a sense of whether this factor extended back into the Classical period, we made an analysis of a sample of the lax vs. tense stops in the tapes accompanying B-N. Park (1968). Our results show that voice quality at the onset of the following vowel (H1−H2) effectively distinguishes this contrast, with lax stops being quite breathy and tense stops creaky. Moreover, the analysis of the Japanese voiceless stops in (10) found them to be relatively breathy. We therefore tentatively conclude that voice quality made the Korean tense series a poor choice for the adaptation of Japanese initial voiceless stops. More study of this question is clearly warranted, however.

In sum, during the Classical period neither the Korean aspirated nor the tense series were phonetically similar enough to match the Japanese word-initial voiceless stops, leaving the lax series as the best alternative. But during the Contemporary period, the VOT shifts in both languages have brought the aspirated stops close enough to the Japanese voiceless stops to serve as an alternative to the traditional lax adaptation. More conservative speakers continue with the lax adaptation, which has become conventionalized for them and more likely to apply in entrenched vocabulary. (14) summarizes this point.

(14)

Classical Period

$/t_{jpn}/$	Ident-VOT	Ident-VQ
→ t		
t*		*
t^h	*	

Contemporary Period

$/t_{jpn}/$	Ident-VOT	Ident-VQ
→ t	✓	
t*		*
→ t^h	✓	

4. Phonetic Correlates: Affricates

We recall from section 2 that affricates have a substantial number of tense adaptations while stops have none. Another puzzling finding was that Japanese /ts/ exhibits a 62% vs. 38% bias to the Korean tense adaptation, while Japanese /tʃ/ shows an inverse 19% vs. 69% tense-aspirate ratio in native loans. These findings raise two questions. First, why are affricates different from stops, and second, why does the alveolar vs. alveo-palatal difference in Japanese translate into a tense vs. aspirate difference in Korean?

A clue to what we believe underlies the tense adaptation of Japanese /ts/ is the finding of Cho et al. (2002) that Korean tense /s*/ has a higher center of gravity (median energy in the frequency spectrum) than lax /s/. (No data on affricates is provided.) The authors speculate that "the channel between the palate and the tongue necessary for the frication of s* may be smaller and thus produce a higher velocity jet of air, which, on striking the incisors, would produce higher frequency" (Cho et al. 2002:215). Due to its more anterior point of articulation, Japanese /ts/ can be expected to have a higher center of gravity than /tʃ/. As a check, four repetitions each of /tsu/ and /tʃi/ by a male Japanese speaker yielded a mean center of gravity difference of 5683 Hz vs. 4202 Hz when analyzed in Praat (Boersma and Weenink 2012).

Several other researchers have observed differences in the articulation of tense vs. lax stops and affricates that could produce a difference in the average frequency of frication. Shin's (1997) EPG study found that Korean tense stops and affricates have the largest contact area among the three laryngeal types as well as the highest convex tongue shape. An MRI investigation by H-S. Kim et al. (2005) reports that the tense stop /t*/ and affricate /c*/ have maximal tongue blade raising compared to the other two laryngeal categories. Both studies thus suggest that the tense affricates have a more narrow constriction channel that could lead to the higher velocity posited by Cho et al. (2002).

The table in (15) below indicates our results from a small pilot study of one female Seoul speaker. The data are based on four repetitions of 15 words containing the five Korean stops and affricates in three word-initial prevocalic contexts: /a, i, ɨ/. The center of gravity measures were made across the entire VOT period (frication plus aspiration) in Praat with LPC smoothing (16 peaks). Figures in parentheses are standard deviations. The data show a consistently higher center of gravity for the tense segments. Sample spectra of the aspirated vs. tense affricates are also shown in (16).

(15) cons	fric dur (ms)	center of gr.	t-test (Welch)	prob.
c	89 (19)	4008 (1919)	c vs. c*	.0029
c^h	100 (9)	4070 (1635)	c^h vs. c*	.0011
c*	40 (14)	6142 (723)	c vs. c^h	.9328
s	118 (27)	3989 (1683)	s vs. s*	<.0001
s*	124 (13)	8409 (458)		

(16)

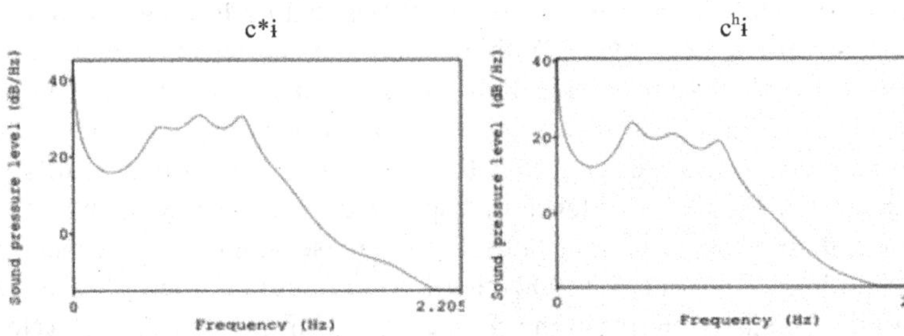

If these data are representative, they suggest that Korean speakers are sensitive to the auditory effects of different frequency distributions in frication and can take this into account when deciding on the appropriate loanword adaptation of an affricate. This hypothesis was anticipated by Kang (2006), who observed that Korean tense /c*/ may be substituted for the otherwise expected aspirated /c^h/ in the adaptation of the alveolar affricates in the loanwords *Mozart* and *Mitsubishi*, while a tense adaptation for the alveo-palatal /tʃ/ would be unnatural. She speculates "the informal use of tense affricates for alveolar affricates of L2 could be interpreted as an interesting way of distinguishing the alveolar input from the palato-alveolar that the lax and aspirate affricates of Korean normally stand for" Kang (2006: 447).

As a final point, we note that since stops lack any substantial frication, the center of gravity effect is not in play, and hence there is no motivation for a tense adaptation for stops.

5. Word-Medial Position: Singletons

For the Classical loans, Ito et al. (2006) found that in intervocalic position Japanese singleton voiced stops mapped to Korean lax while /t/ and /k/ were adapted as Korean lax /t/ and tense /k*/, respectively. The former adaptation makes sense in terms of closure duration and voicing. Relativized to the length of the preceding vowel, Japanese voiced stops (.31) match best to Korean lax (.37) rather than aspirated (.65) and tense (.70). As for the singleton voiceless stops, the relatively long VOT measures reported by Lisker and Abramson (1964) and Kagaya (1974) explain why aspiration is not chosen, just as in word-initial position. The former finds VOT's of 75 ≈ 93 ms and the latter 70 ≈ 140 ms. However, the lax adaptation of /t/ in the face of the tense adaptation of /k/ remains mysterious. Ito et al. (2006) consider various possible explanations; we have nothing to add to their speculations here.

For the Contemporary loans, we find that Japanese voiced stops continue to be adapted as lax, but singleton voiceless stops now vary primarily between tense and aspirated. There is moreover a dialect difference, with more aspirated adaptations for the South Korean speakers compared to our Yanbian consultants. Finally, in both dialects /t/ has a higher aspiration rate than /k/ as well as a greater proportion of lax adaptations. The table below summarizes the medial correspondences in our data.

(17)	Japanese	Lax	Tense	Aspirate
South Korean	t	52 (.09)	169 (.28)	387 (.64)
	k	47 (.02)	1,210 (.54)	1,002 (.44)
Yanbian	t	78 (.25)	132 (.43)	97 (.32)
	k	47 (.04)	845 (.78)	197 (.18)

Phonetic investigations that provide VOT data for both initial and medial position are limited. The table below shows VOT measures for Japanese based on Homma (1981) and Ogasawara (2011). In both studies the medial values are about one-half the initial ones.

(18) Homma	initial	medial	Ogasawara	initial	medial
p	27	7	p	30	11
t	32	16	t	29	13
k	53	24	k	42	23

We are not aware of any recent investigations of the phonetic properties of word-medial Korean stops. The table below shows our VOT measures for two female South Korean speakers based on two repetitions of six different words for each stop consonant.

(19)

	p*	t*	k*	p^h	t^h	k^h
Seoul	10	9	10	16	15	31
Kyungsang	8	11	16	29	27	27

They indicate a much shorter VOT for the aspirated series compared to that reported by Lisker and Abramson (1964) and Kagaya (1974) and suggest the aspirated category has reduced its VOT for younger speakers, just as in word-initial position. There is, however, no merger with the lax series, which is typically voiced in intervocalic position. The shorter medial VOT brings the Korean aspirated category within the range of the Japanese voiceless stops and is presumably responsible for the increased aspiration adaptations compared to the Classical loans. Also, it is well known that velars tend to have longer voicing lags compared to labial and alveolars cross-linguistically. If this asymmetry also holds for word-medial position in Korean then it could help to explain why velars have a smaller rate of aspiration adaptation in both dialects.

Finally, we collected VOT data from our 14 Yanbian consultants. The values for medial position are shown below. They clearly indicate higher values for aspirates than those of our two South Korean speakers. If this represents a true dialect difference, it could help to explain why the word-medial aspiration adaptation rate for Japanese voiceless stops is lower for our Yanbian speakers. Their aspirated stops are more far-removed from the short-lag Japanese compared to the South Korean and hence make poorer correspondents.

(20)

	p*	t*	k*	p^h	t^h	k^h
Yanbian	10	10	22	50	39	59

Also worthy of note in this regard is the finding of Jin (2012) that Yanbian subjects reliably label Japanese word-initial voiced vs. voiceless stops but in word-medial position Japanese /t/ had a significantly higher error rate (38%) compared to /k/ (13%).

6. Word-Medial Position: Geminates

Ito et al. (2006) find only 32 examples of Japanese voiceless geminates in their corpus of Classical loanwords, and all are adapted as Korean tense singletons. The table below summarizes our findings for the adaptation of Japanese voiceless geminate stops in the Contemporary loans.

(21)

		C*	C^h	CC*	t-C*	CC^h	t-C^h	Totals
Native	kk	14	3	43	23	9	9	101
	pp	2	0	5	28	0	1	36
	tt	0	0	23	0	9	0	32
	Totals	16	3	71	51	18	10	169
Western	kk	18	37	24	7	60	9	155
	pp	4	22	3	3	18	6	56
	tt	25	14	63	0	23	0	125
	Totals	47	73	90	10	101	15	336

They evidence greater faithfulness to the Japanese source in that they are overwhelmingly realized as geminates (89%) in native loans as either identical coda-onset sequences (CC) or as a coda alveolar stop-onset (t-C), in which the former often assimilates in place to the following. In Western loans the geminate rate is lower (64%) and presumably indicates competition with a direct adaptation from English, which would lack a geminate in the input source. Conversely, the Western loans show a greater percentage of aspirated adaptations compared to native loans: 56% vs. 18%. On the assumption that the Japanese phonetic realization of a geminate does not differ between a native Japanese word and a Western loan, these striking differences must be explained as competition with the direct mapping of English words into Korean, giving rise to hybrid formations (Kang et al. 2009): cf. native /nat.t*o/ ≈ /nat.t*o:/ < Japanese *nattoo* 'fermented soybeans' vs. /k^hat.t*o/ ≈ /k^hat.t^ho/ ≈ /k^ha.t*o/ < Japanese *katto* 'cut' (cf. direct English > Korean /k^hə.t^hɨ/).

Among the three Korean laryngeal categories, why are tense adaptations favored for Japanese geminates? The primary phonetic correlate of the Japanese geminate stop is closure duration. We reproduce some key references below. While there is considerable variation in the geminate duration across studies, the ratio to the singleton is on average well above twice as long.

(22)

duration (ms)	singleton	geminate	ratio
Homma (1981)	55	160	2.90
Kawahara (2006)	60	129	2.15
Idemaru and Guion (2008)	69	206	2.99

The closure duration of the Korean ternary laryngeal contrast in word-medial stops is surveyed below. The tense consonants are between two and three times as long as the lax ones and fall within the range of the Japanese geminates. Thus, the tense series is the best match for Japanese geminates in terms of the segment-internal cue of closure duration.

(23)

duration (ms)	Lax	Aspirate	Tense
Silva (1992) (p)	48	84	123
Han (1996) (p,t)	56		140
H-S. Kim et al. (2010)	74	139	169

One other finding worthy of note is that Idemaru and Guion (2008) report that for one of their voice quality measures (H1–A1), Japanese vowels are significantly more creaky after geminates than after singletons. This property could also independently encourage the Korean tense adaptation of Japanese geminates and help to explain why this laryngeal state is favored even when the consonant is realized as a coda-onset geminate in the Korean loans and thus a matching for the constriction duration is obtained.

7. Summary and Conclusions

In this paper we compared the loanword adaptation of Japanese voiced vs. voiceless stops and affricates in initial and medial position with regard to the Korean lax–tense–aspirated distinction across two time periods referred to as Classical and Contemporary. Our study was prompted by the discrepancy observed by Shinohara et al. (2011) between productive loanword correspondences, where Japanese initial voiced and voiceless plosives are merged as Korean lax, and speech perception experiments in which Korean speakers readily distinguished the Japanese sounds as lax vs. aspirated. We hypothesized that Korean speakers whose contact with Japanese is more direct and sustained would distinguish these categories in loanwords based on their phonetic correlates. Our hypothesis was supported through the collection and analysis of a corpus of Japanese loanwords used by Korean speakers residing in Japan who use both languages on a daily basis. Our major result is that for many such speakers voiced vs. voiceless stops in loanwords are now distinguished as lax vs. aspirated word initially and as lax vs. aspirated/tense word-medially. We attributed this difference to a change in the VOT correlates of the contrasts in both languages. In the Classical period Korean long-lag aspirates were too disparate from the Japanese short-lag voiceless stops, blocking an aspiration adaptation. We suggested that a tense adaptation was inhibited because of a mismatch in voice quality (relatively breathy voiced Japanese vs. creaky voiced Korean). The voiceless > lax correspondence was conventionalized and persists for speakers whose contact with Japanese is minimal or based initially on written sources. But for speakers with more intimate contact with Japanese, a difference emerges based on presumed judgments of phonetic similarity. A second finding was that, unlike stops, affricates have a significant number of tense adaptations but they are largely confined to Japanese /ts/. We attributed this result to the higher frequency of frication for /ts/ vs. /tʃ/ and tied it to articulatory differences reported in the literature on Korean phonetics where tense affricates and fricatives have a narrower oral constriction that increases the velocity of airflow. Third, for medial position we observed a substantial number of aspirate adaptations that were absent during Classical period. This is also attributed to a shift in VOT that has brought the Korean aspirated category closer to Japanese voiceless stops. This hypothesis was supported by dialect differences and differences in place of articulation with respect to VOT. Finally, Japanese geminate stops are more faithfully realized with coda-onset closure sequences in the Contemporary period compared to singleton geminates in the Classical period. In both periods the tense laryngeal category predominates. We connected this to the longer closure duration of tense stops and more speculatively to creakiness in the vowel following a Japanese geminate.

Tasks for future research include substantiating the phonetic correlates for the laryngeal contrasts with a larger number of speakers. This is particularly critical for the H1−H2 difference proposed to explain why Japanese short-lag voiceless stops were not adapted as tense in the Classical period. For the subjects in Shinohara et al.'s (2011) study, French short-lag voiceless stops were identified as tense. Our speculation was that Japanese voiceless stops were relatively breathy and thus were better matched by the Korean lax than the creaky tense stops. But do French and Japanese really differ in this way?

The more general interest of this research is based on the observation that the same phonological contrast may have different phonetic correlates depending on language or even dialect. Which correlates are primary and which play secondary, enhancing roles? Can these roles change over time? Our results support a typology in which the internal cues of VOT and closure duration are the most important while the external cues of F0 and voice quality in the following vowel come into play when the internal cues are not decisive. In this regard it is interesting that although F0 has become the primary difference for younger Seoul speakers due to the merger of VOT for the lax and aspirated stops, this development has not so far led to a reorganization of the phonological contrast. When placed in medial position in a compound or phrase, the lax and aspirated stops remain distinct, even for the youngest speakers. Will the contrast eventually turn into a tonal distinction, as has happened so many times elsewhere in Asia?

References

Boersma, P. and Weenink, D. 2012. Praat. http://www.fon.hum.uva.nl/praat/.

Cho, T-H., Jun, S-A. and Ladefoged, P. 2002. Acoustic and Aerodynamic Correlates of Korean Stops and Fricatives. *Journal of Phonetics* 30:193–228.

Hardcastle, W. 1973. Some Observations on the Tense–Lax Distinction in Initial Stops in Korean. *Journal of Phonetics* 1:263–272.

Han, J-I. 1996. The Phonetics and Phonology of Plain and Tense Consonants in Korean. Doctoral dissertation, Cornell University.

Han, M. S. and Weitzman, R. S. 1970. Acoustic Features of Korean /P,T,K/, /p,t,k/ and /ph,th,kh/. *Phonetica* 22:112–128.

Homma, Y. 1981. Durational Relationship Between Japanese Stops and Vowels. *Journal of Phonetics* 9:273–281.

Idemaru, K. and Guion, S. 2008. Acoustic Covariants of Length Contrast in Japanese Stops. *Journal of the International Phonetic Association* 38:167–186.

Ito, C., Kang, Y-J. and Kenstowicz, M. 2006. The Adaptation of Japanese Loanwords into Korean. *MIT Working Papers in Linguistics* 52:65–104.

Jin, Z. 2012. Enpen Chōsengo washa ni yoru Nihongo haretsuon ni okeru chikaku to seisei no mekanizumu (Mechanism of Perception and Production of Japanese Stops by Yanbian Korean Speakers). Paper presented at the 26th General Meeting of the Phonetic Society of Japan.

Jun, S-A. 1996. Influence of Microprosody on Macroprosody: A Case of Phrase-initial Strengthening. *UCLA Working Papers in Phonetics* 92:97–116.

Kagaya, R. 1974. A Fiberscopic and Acoustic Study of the Korean Stops, Affricates and Fricatives. *Journal of Phonetics* 2:161–180.

Kang, K-H., and Guion, S. 2008. Clear Speech Production of Korean Stops: Changing Phonetic Targets and Enhancement Strategies. *Journal of the Acoustical Society of America* 124:3909–3917.

Kang, K-S. 2006. Are the Korean Affricates Alveolars or Palatoalveolars? Evidence from Speech Errors and Loanwords. *Studies in Phonetics, Phonology and Morphology* 12:431–451.

Kang, Y-J. and Han, S. 2012. Tonogenesis in Early Contemporary Seoul Korean: A Longitudinal Case Study. Unpublished manuscript.

Kang, Y-J., Kenstowicz, M. and Ito, C. 2008. Hybrid Loans: A Study of English Loanwords Transmitted to Korean via Japanese. *Journal of East Asian Linguistics* 17:299–316.

Kawahara, S. 2006. A Faithfulness Ranking Projected from a Perceptibility Scale: The Case of [+voice] in Japanese. *Language* 82:536–574.

Kim, C-W. 1965. On the Autonomy of the Feature Tense in Stop Classification. *Word* 21:339–359.

Kim, H-S. 1999. The Place of Articulation of Korean Affricates Revisited. *Journal of East Asian Linguistics* 8:313–347.

Kim, H-S., Honda, K. and Maeda, S. 2005. Stroboscopic-Cine MRI Study of the Phasing between the Tongue and the Larynx in the Korean Three-Way Phonation Contrast. *Journal of Phonetics* 33:1–26.

Kim, H-S., Maeda, S. and Honda, K. 2010. Invariant Articulatory Bases of the Features [tense] and [spread glottis] in Korean Plosives: New Stroboscopic Cine-MRI Data. *Journal of Phonetics* 38:90–108.

Kim, M-R. 2012. The [voice] System of Korean Stops Revisited with Special Reference to the Aspirated–Lax Merger. *Studies in Phonetics, Phonology, and Morphology* 18:211–243.

Kim, M-R., Beddor, P. and Horrocks, J. 2002. The Contribution of Consonantal and Vocalic Information to the Perception of Korean Initial Stops. *Journal of Phonetics* 30:77–100.

Kim, M-S., ed. 1997. *Urimal eoweon sajeon* (Korean Etymological Dictionary). Seoul: Taehaksa.

Kong, E-J., Beckman, M. and Edwards, J. 2012. Voice Onset Time is Necessary but Not Always Sufficient to Describe Acquisition of Voiced Stops: The Cases of Greek and Japanese. *Journal of Phonetics* 40:725–744.

Lee, H-J. 2000. Hangugin ilboneo hakseupja-ui ilponeo bareum seupteuk yeongu: yuseong museong payeoreum-ui bareum-eul jungsim-euro (Study on the Acquisition of Japanese Pronunciation by Korean Learners of Japanese: Focusing on the Pronunciation of Voiced/Voiceless Plosives). *Ilboneomunhak* 9:107–137.

Lisker, L. and Abramson, A. 1964. A Cross-Language Study of Voicing in Initial Stops: Acoustical Measurements. *Word* 20:384–422.

Nagato, Y. 2003. Chōsengo Souru hōgen no onsetsu tōshiin to meishi no onchōkei (Onset and Tone Pattern of Nouns in the Seoul Dialect of Korean). *Journal of the Phonetic Society of Japan* 7(2):114–128.

Ogasawara, N. 2011. Acoustic Analysis of Voice-Onset Time in Taiwan Mandarin and Japanese. *Concentric Studies in Linguistics* 37:155–178.

Park, B-N. 1968. *Korean: Basic Course*. Washington: Foreign Service Institute.

Park, H-S. 1982. Kankokugo no onsetsumatsu naihaon no kōtō chōsetsu (Laryngeal Adjustment of Syllable-Final Unexploded Sounds in Korean). *Chōsen Gakuhō* 104:25–60.

Riney, T., Takagi, N., Ota, K. and Uchida, Y. 2007. The Intermediate Degree of VOT in Japanese Initial Voiceless Stops. *Journal of Phonetics* 35:439-443.

Shimizu, K. 1996. *A Cross-Language Study of Voicing Contrasts of Stop Consonants in Asian Languages*. Tokyo: Seibidō Publishing.

Shin, J-Y. 1997. Consonantal Production and Coarticulation in Korean. Doctoral dissertation, University of London (SOAS).

Shinohara, S., Ji, S-R., Ooigawa, T. and Shinya, T. 2011. The Limited Role of Perception in Korean Loanword Adaptation: The Korean Three-Way Laryngeal Categorization of Japanese, English, French, and Chinese Plosives. *Lingua* 121: 1461–1484.

Silva, D. 1992. The Phonetics and Phonology of Stop Lenition in Korean. Doctoral dissertation, Cornell University.

Silva, D. 2006. Acoustic Evidence for the Emergence of Tonal Contrast in Contemporary Korean. *Phonology* 23:287–308.

Sugitō, M. 1996. Chūgokugo washa ni yoru Nihongo no musei shiin, yūsei shiin to, yūkion, mukion (Japanese Voiced/Voiceless Consonants and Aspirates/Unaspirates by Chinese Speakers). *Nihongo no on* (Japanese Sounds), 264–285. Izumi Shoin.

Takada, M. 2012. *Nihongo no gotō heisaon no kenkyū* (A Study on Word-Initial Stops in Japanese). Tokyo: Kuroshio Publishing.

The Society for Teaching Japanese as a Foreign Language. 2003. *Senzen senchū no Nihongo kyōiku kyōzai rekōdo hukkokuban* (Reproduced Version of the Recordings for Japanese Education Textbooks Before and During the War).

Utsugi, A. 2009. Nihongo to Chōsengo no haretsuon: Onkyō onseigaku-teki kenkyū no gaikan (Plosives in Japanese and Korean: A Review of Acoustic Phonetic Studies). *Hokkaidō Gengo Bunka Kenkyū* 7:11–27.

The Phonology of Emphatic Morphology in Japanese Mimetics

KAZUTAKA KURISU*
Kobe College

1. Introduction

Contemporary Japanese has quite productive morphophonological augmentation semantically associated with emphasis. A quite wide range of Japanese vocabulary participates in emphatic morphology, including mimetic items. Of particular interest is the contrastive phonological behavior of reduplicated and suffixed mimetic forms. Phonologically, emphasis is expressed with gemination or nasal epenthesis. There are two reasons for investigating emphatic mimetics. First, several earlier studies devoted to the phonology of emphatic mimetics are not satisfactory. Their description of the data is incomplete and even partially incorrect. Second, previous studies have not exhaustively discussed theoretical issues of significant importance.

With this background in mind, this paper has two main goals. First, this paper describes reduplicated and suffixed emphatic mimetic items in a comprehensive fashion. Two possible emphatic forms exist in many cases and

* For useful discussion and comments on this paper, I thank Haruo Kubozono and Akio Nasu. The author is responsible for all remaining errors and oversights.

Japanese/Korean Linguistics 22.
Edited by Mikio Giriko, Naonori Nagaya, Akiko Takemura, and Timothy J. Vance.

there is no possible emphatic form in certain suffixed forms. The optionality effect is associated with two phonological conditions: sonority and voicing. The absence of emphatic forms is observed in suffixed forms when a liquid occupies the canonical position targeted by gemination.

The second goal of this paper is to explore the theoretical consequences of the two descriptive points raised above. Throughout this paper, my analysis is couched in Optimality Theory (OT; Prince and Smolensky 2004). Regarding optionality, I argue for the combination of free constraint ranking and scalar violation assignment (de Lacy 2002, 2006). Various other proposals have been made to capture optionality, but they do not succeed. Concerning the absence of emphatic forms, I defend Control Theory, originally proposed by Orgun and Sprouse (1999). Two conceivable alternatives are a null parse approach and a paradigmatic approach. However, they encounter serious conceptual problems.

The two theoretical claims mentioned above are not new, but the need for scalar violation assignment and Control Theory has not been proposed in the context of Japanese mimetic phonology. The theoretical contribution of this paper is therefore to lend additional credibility to the two theoretical mechanisms in the OT enterprise.

The rest of this paper is organized as follows. In section 2, I present data and a descriptive generalization for emphatic mimetics. In section 3, I analyze examples without optionality or absolute ungrammaticality. Building on the analysis, section 4 is devoted to an analysis of optionality data. I argue for scalar violation assignment, lending support to de Lacy (2002, 2006). In the course of the discussion, I argue against other analytical possibilities, including the rank-ordered model (Coetzee 2004, 2006) and markedness suppression (Kaplan 2011). The topic of section 5 is absolute ungrammaticality. Among three competing analyses, I argue for the one appealing to Control Theory. Finally, section 6 concludes the paper.

2. Data

This section presents the whole range of data discussed in this paper. Japanese mimetic roots are usually bound, and they are either reduplicated or suffixed in actual use. In this paper, I discuss both reduplicated and suffixed emphatic mimetic forms.

Starting with reduplicated forms, emphasis is phonologically manifested through gemination. The examples in (1) demonstrate the fact that C_2 is usually geminated in reduplicated C_1VC_2V-C_3VC_4V forms. Among obstruents, only voiceless ones may be geminated in Yamato-Japanese and Sino-Japanese (Itô and Mester 1995ab, 1999), but voiced obstruents also undergo gemination in the mimetic vocabulary.

(1) a. C_2 = voiceless stop

Non-emphatic	*Emphatic*	*Gloss*
pika-pika	pikka-pika	shiny
buka-buka	bukka-buka	baggy
hoka-hoka	hokka-hoka	warm
zaku-zaku	zakku-zaku	crunchy
niko-niko	nikko-niko	smiling
waku-waku	wakku-waku	excited

b. C_2 = voiced stop

Non-emphatic	*Emphatic*	*Gloss*
gaba-gaba	gabba-gaba	over-sized
zabu-zabu	zabbu-zabu	splashing
neba-neba	nebba-neba	sticky
jobo-jobo	jobbo-jobo	decrepit

c. C_2 = voiceless fricative

Non-emphatic	*Emphatic*	*Gloss*
çiso-çiso	çisso-çiso	whispering
mosa-mosa	mossa-mosa	hairy
wasa-wasa	wassa-wasa	rustling

d. C_2 = voiced fricative

Non-emphatic	*Emphatic*	*Gloss*
moʒi-moʒi	moʒʒi-moʒi	fidgeting

e. C_2 = nasal

Non-emphatic	*Emphatic*	*Gloss*
muɲa-muɲa	muɲɲa-muɲa	mumbling

f. C_2 = liquid

Non-emphatic	*Emphatic*	*Gloss*
juru-juru	jurru-juru	over-sized
joro-joro	jorro-joro	staggering

g. C_2 = glide

Non-emphatic	*Emphatic*	*Gloss*
jawa-jawa	jawwa-jawa	weak

Besides canonical C_2 gemination, C_3 gemination is also sometimes tolerated, resulting in optionality. There are two such cases. First, this optionality is observed when C_3 is less sonorous than C_2, as exemplified in (2).

(2) a. C_2 = voiceless fricative

Non-emphatic	*Emphatic*		*Gloss*
pasa-pasa	passa-pasa	pasa-ppasa	powdery
kasa-kasa	kassa-kasa	kasa-kkasa	dry
gasa-gasa	gassa-gasa	gasa-ggasa	rustling

b. C_2 = voiced fricative

Non-emphatic	*Emphatic*		*Gloss*
giza-giza	gizza-giza	giza-ggiza	notched
guzu-guzu	guzzu-guzu	guzu-gguzu	unsettled

c. C_2 = nasal

Non-emphatic	*Emphatic*		*Gloss*
guɲa-guɲa	guɲɲa-guɲa	guɲa-gguɲa	spineless
ʒime-ʒime	ʒimme-ʒime	ʒime-ʒʒime	damp

d. C_2 = liquid

Non-emphatic	*Emphatic*		*Gloss*
bara-bara	barra-bara	bara-bbara	to pieces
doro-doro	dorro-doro	doro-ddoro	muddy
gura-gura	gurra-gura	gura-ggura	unsteady
zara-zara	zarra-zara	zara-zzara	rough
nuru-nuru	nurru-nuru	nuru-nnuru	slimy

e. C_2 = glide

Non-emphatic	*Emphatic*		*Gloss*
bojo-bojo	bojjo-bojo	bojo-bbojo	fat
najo-najo	najjo-najo	najo-nnajo	weak
zawa-zawa	zawwa-zawa	zawa-zzawa	noisy

The other case of optionality is conditioned by voicing. As illustrated in (3), optionality arises when C_2 is voiced and C_3 is voiceless.

(3) C_2 = voiced stop

Non-emphatic	*Emphatic*		*Gloss*
keba-keba	kebba-keba	keba-kkeba	gaudy
tsubu-tsubu	tsubbu-tsubu	tsubu-ttsubu	lumpy
sube-sube	subbe-sube	sube-ssube	smooth

Finally, optionality arises when the above two conditions are mixed, as in (4). The generalization above expands on Nasu (2002), who observes that geminated fricatives and geminated voiced obstruents are disfavored.

(4) a. C_2 = voiced fricative

Non-emphatic	*Emphatic*		*Gloss*
taʒi-taʒi	taʒʒi-taʒi	taʒi-ttaʒi	staggering

b. C_2 = nasal

Non-emphatic	*Emphatic*		*Gloss*
puɲo-puɲo	puɲɲo-puɲo	puɲo-ppuɲo	jelly-like
kuɲa-kuɲa	kuɲɲa-kuɲa	kuɲa-kkuɲa	flexible
ɸuɲa-ɸuɲa	ɸuɲɲa-ɸuɲa	ɸuɲa-ɸɸuɲa	flabby

c. C_2 = liquid

Non-emphatic	*Emphatic*		*Gloss*
pari-pari	parri-pari	pari-ppari	crunchy
toro-toro	torro-toro	toro-ttoro	pulpy
ɸura-ɸura	ɸurra-ɸura	ɸura-ɸɸura	dizzy
sara-sara	sarra-sara	sara-ssara	burbling

d. C_2 = glide

Non-emphatic	*Emphatic*		*Gloss*
pojo-pojo	pojjo-pojo	pojo-ppojo	jelly-like
ɸuwa-ɸuwa	ɸuwwa-ɸuwa	ɸuwa-ɸɸuwa	soft

In suffixed C_1VC_2V-ri forms, the descriptive generalization consists of three portions. First, C_2 is geminated if it is voiceless, as in (5a). Second, a nasal is inserted right before C_2 when C_2 is a non-[r] voiced consonant, as in (5b). Finally, no emphatic form is possible when C_2 is a liquid, as in (5c).

(5) a. C_2 = voiceless consonant

Non-emphatic	*Emphatic*	*Gloss*
pika-ri	pikka-ri	flashing
pita-ri	pitta-ri	tight
katʃi-ri	kattʃi-ri	hard
gatʃi-ri	gattʃi-ri	shrewd
basa-ri	bassa-ri	drastic

b. C_2 = voiced consonant other than [r]

Non-emphatic	*Emphatic*	*Gloss*
zabu-ri	zaNbu-ri	splashing
ʃobo-ri	ʃoNbo-ri	depressed
guɲa-ri	guNɲa-ri	limp
jawa-ri	jaNwa-ri	mild
ɸuwa-ri	ɸuNwa-ri	soft

c. C_2 = [r]

Non-emphatic	*Emphatic*		*Gloss*
ɸura-ri	*ɸurra-ri	*ɸuNra-ri	aimless
tsuru-ri	*tsurru-ri	*tsuNru-ri	smooth
gura-ri	*gurra-ri	*guNra-ri	shaky
goro-ri	*gorro-ri	*goNro-ri	slumping
sara-ri	*sarra-ri	*saNra-ri	swimming
jura-ri	*jurra-ri	*juNra-ri	swaying

There are two prominent issues here. One is how the two types of optionality effect in reduplicated forms are to be explained. The other is how the absence of emphatic forms in (5c) is to be analyzed. These two questions are addressed in sections 4 and 5 after presenting in section 3 an OT analysis of the examples without optionality or absolute ungrammaticality.

One note is in order concerning the phonological realization of the emphatic morpheme. Mimetic items are frequently accompanied by vowel lengthening (e.g., [juura-jura] 'swaying'). This vowel lengthening must be differentiated from the emphatic morphology investigated in this paper. Vowel lengthening is associated with spatial or temporal expansion (Hamano 1998). This observation is clearly reflected in the fact that vowel lengthening is incompatible with mimetic items whose meaning has nothing to do with spatial or temporal concepts. For example, vowel lengthening fails to apply to [pika-pika] 'shiny'. Furthermore, vowel lengthening can cooccur with gemination (e.g., [neebba-neba] 'sticky'). This cooccurrence does not make sense if vowel lengthening is a phonological realization of the same morpheme as gemination (Hamano 1998:110). Vowel lengthening is not a phonological realization of the emphatic morpheme general to the entire mimetic vocabulary. Hereafter, I do not discuss how vowel lengthening should be analyzed.

3. Analysis of Basic Data

This section is designed to offer an OT analysis of data that do not involve optionality or absolute ungrammaticality. I assume that the emphatic morpheme is segmentally empty /μ_e/. Subscripted *e* is a mnemonic for the emphatic morpheme. Phonological augmentation occurs for phonological exponence of the morpheme (Davis and Ueda 2002; Kawahara 2007).

I assume the three constraints in (6). The licensing constraint in (6b) is the key. C_2 is geminated or a nasal is inserted before C_2, so the exponent of the emphatic morpheme occupies the coda of the first syllable either way.

(6) a. MAX-μ_e: /μ_e/ must be parsed overtly.
b. LICENSE(μ_e,σ_1): /μ_e/ is licensed by the word-initial syllable.
c. *GEM: Geminates are prohibited.

Default C_2 gemination is analyzed in (7) and (8). MAX-μ_e is positioned above *GEM, so gemination is ruled in. LICENSE(μ_e,σ_1) determines its locus.

(7)

	/RED-pika, μ_e/	MAX-μ_e	LICENSE	*GEM
a.	pika-pika	*!		
b. ☞	pikka-pika			*
c.	pika-ppika		*!	*

(8)

	/pika-ri, μ_e/	MAX-μ_e	LICENSE	*GEM
a.	pika-ri	*!		
b. ☞	pikka-ri			*

Nasal epenthesis occurs in suffixed forms, but not in reduplicated forms. This contrast follows from segregating DEP-IO and DEP-BR. DEP-IO is dominated by *GEM, but DEP-BR is ranked over *GEM. As shown in (9) and (10), the different rankings of the two DEP constraints explain why nasal epenthesis occurs only in suffixed mimetic items.

(9)

	/zabu-ri, μ_e/	LICENSE	*GEM	DEP-IO
a.	zabbu-ri		*!	
b. ☞	zaNbu-ri			*

(10)

	/RED-gaba, μ_e/	DEP-BR	LICENSE	*GEM
a. ☞	gabba-gaba			*
b.	gaba-ggaba		*!	*
c.	gaNba-gaba	*!		

Given low ranked DEP-IO, the question is why nasal epenthesis does not occur in (5a). The answer is: to avoid a phonologically marked representation. Inserting a nasal before C_2 of C_1VC_2V-ri creates a cluster of a nasal and a voiceless obstruent, breaching *NC̥ (Pater 1999). *NC̥ is inviolable in the mimetic vocabulary of Japanese (Itô and Mester 1995ab, 1999). Given undominated *NC̥, nasal epenthesis is blocked when C_2 is voiceless, as in (11).

(11)

	/pika-ri, μ_e/	*NC̥	LICENSE	*GEM	DEP-IO
a. ☞	pikka-ri			*	
b.	piNka-ri	*!			*

This completes my analysis of the examples in (1) and (5a, b).

4. Optionality

In this section, I develop an analysis of the optionality observed in reduplicated emphatic forms. They involve gemination, so susceptibility to gemination must be considered. It is closely associated with sonority: the less sonorous a consonant is, the more susceptible it is to gemination (Kawahara 2007). An immediate analytical possibility is to assume a fixed ranking that penalizes geminated consonants, as in (12).

(12) *GEMGLIDE » *GEMLIQ » *GEMNAS » *GEMFRIC » *GEMSTOP

The fact that optionality arises when C_3 is lower than C_2 in sonority requires free ranking or the equivalent of LICENSE(μ_e,σ_1) and the *GEM constraints. (13a)-(13e) show potential positions where LICENSE(μ_e,σ_1) could be placed.

(13) *GEMGLIDE » *GEMLIQ » *GEMNAS » *GEMFRIC » *GEMSTOP
↑ ↑ ↑ ↑ ↑
(a) (b) (c) (d) (e)

No matter which *GEM constraint is freely ranked with respect to LICENSE(μ_e,σ_1), the entire pattern cannot be captured. Optionality is expected only with the manner referred to by the *GEM constraint ranked freely with respect to LICENSE(μ_e,σ_1). For instance, (13a) predicts optionality only when C_2 is a glide.

In order to overcome the problem, I propose that the *GEM constraints are not ranked in a universally fixed hierarchy. Instead, different degrees of violation marks are assigned to different geminate representations, as illustrated in (14). In (14), the number of *x*'s expresses the degree of markedness and the number of violation marks to be assigned. This idea is the scalar violation assignment proposed by de Lacy (2002, 2006).

(14) a. Geminated stops: *x*Geminate
b. Geminated fricatives: *xx*Geminate
c. Geminated nasals: *xxx*Geminate
d. Geminated liquids: *xxxx*Geminate
e. Geminated glides: *xxxxx*Geminate

I assume that LICENSE(μ_e,σ_1), *GEM, and *VOIGEM are not ranked rigidly—an idea advanced by Anttila (1997, 2007) and Anttila and Cho (1998).

*VOIGEM is well motivated. Articulatorily, geminated voiced obstruents are disfavored because maintaining glottal vibration during long obstruent closure is hard (Jaeger 1978; Westbury 1979; Ohala 1983; Hayes and Steriade 2004). Perceptually, it is difficult to discriminate geminated voiced obstruents, since crucial acoustic properties are largely attenuated

(Kawahara 2005). Finally, sonorants are not good hosts of geminates either, since the duration of sonorous segments is hard to perceive (Kawahara 2006).

The examples in (1) are reanalyzed in (15). C_2 and C_3 are both voiceless stops. Gemination of C_3 gains no benefit in compensation for a violation of LICENSE(μ_e,σ_1). When the voicing and manner of C_2 and C_3 are identical, gemination of C_2 harmonically bounds that of C_3.

(15)

	/RED-pika, μ_e/	LICENSE	*GEM	*VOIGEM
a. ☞	pikka-pika		*	
b.	pika-ppika	*!	*	

My analysis of the data in (2) is given in (16). C_2 and C_3 are voiceless, but they differ in sonority. C_2 is more sonorous than C_3. LICENSE(μ_e,σ_1) » *GEM favors (16a), respecting the default position of μ_e. By contrast, *GEM » LICENSE(μ_e,σ_1) selects (16b), applying gemination to less sonorous C_3.

(16)

	/RED-pasa, μ_e/	LICENSE	*GEM	*VOIGEM
a. ☞	passa-pasa		**	
b. ☞	pasa-ppasa	*	*	

The tableau in (17) presents my analysis of the examples in (3). C_2 and C_3 are both stops, but they differ in voicing. LICENSE(μ_e,σ_1) » *VOIGEM favors (17a), respecting the canonical position of μ_e. The opposite ranking of the two constraints selects (17b), avoiding a voiced geminate.

(17)

	/RED-keba, μ_e/	LICENSE	*GEM	*VOIGEM
a. ☞	kebba-keba		*	*
b. ☞	keba-kkeba	*	*	

Finally, the tableau in (18) represents my analysis of (4). This is a case where both the voicing and manner features of C_2 and C_3 are different. Again, reranking of the three constraints generates either (18a) or (18b).

(18)

	/RED-taʒi, μ_e/	LICENSE	*GEM	*VOIGEM
a. ☞	taʒʒi-taʒi		**	*
b. ☞	taʒi-ttaʒi	*	*	

Before leaving this section, there are several important issues worth addressing. First, Harmonic Grammar (Smolensky and Legendre 2006; Pater 2009ab) is incompatible with the data of optionality. In Harmonic Grammar, each constraint has a certain numerical weight. The performance of a given candidate is expressed as a harmonic score calculated by multiplying the number of violations of the candidate and summing across all constraints. The candidate with the highest harmony score is the winning form. In (17), LICENSE(μ_e,σ_1) and *VOIGEM should have the same weight. In this case, however, (18a) would be harmonically bounded by (18b), suggesting that (18a) has no chance to surface.

Besides partial ordering, there are several other theories of optionality, including the rank-ordered model (Coetzee 2004, 2006) and markedness suppression (Kaplan 2011), but they cannot capture the optionality data in (2)-(4).

In the rank-ordered model, there is a threshold. All candidates that respect the constraints above the cut-off point qualify as output variants. The likelihood of a variant surfacing is determined by its well-formedness relative to other candidates. In (16)-(18), the cut-off point should be between MAX-μ_e and LICENSE(μ_e,σ_1). Optionality is not observed in suffixed forms, but both gemination and nasal epenthesis are wrongly expected to be possible in (5b) regardless of how LICENSE(μ_e,σ_1), *GEM, and *VOIGEM are ranked.

Markedness suppression maintains that EVAL arbitrarily disregards violations of markedness constraints with the suppression operator. This arbitrariness is the source of optionality. The six rankings in (19) exhaust all constraint hierarchies of LICENSE(μ_e,σ_1), *GEM, and *VOIGEM. Markedness suppression must apply to the first or second constraint in each constraint ranking. Otherwise, markedness suppression would have no tangible effect.

(19) a. LICENSE(μ_e,σ_1) » *GEM » *VOIGEM
b. LICENSE(μ_e,σ_1) » *VOIGEM » *GEM
c. *GEM » LICENSE(μ_e,σ_1) » *VOIGEM
d. *GEM » *VOIGEM » LICENSE(μ_e,σ_1)
e. *VOIGEM » LICENSE(μ_e,σ_1) » *GEM
f. *VOIGEM » *GEM » LICENSE(μ_e,σ_1)

All these possibilities encounter empirical problems, as summarized in (20).

(20) *(19a) with LICENSE(μ_e, σ_1) suppressed*
Optionality occurs in (15).

*(19a) with *GEM suppressed*
Optionality does not occur in (16)-(18).

(19b) with LICENSE(μ_e, σ_1) suppressed
Optionality occurs in (15).

*(19b) with *VOIGEM suppressed*
Optionality does not occur in (16)-(18).

*(19c) with *GEM suppressed*
Optionality does not occur in (17).

(19c) with LICENSE(μ_e, σ_1) suppressed
Optionality occurs in (15) and does not occur in (16) and (18).

*(19d) with *GEM suppressed*
Optionality does not occur in (17) and (18).

*(19d) with *VOIGEM suppressed*
Optionality does not occur in (16) and (18).

*(19e) with *VOIGEM suppressed*
Optionality does not occur in (16).

(19e) with LICENSE(μ_e, σ_1) suppressed
Optionality occurs in (15) and does not occur in (17) and (18).

*(19f) with *VOIGEM suppressed*
Optionality does not occur in (16) and (18).

*(19f) with *GEM suppressed*
Optionality does not occur in (17) and (18).

In sum, the data in (2), (3), and (4) are explained with partial ordering of LICENSE(μ_e,σ_1), *GEM, and *VOIGEM. The same data are not explained with Harmonic Grammar, the rank-ordered model, or markedness suppression.

5. Absolute Ungrammaticality

This section deals with the absence of emphatic forms in (5c). The current analysis predicts nasal insertion in (5c). One question is whether the absence of emphatic forms is underparsing of /μ_e/ or absolute ungrammaticality. Absolute ungrammaticality is the right answer. If they were instances of underparsing of /μ_e/, we would predict ambiguity in (5c), contrary to fact.

This absolute ungrammaticality effect should be explained with Control Theory (Orgun and Sprouse 1999, 2009; Bye 2007). In this theory, EVAL always selects the best candidate against a given constraint ranking. The selected candidate is assessed by inviolable constraints in CONTROL. The candidate becomes an output if it satisfies all the constraints in CONTROL. Otherwise, the candidate is abandoned, leading to absolute ungrammaticality.

Davis and Ueda (2002) assume *[nr] as a descriptive constraint. Citing

Mester and Itô (1989), who explain the lack of emphatic forms in (5c) and the non-palatalizability of /r/ with contrastive underspecification, Davis and Ueda (2002) claim that the place feature of [n] is not licensed by [r] (see Itô 1986 and Itô and Mester 1993 for the coda condition in Japanese).

There are two problems. First, the non-palatalizability of /r/ does not necessarily imply the lack of place (see Kurisu 2009). Second, [Nr] is another possibility, where [N] represents a placeless nasal. [N] is not restricted to the word-final position. In Sino-Japanese, morpheme-final coda [N] is not resyllabified (e.g., [geN.iN] 'cause') (Itô and Mester 1996; Kurisu 2000).

I claim that *[NL] is a real constraint, where [N] represents a nasal and [L] is a liquid. *[NL] is justified by the fact that a nasal is elided before a liquid in a number of languages (Flemming 2005). In Bahasa Indonesian, a nasal remains before an obstruent, but a nasal undergoes deletion before a sonorant, including a liquid (Lapoliwa 1981). In Frisian, nasal deletion takes place before a fricative, liquid, or glide (Tiersma 1985).

Let us assume that *[NL] is in CONTROL in Japanese. Equipped with the analysis developed above, EVAL chooses (21b) as the best form. This form is subsequently sent to the CONTROL component. As demonstrated in (22), [ɸuNra-ri] is eliminated there because it breaches inviolable *[NL].

(21)

	/ɸura-ri, μ_e/	LICENSE	*GEM	*VOI GEM	DEP-IO
a.	ɸurra-ri		*!***	*	
b. ☞	ɸuNra-ri				*

(22)

	/ɸura-ri, μ_e/	*[NL]
✖	ɸuNra-ri	*

*[NL] is a domain-sensitive constraint. Examples like [raN-raN] 'glaring' and [riN-riN] 'jingle' show that the sequence of a nasal and a liquid is tolerated across morphemes. Therefore, *[NL] takes a morpheme as its domain. [ɸuNra-ri] violates *[NL]. The relevant nasal and liquid are within the stretch of the root by virtue of the infixal nature of μ_e.

There are two other analytical proposals for analyzing absolute ungrammaticality: an MPARSE approach (Prince and Smolensky 2004; Raffelsiefen 2004; Wolf and McCarthy 2009) and a paradigmatic approach (Rice 2003, 2005, 2007). These two alternatives are unsatisfactory.

In the MPARSE approach, GEN creates a null parse candidate [⊙] as well as candidates with phonological substance. CON contains MPARSE, which requires morphological parsing of input, and [⊙] violates MPARSE. An input is mapped onto some output if a candidate other than [⊙] wins. However, absolute ungrammaticality arises when [⊙] is the most harmonic.

In the paradigmatic approach, each candidate is paradigmatic and candidate assessment is systemic. No gap appears if the winner has a phonological form for the entire paradigm. Absolute ungrammaticality is obtained if the winner has a gap at the cost of a violation of morpheme-specific MAX.

The two alternative approaches are the same in that there is no separate component analogous to the CONTROL component. We need a markedness constraint that rules out [ɸurra-ri]. This is because [ɸurra-ri] would be selected once we include *[NL] as an undominated constraint. The only imaginable constraint would be the conjoined constraint in (23). The OCP is formulated in the sense of Rose (2000): two identical consonants violate the OCP across intervening vowels. As shown in (1f), (2d), and (4c), geminated [r] is possible in reduplicated forms. Penalizing geminated [r] is not enough.

(23) *[rr] & OCP: [rr] may not be preceded or followed by [r].

Once we add the conjoined constraint as a member of the undominated constraints, both the MPARSE approach and the paradigmatic approach generate correct outputs, as shown in (24) and (25).

(24)

	/ɸura-ri, μ_e/	*[rr] & OCP	*[NL]	MPARSE
a.	ɸurra-ri	*!		
b.	ɸuNra-ri		*!	
c. ☞	⊙			*

(25)

	/ɸura-ri, {Ø, μ_e}/	*[rr] & OCP	*[NL]	MAX-μ_e
a.	ɸura-ri, ɸurra-ri	*!		
b.	ɸura-ri, ɸuNra-ri		*!	
c. ☞	ɸura-ri			*

There are conceptual problems with the conjoined constraint. First, it is unclear why geminated [r] is not allowed to violate the OCP. Many mimetic forms violate the OCP (e.g., [sassa-to] 'promptly' and [totto-to] 'promptly'). They breach the OCP, but crucially, the geminates are not liquids.

Second, the mutual relevance of *[rr] and the OCP is unclear. Once we allow for conjunction of unrelated constraints in an arbitrary domain, we predict non-existing crosslinguistic patterns (McCarthy 2007; Pater 2009ab; Potts et al. 2010). This is a general problem with constraint conjunction.

6. Conclusion

Exploring reduplicated and suffixed emphatic mimetic forms together, I addressed two questions: how optionality and absolute ungrammaticality are to be accounted for in OT. Regarding optionality, I proposed combining partial constraint ordering and scalar violation assignment. Concerning absolute ungrammaticality, the absence of emphatic forms in certain suffixed forms is best explained with Control Theory. This conclusion is consistent with an earlier claim of mine. Exploring the systematic absence of any palatal(ized) consonant before [e] in Japanese mimetic vocabulary, Kurisu (2013) argues that Control Theory accommodates the relevant absolute ungrammaticality effect, while MPARSE and paradigmatic approaches encounter empirical problems.

References

Anttila, A. 1997. Variation in Finnish Phonology and Morphology. Doctoral dissertation, Stanford University.

Anttila, A. 2007. Variation and Optionality. *The Cambridge Handbook of Phonology*, ed. P. de Lacy, 519–536. Cambridge: Cambridge University Press.

Anttila, A. and Cho, Y.-M. 1998. Variation and Change in Optimality Theory. *Lingua* 104:31–56.

Bye, P. 2007. Allomorphy – Selection, not Optimization. *Freedom of Analysis?*, ed. S. Blaho, P. Bye, and M. Krämer, 63–91. Berlin and New York: Mouton de Gruyter.

Coetzee, A. 2004. What it Means to be a Loser: Non-optimal Candidates in Optimality Theory. Doctoral dissertation, University of Massachusetts, Amherst.

Coetzee, A. 2006. Variation as Accessing "Non-optimal" Candidates. *Phonology* 23: 337–385.

Davis, S. and Ueda, I. 2002. Mora Augmentation Processes in Japanese. *Journal of Japanese Linguistics* 18:1–23.

de Lacy, P. 2002. The Formal Expression of Markedness. Doctoral dissertation, University of Massachusetts, Amherst.

de Lacy, P. 2006. *Markedness: Reduction and Preservation in Phonology*. Cambridge: Cambridge University Press.

Flemming, E. 2005. Deriving Natural Classes in Phonology. *Lingua* 115:287–309.

Hamano, S. 1998. *The Sound-Symbolic System of Japanese*. Stanford: CSLI.

Hayes, B. and Steriade, D. 2004. Introduction: The Phonetic Bases of Phonological Markedness. *Phonetically Based Phonology*, ed. B. Hayes, R. Kirchner, and D. Steriade, 1–33. Cambridge: Cambridge University Press.

Itô, J. 1986. Syllable Theory in Prosodic Phonology. Doctoral dissertation, University of Massachusetts, Amherst.

Itô, J. and Mester, A. 1993. Licensed Segments and Safe Paths. *Canadian Journal of Linguistics* 38:197–213.

Itô, J. and Mester, A. 1995a. Japanese Phonology. *The Handbook of Phonological Theory*, ed. J. Goldsmith, 817–838. Cambridge: Blackwell.

Itô, J. and Mester, A. 1995b. The Core-Periphery Structure of the Lexicon and Constraints on Reranking. *University of Massachusetts Occasional Papers in Linguistics 18: Papers in Optimality Theory*, ed. J. Beckman, L. Walsh-Dickey, and S. Urbanczyk, 181–209. Amherst: GLSA.

Itô, J. and Mester, A. 1996. Stem and Word in Sino-Japanese. *Phonological Structure and Language Processing: Cross-Linguistic Studies*, ed. T. Otake and A. Cutler, 13–44. Berlin: Mouton de Gruyter.

Itô, J. and Mester, A. 1999. The Phonological Lexicon. *The Handbook of Japanese Linguistics*, ed. N. Tsujimura, 62–100. Cambridge: Blackwell.

Jaeger, J. 1978. Speech Aerodynamics and Phonological Universals. *Proceedings of the Berkeley Linguistics Society* 4:311–329.

Kaplan, A. 2011. Variation through Markedness Suppression. *Phonology* 28:331–370.

Kawahara, S. 2005. Voicing and Geminacy in Japanese: An Acoustic and Perceptual Study. *University of Massachusetts Occasional Papers in Linguistics 31: Papers in Experimental Phonetics and Phonology*, ed. K. Flack and S. Kawahara, 87–120. Amherst: GLSA.

Kawahara, S. 2006. A Faithfulness Ranking Projected from a Perceptibility Scale: The Case of [+voice] in Japanese. *Language* 82:536–574.

Kawahara, S. 2007. Sonorancy and Geminacy. *University of Massachusetts Occasional Papers in Linguistics: Papers in Optimality Theory III*, ed. L. Bateman, A. Werle, E. Reilly, and M. O'Keefe, 145–186. Amherst: GLSA.

Kurisu, K. 2000. Richness of the Base and Root Fusion in Sino-Japanese. *Journal of East Asian Linguistics* 9:147–185.

Kurisu, K. 2009. Palatalisability via Feature Compatibility. *Phonology* 26:437–475.

Kurisu, K. 2013. Constraint Inviolability in Japanese Mimetic Palatalization. *Japanese/Korean Linguistics* 20, ed. B. Frellesvig and P. Sells, 147–162. Stanford: CSLI.

Lapoliwa, H. 1981. *A Generative Approach to the Phonology of Bahasa Indonesia*. Canberra: Australian National University.

McCarthy, J. 2007. *Hidden Generalizations: Phonological Opacity in Optimality Theory*. London: Equinox.

Mester, A. and Itô, J. 1989. Feature Predictability and Underspecification: Palatal Prosody in Japanese Mimetics. *Language* 65:258–293.

Nasu, A. 2002. Nihongo Onomatope no Gokeisei to Inritsukōzō [Word Formation and Prosodic Structure in Japanese Mimetics]. Doctoral dissertation, Tsukuba University.

Ohala, J. 1983. The Origin of Sound Patterns in Vocal Tract Constraints. *The Production of Speech*, ed. P. MacNeilage, 189–216. New York: Springer.

Orgun, O. and Sprouse, R. 1999. From MPARSE to CONTROL: Deriving Ungrammaticality. *Phonology* 16:191–224.

Orgun, O. and Sprouse, R. 2009. Hard Constraints in Optimality Theory. *Modeling*

Ungrammaticality in Optimality Theory, ed. C. Rice and S. Blaho, 97–114. London: Equinox.

Pater, J. 1999. Austronesian Nasal Substitution and Other NÇ Effects. *The Prosody-Morphology Interface*, ed. R. Kager, H. van der Hulst, and W. Zonneveld, 310–343. Cambridge: Cambridge University Press.

Pater, J. 2009a. Review of *The Harmonic Mind*, by P. Smolensky and G. Legendre. *Phonology* 26:217–226.

Pater, J. 2009b. Weighted Constraints in Generative Linguistics. *Cognitive Science* 33:999–1035.

Potts, C., Pater, J., Jesney, K., Bhatt, R., and Becker, M. 2010. Harmonic Grammar with Linear Programming: From Linear Systems to Linguistic Typology. *Phonology* 27:77–117.

Prince, A. and Smolensky, P. 2004. *Optimality Theory: Constraint Interaction in Generative Grammar*. Malden: Blackwell.

Raffelsiefen, R. 2004. Absolute Ill-Formedness and other Morphophonological Effects. *Phonology* 21:91–142.

Rice, C. 2003. Dialectal Variation in Norwegian Imperatives. *Nordlyd* 31:372–384.

Rice, C. 2005. Optimal Gaps in Optimal Paradigms. *Catalan Journal of Linguistics* 4:155–170.

Rice, C. 2007. Gaps and Repairs at the Phonology-Morphology Interface. *Journal of Linguistics* 43:197–221.

Rose, S. 2000. Rethinking Geminates, Long-Distance Geminates, and the OCP. *Linguistic Inquiry* 31:85–122.

Smolensky, P. and Legendre, G. 2006. *The Harmonic Mind*. Cambridge: MIT Press.

Tiersma, P. 1985. *Frisian Reference Grammar*. Dordrecht: Foris.

Westbury, J. 1979. Aspects of the Temporal Control of Voicing in Consonant Clusters in English. Doctoral dissertation, University of Texas, Austin.

Wolf, M. and McCarthy, J. 2009. Less than Zero: Correspondence and the Null Output. *Modeling Ungrammaticality in Optimality Theory*, ed. C. Rice and S. Blaho, 17–66. London: Equinox.

Rendaku Lovers, Rendaku Haters, and the Logistic Curve

MARK IRWIN
Yamagata University

1. Introduction

Rendaku, or sequential voicing, is a productive morphophonemic process found in Japanese. It occurs only in compounds and is restricted to non-initial elements (hereafter NIEs) beginning in a voiceless obstruent, i.e., *k, s, š, t, c, č, h, f* in the standard language. Synchronically, rendaku is not restricted to this standard variety, but is found in all dialects. Diachronically, rendaku is found in texts throughout all stages of the history of the language (Hizume 2010; Kupchik 2012).

When rendaku operates, the initial voiceless obstruent of an NIE voices, as illustrated in (1–4). In addition to voicing, affricatization (5) occurs in the case of *š* [ɕ], and optional deaffricatization (6) in the case of *c* [ts] (*z* may be [z] or [dz]). Despirantization (7) also occurs in the case of *f* [ɸ], while with *h* both despirantization and labialization occur in addition to voicing (8). The complex nature of the additional processes undergone by *f* and *h* are explicable with recourse to diachronic change: both are derived from an earlier *p* (Kiyose 1985; Martin 1987:10–13).

Japanese/Korean Linguistics 22.
Edited by Mikio Giriko, Naonori Nagaya, Akiko Takemura, and Timothy J. Vance.

(1)	*nuri* 'rubbing'	+	*kusuri* 'medicine'	⇒	*nuri.**g**usuri* 'ointment'
(2)	*mukae* 'welcome'	+	*sake* 'alcohol'	⇒	*mukae.**z**ake* 'hair of the dog'
(3)	*uširo* 'behind'	+	*tate* 'shield'	⇒	*uširo.**d**ate* 'backer'
(4)	*hana* 'nose'	+	*či* 'blood'	⇒	*hana.**j**i* 'nosebleed'
(5)	*kome* 'rice'	+	*širuši* 'symbol'	⇒	*kome.**j**iruši* 'asterisk'
(6)	*cuke* 'attach'	+	*cume* 'fingernail'	⇒	*cuke.**z**ume* 'false nail'
(7)	*te* 'hand'	+	*fukoro* 'bag'	⇒	*te.**b**ukoro* 'glove'
(8)	*doru* 'dollar'	+	*hako* 'box'	⇒	*doru.**b**ako* 'money spinner'

More than a century of research on rendaku has shown that the process is hedged with constraints and conditions. There exist many instances where rendaku is resisted. Many of these instances can be explained in a principled manner; this I term *systematic resistance.* However, other instances where rendaku is resisted cannot be explained in a principled manner; this I term *chaotic resistance*.

2. Systematic and Chaotic Resistance

There are at least six sets of constraints governing systematic resistance to rendaku. Their output runs the gamut from almost total blockage through to mere dampening:

MOTOORI/LYMAN'S LAW If an NIE already contains a voiced obstruent, then rendaku is blocked (Motoori 1822; Lyman 1894; Vance 1980a, 2007). This is illustrated in (9). Exceptions are extremely rare and cluster round *hašigo* 'ladder' (Suzuki 2005).

VOCABULARY STRATA Japanese is conventionally divided into four vocabulary strata: native, mimetic, Sino-Japanese and foreign.[1] Rendaku is vigorously resisted, or even blocked, in all strata bar the native. It never occurs when an NIE belongs to the mimetic stratum, only occasionally (around

[1] Non-stratal models have been proposed by Itô and Mester (1995, 1999), Fukuzawa and Kitahara (2005), and others.

10% of the time) with a Sino-Japanese stratum NIE, as in (10), and only very rarely with a foreign stratum NIE, as in (11). The stratum to which the initial element in a compound belongs plays no role in triggering rendaku.[2] For greater detail, see Vance (forthcoming) for the mimetic stratum; Vance (1996) or Irwin (2005) for the Sino-Japanese stratum; Takayama (2005) or Irwin (2011:150–153) for the foreign stratum.

COORDINATE COMPOUNDS Coordinate, or dvandva, compounds generally resist rendaku, as in (12). However, reduplicative coordinate compounds typically do undergo rendaku, as in (13). That said, quasi-mimetic reduplicative coordinate compounds never exhibit rendaku, as in (14), thus suggesting mimesis must be placed higher than reduplication in any putative rendaku resistance ranking.[3] See, *inter alia*, Okumura (1955), Otsu (1980) or Vance (1987:144–145, forthcoming).

RIGHT BRANCHING RULE Rendaku is restricted to elements on the right branch of a constituent structure (Otsu 1980), i.e., rendaku is resisted when a compound is itself part of a larger compound (15). However, this rule is not especially robust and exceptions are not uncommon, as in (16). See Vance (1980b), Itô and Mester (1986), Kozman (1998), and Kubozono (2005) for elaboration and criticism.

BARE NUMERAL INITIAL ELEMENTS When the initial element of a compound is a bare numeral, rendaku is typically blocked, as in (17); see Nakagawa (1966). This is generally not the case with full numerals, as in (18), or with Sino-Japanese numerals. Other elements of a prefix-like nature, such as *kata* 'one of two' or *hacu* 'first, initial', also have a dampening effect on rendaku (Irwin 2012), though probably not to the extent that their behaviour falls under the rubric of systematic resistance.

/m/ FROM ORIGINAL /b/ A few NIEs contain an /m/ derived from an earlier /b/ (e.g., *himo* 'string', *kemuri* 'smoke', *kaNmuri* 'crown'), and here rendaku is blocked (Nakagawa 1966; Martin 1987:31–32). In the even fewer cases where /m/ alternates with /b/ in Modern Japanese, rendaku may be found in NIEs with the /m/ allomorph: *samurai* ~ *saburai* 'warrior', *susamu* ~ *susabu* 'go to seed', *kamači* ~ *kabači* 'frame', etc.

(9)	*ai*	+	***k**agi*	⇒	*ai.**k**agi*
	'matching'		'key'		'passkey'

---

2 As noted by, among others, Ohno (2000) and Vance (forthcoming). Tamaoka et al. (2009) claim that the stratum of the initial element does have a role to play, but their results are contradicted, and Ohno's and Vance's position vindicated, by preliminary analyses to appear in Irwin (forthcoming).

3 Reduplicated baby talk also resists rendaku: *o-te.te* 'hand', *hai.hai* 'crawling'.

(10)	*mizu* 'water'	+	*hoosoo* 'smallpox'	⇒	*mizu.**b**oosoo* 'chickenpox'
(11)	*hi* 'scarlet'	+	*kanakiN*[4] 'cambric'	⇒	*hi.**g**anakiN* 'red cambric'
(12)	*cuki* 'months'	+	*hi* 'days'	⇒	*cuki.**h**i* 'time'
(13)	*šina* 'article for sale'	+	*šina* 'article for sale'	⇒	*šina.**j**ina* 'goods'
(14)	*šiwa* 'wrinkle'	+	*šiwa* 'wrinkle'	⇒	*šiwa.**š**iwa* 'wrinkly'
(15)	*jidoo* 'automatic'	+	*furi.komi* 'money transfer'	⇒	*jidoo.**f**uri.komi* 'automatic transfer'
(16)	*šooka* 'digestion'	+	*ši.ai* 'match'	⇒	*šooka.**j**i.ai* 'meaningless game'
(17)	*hito* 'one'	+	*te* 'hand'	⇒	*hito.**t**e* 'single-handed'
(18)	*icucu* 'five'	+	*hoši* 'star'	⇒	*icucu.**b**oši* '5-star'

Furthermore, parts of speech undergo rendaku to varying degrees. Resistance is significantly high when an NIE is a verb—and particularly conspicuous when all elements in a compound are verbs (Okumura 1955; Vance 2005). It has also been claimed (Yamaguchi 2011) that rendaku is dampened when an NIE is a deverbal noun in an argument-type compound.

Logic thus tells us that, in a non-coordinate compound which does not violate the right-branching rule and whose initial element is not a bare numeral, a native Japanese NIE which is not a verb and which does not contain a voiced obstruent should undergo rendaku. This is not, however, the case. What we witness instead is chaotic resistance.

Individual NIEs undergo rendaku to varying degrees. Most NIEs undergo rendaku most of the time (*kao* 'face', *same* 'shark', *kome* 'rice'), while a far smaller number resist rendaku most of the time (*take* 'mushroom', *ho* 'sail', *či* 'blood'). A few NIEs are rendaku immune, never exhibiting rendaku, e.g., *susuki* 'plume grass', *sumire* 'violet', *hama* 'beach' (Nakagawa 1966; Vance 1979, 1980a; Martin 1987:114–115; Rosen 2003; Irwin 2009). For a few NIEs the small number of compounds in which they appear

[4] From Portuguese *canequim* 'calico' (now obsolete), first attested in the early 17th century.

means that it is difficult to assess with any acceptable level of significance which way they lean: *fuyu* 'winter', *ka* 'mosquito', *kita* 'north'. A few compounds even have alternative pronunciations where the same NIE shows a rendaku and non-rendaku allomorphy: *mizu.tori~mizu.dori* 'waterfowl', *cuke.širu~cuke.jiru* 'dipping sauce', *jimu.cukue~jimu.zukue* 'office desk'.

Clearly, there are at play other inhibiting factors not introduced above. Although little research has been undertaken, it is known that rendaku varies by dialect (Miyara 1996; Sasaki 2008; Tamaoka and Ikeda 2010; Vance, Miyashita and Irwin in press) and thus dialect borrowing cannot be ruled out.[5] Sociolinguistic factors cannot be ignored either, though here too little research has been undertaken. Rendaku may vary by socio-economic group, by age cohort, or by gender (Ōta 2010, 2011). The only data which can be usefully applied are the headwords in dictionaries. Although individual Japanese speakers may disagree with the rendaku status of some of the headwords introduced in this paper, it is on dictionary headwords that the bulk of previous research (and the research I outline here) must rely.

Rosen (2001) coined the terms "rendaku lover" for a morpheme which undergoes rendaku more than two-thirds of the time and "rendaku hater" for a morpheme which undergoes rendaku less than one-third of the time. Provided NIEs are restricted to native nouns, Rosen also claimed there was "a strong apparent tendency for [an NIE] to either strongly prefer to voice, or else to resist voicing, with almost no [NIEs] occupying a middle ground between the two tendencies" (ibid.: 40) and that rendaku lovers far outnumber rendaku haters (ibid.). This "apparent tendency" represents the inverse logistic curve, or inverse S-curve, as grossly schematized in Figure 1 (on the following page). Here, the hypothetical tendency is based on the NOUN DATABASE to be described in Section 4 (cf. Figures 4 and 6).

There are two points to note about Rosen's (2001) research. First, setting out to demonstrate the various proportions of rendaku haters and rendaku lovers was not Rosen's core programme; instead it was an OT analysis of rendaku within a prosodic size criterion. Second, the database Rosen employed was small: just over 800 compounds containing 143 different NIEs, drawn from Martin (1987: 376–599), Chung (1996), and NHK (1999).[6] Although he restricted his analysis to native nouns, he took no account, with the exception of Motoori/Lyman's Law, of the various constraints governing systematic resistance outlined earlier.

---

[5] Miyara (1996) treats rendaku in the Shuri dialect of Okinawa. Depending on one's stance, this is one of the few papers treating rendaku in a Japanese dialect, or the only paper treating rendaku in a language (Ryukyuan) other than Japanese.

[6] Rosen (2001: 28) also cites a "Kodansha Japanese-English dictionary." Not listed in his bibliography, it is unclear to which dictionary this refers.

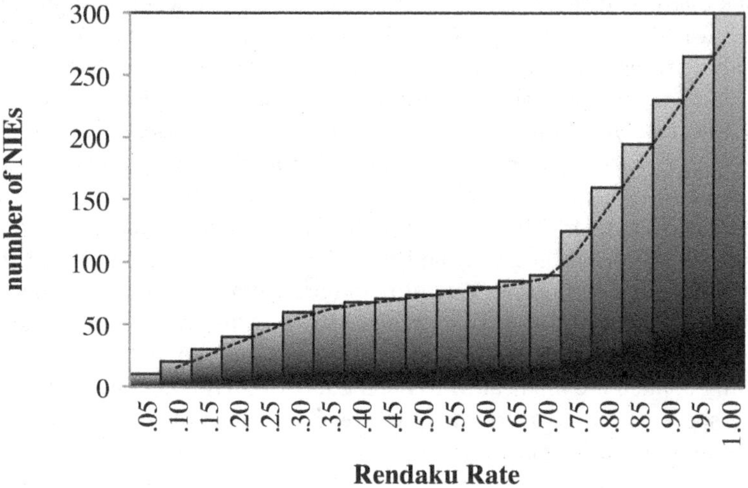

Figure 1: Rosen's (2001) Rendaku Rate "Tendency":
An Inverse Logistic Curve

Irwin (2009) demonstrated that the prosodic size rule proposed by Rosen (2001) holds up to detailed empirical scrutiny and appears robust. Whether Rosen's claim of an "apparent tendency for [an NIE] to either strongly prefer to voice, or else to resist voicing, with almost no [NIEs] occupying a middle ground between the two tendencies" (i.e., the existence of a rendaku lover/hater inverse logistic curve and a dearth of "rendaku waverers") will also hold up to detailed empirical scrutiny will be answered in the following sections.

3. Polysemy and Homophony

Nearly all accounts of rendaku, including Rosen (2001), fail to take into account polysemy, a factor which cannot be ignored in any statistical analysis of NIEs. Examples of polysemy in both English (*program*[*me*]) and Japanese (*te* 'upper limb') are given in Figure 2.

In its general linguistic sense of a 'lexical item with a range of different meanings' (Crystal 2003), distinguishing polysemy from homophony is theoretically problematic (Croft and Cruse 2004; Murphy 2010; Cruse 2011). In English, polysemes are only infrequently distinguished orthographically; *programme* vs. *program* (in British English) is a rare example. In Japanese, however, differing orthographic representations are much more commonly encountered, as in (19), although identical representations are still frequent, as in (20). Two different Japanese polysemes may differ considerably in their rendaku behaviour when they appear as an NIE in a compound, as in

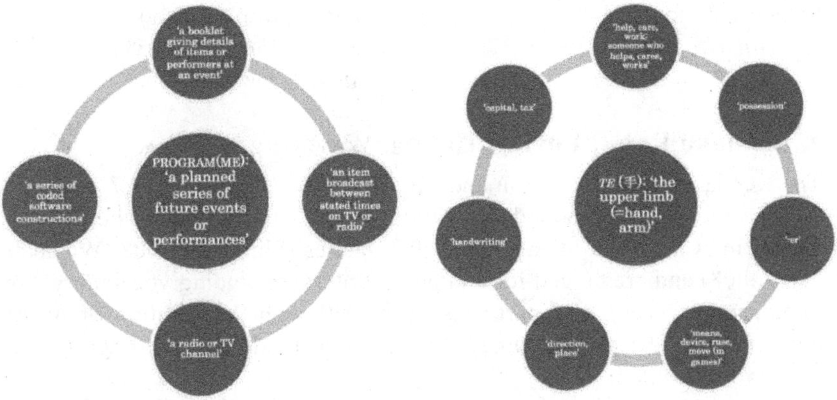

Figure 2. Polysemy in English and Japanese

(21), or they may not, as in (22), a fact first noted by Masuda (1979). As is clear from the examples, such behaviour is independent of orthography.[7]

(19) *šio* 潮 'tide' vs. *šio* 塩 'salt'
cucu 筒 'tube' vs. *cucu* 銃 'gun'
kawa 皮 'skin, film' vs. *kawa* 革 'leather'

(20) *hi* 日 'day' vs. *hi* 日 'sun(light)'
ki 木 'tree' vs. *ki* 木 'wood'
keta 桁 'beam, column' vs. *keta* 桁 'digit, figure'

(21) *kawa* 皮 'skin, film' (72%) vs. *kawa* 革 'leather' (12%)
te 手 'handwriting' (77%) vs. *te* 手 'means, trick' (7%)
ko 子 'child' (66%) vs. *ko* 子 'egg' (15%)

(22) *kuči* 口 'mouth' (72%) vs. *kuči* 口 'entrance' (87%)
ki 木 'tree' (57%) vs. *ki* 木 'wood' (73%)
cuyu 露 'dew' (0%) vs. *cuyu* 汁 'juice' (0%)

NIE homophones (when accent is ignored) may also display broadly similar rendaku rates, as in (23), or, again, they may not, as in (24). There is insufficient evidence to suggest rendaku operates in order to differentiate homophones.

(23) *hana* 花 'flower' (90%) vs. *hana* 鼻 'nose' (89%)
kaki 柿 'persimmon' (100%) vs. *kaki* 牡蠣 'oyster' (100%)
kami 神 'god' (92%) vs. *kami* 紙 'paper' (98%)

[7] The percentages in parentheses in (21)–(24) represent rendaku rates taken from Irwin and Miyashita (2012).

(24) *koi* 恋 'love' (44%) vs. *koi* 鯉 'carp' (100%)
taka 鷹 'hawk' (39%) vs. *taka* 高 'amount' (95%)
su 巣 'nest' (0%) vs. *su* 酢 'vinegar' (90%)

4. Rendaku Rates: Loving, Hating, Wavering

The Rendaku Database (Irwin and Miyashita 2012) contains 33,734 entries, all of which are compounds containing a potential rendaku site.[8] Entries appear in at least one of two major dictionaries (Shinmura 2008; Watanabe et al. 2008) and are tagged for a range of criteria, including vocabulary stratum, length, accent, and part of speech. Although the addition of further dictionaries and tags is planned, the database is already the largest of its kind ever compiled.

In order to obtain an accurate analysis of NIE rendaku rates, a NOUN DATABASE was created. This was done by excising from the Rendaku Database all compounds subject to the six constraints governing systematic resistance to rendaku described in Section 2. Additionally, the following compounds were also removed from the Rendaku Database.

(i) As Rosen (2001) treats only pure nouns, all compounds containing an NIE which is not a pure noun (i.e., deverbal and de-adjectival nouns) were removed.

(ii) NIEs appearing in fewer than 10 compounds were removed. This is too few to come to an accurate conclusion regarding their rendaku rate.

(iii) Since cross-linguistically names often exhibit aberrant behavior, all compounds which are names (but names only) were removed. Thus, *yama.gući* (a name but also a regular noun) was retained, while *yama.zaki* (a name only) was excised.

This left a residue of 15,692 compounds, compared to 800 for Rosen (2001), being 46.5% of the Rendaku Database. This NOUN DATABASE was composed of 300 different NIEs (Rosen: 143), its average rendaku rate was 80%, and the average number of different compounds in which an NIE appeared was 52 (Rosen: 6).

Figure 3 shows the frequency *n* (= number of compounds in which they appear) of the 300 NIEs in the NOUN DATABASE plotted against their rendaku rate. Based on Rosen's (2001) definitions, 77% of NIEs (83% of the NOUN DATABASE) are rendaku lovers, 12% of NIEs (11% of the NOUN DATABASE) rendaku haters, and 11% of NIEs (6% of the NOUN DATABASE)

---

[8] The Rendaku Database is part of the NINJAL 'The Japanese Lexicon: A Rendaku Encyclopedia' Project. The authors would like to express their thanks for all assistance, financial and otherwise, that has been received.

rendaku waverers. Further, if the rendaku rates of the 300 NIEs in the NOUN DATABASE are combined into 5% blocks and stacked cumulatively, we do not find, as predicted by Rosen (2001), an inverse logistic curve. Instead, as illustrated in Figure 4, we find an exponential curve.

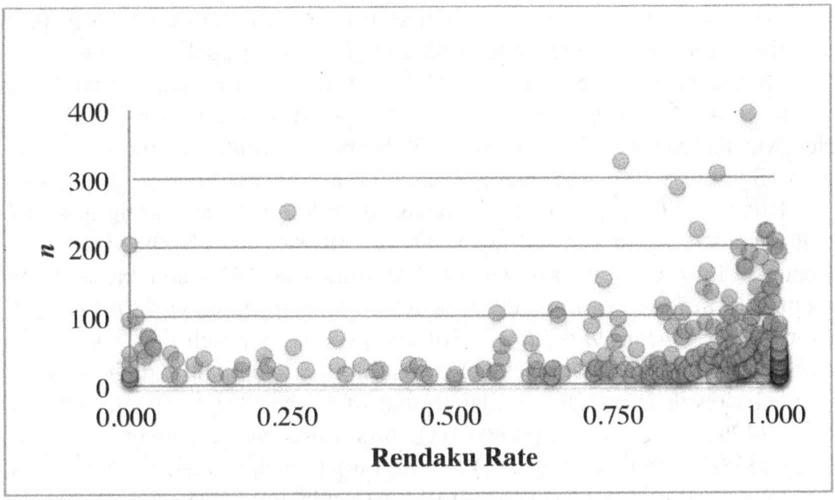

Figure 3. Rendaku Rates of NOUN DATABASE NIEs Plotted Against Frequency

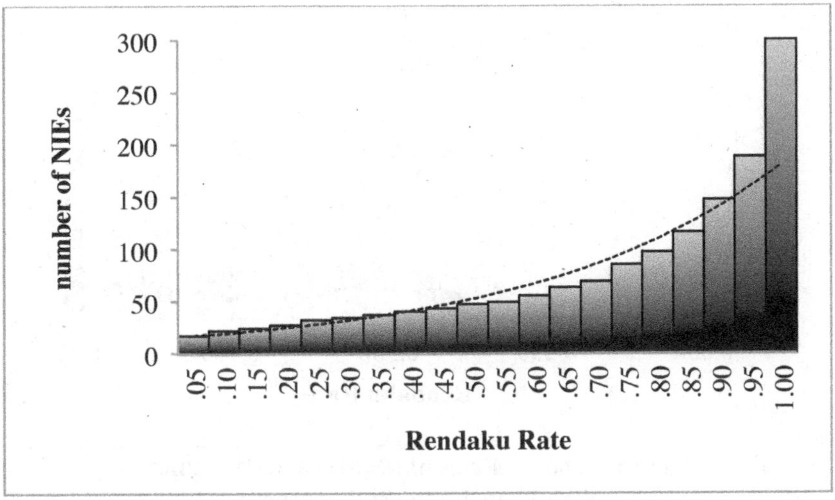

Figure 4. Rendaku Rates of NOUN DATABASE NIEs: 5%-Block Cumulative Stacks

Some compounds in the NOUN DATABASE are obscure or obsolete. An obvious objection might be that the database content does not correspond sufficiently closely to a native speaker's mental lexicon. In response to this, a second smaller NOUN (FREQ) DATABASE was created. This was done by excising from the Rendaku Database all compounds subject to the six constraints governing systematic resistance to rendaku described in Section 2 and then carrying out the three further steps (i)–(iii) applied to the NOUN DATABASE, as described above. Step (ii), however, was relaxed: all NIEs appear in five or more compounds (rather than 10 or more). An extra criterion was then applied: that all compounds appear in both the major dictionaries (Shinmura 2008; Watanabe et al. 2008) used in the Rendaku Database.

This NOUN (FREQ) DATABASE consisted of 240 NIEs appearing in 4,087 compounds (26% the size of the NOUN DATABASE and 12% the size of the Rendaku Database), its average rendaku rate was 79%, and the average number of different compounds in which an NIE appeared was 17. Figure 5 shows the frequency *n* (= number of compounds in which they appear) of the 240 NIEs in the NOUN (FREQ) DATABASE plotted against their rendaku rate. The result is broadly similar to that of the NOUN DATABASE: 77% of NIEs (77% of the NOUN (FREQ) DATABASE) are rendaku lovers, 13% of NIEs (13% of the NOUN (FREQ) DATABASE) rendaku haters, and 10% of NIEs (10% of the NOUN (FREQ) DATABASE) rendaku waverers.

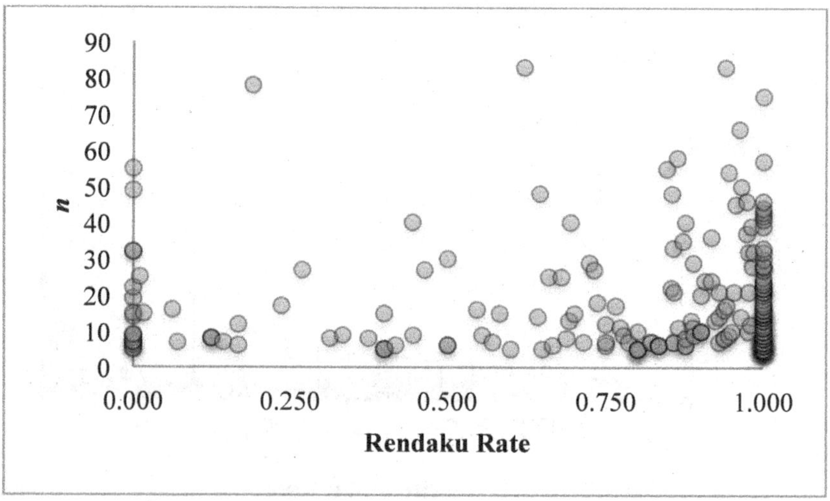

Figure 5. Rendaku Rates of NOUN (FREQ) DATABASE NIEs Plotted Against Frequency

As with the NOUN DATABASE, if the rendaku rates of the NIEs in the NOUN (FREQ) DATABASE are combined into 5% blocks and stacked cumulatively, we do not find, as predicted by Rosen (2001), an inverse logistic curve. Instead, as illustrated in Figure 6, we find, once more, an exponential curve.

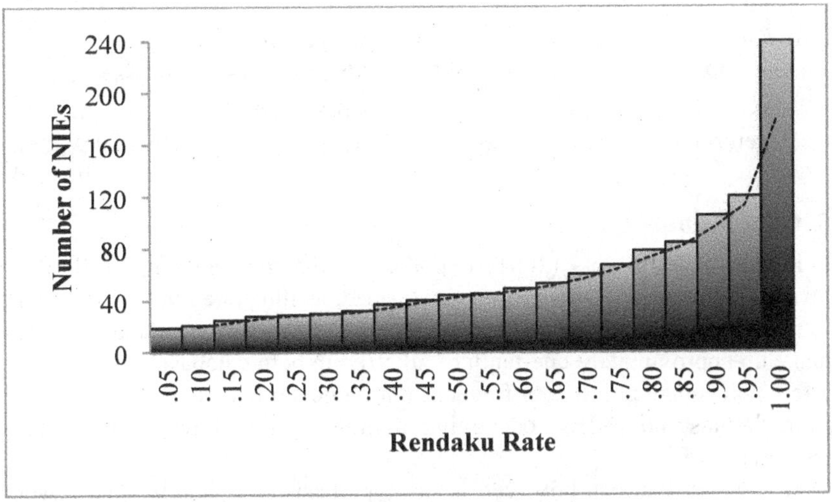

Figure 6. Rendaku Rates of NOUN (FREQ) DATABASE NIEs: 5%-Block Cumulative Stacks

Data for the two databases are summarized in Table 1. Examples of rendaku waverers (in the NOUN (FREQ) DATABASE) are given in (25) and (26).

Table 1. NOUN DATABASE and NOUN (FREQ) DATABASE Statistics

		NOUN DATABASE	NOUN (FREQ) DATABASE
number of NIEs		300	240
number of compounds		15,692	4,087
compounds per NIE		52.3	17.0
average rendaku rate		79.7%	78.7%
lovers	% of NIEs	77.3%	77.1%
waverers		10.7%	10.0%
haters		12.0%	12.9%
lovers	% of database	82.9%	76.8%
waverers		6.3%	9.9%
haters		10.8%	13.3%

(25)	*šira* 'white'	+	*hata* 'flag'	⇒	*šira.**h**ata* 'white flag'
	te 'hand'	+	*hata* 'flag'	⇒	*te.**b**ata* 'hand flag'
(26)	*kara* 'empty'	+	*cuyu* 'rainy season'	⇒	*kara.cuyu* 'drier than usual rainy season'
	modori 'returning'	+	*cuyu* 'rainy season'	⇒	*modori.zuyu* 'rainy season which returns after it's finished'

5. Conclusions

It is clear that Rosen's (2001) hypothesis—that rendaku rates follow an inverse logistic curve—is erroneous. Instead, as illustrated in Figures 4 and 6, rendaku rates exhibit an exponential curve. Moreover, rendaku waverers make up approximately one-tenth of all NIEs in both databases and are only a few percentage points less frequent than rendaku haters. This is a far cry from "almost no [NIEs] occupying a middle ground between the two tendencies."

Rosen was correct, however, in his hypothesis regarding rendaku lovers outweighing rendaku haters. The ratio exhibited by both databases is approximately 6:1 in favour of the former. Rendaku in nouns occurs approximately 80% of the time, with approximately 77% of all nouns being rendaku lovers. Although not a hypothesis put forward by Rosen, the analysis in Section 4 shows that the frequency of a compound (albeit somewhat crudely defined) appears to play no role; the proportion of lovers, haters, and waverers found in both the NOUN DATABASE and NOUN (FREQ) DATABASE were very similar (Pearson's r = .99 for NIE rendaku rates, .99 for DATABASE rendaku rates).

There remain, however, a number of unresolved issues regarding polysemy. The most pertinent of these is that division of dictionary entries by polyseme is unquestionably problematic. Major dictionaries rarely offer sub-entries by polyseme in a uniform fashion. In many cases there is scope for amalgamation or for further sub-division. Naturally, any such refinements are likely to be highly subjective. Moreover, it is not always clear if a given dictionary entry should be divided into polysemes at all, or if a polyseme is in fact a homophone. In spite of these issues, however, it appears unlikely that differing polysemic perspectives would, when analysing NIE rendaku rates database-wide, give rise to an inverse logistic, rather than an exponential, curve.

References

Chung, S. 1996. *A Japanese Word Processor*, version 1.31. http://www.physics.ucla.edu/ ~grosenth/japanese.html.

Croft, W. and Cruse, D. A. 2004. *Cognitive Linguistics*. Cambridge: Cambridge University Press.

Cruse, A. 2011. *Meaning in Language*. Oxford: Oxford University Press.

Crystal, D. 2003. *A Dictionary of Linguistics and Phonetics*, 5th ed. Oxford: Blackwell.

Fukuzawa, H. and Kitahara, M. 2005. Ranking Paradoxes in Consonant Voicing in Japanese. *Voicing in Japanese*, ed. J. van de Weijer, K. Nanjo and T. Nishihara, 105–121. Berlin: Mouton de Gruyter.

Hizume, S. 2010. Kotengo no rendaku. *Kotengo-kenkyū no shōten*, ed. M. Tsukimoto, T. Fujii and S. Hizume, 181–202. Tokyo: Musashino Shoin.

Irwin, M. 2005. Rendaku-Based Lexical Hierarchies in Japanese: The Behaviour of Sino-Japanese Mononoms in Hybrid Noun Compounds. *Journal of East Asian Linguistics* 14:121–153.

Irwin, M. 2009. Prosodic Size and Rendaku Immunity. *Journal of East Asian Linguistics* 18:179–196.

Irwin, M. 2011. *Loanwords in Japanese*. Amsterdam: John Benjamins.

Irwin, M. 2012. Rendaku Dampening and Prefixes. *NINJAL Research Papers* 4:27–36.

Irwin. M. Forthcoming. The Rendaku Database: A Statistical Analysis. *Perspectives on Rendaku: Sequential Voicing in Japanese Compounds*, ed. T. J. Vance and M. Irwin. Berlin: Mouton de Gruyter.

Irwin, M. and Miyashita, M. 2012. *The Rendaku Database*, version 1.0. http://www-h.yamagata-u.ac.jp/~irwin/site/Rendaku_Database.html.

Itô, J. and Mester, A. 1986. The Phonology of Voicing in Japanese: Theoretical Consequences for Morphological Accessibility. *Linguistic Inquiry* 17:49–73.

Itô, J. and Mester, A. 1995. Japanese Phonology. *The Handbook of Phonological Theory*, ed. J. Goldsmith, 817–838. Cambridge: Blackwell.

Itô, J. and Mester, A. 1999. The Phonological Lexicon. *The Handbook of Japanese Linguistics*, ed. N. Tsujimura, 62–100. Oxford: Blackwell.

Kiyose, G. N. 1985. Heianchō hagyō-shiin p-onron. *Onsei no Kenkyū* 21:73–87.

Kozman, T. 1998. The Psychological Status of Syntactic Constraints on Rendaku. *Japanese/Korean Linguistics 8*, ed. D. J. Silva, 107–120. Stanford: CSLI.

Kubozono, H. 2005. Rendaku: Its Domain and Linguistic Conditions. *Voicing in Japanese*, ed. J. van de Weijer, K. Nanjo and T. Nishihara, 5–20. Berlin: Mouton de Gruyter.

Kupchik, J. 2012. Morpheme-Based *Rendaku* as a Rhythmic Stabilizer in Eastern Old Japanese Poetry. *Acta Linguistica Asiatica* 2(1):1–14.

Lyman, B. S. 1894. The Change from Surd to Sonant in Japanese Compounds. Philadelphia: Oriental Club of Philadelphia.

Martin, S. E. 1987. *The Japanese Language Through Time*. New Haven: Yale University Press.

Masuda, Y. 1979. Nihongo ren'on-henka no on'in-kisoku. *Ningen to shakai no shomondai*, ed. S. Suzuki, 1123–1146. Matsuyama: Matsuyama Shōka Daigaku.

Miyara, S. 1996. Okinawahontō shurihōgen ni okeru fukugōgo to rendaku ni tsuite. *Gengo Kenkyū* 110:79–119.

Motoori, N. 1822. *Kojiki-den*. Edo: Maegawa Rokuzaemon.

Murphy, M. 2010. *Lexical Meaning*. Cambridge: Cambridge University Press.

Nakagawa, Y. 1966. Rendaku, rensei (kashō) no keifu. *Kokugo Kokubun* 35:302–314.

NHK, ed. 1999. *Nihongo hatsuon akusento jiten*. Tokyo: Nihon Hōsō Shuppan Kyōkai.

Ohno, K. 2000. The Lexical Nature of Rendaku in Japanese. *Japanese/Korean Linguistics 9*, ed. M. Nakayama and C. Quinn, 151–164. Stanford: CSLI.

Okumura, M. 1955. Rendaku. *Kokugogaku jiten*, ed. Kokugo Gakkai, 961–962. Tokyo: Tōkyōdō.

Ōta, M. 2010. Wakamono ni ooi 'wakashiraga', kō-nensō ni nokoru 'wakajiraga'. *Hōsō Kenkyū to Chōsa* 2010(11):50–70.

Ōta, M. 2011. Onna wa otoko yori mo 'tsumitsukuri'. *Hōsō Kenkyū to Chōsa* 2011(11):26–37.

Otsu, Y. 1980. Some Aspects of Rendaku in Japanese and Related Problems. *Theoretical Issues in Japanese Linguistics* (*MIT Working Papers in Linguistics* 2), ed. Y. Otsu and A. Farmer, 207–227. Cambridge: MIT.

Rosen, E. 2001 *Phonological Processes Interacting with the Lexicon: Variable and Non-Regular Effects in Japanese Phonology*. Doctoral dissertation, University of British Columbia.

Rosen, E. 2003. Systematic Irregularity in Japanese Rendaku: How the Grammar Mediates Patterned Lexical Exceptions. *Canadian Journal of Linguistics/Revue Canadienne de Linguistique* 48:1–37.

Sasaki, K. 2008. Hardening Alternation in the Mitsukaido Dialect of Japanese. *Gengo Kenkyū* 134:85–118.

Shinmura, I., ed. 2008. *Kōjien*, 6th ed. Tokyo: Iwanami.

Suzuki, Y. 2005. Raiman no hōsoku no reigai ni tsuite. *Bunkyō Gakuin Daigaku Gaikokugo Gakubu Bunkyō Gakuin Tanki Daigaku Kiyō* 4:249–265.

Takayama, T. 2005. A Survey of Rendaku in Loanwords. *Voicing in Japanese*, ed. J. van de Weijer, K. Nanjo and T. Nishihara, 177–190. Berlin: Mouton de Gruyter.

Tamaoka, K., Ihara, M., Murata, T. and Lim, H. 2009. Effects of First-Element Phonological Length and Etymological-Type Features on Sequential Voicing (Rendaku) of Second Elements. *Journal of Japanese Linguistics* 25:17–38.

Tamaoka, K. and Ikeda, F. 2010. Whiskey or Bhiskey: Influence of First Element and Dialect Region on Sequential Voicing of *Shoochuu*. *Gengo Kenkyū* 137:65–79.

Vance, T. J. 1979. *Nonsense-Word Experiments in Phonology and Their Application to Rendaku in Japanese*. Doctoral dissertation, University of Chicago.

Vance, T. J. 1980a. The Psychological Status of a Constraint on Japanese Consonant Alternation. *Linguistics* 18:245–267.

Vance, T. J. 1980b. Comments on Ōtsu (1980). *Theoretical Issues in Japanese Linguistics*, ed. Y. Otsu & A. Farmer, 229-236. MIT Working Papers in Linguistics.

Vance, T. J. 1987. *An Introduction to Japanese Phonology*. Albany: State University of New York Press.

Vance, T. J. 1996. Sequential Voicing in Sino-Japanese. *Journal of the Association of Teachers of Japanese* 30:22–43.

Vance, T. J. 2005. Rendaku in Inflected Words. *Voicing in Japanese*, ed. J. van de Weijer, K. Nanjo and T. Nishihara, 89–104. Berlin: Mouton de Gruyter.

Vance, T. J. 2007. Have We Learned Anything about Rendaku that Lyman Didn't Already Know? *Current Issues in the History and Structure of Japanese*, ed. B. Frellesvig, M. Shibatani and J. C. Smith, 153–170. Tokyo: Kurosio.

Vance. T. J. Forthcoming. Rendaku. *Handbook of Japanese Phonetics and Phonology*, ed. H. Kubozono. Berlin: Mouton de Gruyter.

Vance, T. J., Miyashita, M. and Irwin, M. In press. Rendaku in Japanese Dialects that Retain Prenasalization. *Japanese/Korean Linguistics 21*, ed. S. Nam, H. Ko and J. Jun. Stanford: CSLI.

Watanabe, T., Skrzypczak, E. and Snowden, P., eds. 2008. *Kenkyūsha's New Japanese-English Dictionary Digital Supplemented Edition*. Tokyo: Kenkyūsha.

Yamaguchi, K. 2011. Accentedness and Rendaku in Japanese Deverbal Compounds. *Gengo Kenkyū* 140:117–133.

Part II

Psycholinguistics

A Judgment Study on Aspectual Diagnostics in Japanese

KENTARO NAKATANI*
Konan University

NATSUNO AOKI
Konan University

1. Durative and Terminative Temporal Adverbials

Since Vendler (1957), aspectual properties of predicates have been extensively studied through various syntactic diagnostics. Among the most utilized are tests involving the attachment of temporal adverbials. Predicates compatible with durative adverbials (such as *for 30 minutes*) but not with terminative ones (such as *in 30 minutes*) are regarded as atelic, while those compatible with terminative but not with durative adverbials are regarded as telic. For example:

(1) a. She ate an apple in five minutes. (Telic + Terminative Adv.)
b. *She ate an apple for five minutes. (Telic + Durative Adv.)

(2) a. *She ate apples in five minutes. (Atelic + Terminative Adv.)
b. She ate apples for five minutes. (Atelic + Durative Adv.)

The judgments, however, are not as straightforward as one might wish.

* We are indebted to Nigel Duffield and the audience at the 22nd Japanese/Korean Linguistics Conference at NINJAL for their valuable comments on earlier versions of this paper.

Japanese/Korean Linguistics 22.
Edited by Mikio Giriko, Naonori Nagaya, Akiko Takemura, and Timothy J. Vance.

This is particularly true in the case of durative adverbials attached to VPs headed by accomplishment verbs. An example such as (1b) has been judged in quite diverse ways in the literature. Vendler (1957) states that such a combination is "somewhat queer"; Dowty (1979:56) claims that accomplishment predicates "only very marginally" take durative adverbials; however, in the table provided in Dowty (1979:60), the same combination is marked "OK." Smollett (2005) and Piñón (2008), among others, argue that an example like (1b) improves with a proper context. The following is judged acceptable by Smollett (2005:50).

(3) Becky ate an apple for a couple of minutes while talking on the phone.

The judgments on an example like (2a) are not entirely unproblematic either. Krifka (1998:218) points out that a VP headed by *eat* is sometimes acceptable with a terminative adverbial even when the object NP is a bare plural:

(4) Mary is an incredibly fast eater. Yesterday she ate peanuts in 0.43 seconds!

Japanese raises some interesting questions with respect to these issues, because it lacks determiners and a grammatical number system. This has the consequence that bare nominals in Japanese are always ambiguous between definite and indefinite, and between singular and plural interpretations. The present paper sheds some light on the aspectual properties of predicates in Japanese by reporting the results from a questionnaire study on the acceptability of temporal adverbial attachments. We also present a meta-analysis examining the correlation between our data and those of Aoki and Nakatani (2013), which concerns telicity cancellation.

We shall conclude that there are two types of telicity: lexically-encoded telicity and pragmatically-induced telicity. Because of this ambiguity, the terminative adverbial diagnostic cannot by itself provide firm evidence of lexical telicity, at least in Japanese. By contrast, lexically telic predicates tend to resist atelic interpretations, so the durative adverbial test, which is a test for atelicity, is actually useful as a diagnostic of lexical telicity. Aoki and Nakatani's (2013) cancellation data can also be interpreted this way: telicity cancellation provides a reliable diagnostic of atelicity, which in turn points to the degree of lexically-encoded telicity. We also argue, following Krifka (1998), that lexically encoded telicity is a concept that is independent of the duration of the event.

2. Previous Studies on Accomplishment Predicates

This section reviews previous theoretical studies on telicity. We first see how telicity emerges in accomplishment predicates, and then review prior treatments of the exceptions to the temporal adverbial attachment tests.

2.1. Incremental Verbs and Quantized Objects

It is widely accepted in the literature that the telicity in an accomplishment predicate stems from the interaction between (i) the incremental properties of the verb and (ii) the delimitedness in the object NP.

Regarding (i), verbs that can trigger telic interpretations are called by various names, including verbs of the MEASURING-OUT class (Tenny 1994), verbs with an INCREMENTAL THEME (Dowty 1991), DEGREE-OF-CHANGE verbs (Kennedy and Levin 2002), and ACCOMPLISHMENT verbs (Vendler 1957). Formally, Krifka (1989, 1992, 1998) characterizes this type of predicate as one enforcing a mapping relation between the proper parts of the event it denotes and the proper parts of the entity its direct object denotes. For example, *eat* is such a predicate because if *eat x* is true, the subevents of *eat* correspond to bits of *x*. This leads to incrementality, because the progress of the *eat* event in a time course implies incremental changes in *x*. Such a characterization does not apply to *push the cart* because the subevents of *push* do not correspond to bits of *the cart*.

Regarding (ii), it is known that in English-type languages "delimiting" NPs are those with an overt determiner or quantifier, while nondelimiting NPs are bare nominals (Dowty 1979, etc.). Krifka (1989, 1992, 1998) characterizes the former as *quantized* objects and the latter as *cumulative* objects. For example, *wine* is cumulative because parts of *wine* are also *wine* and the sum of the entities each of which is *wine* is also *wine*. By contrast, *a glass of wine* is quantized because a proper part of the entity denoted by *a glass of wine* is not *a glass of wine* (it is less than that). Krifka (1998:200) formally defines cumulative and quantized predicates as below.

(5) $\forall X \subseteq U_P\, [\mathrm{CUM}(X) \leftrightarrow \exists x, y\, [X(x) \wedge X(y) \rightarrow \neg x = y] \wedge \forall x, y\, [X(x) \wedge X(y) \rightarrow X(x \oplus_P y)]]$

(6) $\forall X \subseteq U_P\, [\mathrm{QUA}(X) \leftrightarrow \forall x, y\, [X(x) \wedge X(y) \rightarrow \neg y <_P x]]$

According to (5), if a cumulative predicate X applies to x and to y, it applies to the sum of x and y as well. According to (6), if a quantized predicate X applies to x, x never has a proper part y such that $X(y)$. Telic predicates can then be defined as quantized event predicates.[1]

Note that incremental verbs are generally not telic by themselves: if e is a *drink* event, its proper parts can be said to be *drink* events as well; thus *drink* by itself does not fit the definition given in (6). The same applies to *drink wine*. By contrast, *drink a glass of wine* is quantized because *a glass*

---

[1] Although Krifka's (1998) definition of telicity is slightly different from his definition of the quantized property shown above, this difference is irrelevant to the present study, so we take the above definition as the definition of telicity as well, provided X is an event predicate and x, y are of event type.

of wine is quantized: if *drink a glass of wine* applies to an event *e*, it does not apply to its proper parts, because they each involve an amount of wine smaller than *a glass of wine*.

Another type of potentially telic verb is one denoting a degree of change (Kennedy and Levin 2002; Piñón 2008). For example, *cool x* is clearly not incremental in Krifka's sense because there is no one-to-one mapping between the subevents of *cool* and the subobjects of *x*, but is incremental in a different sense insofar as *x* changes its state along with the progress of the event. We adopt Kennedy and Levin's term *degree-of-change verbs* for this class of incremental verbs. We call incremental verbs in Krifka's sense *incremental mapping verbs*.

Some verbs are inherently telic without being incremental. Vendlerian achievement verbs roughly correspond to this type. *Find*, for example, is not incremental: if *find* applies to an event *e*, it does not apply to any smaller parts of *e*. Note that the lack of incrementality does not necessarily lead to punctuality, which such authors as Verkuyl (1972) and Egg (1995) criticize as a trivial aspectual feature. An achievement predicate (i.e., an inherently nonincremental, quantized predicate) can be nonpunctual. *Kill* is such a predicate: a killing event may span, for example, an hour, but the predicate *kill* does not apply to any proper parts of the event.

2.2. Durative Adverbials

Let us now discuss the compatibility issues between telicity and temporal measure adverbials. First, it is well known that durative adverbials generally require the event predicates to which they adjoin to be atelic, as shown in (1b) above. Krifka (1998) argues that the reason for this is that durative adverbials quantize an event, and thus require nonquantized events. This is taken to be analogous to a more general constraint against double quantitative measuring: *two kilograms of apples* is fine, whereas *two kilograms of seven apples* is awkward (Krifka 1998:202).

If this is true, however, why are telic predicates sometimes compatible with durative adverbials, as in (3)? According to Krifka (1998:215), such cases emerge when the telic predicates optionally allow "incomplete" interpretations, in which case they are regarded atelic. Smollett (2005), by contrast, argues in the opposite direction. She hypothesizes that all the accomplishment predicates are atelic by default, thus allowing durative adverbials to be attached to them; for Smollet, telic interpretations are instead derived from pragmatic inferences we can get from the world knowledge concerning the quantized object NPs in question. For example (Smollett 2005:48):

(7) Thomas mixed the batter {for five minutes/in five minutes}.

Smollett (2005:51) argues that the telic interpretation in (7) is "optionally established by world knowledge": a certain point may optionally be set at which the ingredients are mixed sufficiently that they can be regarded as forming a batter. Although Smollett's approach appears to be very different from Krifka's, they share one crucial assumption, namely, that inferences based on world knowledge play a role in determining the telicity of a predicate.

2.3. Terminative Adverbials

Let us now turn to the question of why terminative adverbials require the predicates to which they adjoin to be telic. Krifka (1998:216–217) argues that terminative adverbials require telic predicates due to scalar implicature, the details of which we cannot review here because of space limitations. The question relevant to the present study is why a case like (4) is acceptable, even though the predicate is atelic. Krifka (1998:200, 217–218) again resorts to pragmatics: although *eat peanuts* and *eat apples* are both atelic by default, it is possible to set a plausible minimal "atomic" event in the former case but not in the latter. This is probably because when we talk about peanuts, we usually talk about more than one peanut, rather than a single peanut. This makes it possible for us to set a minimal amount of peanuts when it comes to a fast eating competition. Because of the availability of this "atomic" interpretation of *eating peanuts*, this eventive predicate gains a possible telic interpretation.

Although Krifka's theory is a formal one, the availability of the atomic interpretation relies on what we can infer from world knowledge. Curiously, this situation is similar to that observed in the acceptable cases of durative adverbials paired with telic predicates. These studies suggest that the role of pragmatic inference in the emergence of (a)telicity may be greater than what has been traditionally assumed. We could even ask this question: If the (a)telicity can be pragmatically determined in certain contexts, can we not assume that (a)telicity is always pragmatically determined? We address this through a questionnaire study on Japanese.

3. Three Hypotheses about Japanese Bare Nominals

As mentioned earlier, Japanese lacks both determiners (Fukui 1995) and a grammatical number system, although it has demonstratives as well as adnominal and adverbial numeral expressions. Thus, bare nominals in Japanese are ambiguous between definite and indefinite and between singular and plural interpretations, especially when there is no preceding context:

(8) kare wa ringo o tabe-ta
he TOP apple ACC eat-PAST
'He ate an apple/apples/the apple/the apples.'

Our concern here is with the aspectual status of such a sentence. The verb *tabe* 'to eat' is incremental, just like English *eat*. How about *ringo* 'apple'? According to Krifka's definitions given in (5) and (6), *ringo* is clearly cumulative: if *x* is *ringo* and *y* is *ringo*, then the sum of *x* and *y* is also *ringo*. Based on this fact, we can make at least three types of competing predictions regarding temporal adverbial attachment.

First, it could be predicted that this type of sentence is always compatible with durative adverbials and not with terminative ones, because its object *ringo* by itself is cumulative by definition.

Alternatively, it could be predicted that (8) is equally compatible with both durative and terminative adverbials, because *ringo* is interpretatively ambiguous between definite and indefinite, and between singular and plural.

Finally, we could hypothesize that the telicity of (8) is brought in by nonlexical, pragmatic inferences about the object itself or the event as a whole (Smollett 2005). If this were the case, compatibility judgments on temporal adverbials would vary depending on individual cases.

4. Telicity Cancellation

A less-studied diagnostic related to aspect is telicity cancellation (Ikegami 1985, Kageyama 1996, Tsujimura 2003), which is exemplified below:

(9) otiba o moyasi-ta kedo moe-na-katta.
fallen.leaf ACC burn(tr)-PAST but burn(intr)-NEG-PAST
'I burnt the fallen leaves, but they didn't burn.'

Here, in the first half of the sentence the burning of the leaves is asserted, while it is negated in the second half. It is often claimed that this type of cancellation is acceptable in Japanese, unlike in English. On the basis of this fact, Tsujimura (2003) argues that in Japanese, telicity is not lexically entailed but rather is conversationally implicated, and thus cancellable. Aoki and Nakatani (2013; henceforth A&N) tested this hypothesis through a questionnaire study and found that Tsujimura's cancellation examples were rated significantly lower than examples with result events not logically entailed, which A&N call *fake telic predicates*, such as (10a) below (note that the English translation is perfectly acceptable here), but still higher than the cancellation of the telicity of typical achievements, such as (10b). See Figure 1 for the mean rating scores of the three types of predicates cited from A&N.

(10) a. te o arat-ta ga kirei-ni nara-na-katta
hand ACC wash-PAST but clean become-NEG-PAST
'He washed his hands but they didn't become clean.'

b. mizu o mitasi-ta ga hanbun sika haira-na-katta.
water ACC fill-PAST but half only(NPI) go.in-NEG-PAST
'She filled (it) with water, but it was filled only halfway.'

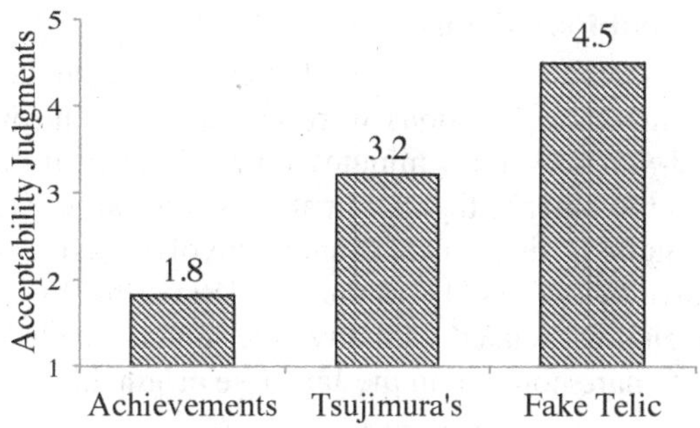

Figure 1. Mean Rating Scores of A&N's Telicity Cancellation Study

A&N thus hypothesize (i) that eventive telicity is actually entailed even in Japanese, and (ii) that the cancellation is acceptable depending on how easily one can infer the process component in the denoted event.

Before proceeding, we must briefly mention the relation between Tsujimura's hypothesis and Smollett's (2005). Although both argue for a pragmatics-based theory of telicity, they do not share the same explanatory goal. Tsujimura's hypothesis is intended to explain the lack of telicity in Japanese as opposed to its presence in English (implying that she is arguing that the telicity in English is *not* pragmatically induced), whereas Smollett applies her theory of pragmatically-induced telicity to English. A&N (2013: fn.3) argue that the contrast between English and Japanese stems from the difference in the degree of leniency that the two languages show in repairing logical contradictions, not from any difference in how the telicity is encoded. This means that one can without inconsistency adopt Smollett's pragmatics-based theory of telicity while rejecting Tsujimura's. The fact that Tsujimura's examples showed varied cancellability judgments in A&N's study could probably be explained along the lines of Smollett's assumption on pragmatically induced telicity.

In this study, we shall present a meta-analysis of the correlation between A&N's results from the cancellation survey and our results from temporal adverbial diagnostics.

5. Questionnaire Study

A questionnaire study was conducted to address the questions outlined above: (i) How varied are judgments on sentences involving the attachment of temporal adverbials, especially when the direct objects are bare nominals? (ii) To what extent do pragmatic inferences influence the availability of telic vs. atelic interpretations? (iii) How are judgments on telicity cancellation reported in A&N associated with those on temporal adverbials?

5.1. Method

5.1.1. Materials and Predictions

We prepared 35 sentences, of which 31 were based on items in A&N's study. For each item, two versions were constructed, one with a durative adverbial (e.g., *3-pun-kan* 'for 3 minutes') placed between the direct object and the verb, and the other with a terminative adverbial (e.g., *3-pun-de* 'in 3 minutes') in the same position. One example involving an incremental mapping verb is shown below in (11). In the translation, the direct object is italicized without being associated with any determiners or plural morphemes, to show that it is a bare nominal in the Japanese original.

(11) Incremental Mapping
Takasi wa ringo o {3-pun de/3-pun-kan} tabe-ta.
Takashi TOP apple ACC {in 3 minutes/for 3 minutes} eat-PAST
'Takashi ate *apple* in 3 minutes/for 3 minutes.'

Among the 35 items, 31 contained direct objects, of which 18 were simple bare nouns (such as *ringo* 'apple') and five were bare NPs consisting of two words (such as *omoi tukue* 'heavy desk' and *kami no ke* 'hair of the head' (as opposed to 'body hair'). The remaining direct objects (eight items) contained either demonstratives (e.g., *sono otoko* 'that man'), possessives (e.g., *mina no iken* 'everybody's opinion'), or a quantified NP (*1-rittoru no gyuunyuu* 'one liter of milk').

Regarding the predicate types involved, 13 items included two kinds of incremental predicates, namely, incremental mapping predicates (such as *tabe* 'to eat') and degree-of-change predicates (such as *kawakas* 'to dry (transitive)'). A sample of the former type is shown above in (11), as well as in (12) below, and a sample of the latter type is shown in (13) below. The effects of an overt quantifier in Japanese could be tested by comparing (11), where the direct object was a bare nominal, with (12) below, which has an overt quantifier.

(12) Taroo wa 1-rittoru no gyuunyuu o {3-pun de/3-pun-kan} non-da
Taro TOP one-liter GEN milk ACC {in/for 3 minutes} drink-PAST
'Taro drank a liter of milk in/for 3 minutes.'

(13) Degree of Change
obasan ga sentakumono o {10-pun-de/10-pun-kan} kawakasi-ta
lady NOM laundry ACC {in 10 minutes/for 10 minutes } dry-PAST
The lady dried *laundry* in 10 minutes/for 10 minutes.'

Closely related to the incremental items were fake telic items such as those in (10) and (14).

(14) ueetaa ga kanbiiru o zyokki ni {5-byo de/5-byo-kan} sosoi-da
waiter NOM canned.beer ACC mug DAT {in/for 5 sec} pour-PAST
'The waiter poured *canned beer* into *mug* in/for 5 seconds.'

The verb *sosog* (conjugated as *sosoi* above) 'to pour' by itself is cumulative and incremental, and can be quantized either by the locatum ('beer') or by the location ('mug'). However, an incomplete interpretation seems to be readily available even in English (e.g., *The waiter poured a bottle of beer into the glass just for a few seconds*). A similar observation applies to *araw* 'to wash' in (10a), which is a cumulative predicate, not an incremental mapping one (although it is not clear if it qualifies as a degree-of-change predicate), and does not fit Krifka's definition of quantization given in (6) above. However, a telic interpretation may be pragmatically induced, even in English (e.g., *He washed his hands in 3 seconds*). The question relevant to the present study was how such fake telic predicates in Japanese would behave with respect to temporal adverbial attachment.

Two types of nonincremental predicates were also included, namely, nonincremental quantized predicates (such as *mitas* 'to fill'), which are inherently telic, and cumulative activity predicates (e.g., *nagame* 'to look at'), which are inherently atelic. We prepared 14 items of the former type and two items of the latter type.[2] Sample items are shown below.

(15) Nonincremental, Quantized (Achievement)
ueetoresu ga koppu ni mizu o {3-byoo de/3-byoo-kan} mitasi-ta
waitress NOM glass DAT water ACC {in/for 3 seconds} fill-PAST
'The waitress filled *glass* with *water* in/for 3 seconds.'[3]

(16) Cumulative (Activity)
watasi wa sono e o {30-pun de/30-pun-kan} nagame-ta
I TOP that painting ACC {in/for 30 minutes} look-PAST
'I looked at that painting in/for 30 minutes.'

We were also interested in examining the effect of adding semantically different objects to the same verb, as in (17)–(19) (adapted from A&N).

[2] Unfortunately, we failed to balance the number of each predicate type, because we used slightly different criteria for the verb classification when preparing the items.

[3] In Japanese, *mitas* 'to fill' is an alternating verb, capable of taking a locatum or a location as its direct object.

(17) zyukensei ga sono rensyuumondai o {10-pun de/10-pun-kan} toi-ta
student NOM that exercise ACC {in/for 10-minutes} solve-PAST
'The student solved the exercise in/for 10 minutes.'

(18) kookoosei ga sono nanmon o {10-pun de/10-pun-kan} toi-ta
high.school.student NOM that hard.problem ACC {in/for 10 minutes} solve-PAST
'The high school student solved the hard problem in/for 10 minutes.'

(19) kanozyo wa karesi no gokai o {2-ka de/2-ka-kan} toi-ta
she TOP boyfriend GEN misunderstanding ACC {in/for 2 days} solve-PAST
'She resolved her boyfriend's misunderstanding in/for 2 days.'

All of the examples in (17)–(19) involve the same verb *tok* (conjugated as *toi*) 'to solve,' while the direct objects differ in each case. Our predictions were as follows. First, we assumed that *tok* is a nonincremental, quantized predicate. However, comparing (17) and (18), the former were expected to be more permissive of durative adverbial attachment than the latter, because we know as a matter of world knowledge that 'exercise' often involves a set or series of problems, while 'hard problem' is often singular. The plural reading of the object available for 'exercise' could yield an iterative, atelic reading. Second, comparing (18) and (19), the former would be relatively more compatible with a durative adverbial than the latter, because we can infer that solving a hard problem (in 10 minutes) involves a more continuous activity than solving a boyfriend's misunderstanding (in two days). Our assumption was that durative adverbials could measure an interval of the event more readily when it was continuous than when it was not.

The total of 70 sentences (35 items × 2 conditions) items were split into two lists, such that the two conditions (the Durative Adverbial and Terminative Adverbial conditions; D and T for short) of each item appeared in separate lists, with each list including the same amount of D and T. In each list, the D and T conditions alternated, so that the participants could easily predict which of the two conditions would come next and would not mistake the crucial temporal markers, *-kan* 'for' and *de* 'in'. The materials in each list were pseudo-randomized.

5.1.2. Participants and Procedure

The participants were 48 native speakers of Japanese, all of whom were undergraduates. Participants were handed an instruction sheet together with three sheets of paper containing the test materials. It was explained on the instruction sheet that all the sentences contained temporal adverbial expressions. Participants were instructed to rate the naturalness of each sentence on a five-point scale by circling one of five numbers, with '5' corresponding ed to 'most natural' and '1' corresponding to 'most unnatural'. The participants were instructed to rate each item quickly, following their immediate intuitions. They were asked to rate one list first, and then, roughly one hour later, were asked to rate the other list, meaning that every participant rated all 70 sentences.

5.2. Results and Discussion

The data from the three subjects who failed to complete the experiment were excluded from the analyses. The data points from one item (×2) were also excluded due to a typographical error in the item.

The grand mean of the 34 items (×2) was 3.4 (SD 1.5). Although a majority (23) of the 34 items contained bare object NPs, the mean rating of condition T was higher than that of D (4.0 (SD 1.3) vs. 2.8 (SD 1.5)). Pearson's χ^2 test revealed this difference to be statistically significant ($\chi^2 = 484.2$, $df = 4$, $p < .001$). Histograms for these two conditions (Figure 2) clearly show that the judgments on D were much more varied than those on T, whose distribution was skewed rightward, suggesting that telic interpretations were more readily available than atelic ones. This overall tendency does not seem to support the first two hypotheses mentioned in Section 3 regarding the aspectual properties of predicates with bare nominals in Japanese. That is to say, the tendency supports neither the hypothesis that incremental predicates with bare nominals are always cumulative, nor the hypothesis that they always allow both telic and atelic interpretations with equal ease. By contrast, this result seems to suggest that telicity was made available through pragmatic inferences in many cases, improving the overall acceptability of T, while atelic interpretations were harder to obtain.

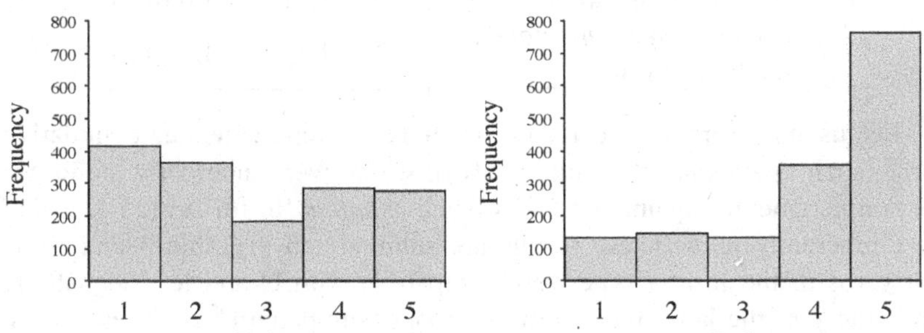

Figure 2. Histograms of Judgments on D (Left) and T (Right)

The results from the items with the three potentially telic verbs, namely, the incremental mapping verbs, the degree-of-change verbs, and the fake telic verbs, are summarized in Table 1. Because the number of the items per verb type was limited, it is not possible to draw any strong conclusion, but it is at least obvious from these results that all of these three types of verbs were highly compatible with T. As for the degree-of-change items and the fake telic items, where the direct objects were always bare nominals, the D condition was also highly acceptable, showing that bare nominals allowed nonquantized interpretations as well.

Table 1. Mean Ratings (SDs) of Potentially Telic Verbs

Type (Number of Items)	D	T
Incremental Mapping (6)	3.0 (1.3)	4.5 (0.9)
Degree of Change (5)	3.9 (1.2)	4.0 (1.2)
Fake Telic (2)	4.4 (1.0)	4.2 (1.0)

What was somewhat unexpected was the lack of any effect of an overt quantifier. The relevant results are shown in Table 2. Here, we can see that 'ate *apple* (bare noun)' was rated almost identically to 'drank a liter of milk (overtly quantified)' both in the D and T conditions, although we had expected that the D condition would be rated higher when the direct object was a bare noun than when it was quantified. This lack of a quantification effect might be due to the fact that *ringo* 'apple' is a count noun with a clear physical boundary in the real world, thus strongly inducing a quantized reading. An interesting comparison could have been made between bare count nouns and bare mass nouns with incremental verbs, which we did not test and leave for future research.

Table 2. Effect of an Overt Quantifier

	D	T
ringo o tabe ta 'ate *apple*'	2.7 (1.1)	4.8 (0.4)
1-rittoru no gyuunyuu o nonda 'drank a liter of milk'	2.7 (1.1)	4.7 (0.5)

Let us now turn to the results from the nonincremental, cumulative verbs (such as *nagame* 'to look' in (16)), which were inherently atelic, vs. the nonincremental, quantized verbs (such as *mitas* 'to fill' in (15)), which were inherently telic. These results are summarized in Table 3 and show that verbs of the former type were compatible with D and less so with T, while those of the latter type showed the opposite pattern.[4] For these verbs, it seems difficult to induce (a)telic interpretation through pragmatic cueing.

[4] The reader may notice that the sum of the items with incremental and nonincremental verbs shown in Tables 1 and 3 is only 29, which is less than the total number of items (34). The reason is that we excluded the items with verbs whose aspectual status was not clear to us, such as *ku* 'to come', *ik* 'to go', and *ugokas* 'to move'.

Table 3. Mean Ratings (SDs) of Nonincremental Verbs

Type (Number of Items)	D	T
Nonincremental, Cumulative (2)	3.9 (1.3)	2.7 (1.5)
Nonincremental, Quantized (14)	1.9 (1.1)	3.7 (1.5)

This point is especially important for the nonincremental, quantized verbs, because for these verbs, it was sometimes easy to pragmatically infer a certain duration in the process. For example, *sosog* 'to pour' (14) and *mitas* 'to fill' (15) denote very similar events, according to our world knowledge. However, these two verbs showed a sharp contrast, as seen in Table 4. This clearly suggests that the unavailability of atelicity in *mitas* 'to fill' cannot be accounted for in terms of our world knowledge. We must assume that the telic property of *mitas* is linguistically determined, thus blocking any effects of pragmatics.

Table 4. *sosog* 'to pour' vs. *mitas* 'to fill'

	D	T
sosog 'to pour'	4.0 (1.1)	4.2 (0.9)
mitas 'to fill'	1.8 (0.9)	3.7 (1.3)

The same point applies to the contrast between *araw* 'to wash' and *kireeni su* 'to clean', summarized in Table 5.

Table 5. *araw* 'to wash' vs. *kireeni su* 'to clean'

	D	T
te o araw 'to wash *hand*'	4.7 (0.9)	4.2 (1.0)
heya o kireeni su 'to clean *room*'	2.5 (1.2)	4.8 (0.5)

Finally, we conducted a correlation analysis between our D ratings and the ratings in A&N to test the hypothesis that the cancellation judgments are a function of the ease in inferring a process component in the event, which is associated with the concept of duration. A simple regression analysis of all the 30 items containing the predicates shared between the two studies failed to reveal a correlation between D and cancellation ($R^2 = .097$, $p > .09$).[5] However, a closer look at the data revealed that the top three items with the highest cancellation scores constituted outliers in the regression analysis.[6] When these three outliers were removed, the correlation between

[5] One item was removed from the analyses due to a typographical error, as noted earlier.

[6] These items showed very high cancellability and very low D compatibility. The verbs in these items were *okur* 'to send' (the cancellation score 4.8 vs. the D score 1.8), *age* 'to give (to a nonspeaker)' (4.4 vs. 1.7), and *kure* 'to give (to the speaker)' (4.4 vs. 1.5). They all involved

the A&N cancallation ratings and our D ratings turned out to be statistically significant ($R^2 = .431$, $p < .001$; see Figure 3).

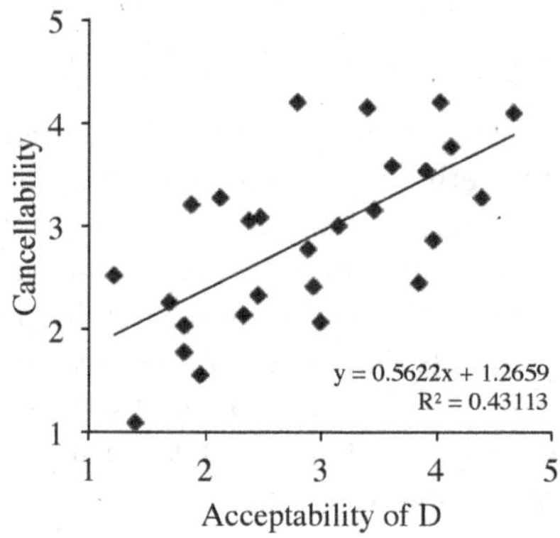

Figure 3. Correlation between Cancellability in A&N and the D Diagnostic

Our predictions were also supported by the results from the varied direct objects used with *tok* 'to solve' in (17)–(19) and a comparison with the A&N cancellation results, summarized in Table 6. In this case, the D diagnostic was a strong predictor of the cancellability judgments, while the T diagnostic was not.

Table 6. Mean Ratings (SDs) for *tok* 'solve' with Different Objects

	Cancellation	D	T
sono rensyuumondai o 'the exercise'	3.6 (1.4)	3.6 (1.4)	5.0 (0.1)
sono nanmon o 'the hard problem'	2.8 (1.4)	2.9 (1.4)	4.9 (0.3)
karesi no gokai o 'boyfriend's misunderstanding'	2.0 (1.1)	1.8 (1.0)	4.0 (1.1)

6. Conclusions

We have reported here the results of a questionnaire study on the compatibility between verbs of various aspectual types and durative/terminative adverbials in Japanese.

It has been shown that incremental verbs, whether they are incremental mapping verbs (Krifka 1998) or degree-of-change verbs (Kennedy and Levin 2002), are highly compatible with terminative adverbials even when their

a dual event, which was comprised of a giving activity of the giver and a receiving activity of the recipient, both of which were quantized/telic.

direct objects are not explicitly quantized. This shows that telicity can be induced by pragmatic inferences for the incremental verbs. Unlike the degree-of-change verbs, however, the incremental mapping verbs show more resistance to an atelic reading even when the direct object is a bare noun. This contrast may reflect the difference in the type of direct objects (i.e., count vs. mass nouns) or in the aspectual properties of these two types of verbs (i.e., the degree-of-change verbs might be more open-ended than the incremental mapping verbs), or both. Further research is required to settle this.

It was also found that the inherently nonincremental verbs (inherently cumulative and inherently quantized verbs) tended to resist the introduction of (a)telicity through pragmatic inferences. This was true for the nonincremental, quantized verbs such as *mitas* 'to fill', *kireeni su* 'to clean', and *koros* 'to kill' (T 4.2; D 1.2), for which certain duration could be easily inferred based on world knowledge. These results show that (a)telicity is not exclusively determined pragmatically. This necessitates the distinction between accomplishment and achievement verbs (but see also Verkuyl 1972 and Egg 1995). Note that our definition of achievements is based on Krifka's criteria of incrementality, cumulativity and quantization, and has nothing to do with the property of instantaneity, which these authors criticize.

Finally, we conducted a meta-analysis on the relation between our results from temporal adverbial diagnostics and the A&N results on telicity cancellation. It was found that telicity cancellation judgments were significantly correlated with the compatibility with durative adverbials, as A&N had predicted. This implies that the telicity cancellation test is better regarded as a diagnostic for atelicity, rather than for telicity. That is to say, to the extent that atelic interpretation is acceptable, cancellation is acceptable. Once again, it should be noted that this characterization is based on the definition of telicity according to Krifka, rather than on the duration of the denoted or inferred event. Although A&N was correct in arguing that telicity cancellation was not really about telicity, the characterization of atelicty based on the "inferred process component of the event" was probably misleading, because inherently telic predicates may be associated with certain activities in the real world.

References

Aoki, N. and Nakatani, K. 2013. Process, Telicity, and Event Cancellability in Japanese: A Questionnaire Study. *JELS* 30:257–263.

Dowty, D. R. 1979. *Word Meaning and Montague Grammar*. Dordrecht: Reidel.

Dowty, D. R. 1991. Thematic Proto-Roles and Argument Selection. *Language* 67: 547–619.

Egg, M. 1995. The Intergressive as a New Category of Verbal Aktionsart. *Journal of Semantics* 12:311–356.

Fukui, N. 1995. *Theory of Projection in Syntax*. Stanford: CSLI.

Ikegami, Y. 1985. 'Activity' – 'Accomplishment' – 'Achievement': a Language that Can't Say 'I Burned It, but It Didn't Burn' and One That Can. *Linguistics and Philosophy: Essays in Honor of Rulon S. Wells*, ed. A. Makkai and A. K. Melby, 265–304. Amsterdam: John Benjamins.

Kageyama, T. 1996. *Dōshi Imiron* (Semantics of Verbs). Tokyo: Kurosio.

Kennedy, C. and Levin, B. 2002. Telicity Corresponds to Degree of Change. Unpublished manuscript, UCLA.

Krifka, M. 1989. Nominal Reference, Temporal Constitution and Quantification in Event Semantics. *Semantics and Contextual Expressions*, ed. R. Bartsch, J. Van Benthem, and P. Van Emde Boas, 75–115. Dordrecht: Foris.

Krifka, M. 1992. Thematic Relations as Links between Nominal Reference and Temporal Constitution. *Lexical Matters*, ed. I. Sag and A. Szabolcsi, 197–235. Stanford: CSLI.

Krifka, M. 1998. The Origins of Telicity. *Events and Grammar*, ed. S. Rothstein, 197–235. Dordrecht: Kluwer.

Martin, F. 2011. Revisiting the Distinction between Accomplishments and Achievements. *From Now to Eternity*, ed. Jesse Mortelmans, Tanja Mortelmans, and Walter de Mulder, 43–64. Amsterdam: Rodopi.

Piñón, C. 2008. Aspectual Composition with Degrees. *Adjectives and Adverbs: Syntax, Semantics, and Discourse*, ed. L. McNally and C. Kennedy, 183–219. Oxford: Oxford University Press.

Smollett, R. 2005. Quantized Direct Objects Don't Delimit After All. *Perspectives on Aspect*, ed. H. J. Verkuyl, H. de Swart, and A. van Hout, 41–59. Dordrecht: Springer.

Tenny, C. 1994. *Aspectual Roles and the Syntax-Semantics Interface*. Dordrecht: Kluwer.

Tsujimura, N. 2003. Event Cancellation and Telicity. *Japanese/Korean Linguistics 12*, ed. W. McClure, 388–399. Stanford: CSLI.

Vendler, Z. 1957. Verbs and Times. *The Philosophical Review* 66:143–60.

Verkuyl, H. J. 1972. *On the Compositional Nature of the Aspects*. Dordrecht: Reidel.

Inferring Verb Meanings from Syntactic Frames by Japanese Two-Year-Old Children: An Experimental Approach Using an IPL Paradigm with a Dialogue Phase

TESSEI KOBAYASHI*
NTT Communication Science Labs

TAKAAKI SUZUKI
Kyoto Sangyo University

1. Syntactic Bootstrapping

Syntactic bootstrapping is the proposal that children make use of syntactic information to learn verb meanings (Gleitman 1990). Learning verb meanings is a complex and challenging task for children. Unlike nouns, verbs refer to ever-changing events, and they often refer to only particular aspects of the events, such as actions, manners, and states. At the onset of verb learning, children need help to focus on the particular aspects that the verb describes, and syntactic bootstrapping helps children in this regard. For example, the meaning of the verb *gorp* in the sentence *The duck is gorping the bunny* is inferable to some extent. Because this sentence consists of an NP, a V, and an NP, the verb is considered transitive, and its meaning is likely to denote a certain kind of causation. Although it is impossible to determine the precise meaning of the verb, syntactic frames act as a kind of "zoom

---

* We thank Kaori Yuruki and Tomoko Kawaguchi for their assistance with data collection and coding, and Miki Terasaka for drawing illustrations used in this paper.

Japanese/Korean Linguistics 22.
Edited by Mikio Giriko, Naonori Nagaya, Akiko Takemura, and Timothy J. Vance.

lens" in directing the listener's attention to certain aspects of the event (Fisher, Gleitman and Gleitman 1991; Gleitman 1990).

A seminal study on syntactic bootstrapping in young children was carried out by Naigles (1990), who used an intermodal preferential looking (IPL) paradigm to demonstrate that English-speaking 25-month-old children are able to use sentence frames to infer a causative/non-causative distinction. Her experiment consisted of two phases. In the training phase, children saw a combination of two different actions performed by two animal entities, one causative (a duck forced a rabbit into a bending position), and the other non-causative (a duck and a rabbit flexed their arms simultaneously). The children in the transitive condition heard a novel verb in the transitive frame (*Look, the duck is gorping the bunny!*), and those in the intransitive condition heard a novel verb in the intransitive frame (*Look, the duck and the bunny are gorping!*). In the following test phase, the causative and non-causative action scenes were presented separately side by side while the children were asked which action was denoted by the novel verb (*Which is gorping?*). Naigles found that the children looked preferentially at the causative scene for the transitive frame (NP-V-NP) and preferentially at the non-causative scene for the intransitive frame (NP-V), providing evidence that English-speaking 2-year-olds can use syntactic frames to infer verb meanings in terms of a causative/non-causative distinction. The original finding has been replicated in English using different methods (e.g., Fisher 1996) and testing different frames (e.g., Naigles 1996).

2. Current Issues

To better understand the nature of syntactic bootstrapping, recent investigations have addressed certain important issues. One is whether syntactic bootstrapping occurs in argument-drop languages. Previous studies on syntactic bootstrapping have been largely limited to English, in which syntactic frames are highly informative about a verb's transitivity because argument NPs must be overtly expressed. On the other hand, in an argument-drop language like Japanese, syntactic frames may not be a robust cue to transitivity. As the following examples show, argument NPs are frequently dropped as long as their information is recoverable from the context or shared by the speaker and the hearer. The transitive verb *homeru* 'praise' can be used in the following ways.

(1) Kyooko ga Saori o hometa.
Kyoko NOM Saori ACC praised
'Kyoko praised Saori.'

(2) Kyooko ga hometa.
Kyoko NOM praised

(3) Saori o hometa.
Saori ACC praised

(4) Hometa.
praised

Both a subject marked with nominative *ga* and a direct object marked with accusative *o* appear in (1), only a subject appears in (2), only a direct object appears in (3), and both the subject and direct object are omitted from (4), all of which are grammatical in Japanese. These patterns suggest that the syntactic frames used for English-type languages, such as NP-V-NP and NP-V, may not work well for identifying the transitivity of a verb. Thus, children learning argument-drop languages may not be able to infer verb meanings from syntactic frames (e.g., Rispoli 1995; Suzuki 2002).

To investigate this issue, Matsuo et al. (2012) examined Japanese-speaking 28-month-old children by adapting Naigle's method to Japanese. Using the same visual stimuli and procedure, this study tested three sentence patterns: the intransitive frame (*Ahiru-san to usagi-san ga neketteru yo* 'The duck and the rabbit are X-ing'), the transitive frame (*Ahiru-san ga usagi-san o neketteru yo* 'The duck is X-ing the rabbit'), and the transitive frame without case markers (*Ahiru-san usagi-san neketteru yo* 'The duck is X-ing the rabbit'). The results showed that Japanese-speaking 2-year-olds associated the sentences provided in the transitive frame with causative events, but the other two types of sentences were not associated with any particular events. On the basis of these results, Matsuo et al. proposed that Japanese 2-year-olds utilize the combination of the number of overt arguments and case markers to infer the meaning of a new verb.

The data from other argument-drop languages are also informative. Göksun, Küntay and Naigles (2008) and Lee and Naigles (2008) examined Turkish-speaking 2- to 5-year-olds and Mandarin-speaking 2- and 3-year-olds, respectively. In an act-out comprehension task, the children were given intransitive verbs in a transitive frame and transitive verbs in an intransitive frame, and then were asked to act-out the scenes by using puppets and props. The results showed that in both languages the children followed the syntactic frames for the interpretation of the sentences, and ignored the verb's original transitivity. These findings indicate early sensitivity to syntactic frames in children learning argument-drop languages, although it is impossible to make a direct comparison with the original IPL studies in English (Naigles 1990) because the Turkish and Mandarin studies used familiar verbs in their act-out tasks, and their participants included relatively older children.

Another important issue in recent research on syntactic bootstrapping is concerned with the availability of visual cues. Although traditional studies on syntactic bootstrapping have shown action events visually in the training phase when providing target sentences (e.g., Naigles 1990), such a procedure is unnecessary. The basic idea of syntactic bootstrapping is that syntactic information itself is informative about verb meanings (Gleitman 1990; Landau and Gleitman 1985), and so children do not need visual information in order to guess the gross meanings of a new verb. Arunachalam and Waxman (2010), and Yuan and Fisher (2009) have succeeded in observing children's syntactic bootstrapping in English by providing syntactic information alone in the absence of visual cues. In their "dialogue method," children did not see an action event but instead saw a two-woman dialogue scene in the training phase. In the dialogue, two women used a novel verb embedded in a transitive or intransitive frame. Then, causative and non-causative action scenes were simultaneously presented in the test phase. The results of both studies showed that English-speaking 27- to 28-month-old toddlers looked longer or pointed more often at the causative action in the transitive frame, providing evidence that children can infer verb meanings from syntactic information alone in the absence of visual cues.

3. Aims of the Present Study

In the present study, we investigated whether syntactic bootstrapping occurs in children learning Japanese by using a dialogue method in an IPL paradigm. A critical issue here is to determine whether the children can infer verb meanings from syntactic information alone in the absence of visual cues. The syntactic information includes morphological or morpho-syntactic properties such as case markers, and the position and the number of argument NPs. In this study, we use the term syntactic bootstrapping to refer to the utilization of these aspects of the language. Our participants were given two-woman dialogue-clips including a novel verb embedded in either transitive or intransitive frames and asked which of the events shown in the two adjacent scenes (causative scene vs. non-causative scene) indicated the meaning of the novel verb. We predicted that if the children infer the meaning of the novel verb from syntactic information alone during the training phase, those hearing the transitive frame should look longer at the causative scene and those hearing the intransitive frame should look longer at the non-causative scene in the test phase.

4. Experiment

4.1. Participants

Thirty-two Japanese-speaking children (16 boys and 16 girls) with a mean age of 27.5 months (range: 27.1 to 28.7 months) completed this study. Four additional children were tested but excluded from the present analysis due to fussiness. All the children grew up in a monolingual environment where they learned Japanese as their native language. They were recruited from the Kyoto area. Parents completed the Japanese version of the MacArthur-Bates Communicative Development Inventory (CDI): Words and Grammar (Watamaki and Ogura 2004). The mean productive vocabulary was 364.3 words (range: 72–621).

4.2. Apparatus and Stimuli

The children sat on their mothers' laps in a dimly lit testing room (250 × 250 cm) facing a 40-in. monitor about 150 cm away. Visual stimuli were presented on the monitor using Microsoft PowerPoint installed on a Macintosh G4 computer. Audio stimuli were presented through a speaker located under the monitor behind black curtains. A digital video camera was placed behind a small opening in the black curtains, and about 3 cm below the monitor. The camera was connected to a 20-in. monitor and a digital video recorder to record the direction of the children's eye fixation and to allow an experimenter in an adjacent room to observe the children's behaviors.

Visual stimuli were created for the dialogue scene in which two women were engaged in conversation with natural gestures, and for the causative and non-causative scenes in which a man and a woman were engaged in novel actions. The audio stimuli for the action scenes were produced and recorded by a female native Japanese speaker in a soundproof booth, and then synchronized with the visual stimuli using movie-editing software.

4.3. Design and Procedure

Sixteen children were randomly assigned to a Transitive condition and sixteen to an Intransitive condition. Within each condition, they were randomly assigned one of two novel verbs (*nemaru* or *wageru*). A session consisted of a dialogue phase, a baseline phase, and a test phase. All the children completed two consecutive sessions.

4.3.1. Dialogue Phase

In the dialogue phase, the children saw a color video clip of two women engaged in conversation (Figure 1). The dialogue video appeared in the center of the monitor (size: 26.1 cm × 46.3 cm). While the children in the Transitive condition heard the novel verb embedded in transitive sentence frames (5), those in the Intransitive condition heard the novel verb embedded in conjoined-subject intransitive sentence frames (6). Each trial consisted of a 17-second dialogue including the novel verb in four sentences (Table 1). The children saw the same video clip three times in succession. At the end of each trial, the scene was blank for 3 seconds before the next trial began.

(5) Tomo-kun ga Yuu-chan o nemat-teiru/waget-teiru yo.
Tomo-Mr. NOM Yu-Ms. ACC verb-PROG PCL
'Tomo is X-ing Yu.'

(6) Tomo-kun to Yuu-chan ga nemat-teiru/waget-teiru yo.
Tomo-Mr. and Yu-Ms. NOM verb-PROG PCL
'Tomo and Yu are X-ing.'

Table 1. Two-Woman Dialogues Including Novel Verbs in the Transitive Condition and the Intransitive Condition

Transitive Condition ($N = 16$)	Intransitive Condition ($N = 16$)
A: *Nee nee.* *Tomo-kun ga Yuu-chan o nematteiru yo.* 'Hey. Tomo is X-ing Yu.'	A: *Nee nee.* *Tomo-kun to Yuu-chan ga nematteiru yo.* 'Hey. Tomo and Yu are X-ing.'
B: *E? Dare ga dare o nematteiru no?* 'Huh? Who is X-ing whom?'	B: *E? Dare to dare ga nematteiru no?* 'Huh? Who are X-ing?'
A: *Tomo-kun ga Yuu-chan o nemattan yo.* 'Tomo is X-ing Yu.'	A: *Tomo-kun to Yuu-chan ga nemattan yo.* 'Tomo and Yu are X-ing.'
B: *Honma?* *Tomo-kun ga Yuu-chan o nemattan ya.* *Sugoi ne.* 'Really? Tomo is X-ing Yu. Good.'	B: *Honma?* *Tomo-kun to Yuu-chan ga nemattan ya.* *Sugoi ne.* 'Really? Tomo and Yu are X-ing. Good.'
A: *Un, sugoi ne.* 'Yeah, I think so.'	A: *Un, sugoi ne.* 'Yeah, I think so.'

Figure 1. Illustration of Movie Clip Used in Dialogue Phase

4.3.2. Baseline Phase

Following the dialogue phase, the children were given two baseline trials. While the children in both conditions were watching two side-by-side video clips, they heard an arousal phrase such as *Mite-mite!* ('Look!'). One video clip showed a causative scene in which a man spun a woman around on a chair. The other showed a synchronous non-causative scene in which the same man and woman each waved a hand in circles (Figure 2). The size of each clip was 39.2 cm wide by 22.1 cm high, and the two clips were shown with a space of 10 cm between them. We chose this action pair because Arunachalam and Waxman (2010) used the same action pair to provide clear evidence for inferring verb meanings from syntactic frames alone.

Figure 2. Movie Clip of Causative Action (Left) and Non-causative Action (Right) Used for Baseline Phase and Test Phase

4.3.3. Test Phase

The children were given two test trials in which they watched two side-by-side clips while hearing a sentence including the novel verb without syntactic frames (7).

(7) Nemat-/waget-teiru no dotchi
VERB-PROG NML which
'Which is X-ing?'

We predicted that if the children were able to infer the meaning of the novel verb that they heard during the dialogue phase, the children in the Transitive condition would look longer at the causative scene than at the non-causative scene in the test phase. In contrast, the children in the Intransitive condition would look longer at the non-causative scene than at the causative scene.

Each trial in the baseline and the test trial lasted 12 seconds. At the end of each trial, the scene became blank for 1.5 seconds before the next trial began. The left-right position of each video clip was randomized in a predetermined order.

4.4. Data Analysis

A coder who was not informed of the experimental design and condition performed an offline frame-by-frame coding (30 frames/second) to calculate how long the children looked at each scene (left and right) during the baseline and the test trials from a video recording. To assess data reliability, a different coder did offline coding of a random selection of about 20% of the primary sample. The inter-coder correlations were high (mean = .97). We calculated the proportion of time spent looking at the causative scene in each trial.

5. Results

The time spent looking at the causative scene in the test phase was analyzed with a mixed-design ANOVA with condition (Transitive vs. Intransitive) and word type (*nemaru* vs. *wageru*) as between-subjects factors, and test phase (baseline vs. test) and trial block (first vs. second) as within-subjects factors. The analysis revealed a significant main effect of test phase, F (1, 28) = 14.978, $p = .001$, $\eta_p^2 = .349$, and a significant interaction between test phase and condition, F (1, 28) = 24.788, $p < .001$, $\eta_p^2 = .469$. No other main effects or interactions were significant.

Further analysis with Bonferroni correction indicated that the children in the Transitive condition looked significantly longer at the causative scene in the test trials (M = 66.1%, SD 11.2) than in the baseline (M = 56.4%, SD 10.6), F (1, 28) = 9.864, $p = .004$, $\eta_p^2 = .261$. In contrast, those in the Intransitive condition looked significantly shorter at the causative scene in the test trials (M = 45.5%, SD 14.8) than in the baseline trials (M = 57.5%, SD 13.7), F (1, 28) = 15.201, $p = .001$, $\eta_p^2 = .352$, indicating that they looked preferentially at the non-causative scene in the test trials than in the baseline trials. These results are shown in Figure 3.

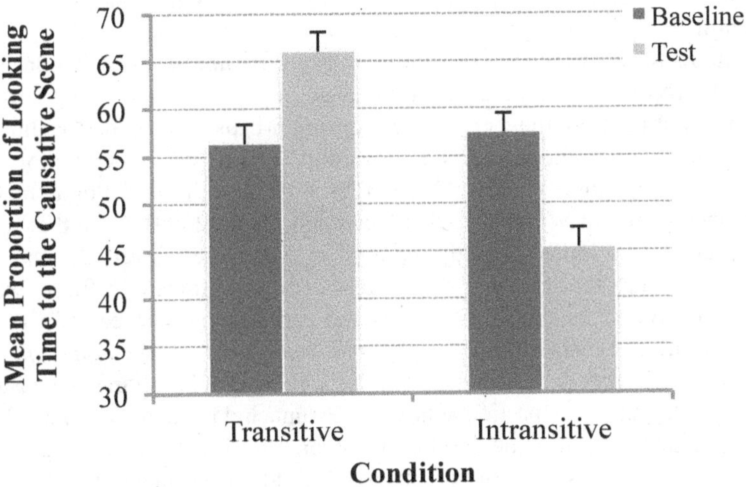

Figure 3. Mean Proportion of Looking Time to Causative Scene in Baseline Phase and Test Phase in Transitive Condition and Intransitive Condition (Error bars show standard errors.)

6. Discussion

Using an IPL paradigm that adopts a dialogue phase similar to that reported by Yuan and Fisher (2009), the present study demonstrates that the Japanese-speaking 27-month-old children hearing transitive frames during the dialogue phase looked preferentially at a causative scene over a non-causative scene, while those hearing the intransitive frames looked preferentially at a non-causative scene over a causative scene. These results reveal syntactic bootstrapping in Japanese. While previous studies using act-out tasks had reported children's sensitivity to syntactic frames in argument-drop languages such as Turkish and Mandarin (Göksun et al. 2008; Lee and Naigles 2008), the present study, using the IPL paradigm, provides additional support for Matsuo et al. (2012), which suggested that syntactic bootstrapping works in children learning Japanese as a first language.

Moreover, by using the dialogue method, we have demonstrated that Japanese-speaking children can infer verb meanings from syntactic information alone in the absence of visual cues. This finding, which parallels English studies (Arunachalam and Waxman 2010; Yuan and Fisher 2009), supports Gleitman's original idea that syntactic information is independently informative in early verb learning (Gleitman 1990), and extends this proposal to argument-drop languages. Our results indicate that Japanese-speaking children can associate causative meaning with the transitive frame and non-causative meaning with the intransitive frame in Japanese, which is certainly consistent with the results of Naigle's original experimental study in English.

Interestingly, however, these observations are not necessarily consistent with the results of a number of previous studies. English-speaking children often failed to show their preference for a non-causative scene for intransitive frames with the traditional procedure (Hirsh-Pasek, Golinkoff and Naigles 1996; Naigles and Kako 1993) as well as with the dialogue method (Arunachalam and Waxman 2010; Yuan and Fisher 2009). Note that this is also true for the Japanese study reported by Matsuo et al. (2012). Some researchers claim that children do not associate an intransitive frame with a non-causative scene because intransitive verbs do not necessarily denote non-causative events. For example, *play* and *fight*, as in *John and Bill played/fought together*, can be a reciprocal action involving a causative meaning by the two participants (e.g., Arunachalam and Waxman 2010; Noble, Rowland and Pine 2011). However, this line of reasoning cannot explain why only some studies observed children's preference for a non-causative scene with an intransitive frame (Kidd, Bavin and Rhodes 2001; Naigles 1990). We must wait for future studies to resolve this issue, but it is important to note that this fact in itself does not undermine the possibility of syntactic bootstrapping, because all the previous studies mentioned above observed that children figured out the distinction between transitive and intransitive frames for causative/non-causative events.

7. Concluding Remarks

In summary, we suggest that Japanese 27-month-olds can make inferences about the meanings of novel verbs from syntactic information alone in the absence of visual cues about referents. This is the first evidence to show that syntactic bootstrapping works in young children learning an argument-drop language under highly controlled experimental conditions.

A further question arises as to what exactly the syntactic cues are for Japanese-speaking children. As with English, the number and the position of argument NPs may be crucial, but Matsuo et al.'s study provides evidence against this possibility. Their experimental sentences included a sentence pattern involving two NPs without case markers, and they found that this type of the sentences was not associated with either a causative or non-causative event. This leaves us with the idea that the existence of case markers is essential. To ascertain whether case markers alone can be robust cues, we need to look at single-argument sentences, namely, sentences involving only one argument with a case marker and a verb (e.g., NP NOM V / NP ACC V) (e.g., Suzuki 2007). This remains a topic for further research. Alternatively, it may be true that both the number of argument NPs and case markers provide the essential information required for syntactic bootstrapping in Japanese.

References

Arunachalam, S. and Waxman, S. R. 2010. Meaning from Syntax: Evidence from 2-year-olds. *Cognition* 114:442–446.

Fisher, C. 1996. Structural Limits on Verb Mapping: The Role of Analogy in Children's Interpretations of Sentences. *Cognitive Psychology* 31:41–81.

Fisher, C., Gleitman, H. and Gleitman, L. 1991. On the Semantic Content of Subcategorization Frames. *Cognitive Psychology* 23:331–392.

Gleitman, L. 1990. The Structural Sources of Verb Meanings. *Language Acquisition* 1:3–55.

Göksun, T., Kuntay, A. C. and Naigles, L. R. 2008. Turkish Children Use Morphosyntactic Bootstrapping in Interpreting Verb Meaning. *Journal of Child Language* 35:291–323.

Hirsh-Pasek, K., Golinkoff, R. and Naigles, L. 1996. Young Children's Use of Syntactic Frames to Derive Meaning. *The Origins of Grammar*, ed. K. Hirsh-Pasek and R. Golinkoff, 123–158. Cambridge: MIT Press.

Kidd, E., Bavin, E. L. and Rhodes, B. 2001. Two-year-olds' Knowledge of Verbs and Argument Structures. *Research on Child Language Acquisition: Proceedings of the 8th Conference of the International Association for the Study of Child Language*, ed. M. Almgren, A. Barrena, M.-J. Ezeiz-abarrena, I. Idiazabal, and B. MacWhinney, 1368–1382. Somerville: Cascadilla Press.

Landau, B. and Gleitman, L. 1985. *Language and Experience: Evidence from the Blind Child.* Cambridge: Harvard University Press.

Lee, J. N. and Naigles, L. R. 2008. Mandarin Learners Use Syntactic Bootstrapping in Verb Acquisition. *Cognition* 106:1028–1037.

Matsuo, A., Kita, S., Shinya, Y., Wood, G. C. and Naigles, L. 2012. Japanese Two-year-olds Use Morphosyntax to Learn Novel Verb Meanings. *Journal of Child Language* 39:637–663.

Naigles, L. R. 1990. Children Use Syntax to Learn Verb Meanings. *Journal of Child Language* 17:357–374.

Naigles, L. R. 1996. The Use of Multiple Frames in Verb Learning via Syntactic Bootstrapping. *Cognition* 58:221–251.

Naigles, L. R. and Kako, E. T. 1993. First Contact in Verb Acquisition: Defining a Role for Syntax. *Cognitive Development* 64:1665–1687.

Noble, C. H., Rowland, C. F. and Pine, J. M. 2011. Comprehension of Argument Structure and Semantic Roles: Evidence from English-Learning Children and the Forced-Choice Pointing Paradigm. *Cognitive Science* 35:963–982.

Rispoli, M. 1995. Missing Arguments and the Acquisition of Predicate Meanings. *Beyond Names for Things: Young Children's Acquisition of Verbs*, ed. M. Tomasello and W. E. Merriman, 331–352. Hillsdale: Lawrence Erlbaum.

Suzuki, T. 2002. Bootstrapping from Case-marking Morphology in Japanese. *Studies in Language Sciences 2*, ed. Y. Shirai, H. Kobayashi, S. Miyata, K. Nakamura, T. Ogura, and H. Sirai, 157–174. Tokyo: Kuroshio.

Suzuki, T. 2007. Tan'itsu-kōbun no rikai kara saguru yōji no kakujosi rikai (The Development of Japanese Case Markers Observed through Children's Comprehension of Single-Argument Sentences). *Gengo Kenkyū* 132: 55–76.

Watamaki, T. and Ogura, T. 2004. *The Japanese MacArthur-Bates Communicative Development Inventory: Words and Grammar*. Kyoto: Kyoto International Social Welfare Exchange Center.

Yuan, S. and Fisher, C. 2009. "Really?" She Blicked the Baby?: Two-year-olds Learn Combinational Facts about Verbs by Listening. *Psychological Science* 20: 619–626.

The Tensed-S Condition (TSC) and the Determination of the Binding Domain of Anaphors in Korean

JI-HYE KIM[*]
Baird University College, Soongsil University
JAMES H. YOON
University of Illinois at Urbana-Champaign

1. Introduction

In the classical formulation of the Binding Theory (BT) proposed in Chomsky (1980, 1981) both the Tensed-S Condition (TSC) and the Specified Subject Condition (SSC) figure in the definition of the Binding Domain (BD) of anaphors. The relevance of SSC in defining BD is seen in (1), where an anaphor cannot be bound by non-local c-commanding antecedents if there is a Subject that locally c-commands it.

(1) *John$_i$ thinks that Bill hates himself$_{*i}$

The decision to incorporate TSC into the definition of BD seems justified in view of the ungrammaticality of (2a), but then (2b), which is well-formed despite violating TSC, immediately challenges the wisdom of this decision.

[*] This work was supported by the National Research Foundation of Korea Grant funded by the Korean Government (NRF332-2011-1-A00087) awarded to Ji-Hye Kim.

Japanese/Korean Linguistics 22.
Edited by MikioGiriko, Naonori Nagaya, AkikoTakemura, and Timothy J. Vance.

(2) a. *John$_i$ thinks [that himself$_i$ is to blame]
b. John$_i$ said [that pictures of himself$_i$ are on display]

The paradox posed by TSC has been addressed in two ways. Chomsky (1980, 1981) chose to treat (2b) as a principled exception to TSC, and maintained that TSC figures in the determination of BD, which is supported by the ungrammaticality of (2a). By contrast, the Binding Theory developed in Pollard and Sag (1992) is based only on (the argument structural equivalent of) SSC, because it requires an anaphor to be "locally o-bound" only when it is "locally o-commanded," which means only when it has a structurally more prominent co-argument.

The theory correctly prevents SSC-violating anaphors like *himself* in (1) from being bound by the matrix subject. TSC-violating anaphors in (2a) and (2b) are not locally o-commanded and hence do not meet the pre-condition for BT to apply. Pollard and Sag interpret this to mean that TSC-violating anaphors fall outside of syntactic BT. Anaphors that fall outside of syntactic BT are categorized as "exempt" anaphors. In their system, exempt anaphors are licensed extra-grammatically.[1] The theory predicts that both (2a) and (2b) should be well-formed as instances of exempt binding. Why, then, is (2a) out? Pollard and Sag attribute the ungrammaticality of (2a) not to violation of BT, but to the anaphor *himself*, which is in the wrong case form for a subject of a finite clause.

The two theories make different predictions about whether nominative-marked anaphors can exist in a language. Chomsky's theory predicts that nominative anaphors should be disallowed altogether, while Pollard and Sag's system predicts that if case-marking is not a problem, nominative anaphors should be possible. Korean is a language that has both locally bound anaphors (*caki-casin, pronoun-casin*) and long-distance anaphors (LDAs, *caki, casin*). Interestingly, even local anaphors can violate TSC, as shown in (3a), while SSC violations are acceptable for LDAs but marginal for local anaphors, as shown in (3b).

(3) a. John$_i$-un [caki$_i$-ka/caki-casin$_i$-i chencayla-ko] mitnunta
J-TOP self-NOM genius-COMP believes
'John believes himself (=John) to be a genius.'

b. John$_i$-un [Bill-i caki$_i$-lul/*?caki-casin$_i$-ul coahantako] mitnuta
J-TOP B-NOM self-ACC likes believes
'John believes that Bill likes self (=John).'

The fact that TSC-violating local anaphors are possible, as in (3a),

[1] SSC-violating anaphors satisfy the preconditions of syntactic BT, and therefore have no option of becoming exempt.

seems to settle the score in favor of Pollard/Sag once and for all, since local anaphors do occur as subjects of finite clauses when case-marking is not a problem.

However, it would be premature to call the game in favor of Pollard and Sag's theory, because their theory also predicts that the nominative-marked local anaphor in (3a) should be an exempt anaphor, and so far this demonstration has not been made for Korean. In fact, the well-formedness of (3a) has not caused researchers to rethink the role of TSC in defining BD. A well-known line of thinking within work that stems from classical BT has viewed TSC as a parameter (Yang 1983; Manzini and Wexler 1987). The reason TSC is ineffective even for local anaphors in Korean is because TSC does not figure in defining BD in Korean. In English, by contrast, both SSC and TSC are active in the characterization of BD. Under this view, TSC-violating anaphors in Korean are licensed syntactically as core anaphors, rather than extra-syntactically as exempt anaphors.

The question we are interested in answering is whether TSC-violating local anaphors in Korean are licensed as exempt anaphors or as core anaphors (in a parameterized BD). Now, in phrasing the question this way, we have made an assumption that local anaphors in Korean could in principle function as exempt anaphors. This is not an innocuous assumption, since while much work has shown that local anaphors in English can function as exempt anaphors in certain contexts, there is potential danger in generalizing this assumption for all languages (Huang and Liu 2001). Fortunately, Kim and Yoon (2009) provide convincing arguments that certain types of SSC-violating *caki-casin* should be viewed as exempt anaphors, giving support for the assumption.[2]

How do we know that *caki-casin* functions as an exempt anaphor? According to Kim and Yoon (2009), determination that the anaphor is exempt can be made in two ways. First, sloppy vs. strict readings in VP ellipsis can differentiate core vs. exempt anaphors, because an elliptical VP with a core anaphor is predominantly interpreted in the sloppy sense, but strict readings become readily available when the VP contains an exempt anaphor (Huang and Liu 2001; Runner et al. 2006). Second, exempt *caki-casin* is sensitive to logophoricity. Specifically, sentences containing exempt anaphors bound by

[2] This seems to contradict the previous claim—cf. (3)—that local anaphors cannot violate SSC easily. In the sentences employed in Kim and Yoon (2009), which were judged acceptable even though *caki-casin* violates SSC, the local subject was not a possible antecedent of the anaphor, because of mismatched features. Only the SSC-violating LD antecedent matched the anaphor in features. It seems that in Korean, local anaphors can bypass the local subject and be bound LD as exempt anaphors in this situation. What is different in (3) is that the local subject (*Bill*) is a possible, feature-matched, antecedent of *caki-casin*, which prevents the anaphor from bypassing the subject and being bound LD as an exempt anaphor.

antecedents that bear canonical logophoric roles (in the sense of Sells 1987) are judged to be highly acceptable, while those with less canonical logophoric roles are judged to have lowered degrees of acceptability.[3]

Interestingly, while Kim and Yoon (2009) argued that SSC-violating *caki-casin* is an exempt anaphor, they assumed that TSC-violating *caki-casin* is a core anaphor, following earlier researchers, and used TSC as the control condition to compute the rate of sloppy vs. strict readings in VP ellipsis in core vs. exempt binding. Now, if TSC-violating *caki-casin* is a core anaphor, it is predicted to show a high rate of sloppy readings, but that is not what they found. They found a high rate of strict readings in VP ellipsis containing TSC-violating *caki-casin*. This implies that TSC-violating *caki-casin* might be an exempt anaphor, and if that is the case, the study did not have genuine controls with core binding. But since it could be that even unambiguous instances of core anaphors bound by co-arguments yield a high rate of strict readings under VP ellipsis, without further investigation, we have no way of knowing whether the high incidence of strict readings with TSC-violating local anaphors in their study is due to their exempt status or reflects a general property of anaphors in Korean.

Our goal in this paper is to settle the issue of core vs. exempt status of TSC-violating local anaphors in Korean through a properly designed empirical study. We will compare the properties of TSC-violating local anaphors with the properties of locally bound core anaphors on the one hand, and of SSC-violating exempt anaphors on the other. The results of our study are consistent with the position that views TSC-violating local anaphors in Korean as exempt anaphors, although there are factors that compromise the strength of this conclusion.

2. Empirical Study

2.1. Research Question

The research question of our study is: Are TSC-violating local anaphors in Korean (*caki-casin* and *pronoun-casin*) core or exempt anaphors?

2.2. Experiment

2.2.1. Hypotheses and Predictions

Regarding the question above, we hypothesize the following.

Hypothesis

TSC-violating local anaphors in Korean are exempt anaphors.

---

[3] The antecedents of exempt *caki-casin* were categorized in that study along the following hierarchy drawn from Sells (1987) and Huang and Liu (2001): Source>Self>Pivot>Less Logophoric. Roles higher in the hierarchy were judged as more optimal antecedents compared to those lower in the hierarchy.

Our specific predictions were as follows.

Prediction 1: Acceptability Rating
If TSC violations fall under exempt binding, the acceptability rating for TSC-violating local anaphors may be lower than that for local binding.[4] This prediction is based on the following logic. It has been claimed that, other things being equal, the on-line processing of exempt binding is more resource-consuming than that of local binding (Reuland 2011; Koorneef 2008). We may thus expect the extra processing cost involved in exempt binding to be reflected in a lowered rating of acceptability compared to core binding.

Prediction 2: Strict vs. Sloppy Reading
Ellipsis of VPs containing TSC-violating local anaphors will behave similarly to that of VPs containing SSC-violating local anaphors, and differently from ellipsis of VPs with local (core) anaphors. A higher rate of strict readings should become available in both TSC and SSC conditions compared to the local binding condition.

2.2.2. Method

Participants

Forty Korean native speakers (age range: 20–29) residing in and near Seoul and attending a university there participated in the experiment.

Task and Materials

The task in the experiment was an Acceptability Judgment Task using a 4-point Likert scale coupled with a Preferential Sentence Interpretation Task. The first part of each task asked the subjects to judge the degree of acceptability of a given sentence on the 4-point scale (1 = completely unacceptable, 2 = relatively unacceptable, 3 = relatively acceptable, 4 = completely acceptable). The second part was designed to test the strict vs. sloppy readings in the context of VP-ellipsis, as this could not be ascertained from the first

---

[4] Since SSC violations constitute clear cases of exempt binding, do we expect the rating given to TSC to be similar to that given for SSC? Not necessarily.

There were too many differences between the TSC and SSC conditions. In the SSC condition, the distance between antecedent and anaphor was greater than in the TSC condition, there were intervening NPs between anaphor and antecedents, and logophoricity was manipulated so that not all SSC violations had antecedents with optimal logophoric roles, which could have contributed to lowering the aggregate acceptability rating. In the TSC condition, the distance between the anaphor and antecedent was short, there were no intervening potential antecedents, and the antecedent (matrix subject) always had a robust logophoric role (Source).

On the other hand, the local binding conditions and the TSC condition are similar enough to expect an effect to surface that may be attributable to the difference between core and exempt binding. This is why we are not predicting that ratings for TSC violations should be closer to those given for the SSC condition.

part. The subjects were asked to respond to determine if the sentence allowed only the sloppy reading, only the strict reading, or both readings. If the subjects indicated that both readings were possible, they were asked to choose the preferred reading. If they could not get either of the two readings, they were asked to describe the reading they got of the sentence containing VP-ellipsis.

The test materials consisted of 175 items: 87 target items and 88 non-target items. There were four types of binding conditions: local co-argument (clause-mate) binding, local binding of possessor of NP by the co-argument of the NP, TSC-violating binding, and SSC-violating binding (which also violated TSC). Each binding condition was presented with four pro-forms: two local anaphors (*caki-casin*, *pronoun-casin*), a long-distance anaphor (*caki*), and a pronoun. (A pronoun was used in only three of the four conditions, since pronouns cannot be locally bound by co-arguments.) Although the main target items were designed to test local anaphors, we also included items with long-distance anaphors and pronouns to compare the pattern of responses of local and long-distance anaphors, and of anaphors and pronouns.

Sample target items are shown below. (4a) and (4b) show the local co-argument binding condition and local binding of possessor, respectively. (4c) exemplifies the TSC-violating condition. In (4d), *kyengchalcheng* (police agency) is inanimate, an impossible antecedent of *caki-casin.* Therefore, *caki-casin* can be bound by the LD matrix subject *Mary*, in violation of SSC.

(4) a. ***Mary**-nun* salamtul aph-eyse ***caki-casin**-ul* piphanhayssta
Mary-TOP people front-LOC self-ACC criticized
'Mary criticized self in front of people.'

b. ***Mary**-nun* salamtul aph-eyse ***caki-casin**-uy* *pimil-ul*
Mary-TOP people front-LOC self-GEN secret-ACC
swumkyessta
hid
'Mary hid her (=self's) secret in front of people.'

c. ***Mary**-nun* [***caki-casin**-i* maylekcekin yeca-la-ko]
Mary-TOP self-NOM attractive woman-COP-COMP
malhayssta
said
'Mary said that self was an attractive woman.'

d. ***Inswu-nun*** [hoysa-eyse ***caki-casin-ul*** uysimhanunkes
Inswu-TOP company-LOC self-ACC doubt
kathta-ko] malhayssta
seems-COMP said
'Inswu said that the company seemed to be suspecting self (=Inswu).'

For the interpretation part, as shown in (5), the subjects were instructed to determine the possibility of each reading and check the appropriate box. They were also instructed to choose the preferred interpretation between A and B only if they accepted both readings.

(5)

Hanna-nun [Samsung Caytan-eyse *caki-casin-ul*
Hanna-TOP S-Foundation-LOC self-ACC
canghaksayng-ulo ppopassta-ko] malhayssta
scholarship.student-INST selected-COMP said
'Hanna said that Samsung foundation selected self (=Hanna) for a scholarship.'

Unacceptable			**Acceptable**
1	2	(√)3	(√)4

Laura-to kulayssta
Laura-too did (so)
'Laura did so too.'

Interpretations:
A. Laura-nun [Samsung caytan-i Laura-lulcanghaksayng-uloppopassta-ko] malhayssta: (Possible__√__ Impossible____).
'Laura said that Samsung foundation selected Laura for a scholarship.'
B. Laura-nun [Samsung caytan-i Hanna-lulcanghaksayng-uloppopassta-ko] malhayssta: (Possible__√__ Impossible____).
'Laura said that Samsung foundation selected Hanna for a scholarship.'
C. If both are possible indicate the preferred interpretation:__B__
D. Neither of the above is a possible interpretation: Comments____

For this particular test item, we expect that subjects will rate it close to acceptable (that is, 3 or 4), although the rating should be somewhat lower than the ratings they give for instances of core binding. We also expect they will mark both A (the sloppy reading) and B (the strict reading) as possible, which means they will indicate a preferred reading between A and B in the response to item C.

Procedure

Participants were first asked to fill out a simple one-page questionnaire to provide biographical information such as age, gender, and dialect(s) spoken. They were then asked to proceed to take the main task.

There was a screening procedure. If the subjects judged the target sentence as unacceptable but still chose an interpretation, the responses were judged to be unreliable, because what the subjects likely did in such cases was to make inferences to the nearest grammatical/acceptable sentence and then give answers based on those inferences. We were interested in the range of interpretations of acceptable (hence, grammatical) sentences, and not the interpretations subjects may get from unacceptable sentences. So, responses like this were discarded.

Analysis

The mean acceptability score and standard deviation for each sentence was calculated across subjects. The responses were then grouped according to the sentence type (i.e., by binding type: local, TSC, SSC; and by anaphor type: simple vs. complex) and averaged by sentence type. Repeated measures ANOVAs and paired sample *t*-tests were run to determine the statistical significance of the differences for distinct within-subject factors.

The results for VP ellipsis were analyzed in the following manner. First, subjects' responses were coded into six different categories: A (sloppy reading only), B (strict reading only), CA (both readings and sloppy reading as preferred interpretation), CB (both readings and strict reading as preferred interpretation), C (both readings but no choice of a preferred reading), D (responses which did not agree with any of the provided answers). To calculate the rate of sloppy reading *possibility*, categories A, CA, C, and CB were added; for strict reading possibility, categories B, CB, C, and CA were added. To calculate the rate of sloppy reading *preference*, only the categories A and CA were combined. The same procedure was followed to compute strict reading preference; only the categories B and CB were added together. The rates were analyzed based on the frequency of the choice divided by the total number of the responses in each type of sentence. A chi-square test was conducted to examine the statistical significance of the interaction between the binding conditions and sloppy vs. strict reading rates.

2.2.3. Results

(i) Acceptability Rating Results

The test items in all four conditions (local co-argument; local possessor/non-co-argument; TSC; SSC) were judged as acceptable, garnering scores higher than 3 (relatively acceptable). Mean responses for the different sentence types on the Acceptability Judgment Task were compared by repeated measures ANOVAs (Binding 4, Anaphor 4, df = 102). There was a main effect for binding type (F(3, 102) = 3.100, p = 0.030), and a main effect for anaphor type (F(3, 102) = 4.973, p = 0.003). The interaction of binding by anaphor type was also significant (F(9, 306) = 3.391, p = 0.001).

As for the main effect by anaphor type on acceptability, a significant effect was found between *caki* and *caki-casin* (p = .022), *casin* and *pronoun-casin* (p = .009), and between *caki-casin* and *pronoun-casin* (p = .002). As for the main effect by binding type, pairwise comparisons revealed that no significant difference exists between the two local binding conditions, i.e., the co-argument and non-co-argument conditions (p = .864, n.s.). Also, no significant difference between local binding conditions and the TSC condition was found (local co-argument condition vs. TSC: p = .703, n.s.; local non-co-argument condition vs. TSC: p = .564, n.s.). On the other hand, SSC-violating anaphors were judged significantly less acceptable than TSC conditions (p = .037) and local binding conditions (SSC vs. local co-argument condition: p = .015; SSC vs. local non-co-argument condition: p = .007). Paired sample *t*-tests also revealed the same pattern, where TSC-violation patterned with local binding conditions rather than the SSC violation condition. The results are shown in Figure 1.

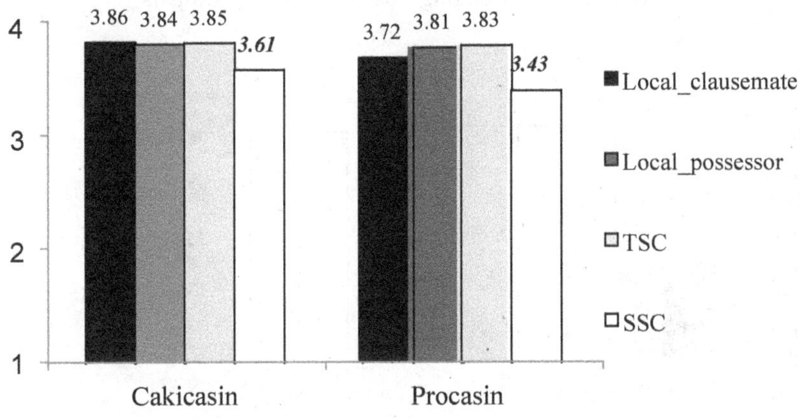

Figure 1. Acceptability by Binding Type for *caki-casin* and *pro-casin*

(ii) VP Ellipsis Results

The overall results with VP ellipsis were as follows. Sloppy readings were judged to be possible in all binding conditions. The possibility of strict readings increased considerably in the TSC condition, compared to the local binding conditions. The rate of strict reading possibility in the TSC condition was similar to that in the SSC condition, which was also higher than that in the local binding condition. Figure 2 shows that all conditions were judged to allow more than 90% of sloppy readings, while Figure 3 shows that the TSC conditions (the light grey bars) and the SSC conditions (the white bars) got very similar and significantly higher ratings compared to the two local binding conditions. A chi-square test revealed that there was a significant association between the type of binding and the increase in the possibility of sloppy vs. strict readings in each condition ($\chi^2(2) = 12.605$, $p = .002$).

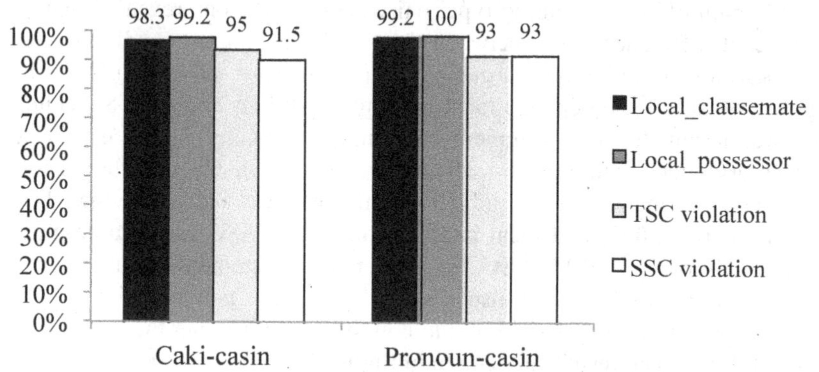

Figure 2. Sloppy Reading Possibility in VP Ellipsis

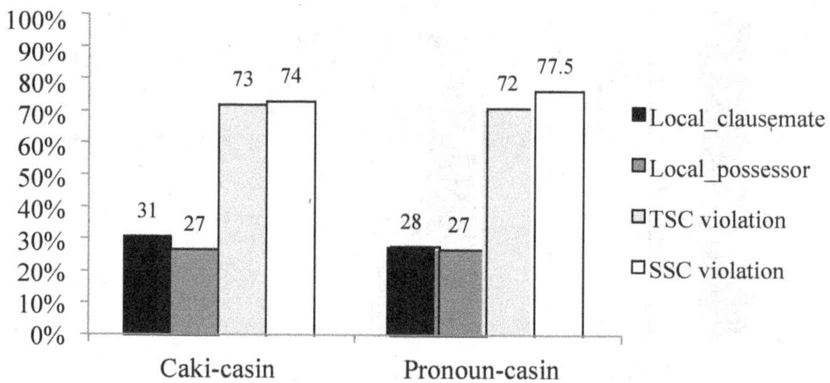

Figure 3. Strict Reading Possibility in VP Ellipsis

3. Discussion

According to the results in (i), the first prediction of our hypothesis, which stated that acceptability ratings for TSC-violations may be lower than those for local binding conditions, is not borne out. On the other hand, results in (ii) seem to support the second prediction that the rate of emergence of the strict reading will be similar in the TSC and SSC conditions, compared to the local binding conditions.

Let us consider the acceptability ratings first. The results show that the

SSC condition was rated significantly lower than local and TSC conditions, but the difference between the local binding condition and the TSC condition was not significant. Now, for reasons given earlier (note 3), we do not expect ratings for TSC to parallel those for the SSC condition, even if TSC-violating anaphors are exempt anaphors. However, we predicted a difference in acceptability rating between local vs. TSC-violating anaphors, which did not surface in the results.

The fact that there was no significant difference between the local binding and TSC conditions may be blamed on several factors. For one thing, the 4-point scale we used may not have been fine-grained enough. A finer-grained (7-point) scale might have yielded a significant difference. Another consideration is that both structural and logophoric factors conspired to make the identification of the antecedent of TSC-violating anaphors easy. Han and Storoshenko (2014) found that while logophoric factors and feature compatibility with antecedents help in making non-Subjects available as antecedents for TSC-violating anaphors, Subjects are always better than Objects as antecedents, and when logophoric (being a Source) and structural (being a Subject) factors converge on an antecedent, participants give the highest ratings. The TSC-conditions in our task had exactly this property, and it is no wonder that participants found the binding relation in this condition easy.[5]

Although the acceptability rating of TSC-violating local anaphors did not differ from that of local anaphors, there may yet be a way to ascertain whether TSC-violating local anaphors are core or exempt anaphors, and that is by comparing the ratings that subjects gave to local vs. long-distance anaphors in the TSC condition. An LDA that violates TSC is by assumption a core anaphor. Recall that that processing core anaphors is less resource-draining than processing exempt anaphors. Therefore, we could possibly find a difference in rating between local (core) and long-distance (exempt) anaphors in the TSC condition. If the difference is significant, we may chalk it up to different types of binding involved (core vs. exempt). The LDA *caki* is most likely a core anaphor, at least in cases where it has a sentence-internal c-commanding antecedent.[6] Given these assumptions, it is conceivable that subjects will rate *caki* higher than *caki-casin*/*pronoun-casin* in the TSC condition.

The place to start our investigation is the SSC condition. This is because

---

[5] It should be noted, however, that Han and Storoshenko's (2014) experiment was done with *caki*, not *caki-casin*.

[6] *Caki* can occur unbound, or with non-c-commanding antecedents. It is conceivable that in such cases, *caki* is an exempt anaphor, if we assume that being bound is necessary for a syntactically licensed anaphor (Core, Hermon and Huang 2001).

Kim and Yoon (2009) showed that SSC-violating *caki-casin* is an exempt anaphor. If *caki* in the same condition is a core anaphor, as we are now hypothesizing, then it should be judged more acceptable than *caki-casin*. The rating of 3.7 for *caki* in the SSC condition (see Figure 4 below) was indeed higher than the ratings of the two local anaphors (3.61 for *cakicasin*, 3.43 for *pro-casin*). A paired sample *t*-test revealed the rating difference between *caki* in SSC condition and *caki-casin* was significant (p = .005), as was the difference between *caki* and *pronoun-casin* (p = .001). Thus, our assumption that, when *caki-casin* is bound long-distance in violation of SSC it is an exempt anaphor, while LD-bound *caki* in the same configuration is a core anaphor, seems to be supported. The question now is if a similar difference emerges in the TSC condition.

In the TSC condition, subjects gave a slightly higher acceptability rating for *caki* (mean = 3.87) compared to *caki-casin* (mean = 3.85) and *pronoun-casin* (mean = 3.83) (see Figure 4). However, pairwise comparisons of *caki* and local anaphors revealed that the difference was not significant. Again, a finer-grained rating scale might have yielded different results, and manipulating the logophoric role of the antecedent of the anaphors in the TSC condition might have helped. But as things stand, we do not have confirmation of the first prediction of our hypothesis that TSC-violating local anaphors are exempt anaphors by comparing the acceptability ratings of local and long-distance anaphors in the TSC condition.

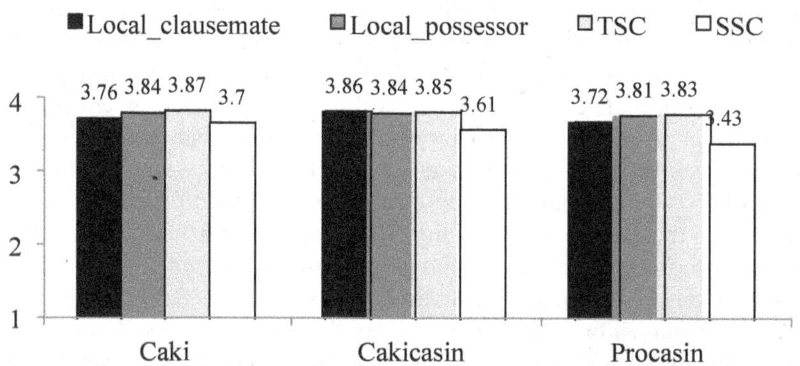

Figure 4. Acceptability Scores with *Caki* Compared to Complex Anaphors

This makes the results bearing on the second prediction (the rate of strict vs. sloppy readings in VP-ellipsis contexts) all the more important. On the face of it, the second prediction of our hypothesis seems to be confirmed robustly, in that the rate of strict reading increase was similar between the TSC and SSC conditions, both of which allowed significantly higher rates of strict readings compared to the local binding conditions. The local binding conditions still admitted around 30% strict readings, but while many subjects reported that the strict reading is possible, no one reported that the strict reading was preferred to the sloppy reading in local binding. On the other hand, in the TSC and SSC conditions, there were subjects who preferred strict readings over sloppy readings. (The percentages of subjects reporting preference for strict reading were: *caki-casin* – TSC 22%, SSC 28%; *pronoun-casin* – TSC 25%, SSC 36%.) With regard to this measure, TSC patterns with SSC and not with local binding, which is consistent with taking local anaphors in these two conditions as exempt anaphors.

Before we can take the result from VP ellipsis to constitute confirmation that TSC-violating local anaphors are exempt anaphors, we need to know how *caki*, which we took to be a core anaphor, behaves under VP ellipsis. Specifically, if *caki* is a core anaphor that is bound in a larger domain, as a Type I LDA, in the typology of Cole, Hermon and Huang (2001), it is predicted always to have a strong preference for sloppy readings, regardless of whether it is locally bound or LD-bound. Alternatively, if Han and Storoshenko (2012) are correct that *caki* is semantically a bound variable, we expect the same result. *Caki* should not allow strict readings to any significant degree regardless of the binding condition. If *caki* indeed patterns this way, the significant increase in the possibility of strict readings in the TSC and SSC conditions with local anaphors (see Figure 3) could be taken as evidence that, in these conditions, local anaphors are exempt anaphors.

Unfortunately, the behavior of *caki* with VP ellipsis did not bear out the expectation that it would not allow a significant degree of strict reading in any binding condition, and that the sloppy reading would be the dominant in all cases. Figure 6 shows that the possibility of strict reading increases significantly for *caki* in the TSC and SSC conditions, compared to the local binding conditions, although the rate of increase is less dramatic than the local anaphors, because *caki* actually allows a higher rate of strict readings even in local binding (Figure 5). This last fact tells us that the assumption we made about *caki*, that it would show sloppy reading dominance in all contexts (either because it is a Type I LDA or because it is a bound variable semantically), is simply wrong.[7]

This considerably weakens the case for interpreting the marked difference in the availability of strict readings in the LD-binding conditions (TSC and SSC) with local anaphors as being due to the difference between core and exempt binding, because we simply do not have a genuine LDA that

[7] The behavior of *caki* is quite damaging to Han and Storoshenko's (2012) central thesis that *caki* is semantically a bound variable (in all cases where it has an accessible sentence-internal antecedent). It is less of a challenge for Cole, Hermon and Huang (2001), who could simply reclassify *caki* as Type 2 or Type 3 LDA.

maintains a strong degree of sloppy preference in all binding conditions that could have provided an independent verification of this interpretation.

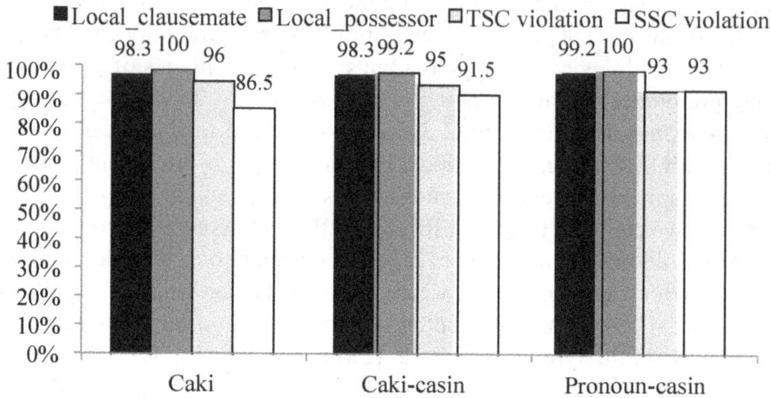

Figure 5. Sloppy Reading Possibility with *Caki* and Other Anaphors

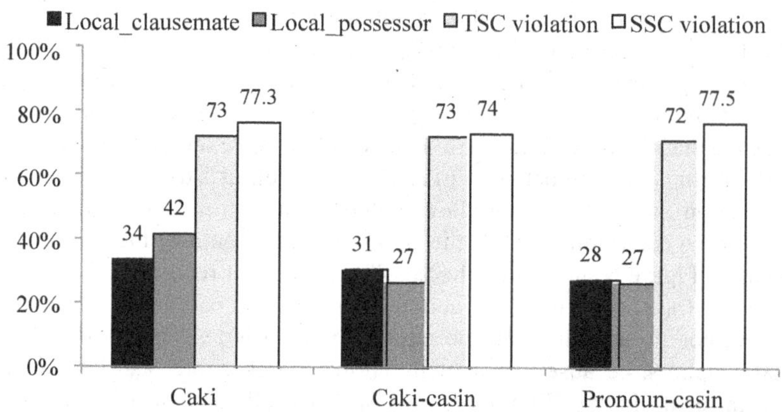

Figure 6. Strict Reading Possibility with *Caki* and Other Anaphors

To conclude, the current study investigated whether a TSC-violating local anaphor is a core anaphor or an exempt anaphor. The results of the experiment do not necessarily contradict the conclusion that TSC-violating local anaphors are exempt anaphors rather than core anaphors. However, the conclusion is a weak one at best. Additional research and follow-up experimentation are called for.

References

Chomsky, N. 1980. On Binding. *Linguistic Inquiry* 11:1–46.

Chomsky, N. 1981. *Lectures in Government and Binding*. Dordrecht: Foris.

Cole, P., Hermon G. and Huang, C.-T. J. 2001. Introduction. *Long-Distance Reflexives* (*Syntax and Semantics*, vol. 33), ed. P. Cole, G. Hermon, and C.-T. J. Huang, xiii–xlvii. New York: Academic Press.

Kim, J-H. and Yoon, H-S. J. 2009. Long-Distance Bound Local Anaphors in Korean: An Empirical Study of the Korean Anaphor *Caki-casin*. *Lingua* 119:733–755.

Koorneef, A. W. 2008. Eye-Catching Anaphora. Doctoral dissertation, University of Utrecht.

Han, C-H. and Storoshenko, D. R. 2012. Semantic Binding of Long-Distance Anaphor *Caki* in Korean. *Language* 88:764–790.

Han, C-H. and Storoshenko, D. R. 2014. Non-Subject Antecedent Potential of *Caki* in Korean. *Japanese/Korean Linguistics 21*, ed. S. Nam, H. Ko, and J. Jun. Stanford: CSLI.

Huang, C.-T. J. and Liu, C-S. L. 2001. Logophoricity, Attitude, and *Ziji* at the Interface. *Long-Distance Reflexives* (*Syntax and Semantics*, vol. 33), ed. P. Cole, G. Hermon, and C.-T. J. Huang, 141–195. New York: Academic Press.

Manzini, R. and Wexler, K. 1987. Parameters, Binding Theory and Learnability. *Linguistic Inquiry* 18:413–444.

Pollard, C. J. and Sag, I. A. 1992. Anaphors in English and the Scope of Binding Theory. *Linguistic Inquiry* 23:261–303.

Reuland, E. 2011. *Anaphora and Language Design*. Cambridge: MIT Press.

Runner, J. T., Sussman, R. S. and Tanenhaus, M. K. 2006. Processing Reflexives and Pronouns in Picture Noun Phrases. *Cognitive Science* 30:193–241.

Sells, P. 1987. Aspects of Logophoricity. *Linguistic Inquiry* 18:445–479.

Yang, D-W. 1983. The Extended Binding Theory of Anaphors. *Language Research* 19:169–192.

An Experimental Investigation of Online and Offline Binding Properties of Korean Reflexives

EUNAH KIM
University of Illinois at Urbana-Champaign

MYEONG HYEON KIM
University of Illinois at Urbana-Champaign

JAMES H. YOON
University of Illinois at Urbana-Champaign

1. Introduction

Korean is a language that has a rich inventory of reflexives. The most representative and most frequently used reflexive is *caki*, a morphologically simple reflexive. The language also possesses several other reflexives, both morphologically simple and complex, such as *casin*, *caki-casin*, pronoun-*casin*, *tangsin*, and *susulo*. Given this complex reflexive system of Korean, an important question that needs to be answered is what the functions of the different reflexives are. Why are there so many reflexives and how are they distinguished from each other?

This paper reports the results of an experimental study conducted to provide some insight on this issue. Crosslinguistically, we know that reflexives may be differentiated at multiple levels of linguistic categorization (lexical, syntactic, and discourse-pragmatic). Among the dimensions along which the reflexives can potentially vary, we focused on the syntactic dimension (the binding distance of the reflexives) in our study. We investigated whether a reflexive can be bound by a local antecedent or by a long-distance antecedent, and if both types of binding are possible, which of the

Japanese/Korean Linguistics 22.
Edited by Mikio Giriko, Naonori Nagaya, Akiko Takemura, and Timothy J. Vance.

two interpretations is preferred. We focused on three reflexives among those mentioned above: *caki*, *casin*, and *caki-casin*.

Although the binding distance preference of these three reflexives has been addressed in previous literature (e.g., Kim 2000; Moon 1995; Yoon 1989), most studies have based their claims on informal intuitions. Kang (1998) is a notable exception. Kang conducted a corpus study to check whether the claims made in previous studies are confirmed in real-life examples. Focusing on the accusative marked forms of *caki*, *casin*, and *caki-casin*, he examined how often these reflexives are used with local and long-distance antecedents in a Korean corpus of about 10 million words. He found that *caki* occurred about equally with long-distance and local antecedents (151 local vs. 165 long-distance antecedents, out of 316 total tokens). *Casin* preferred local antecedents to long-distance antecedents (311 local vs. 123 long-distance antecedents, out of 434 tokens), and *caki-casin* was locally bound most of the time (66 local vs. 5 long-distance antecedents, out of 71 tokens).

In addition to Kang's (1998) corpus study, a few experimental studies have been conducted recently to investigate the binding distance of reflexives. Kim and Yoon (2008) and Kim, Montrul and Yoon (2009) examined the binding distance of *caki*, *casin* and *caki-casin* using an offline truth value judgment task. Native Korean speakers were given sentences such as (1).

(1) Cheli-nun [Minswu-ka caki/casin/caki-casin-(l)ul
Cheli-TOP Minswu-NOM self-ACC
kuli-ess-ta-ko] malhay-ss-ta
draw-PAST-DECL-COMP say-PAST-DECL
'Cheli said that Minswu drew self.'

The sentences were presented together with pictures that represent either the local binding interpretation or the long-distance binding interpretation of the reflexive, and participants were asked to judge whether the sentences were true descriptions of the pictures. The results showed that participants strongly preferred long-distance binding for *caki*. For *casin*, there was either a slight preference for long-distance binding (Kim and Yoon 2008) or no preference in binding distance (Kim, Montrul, and Yoon 2009), while for *caki-casin*, there was a strong preference for local binding. By and large, both corpus and experimental studies confirm the claims made in the previous theoretical literature that there is a three-way distinction among these reflexives in terms of preferred binding distance.

Little is known, however, about how these reflexives are processed in real time. In one of few studies on online processing of multiple reflexives, Choi and Kim (2007) conducted an eye-tracking study of *caki* and *casin*. Participants' eye movements were recorded while they read biclausal sentences such as (2), where the embedded verbs disambiguated the interpretation of the reflexives.

(2) a. Halu-nun hoysawen-i [annaywen-i
one day-TOP company worker-NOM receptionist-NOM
caki/casin-ul pyelankan hoyphihay-ss-ta-ko]
self-ACC suddenly avoid-PAST-DECL-COMP
malhay-ss-ta
say-PAST-DECL
'One day, the company worker said the receptionist avoided self suddenly.

b. Halu-nun hoysawen-i [annaywen-i
one day-TOP company worker-NOM receptionist-NOM
caki/casin-ul pyelankan kwasihay-ss-ta-ko]
self-ACC suddenly show off-PAST-DECL-COMP
malhay-ss-ta
say-PAST-DECL
'One day, the company worker said the receptionist showed self off suddenly.'

At the disambiguating embedded verb, the first pass reading times, which are usually considered to reflect early processes of sentence comprehension, were shorter in (2a) than in (2b) for *caki* sentences, but for *casin* sentences, no difference was found between the conditions. The same pattern of interaction between the reflexive and verb type was found in total reading times (an indicator of later processes) at the reflexive region and the embedded verb region. Based on these results, Choi and Kim (2007) concluded that *caki* is immediately assigned a long-distance interpretation (hence a longer first pass reading time for (2b), in which this initial interpretation must be revised), whereas *casin* does not have an immediate preference for either binding interpretation. Again, their results do not contradict the conclusions drawn in the previous literature, including those of corpus and experimental research.

Previous studies provide emerging experimental confirmation that binding distance is a factor discriminating among *caki*, *casin*, and *caki-casin*, and more experiments are needed to obtain a complete picture of the preference in binding distance that different Korean reflexives have. Investigation of online interpretation of multiple reflexives is called for in particular, since online behavior of reflexives other than *caki* and *casin* has not been investigated so far. Also, while Choi and Kim (2007) came to their conclusion by introducing a bias involving the embedded verb, we do not know how different reflexives are processed in the absence of such biases. The present study conducted an experiment on the binding distance preference of all three reflexives (*caki, casin,* and *caki-casin*) in both online and offline comprehension. The online task (visual world eye-tracking) examined the time course of antecedent search, and the offline task (antecedent identification) investigated the final interpretations possibly given to the reflexives. The online task results show evidence suggesting that *caki* and *casin* do not immediately select between the local and long-distance antecedent and maintain the ambiguity in interpretation if no disambiguating information follows. *Caki-casin,* however, is immediately bound by the local antecedent. The offline task results reveal a three-way distinction between the reflexives in final interpretation, as in the previous studies.

This paper is organized as follows. Section 2 describes the study, in the order of the norming test (2.1), the participants in the study (2.2), the methods and results of the eye-tracking task (2.3), and those of the antecedent identification task (2.4). The results of the study are discussed in Section 3.

2. The Study

2.1. Norming Test for the Materials

Biclausal sentences such as (3) were used for the two main tasks of this study, where three reflexives (*caki, casin,* and *caki-casin*) replaced the embedded object (marked as X). The matrix subject (*Peterpan*) and the embedded subject (*Shrek*) served as long-distance and local antecedents, respectively. More detailed descriptions of the experimental sentences will be given when we describe the eye-tracking task. Since we were interested in testing the long-distance or local interpretation of the reflexives, we made sure that the embedded verb and any other elements of the sentence do not introduce a bias in favor of local or long-distance interpretation. For this purpose, a norming test was conducted. Ten native speakers of Korean, who did not participate in the main task but had comparable linguistic and biographical profiles to the subjects for the main task, were given 73 sentences such as (3) and were asked to judge whether the embedded object (X) can refer to the matrix subject or the embedded subject. The two questions for each test item were spaced far apart, intermixed with questions about other items, to reduce the possibility of the answer to one question affecting the response to the other. Participants were asked to choose a number on a 7-point Likert scale, where 1 indicated that X could never refer to the character mentioned in the question and 7 meant that X can refer to the character naturally.

(3) Peterpan-un [Shrek-i ppyocokhan panul-lo **X-lul** silswulo
P-TOP S-NOM sharp needle-INS X-ACC by mistake
ccille-ss-ta-ko] malhay-ss-sup-ni-ta.
prick-PAST-DECL-COMP say-PAST-HON-IND-DECL
'Peterpan said Shrek pricked X with a sharp needle by mistake.'

Question 1: 'Can X be Peter Pan in this sentence?'
Question 2: 'Can X be Shrek in this sentence?'

Among the 73 sentences we piloted, 21 sentences for which the matrix subject interpretation and the embedded subject interpretation received similar scores ($t1(9)=1.027$, $p>.05$; $t2(20)=1.623$, $p>.05$) were selected as target items for the main tasks. The selected sentences were not inherently biased for one of the two binding interpretations of objects. Therefore, if any bias in the interpretation emerges, we can conclude that it arises from the inherent lexical properties of the reflexives.

2.2. Participants

The participants of the main tasks were 16 native speakers of Korean who did not participate in the norming test. The participants were residing in the United States at the time of testing (mean age=29.2, range=23–37). According to the language background questionnaire filled out by the participants, they were born in Korea and moved to the United States as adults (mean age of arrival=27.2, range=21–37). Three of them had lived in an English-speaking country before they moved to the United States, but this was when they reached adulthood (one participant spent 10 months in the United Kingdom at age 22, one 13 months in Singapore at age 35, and another 12 months in Singapore at age 37). The total duration of stay in the United States and in the other English-speaking countries ranged from one month to 59 months (mean=25.9 months).

2.3. Eye-Tracking Task

2.3.1. Design, Materials, and Procedures

A visual world paradigm eye-tracking task was conducted in order to examine the process of moment-by-moment antecedent search involving reflexives. The study adapted the design used in Clackson, Felser, and Clahsen (2011), which investigated processing of English reflexives and pronouns. Participants listened to Korean sentences while looking at a computer monitor showing pictures. An example aural stimulus and the corresponding visual display are presented in (4) and Figure 1.

(4) a. Peterpan-un [Shrek-i ppyocokhan panul-lo **caki-lul**
P-TOP S-NOM sharp needle-INS self-ACC
silswulo ccille-ss-ta-ko] malhay-ss-sup-ni-ta.
by mistake prick-PAST-DECL-COMP say-PAST-HON-IND-DECL

b. Peterpan-un [Shrek-i ppyocokhan panul-lo **casin-ul** silswulo ccille-ss-ta-ko] malhay-ss-sup-ni-ta.

c. Peterpan-un [Shrek-i ppyocokhan panul-lo **caki-casin-ul** silswulo ccille-ss-ta-ko] malhay-ss-sup-ni-ta.

'Peter Pan said Shrek pricked **self** with a sharp needle by mistake.'

Figure 1. Visual Display Corresponding to (4)

The experimental sentences were biclausal sentences where the embedded object was one of the three reflexives (*caki/casin/caki-casin*). Both the matrix subject and the embedded subject denoted third-person singular masculine animation characters, which matched the reflexives in phi-features. Six well-known animation characters were selected and used an equal number of times, half of the times as the matrix subject and half of the times as the embedded subject. A postpositional phrase (such as *pyocokhan panul-lo* 'with a sharp needle') was inserted before the reflexive. This phrase was added to direct the participants' gaze to a single position in the display (the picture denoted by the NP within the PP) that is neither the picture of the matrix subject or that of the embedded subject, at the onset of the reflexive. After the reflexive, an adverb (such as *silswulo* 'by mistake') was inserted to create a 'spill-over' region, in order to secure some time to capture the effect of the reflexive before the participants hear the embedded verb. Twenty-one sets of experimental items were constructed and distributed among three lists in a Latin Square design. Each list also contained 59 filler sentences, intermixed with the experimental sentences in a pseudorandomized order. Participants were randomly assigned to one of the lists.

The visual display showed four pictures in the middle of the computer monitor: the picture of the matrix subject, the picture of the embedded subject, the picture depicting the object mentioned by the NP within the PP that occurred right before the reflexive (in the example display, *pyocokhan panul* 'a sharp needle'), and the picture of an object that was not mentioned in the aural stimuli. The four pictures were arranged to be displayed equally often in each position (i.e., the subject picture was shown in the first quadrant in one fourth of the trials, in the second quadrant in another one fourth of the trials, etc.).

The expected fixation patterns were as follows. It was expected that fixations would be directed to the matrix subject picture and the embedded subject picture, respectively, upon hearing the matrix subject and the embedded subject. On hearing the PP, fixations would move to the picture representing the NP within the PP. As we discussed earlier, this step was created to direct fixations away from pictures of the potential antecedents of the reflexive (the matrix subject picture or the embedded subject picture) before participants heard the reflexive. The search for the antecedent would begin upon hearing the reflexive. The proportion of fixations on the matrix subject picture and on the embedded subject picture would change depending on which of the two subjects is considered the antecedent. We thus compared the proportions of the two fixations from the onset of the reflexive.

From the reflexive onset, two possible time courses of antecedent search were predicted. First, it is possible that one of the two binding interpretations is assigned immediately when the reflexive is heard (or at the adverb, which is the spill-over word). The initially assigned interpretation will then be confirmed or revised as more information follows the reflexive. Note that in our stimuli, the information following the reflexive is not likely to cause a noticeable revision of the initial interpretation because we normed our stimuli so that they do not have a bias either for the local binding interpretation or for the long-distance binding interpretation. Alternatively, it is possible that the antecedent selection is not immediately done at the reflexive (or at the spill-over word) but is delayed until potentially important information is given, for instance, at the embedded verb. In this case, due to the nature of our stimuli, the ambiguity of the reflexive will not be resolved even after additional words are given beyond the reflexive.

The proportions of fixations on the two potential antecedents were analyzed in two consecutive timing windows. The first window included the reflexive and the following adverb, and was expected to show the initial interpretation of the reflexives. The next window, which included the embedded verb, was expected to show the influence of the embedded verb in determining the interpretation of reflexives. The next word (the matrix verb) was excluded from the analysis because it could involve the sentence wrap-up effect, being the last word of the sentence.

The experiment was conducted using a computer connected to the EyeLink 1000 system. After the participants were familiarized with the experiment through a practice session, they proceeded to the main session. At the beginning of each trial the visual display to be used in the trial was shown briefly (for 2.5 seconds) on the screen. This was done so that the participants would become familiar with the picture arrays in the display. The next screen was a blank screen with a fixation cross in the middle (700msec). This screen was included to direct the participants' gaze to the center of the screen before they began to hear the aural stimuli. On the next screen, the visual display shown earlier was presented again, and the aural stimulus, recorded by a female native Korean speaker, was played at the same time. Participants were told that they could look anywhere they liked on the screen while trying to comprehend the meaning of the aural stimulus. 3.5 seconds after the stimulus ended, participants heard a comprehension question. It was a short description of the aural stimuli (e.g., *Shrek-i panul-lo ccillesssupnita* 'Shrek pricked (someone) with a needle' for (4)), and participants were asked to judge whether it was a true or a false description of the sentence they had heard by pressing one of two keys on the keyboard. When a key was pressed, the next trial began. The eye-tracker was calibrated at least four designated times (at the beginning of the practice session, at the beginning of the main session, and twice in the middle of the eye-tracking experiment). Calibration was monitored by one of the experimenters, and the eye-tracker was additionally calibrated when necessary (e.g., in cases where the eye-tracker lost track of the eye or clear miscalibration was observed). Viewing was binocular, but only the movement of the right eye was recorded and analyzed.

2.3.2. Results

The mean accuracy on the comprehension questions was high (97.1%), suggesting that the participants were paying attention to the task. Questions for *caki* sentences and *casin* sentences had slightly lower accuracy than those for *caki-casin* sentences (*caki* 96%, *casin* 95.2%, *caki-casin* 100%), but a repeated-measures ANOVA performed on percent accuracy revealed that the accuracy was not significantly different across the three reflexives ($F1(2,30)=2.015, p>.05$; $F2(2,40)=1.727, p>.05$).

Turning to the fixation data, the proportion of fixations on the four pictures was first calculated. When the fixation patterns were visually examined from the onset of the stimulus sentence to the reflexive onset (i.e., the end of the PP) (*Peterpan-un Shrek-i ppyocokhan panul-lo* 'Peter Pan-TOP Shrek-NOM sharp needle-INS' in (4)), the patterns generally confirmed our expectations: proportions of fixations increased in the order of the matrix subject picture, embedded subject picture, and the picture depicting the NP in the PP. However, it turned out that the insertion of the PP before the reflexive was not entirely successful in directing fixations away from the pictures of the two potential antecedents of the reflexive. At reflexive onset, although the proportion of looks to the picture depicting the NP in the PP was the highest (0.45), the proportion of looks to the embedded subject was not reduced enough to be comparable to the proportion of looks to the matrix subject (matrix subject 0.07 vs. embedded subject 0.22; cf. object not mentioned 0.04). Due to the difference between the proportions of looks to the two potential antecedents at reflexive onset, comparison of the two in the critical windows was not possible. Such a baseline difference is sometimes found in visual world paradigm studies (Barr 2011). As a way to deal with the baseline difference, we eliminated the trials where fixations were on the matrix subject picture or on the embedded subject picture at reflexive onset and analyzed the remaining trials (a suggestion made by Tanenhaus, Frank, Jaeger, Masharov, and Salverda 2008; cited in Barr 2011). This made the proportion of fixations for the two subject pictures start from 0 at reflexive onset and allowed clearer interpretations of the trajectory of looks to the potential antecedents. The analyzed data constituted 69.9% of the total trials. Figures 2, 3 and 4 show the proportion of fixations on the matrix subject picture and the embedded subject picture in the critical timing windows for sentences including *caki*, *casin*, and *caki-casin*, respectively. The x-axis represents time in msec. Note that the x-axis is longer for the *caki-casin* sentences, due to the fact that *caki-casin* is longer than *caki* or *casin*.

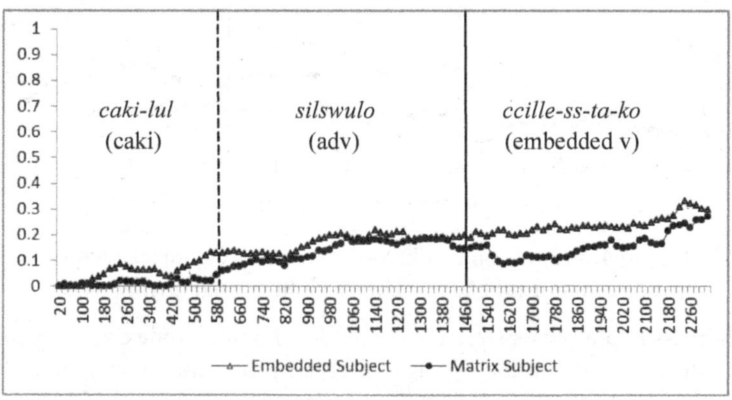

Figure 2. Proportion of Fixations on Matrix Subject Picture and Embedded Subject Picture: *caki*

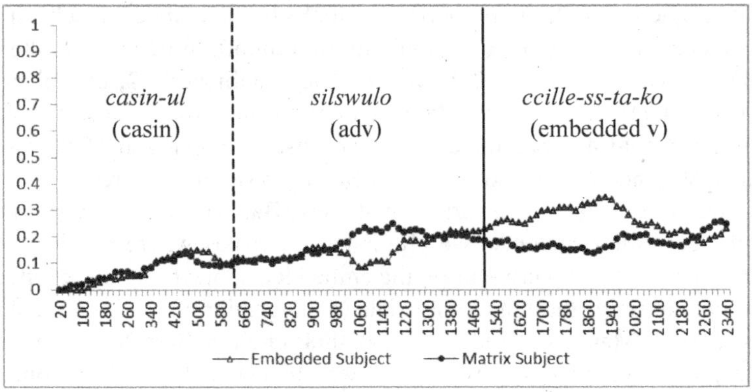

Figure 3. Proportion of Fixations on Matrix Subject Picture and Embedded Subject Picture: *casin*

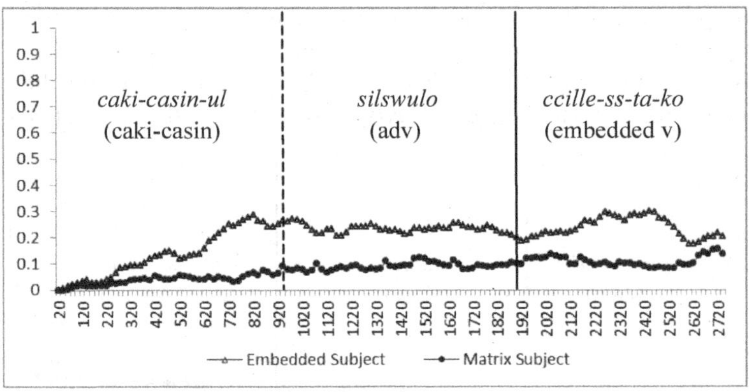

Figure 4. Proportion of Fixations on Matrix Subject Picture and Embedded Subject Picture: *caki-casin*

Paired-sample t-tests were conducted for the three reflexives separately, to statistically compare the averaged fixation proportion of the matrix subject picture and the averaged fixation proportion of the embedded subject picture in each timing window. Considering that it takes about 300ms to program and launch an eye movement, the analyses were conducted from 300ms after the reflexive onset. The results revealed that in *caki* sentences, the proportion of fixations on the matrix subject picture was not significantly different from the proportion of fixations on the embedded subject picture in the reflexive+adverb window ($t1(15)=-.574$, $p>.05$; $t2(20)=-.812$, $p>.05$). The two fixation proportions were not significantly different in the embedded verb window, either ($t1(15)=-1.477$, $p>.05$; $t2(20)=-1.469$, $p>.05$). The same statistical results were found in *casin* sentences, with fixation proportions on the two subjects not significantly different in the two timing windows (reflexive+adverb: $t1(15)=.480$, $p>.05$; $t2(20)=.168$, $p>.05$; embedded verb: $t1(15)=-1.165$, $p>.05$; $t2(20)=-1.296$, $p>.05$). A different pattern was found in *caki-casin* sentences. The fixation proportion on the embedded subject picture was significantly higher than that on the matrix subject picture in the reflexive+adverb window ($t1(15)=-2.999$, $p<.01$; $t2(20)=-4.012$, $p<.01$), and the difference was maintained in the embedded verb window ($t1(15)=-2.844$, $p<.05$; $t2(20)=-3.092$, $p<.01$).

2.4. Antecedent Identification Task

2.4.1. Design, Materials, and Procedures

After the eye-tracking task was conducted, participants were given a written antecedent identification task. The experimental items from the eye-tracking task were used for this task, distributed among the same three lists as in the eye-tracking task. The filler items were not included for the antecedent identification task. Each sentence was accompanied by two questions explicitly asking whether the reflexive can refer to one of the two subjects. Since there were two questions for each sentence, each participant was given 42 sentence-question pairs in total (21 sentences × 2 questions). The within-list order was pseudorandomized so that the two questions for a sentence were placed far apart. Participants were assigned to a list that was different from the list they were given in the eye-tracking task. They gave 1 to the question if the answer was “Yes” and 0 if it was “No.”

2.4.2. Results

Table 1 shows the average response scores for the two binding interpretations for each reflexive.

Table 1. Average Response Scores for Local Binding and Long-Distance Binding Interpretation for *caki*, *casin*, and *caki-casin*

	caki	*casin*	*caki-casin*
Matrix subject-binding interpretation	0.74	0.58	0.24
Embedded subject-binding interpretation	0.74	0.82	0.96

Paired-sample t-tests comparing the scores for the two binding interpretation revealed that for *caki*, the two binding interpretations did not receive significantly different scores ($t1(15)=.000$, $p>.05$; $t2(20)=.438$, $p>.05$). For *casin*, however, the matrix subject interpretation received significantly lower scores than the embedded subject interpretation ($t1(15)=-2.649$, $p<.05$; $t2(20)=-2.642$, $p<.05$). For *caki-casin*, the difference was even more highly significant ($t1(15)=-8.676$, $p<.001$; $t2(20)=-11.204$, $p<.001$).

3. Discussion

The present study investigated the binding distance preferences of the Korean reflexives *caki*, *casin*, and *caki-casin* in online antecedent search process and in final interpretation. In the online eye-tracking task, we examined whether the three reflexives are incrementally interpreted, that is, whether they select their antecedents immediately after they are heard, and if so, which of the two antecedents they select. Our study did not find evidence that *caki* and *casin* immediately activate a preferred antecedent. Rather, the fixation patterns suggest that both local and long-distance antecedents are initially considered as potential antecedents for *caki* and *casin*. These reflexives continued to be ambiguous even after the embedded verb was heard, probably because the embedded verbs used in our study were not helpful in disambiguating them. By contrast, with *caki-casin*, participants' gaze was immediately directed to the embedded subject picture, suggesting that *caki-casin* is initially assigned the local binding interpretation. The initial interpretation was maintained after the (neutral) embedded verb was heard.

In the offline antecedent identification task, we examined the final interpretations given to the reflexives. The results showed that *caki* was judged to be ambiguous between the local and long-distance binding interpretations. *Casin* was also ambiguous, but the local binding interpretation was preferred. *Caki-casin* strongly preferred the local binding interpretation.

Putting the results of the online and the offline tasks together, what is interesting is that *casin* showed a discrepancy between the initial and the final interpretation. In the online task, both the local and the long-distance antecedents were equally weighed as the potential antecedents of *casin*, but the offline judgment suggests that the local binding interpretation is slightly preferred. Relevant to this discrepancy might be the fact that *casin* is structurally ambiguous, unlike *caki* or *caki-casin*. Although *casin* is morphologically simple, it can also be analyzed as a complex anaphor, containing a null pronoun as non-head—i.e., pro-*casin* (Kim 2000; Kim and Yoon 2008), since Korean is a pro-drop language. It is possible that the indeterminacy in the structural analysis of *casin* is what contributes to a delay in online antecedent resolution until after the entire sentence has been presented, at which point the possibility of the complex-form analysis might increase the acceptability of the local binding interpretation.

The offline results of our study are not the same as the results of previous (offline) experimental studies. Kim and Yoon (2008) and Kim, Montrul, and Yoon (2009) found that *caki* has a strong long-distance binding preference, *casin* has a slight long-distance binding preference or no preference, and *caki-casin* has a strong local preference. However, this is not entirely incompatible with the results of our antecedent identification task in that all of the studies show a three-way distinction in binding distance among *caki*, *casin*, and *caki-casin*. In our study, the preferences are pushed toward the side of local binding for reasons that are not currently clear. It is more difficult to reconcile our online results with Choi and Kim (2007), who found evidence of immediate long-distance binding preference with *caki*. There are several differences between the two studies, such as the eye-tracking paradigm (visual world vs. sentence reading), the stimulus modality (aural vs. written), the structure of the stimuli (e.g., topic marking vs. case-marking of the matrix subject), etc., which may be worth considering in future studies.

Finally, it should be noted that the participants in our study were living in the United States at the time of testing. Judging from their language background, it is clear that they had fully acquired and consolidated Korean before they left Korea. However, at the time of testing, they were probably using Korean less and were being exposed in daily life to English, a language that has a different, simpler reflexive system with a single local reflexive. We acknowledge that the possibility should be taken into account that the participants' experience of living in the United States might have influenced our results to a certain degree.

References

Barr, D. J., Gann, T. M. and Pierce, R. S. 2011. Anticipatory Baseline Effects and Information Integration in Visual World Studies. *Acta Psychologica* 137(2):201–207.

Choi, K. and Kim, Y. 2007. Caykwitaymyengsa-uy Ta.uyseng Hayso-Kwaceng: Ankwu-Wuntong Pwunsek (Ambiguity Resolution Processes of Reflexives: Eye-tracking Data). *The Korean Journal of Experimental Psychology* 19(4): 263–277.

Clackson, K., Felser, D. and Clahsen, H. 2011. Children's Processing of Reflexives and Pronouns in English: Evidence from Eye-Movements During Listening. *Journal of Memory and Language* 65(2):128–144.

Kang, B-M. 1998. Mwunpep-kwa Ene Sayong: Khophes-ey Kipanhan Caykwisa 'caki', 'casin', 'caki-casin'-uy Kinung Pwunsek-ul Cwungsim-ulo (Grammar and the Use of Language: Korean Reflexives 'caki, 'casin', and 'caki-casin'). *Kwuk-e-hak* (Korean Linguistics) 31:165–204.

Kim, J-H., Montrul, S. and Yoon, J. H-S. 2009. Binding Interpretations of Anaphors by Korean Heritage Speakers. *Language Acquisition* 16:3–35.

Kim, J-H. and Yoon, J. H-S. 2008. An Experimental Syntactic Study of Binding of Multiple Anaphors in Korean. *Journal of Cognitive Science* 9(1):1–30.

Kim, Y-S. 2000. Caykwitaymyengsa-uy Hyengthay-thongsaloncek Pwunsek: Choy-socwu.uycek Cepkun (A Morphosyntactic Analysis of Reflexives: A Minimalist Approach). *Studies in Modern Grammar* 19:1–26.

Moon, S-C. 1995. An Optimality Approach to Long-Distance Anaphors. Doctoral dissertation, University of Washington, Seattle.

Yoon, J-M. 1989. Long-Distance Anaphors in Korean and their Crosslinguistic Implications. *Chicago Linguistic Society* 25: 479–495.

Part III

Historical Linguistics

Some Korean/Japanese Linguistic Implications of Korean Wooden Tablet Inscriptions

SEUNGJAE LEE*
Seoul National University

1. Introduction

The term *wooden tablet* refers to a piece of processed wood specifically used to inscribe a text. Over 600 wooden tablet pieces have been excavated in Korea, of which around 430 contain writing. While the recorded dates on these tablets range from the mid-6th century to the 13th century, this paper only considers writings from the mid-6th century to the late 8th century.

Based on new decipherments of the inscriptions, this paper claims that, unlike Japanese, Old Korean contained CVC syllables, i.e., closed syllables, and explains how and when Middle Chinese syllable-final */t/ became */l/ in Sino-Korean pronunciation.

Before beginning, it will be helpful to define a few frequently employed

* This paper was supported by the Seoul National University Study Abroad Fund for Humanities and Social Science Research in 2009. I am deeply grateful to Professor John Whitman (NINJAL) for encouraging me to present this paper at the 22nd annual Japanese/Korean Linguistics Conference, hosted by NINJAL. In writing this paper, I received great help from Yun Suyeon (MIT) and Kim Migyeong (SNU). Finally, I wish to thank Professor Zev Handel (University of Washington) for proofreading this paper and giving me useful questions and comments. However, all remaining errors and misjudgments are my sole responsibility.

Japanese/Korean Linguistics 22.
Edited by Mikio Giriko, Naonori Nagaya, Akiko Takemura, and Timothy J. Vance.

terms. It is well known that Chinese characters used in the writing of non-Chinese languages have two kinds of reading, *phonetic* and *semantic*. For example, the Chinese character 人 can be semantically read as /hito/ in Japanese, and phonetically read as /zin/ in Kan'on 漢音 and as /nin/ in Go'on 呉音. Similarly, the same character in 15th-century Korean could be semantically read as /sarʌm/ and phonetically read as /zin/.[1] Where the syllable /zin/ in both Japanese and Korean is represented by the graph 人, we say this is an instance of *phonetic adaptation* of 人, and where /hito/ in Japanese and /sarʌm/ in Korean are represented by the graph 人, we say this is an instance of *semantic adaptation* of 人 (see Handel 2009 for details).

2. Syllable-Final Consonants in Old Korean

One notable phonological difference between the Korean and Japanese languages lies in their syllable structures. Korean contains many closed (i.e., CVC) syllables, while such syllables are almost completely absent in Japanese.

Some scholars of the Japanese language hypothesize that the Old Korean language, like the Old Japanese language, did not have any closed syllables. They argue that the CVC syllables of Middle Korean arose from the deletion of word-final vowels in Old Korean CVCV structures. For example, they argue that the second vowel was dropped from the Old Korean words */goma/ *고마 'bear' and */dɨrɨ/ *드르 'field', resulting in the attested Middle Korean forms /go:m/ 곰 and /dɨ:l/ 들. However, this argument is not generalizable across the entire Korean lexicon. The argument is only applicable to some Middle Korean monosyllabic words with a rising tone. Many monosyllabic words in Middle Korean had either a low tone or a high tone, which supports the claim that CVC syllable structure should be hypothesized in Old Korean. In fact, there are a number of different types of evidence that support the idea that CVC syllable structure was present in Old Korean.

First, CVC syllables are prevalent in various Old Korean words. Second, some Chinese characters employed in the Sino-graphic representation of Old Korean were specifically designated to write syllable-final consonants. Third, in Sino-Korean pronunciation, syllable-final consonants /p/, /l/, /k/,

[1] In this paper, the International Phonetic Alphabet (IPA) is used for transcriptions of both attested Middle Korean forms and reconstructed forms of Korean, except that the palatal semivowel is transcribed as /y/. However, the letters ⟨ㄱ⟩, ⟨ㄷ⟩, ⟨ㅂ⟩, and ⟨ㄹ⟩ of the Korean alphabet are transcribed as /g/, /d/, /b/, and /r/ in syllable-initial position and as /k/, /t/, /p/, and /l/ in syllable-final position, following the practice of the Revised Romanization System promulgated by the Korean government in 2000. Proper nouns and academic terms have been transcribed following the Revised Romanization System.

/m/, /n/, and /ŋ/ have clearly been extant throughout the entire period from Old Korean to Modern Korean.

Regarding the first point, a few supporting examples from wooden tablet inscriptions are presented here. As seen in Table 3 below, numerals in the Southern Korean language were written on a wooden tablet from the Iksan 益山 Mireuksa Temple Site 彌勒寺址, and the suffix 〈邑〉 following these numerals was read as syllable-final */p/ (Lee 2012). On this wooden tablet, the semantically adapted graphs 〈今〉 and 〈毛〉 can be assigned a reconstructed pronunciation by projecting backward from later forms */yət/ and */təl/, and the phonetically adapted graph 〈日〉 must have been read as */nil/ (Lee 2012). Another example comes from wooden tablet no. 119 excavated from Haman 咸安 Seongsan sanseong 城山山城, which contains the sequence of graphs 〈器尺一石〉. The graphs 〈器尺〉 write the name of a type of grain, */gidzak/ 'millet'. These examples all contain syllable-final consonants, and demonstrate that syllable-final consonants */p/, */l/, */t/, and */k/ existed in the Old Southern Korean language.

The second type of evidence is related to Sino-graphic orthography. Under this notational system, certain graphs were designated to represent syllable-final consonants. These graphs are presented in Table 1. The row headings *Hyangchal* 鄕札, *Idu* 吏讀, and *Gugyeol* 口訣 refer to different traditions of Sino-graphic orthography used in pre-modern Korea.[2]

Table 1. Graphs that Represent Syllable-Final Consonants

	/k/	/n/	/l/	/m/	/p/	/s/	/ŋ/
Hyangchal	只	隱, 焉	乙, 尸	音		叱	
Idu	只		乙	音	(邑)	叱	(應)
Gugyeol	ハ	㇐	乙, 尸	亠	(邑)	七	(應)

Table 1 encompasses data from Old Korea to the Goryeo 高麗 dynasty (918–1392). Data from the Joseon 朝鮮 dynasty (1392–1910) are placed in parentheses. The graphs in Table 1 were never used to write syllable-initial consonants, only syllable-final consonants. These graphs were used as alphabetic letters representing segmental phonemes from Old Korea to the Joseon dynasty. Since such a system was in continuous use from early on, it should be concluded that syllable-final consonants existed in Old Korean.

Third, the pronunciation of Chinese characters also proves that syllable-final consonants existed in Old Korean. Sino-Korean pronunciation is well

---

2 Hyangchal refers to a notational system of transcribing Korean songs of the Silla 新羅 kingdom, i.e., Hyangga 鄕歌, and Idu refers to a system of writing down personal and official documents. Gugyeol refers to the Korean readings of Chinese texts in a broad sense, and to a glossing system annotated onto Chinese texts in a narrow sense.

known for retaining syllable-final sounds. According to Kōno (1968/1979), Sino-Korean pronunciation in Middle Korean was initially based on the pronunciation of Chinese characters in late 8th-century Cháng'ān 長安, the capital of China's Tang 唐 dynasty (618–907). Chinese during this time contained syllable-final consonants */p/, */t/, */k/, */m/, */n/, and */ŋ/, but Modern Mandarin Chinese shows complete loss of the stops and reduction of the nasals, so that only the two consonants /n/ and /ŋ/ now occur in syllable-final position. In contrast, the pronunciation of Sino-Korean has been much more conservative, retaining six distinct consonants in syllable-final position. Therefore, the claim that syllable-final consonants did not exist in Old Korean should be dismissed.

3. How Syllable-Final */t/ of Middle Chinese Became */l/ in Sino-Korean

Another well-known characteristic of Sino-Korean pronunciation is that syllable-final */t/ consonants have all been replaced by /l/. For example, the Chinese character 鐵 'iron' is pronounced as /tetu/ in Sino-Japanese, but as /t^hyəl/ in Sino-Korean. Where Middle Chinese syllable-final */t/ has become /tu/ [tsu] or /ti/ [tɕi] in Sino-Japanese, it has become /l/ in Sino-Korean.

In Sino-Japanese pronunciation, */u/ or */i/ was added after */t/ to conform to the open syllable structure of Japanese, after which *[tu] and *[ti] changed to [tsu] and [tɕi], respectively. Under the principle of loan phonology where borrowed words are modified to fit the phoneme inventory and phonological structure of the borrowing language, these developments can easily be understood.

Circumstances greatly differ in the pronunciation of Sino-Korean. For example, it is unclear whether the graph 〈乞〉 in the personal name 乞負支 found on the Haman wooden tablet from the mid-6th century was a written representation of */gət/ or */gəl/. Moreover, it has been very difficult for scholars to explain exactly when and how syllable-final */t/ in Middle Chinese pronunciation became */l/ in Sino-Korean. Because linguistic data indigenous to Korea have been insufficient to resolve these issues, Lee Ki-Moon (1981) claimed that syllable-final */t/ changed to */l/ initially in Northern Wei 北魏 (386–534), a Chinese dynasty ruled by a Mongolic-speaking people, and it was this */l/ that was accepted into Sino-Korean pronunciation. According to this hypothesis, the */t/ to */l/ change did not take place in Korean.

Taking the opposite view, Kōno (1968/1979) considered the change to be internal to the Korean language. He presented the examples shown in (1) to support his claim.

(1) a. 次ᄎᆞh 第뎨r: */tsʌtyəy/ > /tsʌryəy/, 定母 (ᄎᆞ뎨 > ᄎᆞ례, 'order')
    b. 牧모h 丹단l: */motan/ > /moran/, 端母 (모단 > 모란, 'peony')
    c. 道도r 場댱l: */dotyaŋ/ > /doryaŋ/, 澄母 (도댱 > 도량 , 'school')
    d. 菩보l 提뎨l: */botyey/ > /bori/, 端母 (보뎨 > 보리, 'Buddhahood')

However, the examples in (1) illustrate a change not in syllable-final position but rather in syllable-initial position, or more specifically, in an intervocalic environment. In other words, it is not appropriate to regard this change in the same light as the shift from */t/ to */l/ in the final position of monosyllables. Moreover, since only a limited number of words fall into this category, the change exemplified in (1) should be considered a sub-rule. Given that the change from */t/ to */l/ is a characteristic seen across the entire Sino-Korean lexicon, the examples in (1) are not relevant to discussion of the cause and timing of the change.

Setting aside the examples in (1), it is necessary to seek some other empirical evidence to explain how and when the coda */t/ in Middle Chinese became the coda */l/ of Sino-Korean. To resolve the first question, this paper points out that there is a significant tendency in the Korean language to avoid syllable-final /t/ in underlying forms. Taking a close look at native Korean words, it is clear that many of them contain syllable-final /l/, whereas only a small number of words contain syllable-final /t/. For example, among nouns that refer to parts of the human body, syllable-final /l/ is common: /t^həl/ 'body hair', /gol/ 'marrow', /bol/ 'cheek', /p^hʌl/ 'arm', /sʌl/ 'flesh', and /bal/ 'foot' are examples. But syllable-final /t/ is seen only in the word /sat/ 'groin'. This tendency is also reflected in graphs used to notate words in Old Korean. As shown in Table 1, syllable-final */l/ was notated either with ⟨尸⟩ or with ⟨乙⟩, and syllable-final */s/ with ⟨叱⟩. But no graph designated to notate syllable-final */t/ has been discovered to date. While notational systems using adapted graphs date as far back as the 6th century, syllable-final */t/ seems to have been excluded from these systems. This must reflect the fact that only a few words in Old Korean ended with coda */t/. If Chinese words were adopted under such circumstances, it is reasonable to suppose that syllable-final */t/ would have been avoided (Park 1971: 234–235).

The strong tendency to avoid syllable-final /t/ is also observed in contemporary loanwords from English. For example, the English word *foot* is adopted as /p^hus/ 풋 or /p^hut^hɨ/ 푸트 in Korean (cf. Japanese /hutto/ フット). It is apparent that borrowed words undergo phonological changes during the borrowing process in order to conform to the phoneme inventory and syllable structure of the recipient language. In the case of Korean, syllable-final /t/ in English words is converted to /s/ ㅅ or /t^hɨ/ 트 in the underlying representation, and in Hangeul orthography as well. The CVC forms in row 1 in

Table 2 are typically used when the borrowed English word is followed by the subject marker /-i/ or the object marker /-ɨl/, and the CVCV forms in row 2 are typically used when the speaker intends to pronounce the word as closely to the original English pronunciation as possible.

Table 2. Modern Korean Pronunciation of English Syllable-Final /t/

	shoot	*set*	*cut*	*bat*	*that*	*food*	*good*
1. CVC	/syus/ 슛	/ses/ 셋	/kʰəs/ 컷	/bɛs/ 뱃	/dɛs/ 댓	/pʰus/ 풋	/gus/ 굿
2. CVCV		/setʰɨ/ 세트	/kʰətʰɨ/ 커트	/bɛtʰɨ/ 배트	/dɛtʰɨ/ 대트	/pʰudɨ/ 푸드	

The key point here is the fact that, in row 1, syllable-final /t/ in English is adapted as /s/ in Korean. For a native speaker of Korean this is a very natural process, and it might be due to the fact that not many words in Modern Korean have a word-final /t/ in their underlying forms, whereas many words end in /s/. Most Korean words that seemingly end in /t/ are the result of phonetic realization of underlying /s/. For example, a native Korean would take /ses/ as the underlying form of the English word *set*, and apply the coda neutralization rule to derive the phonetic form [set] when uttering it in isolation.

It is not uncommon for analogy to play a crucial role in the adoption of foreign words and the formation of underlying forms. It is reasonable to assume that this same kind of process occurred in Old Korean. As syllable-final */t/ was scarce but syllable-final */l/ was abundant in native Old Korean words, an analogy to the native phonological pattern might have interfered with the process of borrowing Middle Chinese words that ended in the coda */t/. It is highly probable that an analogical change occurred in Old Korean as part of the loanword adaptation process, altering the syllable-final */t/ of Middle Chinese to */l/. For example, when native speakers of Old Korean borrowed the Chinese word */tat/ 達 'reach', they would have established the underlying form */tal/ instead of */tat/. Such a shift is similar to the shift of the English word *set* from /set/ to underlying /ses/ in Modern Korean.

The examples in (2) present Tibetan data which show the phonetic representation of Chinese words with Middle Chinese syllable-final */t/ as perceived by Tibetans from the mid-8th to mid-9th century. This set of data indicates that during this period, a change of coda */t/ to */r/ occurred in the dialect of northwest China.

(2) Tibetan: 節 tser, 切 ts'er, 鬱 gur, 密 'bir, 勿 'bur, 滅 'byar, 厥 kwar, 悅 war, 弗 p'ur, 逸 yir, 察 c'ar (Luó 1933)

The examples in (3) present Chinese data which show the phonetic representation of Turkic words as perceived by the Chinese. Syllable-final Turkic /l/ and /r/ are represented by Chinese characters with Middle Chinese syllable-final */t/.

(3) a. Turkic Monuments: bilgä 苾伽, bolmis 沒密施, tarqan 達干, türk 突厥; Uigur: pusar 菩薩, cirki/sirki 節氣, bir/biir 筆, mir 密 (Song 1995)
    b. Turkic: tar 達, Uigur: bur 佛 (Lee 2006:276)

However, the data in (3) do not necessarily show that */l/ and */r/ were the phonetic representations of the Chinese syllable-final sounds of the graphs ⟨苾⟩ and ⟨達⟩, respectively. Since there were no Chinese characters whose pronunciation could represent syllable-final */l/ and */r/ accurately, the Chinese had to either use characters with the coda */t/ or add an additional CV syllable beginning with */l/. The former solution, the phonetic representation of foreign words with */l/ or */r/ as */t/ in Chinese, can be also considered an instance of analogical change. In other words, syllable-final */l/ and */r/, which did not exist in Middle Chinese, were interpreted as */t/ in order to fit into Chinese syllable structure.

So far in this paper, it has been suggested that the shift from */t/ to */l/ in the Sino-Korean reading system was an analogical change involving loanword adaptation. Assuming this suggestion is correct, it is clear why Sino-Korean syllable-final */p/ and */k/ remained unchanged from the Old Korean era up to the present, whereas syllable-final */t/ was replaced by */l/. Since there have always been many native Korean words ending with */p/ and */k/, it would have been quite natural to adopt Chinese words that ended in */p/ and */k/ without any modification. In contrast, words ending with */t/ were scarce, while those ending with */l/ were abundant in Old Korean, which explains why the analogical change applied only to */t/ and not to other codas.[3]

4. When Syllable-Final */t/ of Middle Chinese Became */l/ in Sino-Korean

We now turn to the discussion of when this analogical change may have occurred. It will be argued that it happened during the mid-7th century. Empirical evidence from Korean wooden tablet inscriptions will be presented to support this claim. The primary evidence comes from the two graphs

[3] Wei (2012) claims that Old Koreans accepted /t/-final syllables as "CVtV," which underwent the change "CVtV>CVrV>CVr." However, he does not explain why the intervocalic weakening did not occur in the case of */p/ and */k/ but only in the case of */t/. In contrast, the hypothesis based on analogical change does explain why the change did not occur for */p/ and */k/.

〈本〉 and 〈原〉 written on Haman Seongsan sanseong wooden tablets (see Figures 1 below).

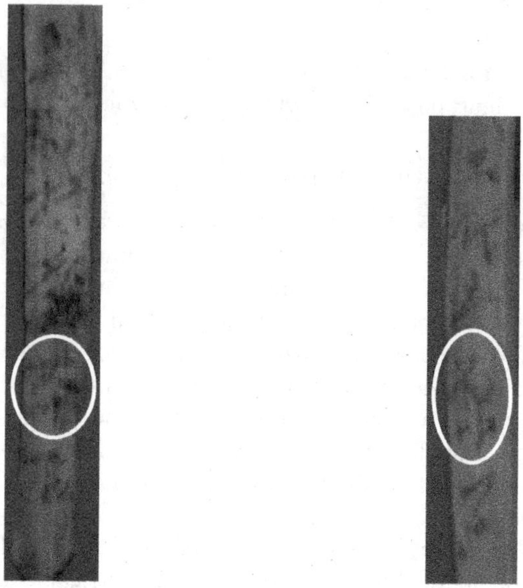

[···■■村以■本石]
'(one) *seom* of wheat (sent by) I■ at ■■ village'

[···只伐支原石]
'(one) *seom* of wheat (sent by) Gibeoldzi'

Figure 1. Haman no. 53 (Left) and Haman no. 195 (Right)

The sequences of graphs 〈以■〉 and 〈只伐支〉 that precede 〈本〉 and 〈原〉 in Figure 1 are personal names. The following graph 〈石〉, semantically read as */syəm/ *셤, is a measure noun. Other inscriptions on the Haman wooden tablets show that a word referring to a type of grain typically comes between a personal name and a measure noun. Therefore, the graphs 〈本〉 and 〈原〉 are assumed to name kinds of grain. Normally, a numeral would precede a measure noun like 〈石〉. However, many other wooden tablets containing numeral+measure-noun structures show that the graph 〈一〉, indicating the numeral 1, could generally be omitted before a measure noun, whereas graphs indicating other numbers such as 〈二〉 '2' or 〈三〉 '3' could not. Thus, the single graph 〈石〉 in Figure 1 would presumably be read as */hʌn syəm/ 'one *seom*'.

The next question is which types of grain the graphs 〈本〉 and 〈原〉 represented. This paper assumes that these two graphs were both representations of */mit/ 'wheat'. The reading */mit/ is based on the fact that they share the same semantic reading /mit/ in Middle Korean, which is clear from the fact that they were transcribed as the native Korean word /mit/ 믿, meaning 'base' or 'origin' in Middle Korean. This semantic reading is also supported by the fact that both graphs have the same semantic reading, /moto/, in Japanese.[4]

If this assumption is correct, then the graphs 〈本〉 and 〈原〉 constitute invaluable evidence that syllable-final */t/ went through an analogical change to */l/ in Sino-Korean pronunciation. In other words, the reconstructed form */mit/ for the word in these inscriptions leads to the conclusion that the */mit/ in Old Korean became /mil/ 밀 'wheat' in Middle Korean. This implies that an analogical change occurred internally in the Korean language. Data that reveal such a change have been unavailable until quite recently, highlighting the importance of the graphs 〈本〉 and 〈原〉 on the Haman wooden tablets.

How can we be certain that the graphs 〈本〉 and 〈原〉 designated 'wheat' instead of some other type of grain? Given that the Middle Korean word for 'wheat' was /mil/ and that the Chinese character 〈麥〉 was normally used to designate it, the claim may seem baseless at a first glance. *Jīlínlèishì* 鷄林類事, written in the early 12th century, gives the notation 麥曰密 '麥 is pronounced /mil/', and *Hunmong jahoe* 訓蒙字會, written in the 16th century, also says that the semantic reading of 〈麥〉 was /mil/ 'wheat'. However, the character 〈麥〉 did not mean 'wheat' only. In Modern Korean Sino-graphic orthography, the grain /mil/ 'wheat' is typically written as 〈小麥〉, and the grain /bori/ 'barley' as 〈大麥〉. This shows that the Chinese character 〈麥〉 was a generic word for several types of grain. In Korea, many types of grain, including /mil/ 'wheat' and /bori/ 'barley', have been cultivated from ancient times. Thus, for any particular instance of the graph 〈麥〉, it is unclear whether it was intended to be read as /mil/ or /bori/.

The author of the Haman wooden tablets used both 〈本〉 and 〈原〉 to indicate 'wheat' and 〈麥〉 to indicate 'barley'. As these wooden tablets were used as a confirmation of the fulfillment of a duty, there was a need to be precise about which people dispatched which items. Other major cereals have their own notations, and the only major cereal crop that is not identified in wooden tablet texts is 'wheat'. The phonological similarity between */mit/ and /mil/, the tendency to avoid */t/ in coda position, and the differentiated usage of 〈本/原〉 and 〈麥〉 all lead to the conclusion that 〈本/原〉 designated 'wheat' with the semantic reading */mit/. On the Haman wooden tablets, the graph 〈麥〉 and the sequence of graphs 〈艹里〉 are assumed to be written expressions of 'barley' */bori/ *보리. Noticing that the two types of grain are strictly distinguished in writing, it can be reaffirmed that the graphs 〈本〉 and 〈原〉 represent */mit/.

---

4 It has already been argued that /mit/ in Korean is cognate with /moto/ in Japanese.

The next question is, When was this */mit/ most likely written? The wooden tablets on which 'wheat' was written as */mit/ were all excavated from Haman Seongsan sanseong. The wooden tablets excavated from Haman are closely related to the construction of a castle; most of the texts found on Haman wooden tablets document the many types of grain that were consumed during its construction. If the timing of this fortification can be determined from historical data, we can also determine when the Haman wooden tablets were made. No historical record of the construction of the castle survives in any Korean texts, but such a record is found in the 8th-century Japanese historical work *Nihonshoki* 日本書紀, as shown in (4).

(4) 故新羅築城於阿羅波斯山以備日本 (巻19 欽明紀 22年)
'Hence Silla built a castle on Pasasan mountain at Ara to prepare against Japan (561 CE).'

According to this record, the construction of a castle on Pasasan (present-day Seongsan) of Ara (present-day Haman) must have been finished by around 561 CE. Most historians consider this date to be valid. For example, Lee (2000) has proposed that the Haman wooden tablets were created between the years 545 and 561 CE, in the mid-6th century. According to his interpretation, it can be concluded that the Old Korean word */mit/ 'wheat' must have been in use at least up to that time.

A remaining question is how and why */mit/ became /mil/ in Middle Korean. This paper suggests that this word underwent the same analogical change which occurred in the process of borrowing Chinese words and the development of Sino-Korean pronunciation. People in the southern region of the Korean peninsula mainly cultivated /bori/ 'barley'. Wheat, which was mainly cultivated in the northern region, was newly introduced to them. It is very likely that the northern word for 'wheat' was considered to be a foreign borrowing, and was converted to /mil/ by the same process which occurred in the borrowing of Chinese words ending in */t/. In contrast, the homophonous native word */mit/ meaning 'base' or 'origin' would not have been considered a foreign borrowing, and its original pronunciation /mit/ 믿 or /mit^h/ 밑 is retained even today.

Now, let us discuss when this change came to a halt. Lee (2012) has argued that the change took place either in the late 7th century or in the early 8th century, based on the analysis of Old Korean numerals written on a wooden tablet from Iksan 益山 Mireuksa Temple Site 彌勒寺址. Examples of the identification and phonological reconstruction of these numerals are given in Table 3. They serve as critical evidence in determining the timing of the analogical change.

Table 3. Identification and Reconstruction of Old Korean Numerals

	Identification	External Reconstruction	Internal Reconstruction	Final Reconstruction
1	(坐)伽第巳	(*dzwɑ)gɪɑdeip	(*dzwa)gadəp	*gadəp/*가덥
2	矣毛巳	*ɦiĕitəriĕp	*itərɨp	*itərɨp/*이더릅
3	新台巳	*sayt'ʌip	*saydʌp	*saydʌp/*새ᄃᆞᆸ
5	刀士巳	*tɑudẓiĕp	*dasʌp	*dasip/*다십
7	日古巳	*ɲɪĕtkop	*nilgop	*nilgop/*닐곱
	二■口巳	*ɲɪĕi■k'əup	*ni■gup	*ni■gup/*닐굽
8	今毛巳		*yətərɨp	*yətərɨp/*여더릅
	以[?]如巳 (⺀ 十)	*jɪĕitap(agʌy), *jɪĕitəp(agʌy)	*yʌtap(agʌy), *yətəp(agʌy)	*yʌtap/*ᄋᆢ답, *yətəp/*여덥

What is most notable in Table 3 that the Old Korean numeral 7 is written with the two sequences 〈日古巳〉 and 〈二■口巳〉. The phonetic reading of these graphs yields the same result corresponding to Middle Korean /nilgop/ or /nilgup/ 'seventh'. This indicates that both the graph 〈日〉 and the sequence of graphs 〈二■〉 correspond to */nil/.

This correspondence opens up a way of reconstructing the Old Korean sound value of Middle Chinese ńź-initial 日母, the initial consonant of the two graphs 〈日〉 and 〈二〉. Whereas the ńź-initial is regularly realized as /z/ in the Sino-Korean reading system of Middle Korean, the Old Korean sound value of the ńź-initial is clearly shown to be */n/ by the examples of */nil/ 日 and */ni/ 二 inscribed on the wooden tablet. This shows that Sino-Korean had at least two layers of reading systems: one with the initial sound */n/ and the other with initial sound /z/. The first layer is comparable to the Sino-Japanese layer Go'on 呉音 and the second to the Sino-Japanese layer Kan'on 漢音 (Lee 2012).

These inscriptions also show that Middle Chinese coda */t/ was */l/ in the Sino-Korean pronunciation of the time. If the graph 〈日〉 were */nit/, with a coda */t/, the Korean numeral 7 would have to be reconstructed as */nitgup/. However, the graph 〈日〉 in Table 3 cannot be reconstructed as */nit/. In the history of Korean phonology, obstruent consonant */t/ followed by */g/ or */k/ has never changed to */l/, so */nitgup/ is not a possible precursor of Middle Korean /nilgup/. Instead, reconstructing the graph 〈日〉 as */nil/ allows it to accord perfectly with the normal developments of Korean historical phonology. Therefore, it must have been before the late 7th century or the early 8th century that syllable-final */t/ analogically changed to */l/

in Sino-Korean pronunciation. Many artifacts excavated from the Mireuksa Temple Site also seem to come from before this time period.

Based on the wooden tablet inscriptions shown in Figure 1 and Table 3, the period in which the analogical change from */t/ to */l/ took place can be narrowed down to between the mid-6th century and the early 8th century. This conclusion is also supported by evidence from the regional names that appear in the 12th-century Korean historical work *Samguksagi* 三國史記, which allows us to narrow down the time period even further.

About one hundred years after the mid-6th century, there was an outbreak of international warfare in northeast Asia. Silla 新羅, in alliance with the Tang 唐 dynasty of China, attacked Baekje 百濟 and Goguryeo 高句麗. Baekje aligned with Japan to counter the attack but fell in 660 CE, followed by Goguryeo in 668 CE. With hundreds of thousands of Tang Chinese troops invading the Korean peninsula, the people of Silla were exposed to numerous Chinese words for the first time. It is likely that they learned and adopted Chinese sounds and words during the process.

Another hundred years later, in 757 CE, King Gyeongdeọk 景德王 of Silla rectified all regional names to conform to Chinese norms. For example, as shown in (5), 吉同 was changed to 永同, 推火 to 密城, 德勿 to 德水, 勿居 to 淸渠, and 毛乙冬非 to 鐵圓.

(5) a. 永同郡 本吉同郡 (vol. 34) '永同郡 originated from 吉同郡'
b. 密城郡 本推火郡 (vol. 34) '密城郡 originated from 推火郡'
c. 德水縣 本高句麗德勿縣 (vol. 35) '德水縣 originated from 德勿縣 of Goguryeo'
d. 淸渠縣 本百濟勿居縣 (vol. 36) '淸渠縣 originated from 勿居縣 of Baekje'
e. 鐵圓郡一云毛乙冬非 (vol. 37) '鐵圓郡 is also called 毛乙冬非'

The graph 〈吉〉 in (5a) is an example of phonetic adaptation, read as */gil/. It corresponds to a semantic adaptation */gil/ of the graph 〈永〉. The following similar correspondences are also found: the phonetic adaptation of 〈密〉 */mil/ matches the semantic adaptation of 〈推〉 */mil/ in (5b), the phonetic adaptation of 〈勿〉 */mɨl/ matches the semantic adaptation of 〈水〉 */mɨl/ in (5c), and the phonetic adaptation of 〈勿〉 */mɨl/ matches the semantic adaptation of 〈淸〉 */mʌl(g)/ in (5d). Of these, the graphs that were read semantically were used to represent native Korean morphemes or words including the adjective stem */gil-/ 永 'long', the verb stem */mil-/ 推 'push', the noun */mɨl/ 水 'water', and the adjective stem */mʌl(g)-/ 淸 'clean, clear'.

These native Korean morphemes were also written with the phonetically adapted graphs 〈吉〉, 〈密〉, 〈勿〉, and 〈勿〉, as shown in (5). Regarding the phonetic readings, it has to be determined whether the coda was */t/ or */l/.

The former would be chosen if one accepts the hypothesis that Sino-Korean pronunciations were based on Chinese of the late 8th century (Kōno 1968/1979) or as late as the 10th century (Arisaka 1936/1957; Itō 2002). However, this conclusion is not in accord with the evidence. Textual evidence from Korea does not support the idea that the native Korean morphemes */gil-/, */mil-/, */mɨl/, and */mʌl(g)-/ trace back to earlier */git-/, */mit-/, */mɨt/, and */mʌt(g)-/. Claiming that the morphemes should be reconstructed as */git-/, */mit-/, */mɨt/, and */mʌt(g)-/ because their syllable-final consonant must have reflected Middle Chinese */t/ would be making the same mistake as claiming that syllable-final consonant */r/ did not exist in the Turkic languages because a Chinese author wrote 〈達干〉 */tatqan/ to transcribe the Turkic word /tarqan/, as in (3a). Neither claim is plausible. Therefore, these native Korean morphemes are reconstructed as */gil-/, */mil-/, */mɨl/, and */mʌl(g)-/.

The graph 〈鐵〉 and the sequence of graphs 〈毛乙〉 in (5e) are decisive evidence in support of the reconstructions with syllable-final */l/. The sequence 〈毛乙〉 is an example of a Korean orthographic convention which combines semantic and phonetic readings of graphs to express a single word. By this convention, the first graph is read semantically and the second graph is read phonetically. This way of writing is called *hunju-eumjong* 訓主音從. The second graph 〈乙〉 does not represent a full syllable but only the coda sound /l/. This reiteration of the coda sound of the preceding syllable is referred to *mareum-cheomgi* 末音添記 'final-sound addition'. Both 〈鐵〉 and 〈毛乙〉 represent the native Korean word */təl/ *덜 'hair'. This word has retained the syllable-final /l/ since the Old Korean era. In other words, the graph 〈鐵〉 should be seen as a representation of the word form */təl/ or */tyəl/, written some time after the analogical change of */t/ to */l/ was completed.

To sum up all the data related to the completion of the analogical change of */t/ to */l/, it has been argued that (1) the graphs 〈吉〉, 〈密〉, 〈勿〉, and 〈鐵〉 were read phonetically and represented Korean native morphemes ending in the coda */l/, (2) the graph 〈日〉 was phonetically read as */nil/ and was used to represent the Korean native numeral */nilgup/ or */nilgop/ 'seventh', and (3) the graphs 〈本〉 and 〈原〉 were semantically read as */mit/ and represented the Korean word */mit/ for 'wheat'. These data are summarized in chronological order in Table 4.

Table 4. Data on the Timing of the Analogical Change from */t/ to */l/[5]

Example Number	Reconstructed Form	6th C	7th C	8th C	15th C Hangeul
6.1	*mit 'wheat'	本$_{SR}$			mil
6.2	*mit 'wheat'	原$_{SR}$			mil
8.2	*təl 'hair'		毛$_{SR}$		tʰəl
8.7	*nil 'date, sun'		日$_{PR}$		nil
9.1	*gil- 'long'		吉$_{PR}$	永$_{SR}$	gil-
9.2	*mil- 'push'		推$_{SR}$	密$_{PR}$	mil-
9.3	*mɨl 'water'		勿$_{PR}$	水$_{SR}$	mɨl
9.4	*mʌl(g-) 'clean'		勿$_{PR}$	淸$_{SR}$	mʌlg-
9.5	*təl 'hair'		毛$_{SR}$乙$_{PR}$	鐵$_{PR}$	tʰəl

The writing on the Haman wooden tablets (examples 6.1 and 6.2) was inscribed in the mid-6th century, and the writing on the Mireuksa Temple Site wooden tablet (examples 8.7 and 8.7) was inscribed in the late 7th century or early 8th century. As shown in examples 9.1–9.5, King Gyeongdeok of Silla rectified regional names in the mid-8th century. The regional names in use prior to this rectification are also listed in Table 4, and it is reasonable to suppose that these earlier names were in use until the mid-7th century. This is because they include place names used before the demise of Baekje and Goguryeo in the latter half of the 7th century. In writing the earlier regional names, the phonetically adapted graphs ⟨吉⟩, ⟨勿⟩, ⟨鐵⟩, and ⟨乙⟩ were used. Thus, it is highly probable that the change from */t/ to */l/ took place in the mid-7th century.

Combining evidence from the words written on wooden tablets and the regional names from *Samguksagi*, it can be concluded that the analogical change had not yet occurred in the mid-6th century but had taken place by the mid-7th century. It follows from this conclusion that Sino-Korean pronunciations most likely developed based on the Chinese pronunciations encoded in the sound glosses of the Chinese Buddhist dictionary *Yīqièjīngyīnyì* 一切經音義 by Xuányīng 玄應, which came out in the 640s.

Publications that describe graphic forms and meanings of Chinese characters were already available in the pre-Qín 先秦 period (before the Common Era), but books that illustrated phonetic values of Chinese characters only began to appear from the mid-6th century. It was not until 601 CE that Lù Fǎyán 陸法言 published the first still-extant rhyme book (yùnshū 韻書)

[5] Subscript SR indicates a semantic reading; subscript PR indicates a phonetic reading.

titled *Qiēyùn* 切韻. *Yīqièjīngyīnyì* was the first Chinese Buddhist dictionary, and as noted in the preceding paragraph, it was published in the 640s. This implies that it was difficult even for Chinese intellectuals to decide upon a standard pronunciation for each Chinese character. The three kingdoms of Old Korea must have experienced similar difficulties. In 6th-century Korea, it had not been decided which pronunciations should be deemed standard or correct for each character. At the same time, it would have been too early for Koreans to decide on certain pronunciations autonomously; they would have looked to a Chinese model.

By the 7th century circumstances had changed considerably, especially with the unification of the Chinese polity. Given that *Qiēyùn* provided a standardized pronunciation for Chinese characters, it must have acted as an influential reference for both Chinese and Korean intellectuals. *Yīqièjīngyīnyì* would undeniably have been influential as well, since all three kingdoms in Korea at the time were Buddhist. It is also certain that Korean intellectuals studied both *Qiēyùn* and *Yīqièjīngyīnyì*, which helped them to become more linguistically refined. For example, the Silla monk Sungyeong 順璟 went to China in 667 CE to study under Xuánzàng 玄奘, after which he added linguistic annotations to many Buddhist scriptures. The Baekje-born Silla monk Gyeongheung 璟興, a national leader of Buddhism in Unified Silla in 681 CE, also left many linguistically-annotated scriptures. Some of their annotations and scriptures, referred to as *Sungyeong Yīnyì* 順璟 音義 and *Gyeongheung Yīnyì* 璟興 音義, are cited in Old Japanese dictionaries (Nam 2003).[6] *Yeonui sulmunchan* 連義述文贊, Gyeongheung's annotations on the *Infinite Life Sutra*, contains around 300 entries of lexicographic description including 13 orthographic, 53 phonological, and 230 semantic annotations (Lee 2008).

The 53 phonological annotations by Gyeongheung are of two types; one is his original addition of *fǎnqiē* 反切 (a method of indicating the pronunciation of a character by means of two other characters) in 23 annotations, and the other is direct citation of *fǎnqiē* from *Yīqièjīngyīnyì* in 27 annotations (Lee 2008). It is apparent that *Yīqièjīngyīnyì* was the text most frequently referred to by Gyeongheung, and it was the most important reference on the phonological description of Chinese characters for Silla intellectuals in the late 7th century.

The *fǎnqiē* characters used in the Gyeongheung's independent system were all found in Hyangchal. This implies that he was quite literate in Hyangchal and that he was capable of accurate phonological analysis of Sino-Korean (Lee 2008). Unless a complete phonological analysis had al-

---

[6] Yīnyì is a Chinese term referring to a text-dependent linguistic dictionary containing both meaning and sound glosses.

ready been conducted, it would not have been possible for him to accurately create sound annotations for each character, and this indicates that the analysis of Sino-Korean pronunciation had already been completed by the late 7th century.

Summarizing the discussion so far, it can be concluded that the analogical change from */t/ to */l/ occurred in the mid-7th century. Since there are no exceptions to syllable-final /l/ for Middle Chinese */t/ in Sino-Korean, it would not be an exaggeration to conclude that the formative period for the development of Sino-Korean pronunciation as a whole was the mid-7th century.

Based on this conclusion, a more precise analysis becomes possible concerning the Japanese development of */ti/ (modern [tɕi]) or */tu/ (modern [tsu]) corresponding the coda */t/ of Middle Chinese. In other words, there is a logical explanation for why Sino-Korean */l/ does not appear in either of the two layers of Sino-Japanese pronunciation, Go'on and Kan'on.

Of the two layers, Go'on is said to have been used mainly in Buddhist terminology for a longer period of time, and to have been transmitted to Japan through Baekje rather than directly from China. This brings our attention to the Sino-Korean pronunciation of Baekje. As the analogical change of */t/ to */l/ did not occur until around the time of the demise of Baekje, the coda */t/ was present in the Baekje pronunciation of Chinese characters. Japanese Go'on */t/ was taken from the */t/ of Baekje. The vowel */i/ was added to fit the open syllable structure of Japanese, and this */ti/ in turn became [tɕi] by the application of a Japanese phonological rule.

On the other hand, Kan'on in Japanese is said to have been taken directly from China during the Tang dynasty. Japan dispatched diplomats and many scholars to the Tang dynasty for the first time in 630 CE, which would imply that Japanese Kan'on developed some time after the mid-7th century. It is clear that syllable-final */t/ was in use in contemporary Tang, which would explain how Chinese */t/ became Japanese Kan'on */tu/.

The change of borrowing source from Baekje to Tang explains why the Middle Chinese sound */t/ was rendered as */t/ in both Go'on and Kan'on, bypassing the change that meanwhile had occurred in Korea. While the changed syllable-final */l/ was generalized in Unified Silla, the coda */l/ had no pathway to adoption in Japanese because, after the demise of Baekje, the Japanese people no longer accepted Chinese pronunciation through the medium of Korea.

5. Conclusion

Old Korean wooden tablets have only been a topic of linguistic research in Korea since the early 2000s, but the inscriptions on these wooden tablets have already played a critical role in the study of the Old Korean language.

This paper has mainly discussed the implications of wooden tablet inscriptions for our understanding of the Old Korean and Japanese languages.

The first conclusion is that unlike Old Japanese, Old Korean had CVC (i.e., closed) syllables. Many examples of CVC syllables within Old Korean words have been found on wooden tablets. Notational rules in Sino-graphic orthography have traditionally designated a set of specific graphs to write syllable-final consonants. Moreover, the syllable-final consonants /p/, /l/, /k/, /m/, /n/, and /ŋ/ in Sino-Korean pronunciation have been in continuous use from Old Korean until Modern Korean today. Thus, the hypothesis that Old Korean, like Old Japanese, had only open syllables is disproved.

The second conclusion concerns how and when syllable-final */t/ in Middle Chinese changed to */l/ in Sino-Korean pronunciation. Korean words, from Old Korean to Modern Korean, have strongly tended to avoid syllable-final */t/ in their underlying forms. Focusing on this particular aspect, it has been argued that */t/ went through an analogical change and became */l/ in Sino-Korean pronunciation.

The two graphs 〈本〉 and 〈原〉 found in the Haman wooden tablet inscriptions are reconstructed as */mit/ *믿, 'wheat', and this */mit/ later became /mil/ through the same kind of analogical change. In addition, the graphic sequences 〈日古巳〉 and 〈二■口巳〉 written on the Mireuksa Temple Site wooden tablet are shown to be transcriptions of the numeral 7, and the sub-sequences 〈日〉 and 〈二■〉 are clearly reconstructed as containing phonetic representations of */nil/. Since the Haman wooden tablets were manufactured in the mid-6th century and the Mireuksa Temple Site wooden tablets either in the late 7th century or the early 8th century, the analogical change in Sino-Korean pronunciation is estimated to have occurred during the mid-7th century.

This conclusion is supported by the fact that Silla's scholars, including Sungyeong and Gyeongheung in the late 7th century, had a sufficiently refined and sophisticated understanding of the phonological system to autonomously describe Sino-Korean pronunciation. Moreover, this conclusion is in conformity with previous assertions that Japanese Go'on was imported from Baekje before the early 7th century, while Kan'on was imported from Tang-dynasty China after the mid-7th century.

References

Arisaka, H. 1936/1957. *Kokugo on'inshi no kenkyū* (A Historical Study of Japanese Phonology). Tokyo: Sanseidō.

Handel, Z. 2009. Towards a Comparative Study of Sinographic Writing Strategies in Korean, Japanese, and Vietnamese. *Scripta* 1: 89–125.

Itō, C. 2002. *Chōsen kanjion kenkyū* (A Study of Sino-Korean Pronunciations). Doctoral dissertation, University of Tokyo.

Kōno, R. 1968/1979. *Chōsen kanjion no kenkyū* (A Study of Sino-Korean Pronunciations). Tokyo: Heibonsha.

Lee, D. 2006. Hanguk Hanja-eum-ui Myeot Gaji Teukjing (Some Properties of Sino-Korean Pronunciations). *Gugeosa Yeongu*, ed. Y. Yim and Y. Hong, 261–290. Seoul: Taehaksa.

Lee, K.-M. 1981. Idu-ui Giwon-e Daehan Il Gochal (An Inquiry into the Origin of Idu Writings). *Chindan Hakbo* 52:65–78.

Lee, S.J. 2008. Chil Segi Malyeop-ui Hangugeo Jaryo (Philological Remarks on the Linguistic Annotations Written by Gyeong-heung in the Late 7th Century). *Kugyol Yeongu* 20:123–178.

Lee, S.J. 2012. On the Old Korean Numerals Inscribed on Wooden Tablet no. 318. *Scripta* 4:27–68.

Lee, S. 2000. Hanguk Mokgan Yeongu-ui Hyeonhwang-gwa Haman Seongsan Sanseong Chulto-ui Mokgan (Current Issues in the Study of Korean Wooden Documents and Wooden Tablets from Seongsan Sanseong at Haman). *Hanguk Godaesa Yeongu* 19:77–121.

Luó, C. 1933. *Táng Wŭdài Xībĕi Fāngyán* (The Northwestern Dialects of the Tang and Five Dynasties Period). Táibĕi: Academia Sinica.

Nam, P. 2003. Silla Seung Sungyeong-gwa Gyeongheung-ui *Beophwa-gyeong* Juseokseo-e Daehayeo (On the Commentaries on *Saddharma Pundarîka* Written by the Monks Sungyeong and Gyeongheung of Silla). *Kugyol Yeongu* 10:31–46.

Park B. 1971. *Godae Gugeo-ui Yeongu* (A Study of Old Korean). Seoul: Korea University Press.

Song, K.-J. 1995. Dang-dae Dolgweoreo-ui Gacha Pyogi-wa Gugeo Hanja-eum-ui Jongseong (Jiăjiè Transcriptions of Türük Words in the Tang Dynasty and Syllable-final Consonants in Sino-Korean Pronunciations). *Gugeosa-wa Chaja Pyogi* (The History of the Korean Language and Sino-graphic Orthography). Seoul: Taehaksa.

Wei, G. 2012. Hanguk Hanja-eum Seolnae Ipseong Unmi-e Daehan Gochal (A Study of Entering Tone Alveolar Coda in Sino-Korean Pronunciation). *Gugeohak* 63:221–246.

How Adessive Becomes Nominative in Korean Honorifics

ALAN HYUN-OAK KIM*
Southern Illinois University at Carbondale

1. Introduction

Korean has a special set of case markers that are exclusively assigned to the exalted persons in a sentence: the dative *kkey* for an exalted recipient and the nominative *kkeyse* for an exalted agent. The question of how these two honorific case markers evolved has been a main concern in the literature.[1] The general consensus in previous studies is that the dative *kkey* has a

* I express my thanks to Professors J.R.P. King and Chungmin Lee in the audience for their valuable comments. This research is partially supported by a travel fund of the Liberal Arts College of Southern Illinois University Carbondale, to which I am grateful. My appreciation is also extended to Mary Lou Wilshaw-Watts and Dale B. Budslick for their editing of this manuscript. The remaining errors are all mine.

[1] General references to Korean honorifics are found in works such as Rhee (1979), Lee and Hong (1983), Sŏ (1984), Martin (1997), and, more recently, Lee and Ramsey (2000), Rhee (2006), and Song (2005), among many others. Paek (2003) is a rare work on Japanese honorifics by a Korean researcher. Aside from the recent Sohn and Strauss (1998) and Sohn (2002), Yu (1984) is one of the few papers devoted to the historical aspects of the Korean nominative marker *kkeyse*. In a series of papers (Kim 2004, 2006a, 2006b, 2008, 2010a, 2010b) and in a book-length manuscript, the present author suggests some highly probable morphological relationships in the honorific systems of Japanese and Korean.

Japanese/Korean Linguistics 22.
Edited by Mikio Giriko, Naonori Nagaya, Akiko Takemura, and Timothy J. Vance.

base construction composed of a genitive marker and a locational noun, while the nominative *kkeyse* is viewed as a result of coalescence of the dative *kkey* plus two verbal sources, i.e., the unmarked existential verb *isi-ta* and the honorific existential verb *kyesi-ta.* A closer look at the previous studies, including the recent methodologically refined work by Sohn (2002), reveals problems that cannot pass unremarked. Many such problems come from establishing underlying constructions of these particles on narrow morphological bases without recourse to the existing general system of rules regarding locational postpositions (including case markers) operative in Korean. Such locally confined analyses inevitably lead to piecemeal solutions. This paper attempts to propose an alternative to the honorific case marking phenomena in a systematic, principled, and therefore economically tidier way.

The present paper is organized in five parts. Section 2, which follows this introduction, is a critical review of previous studies focusing on Sohn's (2002) analysis. Section 3 introduces the theoretical basis adopted in this paper. Section 4 demonstrates that the emergence of the two case particles is an instance of grammatical synthesis of three kinds of fundamental factors operative in higher levels of Korean. Such an approach enables one to explain even various previously unaddressed phenomena. Section 5 concludes the paper with a brief summary and remarks about the theoretical implications of the proposed analysis.

2. Review of Previous Studies

2.1. Genitive-Based *kkey* Analyses

Following analyses in Hŏ (1975:297), S.-K. Kim (1992:149), Nam (1997: 176) and others, Sohn (2002) proposes that the diachronic changes in Korean dative case markers had two separate paths, as shown in (1).

(1) Development of Plain and Honorific Dative Markers (Sohn 2002:315)
  a. plain dative: *-uy* (genitive) + *kuey* 'there' > *-eykey* (dative)[2]
  b. honorific dative: *-s* (genitive) + *kuey* 'there' > *-kkey* (dative)

There are confusions about the morpheme *kuey* in (1). It may be either *ku.ey* or *ku.ŋey*, but only the latter (with nasalized velar /ŋ/) has the meaning of the locative pronoun 'at the place' or the dative case marker corresponding to the present-day *eykey* or *key*. (We do not find the entry form *ku.ey* in Nam's [1997] Middle Korean dictionary.) The monosyllabic morpheme *-s*, known as *sai.sios*, is a 'mediating fricative' and typically functions to mark

[2] The genitive status of *-uy* in (1a) is still in dispute in the literature, and some (e.g.,Yang 1965:148–149; S.-H. Chwe 1964:23) argue that it was originally adverbial, while others insist that it was genitive in origin.

the genitive case. According to Nam (1997:963), the form *kkey* 께 has several older versions: *-s kuy*, *skuy*, and even *pskuy*. The variant *skuy*, from [*-s* + *kuy*], becomes *kkuy*, the later honorific dative *kkey*.

In the analysis in (1), the plain dative and honorific dative have gone through two separate paths in a somewhat parallel way. How have the plain *eykey* and honorific *kkey* acquired their dative function? In Sohn's view, the dative form evolved from the locational noun preceded by the genitive suffix, which is regarded as "an instance of grammatical realization of unidirectionality and metonymy' (Sohn 2002:315). Sohn takes metonymy as being a major factor in the development of the dative form and adds that "the development of dative in Korean supports the localist hypothesis (Anderson 1971; Lyons 1977; Heine et al. 1991)." Sohn claims the underlying morphological construction is [(an esteemed person)-*s* + *kuey*], where -*s* is a genitive marker and *kuey* a locational noun meaning 'there'. The construction yields the tensed velar geminate and also licenses an honorific reading for the construction.

In Middle Korean, however, the particle -*skuy* (Sohn's [-*s* + *kuey*]) operates as a locative marker independent of the honorific usage, as shown in Nam (1997:194), Hŏ (1975:299,347), and Rhee (1979). The following examples are from Nam (1997:963).

(2) *Tyecwum-**skuy** ku sicel-ey pichi-teni* (first edition of *Tusi.Ŏnhay* 24: 27.1481)
'As (it) shows up around that time, . . .'

(3) *Anpyeng.sipuk-un ce cum-**skuy** hoci le-ni . . .* (*Chwulsey.kok*)
'Though the Anpyeng area to the north used to be considered Chinese territory in those days, . . .'

(4) *Polum-**skuy** chwi.ha-ye tAlye-wa ipati.ha-ko* (*Pak Thongsa Ŏnhay* 1: 41.1677)
'Around the 15th of the month, (he) married and brought back the bride to serve . . .'

The Middle Korean lexical item *skuy* in these examples is suffixed to a noun denoting a general vague area ('around, nearby') or an approximate point in time ('around, about, approximately'). The particle *kkey* as a locative marker is observed in unmarked (non-honorific) contexts in Modern Korean as well, as shown in (5). These examples are from Martin (1992:107).

(5) [Postposition 1]: about (around), towards (a time): *polum-kkey* 'about (towards) the middle of the month'; *kumum-kkey* 'about (towards) the end of the month'; *mence-kkey* 'the other day, some time ago'; *oceng.ccum-kkey* 'around noontime, towards noon'

> [Postposition 2] around, in the vicinity (neighborhood) of, near (a place): *Namtaemun-kkey*: 'in the vicinity of South Gate'; *Conglo-nay-keli-kkey*; 'in the neighborhood of Bell Street Cross'; *wumul-kkey*; 'around the well'

Examples like these indicate four things. First, the phonological tensification in the velar geminate /kk/ cannot necessarily be attributed to a special class of host noun with a meaning like 'esteemed person'. Second, the semantics of *kkey* is not entirely contingent on a host noun meaning 'a superior.' Third, Sohn's gloss '(an esteemed person)'s there' for [(an esteemed person)-*s kuy*] is not necessarily faithful because the morpheme *kuŋey* (Sohn's *kuey*) might have completed its shift to a locational case particle equivalent to *eykey* (Modern Korean dative/allative) by the time the honorific *kkey* started to appear. Fourth, the morpheme *kuy* is also regarded as a shortened form of *ʌy/uykuy* (<*ʌy/uy+ku+ŋey*) via the deletion of *ʌy/uy*. (Nam 1997:1150; T.-S. Kim 2003:200; among others.) All this suggests that the dative feature of [X-*s kuy*] in (1b) might have come from a previously established dative case, namely *eykey* or its shortened form *key* before its cooccurrence with the (a superior)-*s* phrase. This point will be further discussed in Section 4. Hŏ (1975:298) and S.-K Kim (1992:250) remark that *kuŋuy* (>*key*) had been found only as dative case marker (but not as a locational pronoun) as early as in Middle Korean *Taemyŏngyul jikhae* (1395). The development of the honorific nominative case particle *kkeyse* will be pursued along the same line of thinking in the following two sections.

2.2. Existential Verb-Based Analysis: *kkeyse*

Sohn (2002:316) argues that the particle *kkeyse* is derived from a bimorphemic base: [X-*s kuy* + *si-e*], where X is an honored person, *kuy* is 'there', and *si-e* is the infinitive form of an existential verb.

Following Sohn and Strauss (1998), Sohn discusses two critical triggering factors involved in the morphological derivation. The genitive *-s* and *kuey* subsequently were fused to yield *kkeysye* 'be at there.' As far as the semantic shift is concerned, the underlying construction [X-*s kuy* + *si-e*] goes through three distinct stages to become the subject marker *kkeyse*: [X exists at Y's place] > [X is from Y's place] > [Y instigates X] (Sohn 2002:319).

Sohn's analysis above calls for clarification. First, Sohn's orthographic representation (*i*)*si-ta* of the existential verb with no provision of proper conditions associated with the deletion of /i/ may cause misleading interpretations. And that is exactly what one finds in Sohn's analysis. Namely, of the variant forms *isi-ta* and *si-ta*, the latter occurs only when it is preceded by the continuative form of a verb /ie/ or /-a/, or even /-ko/, but never in stand-alone environments. For example, Nam (1997:916) gives 16 Middle Korean examples under the lexical entry *si-ta* (= *iss-ta*/*is-ta*), which are all in the syntactic environment of [V-*e*/-*a*/-*ko* **si-*ta***] without exception. Thus, one may tentatively assume that the onset vowel /-i/ of the existential verb *isi-ta* may optionally be deleted only if it is preceded by another verb in the continuative form. In other words, the base construction [(a superior)'s *kuy si-e*], which Sohn proposes, is inconsistent with the constraint above.

Besides the genitive-based *kkeyse* discussed above, Sohn makes the case for additional sources contributing to subject marker formation, i.e., *kyesi-ta* and the lexical honorific existential verb: *kyesi-ta* '(an honored person) be at', as shown in (6b) below.[3] (Both verbs are in the infinitival form.) Thus, present-day *kkeyse* is characterized as a merger of two distinct sources, as shown in (6).

(6) Merger of Honorific Subject Marker (Sohn 2002:321,322)
   a. [-*s kuey* + *si-e* 'exist-and'] > -*kkeysye* > -*kkeyse*
   b. *kyeysi-e* > -*keysye* > -*kyeysye* ('exists and')

The derivational path of the verbal form *kyesi-e* is simpler than that of the genitive-based form (6a) in that the verb *kyesi-e* (the infinitival form of *kyesi-ta* 'be and') is directly adopted from the lexicon. The two forms—*kkeysye* 꼐셔 in (6a) and *kyeysye* 계셔 in (6b)—show a remarkable resemblance, which made them converge, as Sohn (2002:321) characterizes it, "triggered at first by the structural and semantic parallel of the two source forms." The existential function of the honorific *kyesi-* was subsequently "weakened in contexts where there is no explicit reference for a location of the honored person."

As seen above, the presence of *si-e* in Sohn's construction seems to be critical in its shifting to the subject case particle. Sohn (2002:318) illustrates her proposed process with (7a) and its paraphrase (7b).

(7) a. Halapeci-kkeyse chayk-ul tuli-ess-ta
   grandfather-HONSUB book-ACC give-PAST-DEC
   'My grandfather gave a book to someone (an honored person)'
   b. [[My grandfather was there] and [he gave a book to someone there]]

(8) [(an honored person)-*s*+*kuy*+*si-e*] > [*skuy-sye*] > [-*kkey-se*] > [*kkeyse*]

Sentence (7a) is paraphrased as having two clauses, as in (6b): [*My grand-*

[3] Sohn (2002:316,319) twice gives the English gloss 'be at' for *isi-e*; however, these must be typos for 'be and'. Incidentally, Martin's (1992:673) definition of *kyesi-ta* is as follows: '*kyeysita* (<*kyesi-ta*) — (i) (one esteemed) is, there is, is located, stays, lives . . . (ii) stays, stops, waits (around/ momentarily), pauses . . .' The existential verb analysis that Sohn adopts can also be found in traditional works, such as those by S. N. Lee (1979) and T.-S. Kim (2003:302).

father was there] and [*he gave a book to someone there*]. Two questions immediately arise. First, what is referred to by 'there' in (7b)? And second, why does (7a) need to have an assertion like (7b)? It seems superfluous or even tautological, since the location of the person referred to as 'my grandfather' is implicated as part of background information in normal discourse. Furthermore, the derivational process given in (8) contains *si-e*, an inflected form (the infinitive or continuative) of the verb *si-ta*. The conjugated form *si-e* presupposes a bi-clausal construction. The problem here, aside from the dubious analysis of *si-e* (> *sye* > *se*), is the burden of explaining how a complete clause like 'my grandfather was there' is reduced to a bound morpheme like a case marker. Sohn (2002:319) argues by stating that "[s]yntactic contiguity of the locational noun and the *sye* form is also ascribed to the coalescence." However, we have no clue about what syntactic conditions license a semantic conversion of [*halapeci-ka keki-ey kyesi-e-ss-ta* 'my grandfather was there'] to [*halapeci-kkeyse* 'my grandfather's there/ place']. Sohn's characterization (mentioned above) of the third stage as 'Y *instigates* X' is hard to follow when one does not know what exactly is meant by "instigates" in this context. Although several examples are given, they are useful only for showing what is shifted to other forms but not how they shifted or what drives such a shift.

Should Sohn's analysis be theoretically valid, we would still be left in the dark about why a grammar complicates itself with a tautological self-explanatory statement like [X exists at X's place]. What Sohn, along with most of her predecessors, assumes is in fact pervasively used in Middle Korean. The morpheme *sye* (> *se*) functions as a productive postpositional suffix for the locative or ablative with the [+Dynamic] feature, as in *Seoul-(ey)-se* 'in Seoul' or 'from Seoul' (Nam 1997:837). As proposed in the following sections, *kkeyse* is to be analyzed as a direct morphological expansion of the locative/allative *kkey* through the suffixation of dynamic *sye* (> *se*), which is not only simpler but also far less costly in terms of operational economy. Furthermore, one noteworthy observation from Table 1 below in Section 3.3 is the absence of the "honorific accusative" case particle in the system. This is rather surprising considering the accusative's primary status of presenting the internal thematic role of an argument. There must be some compelling reason for this, which Sohn (2002), like her predecessors, has failed to address. Last, but not least, Sohn's analysis requires a formidably powerful interface mechanism that allows for operations that cross the grammatical boundaries of syntax, semantics, morphology, and the lexical domain in a relatively short 200-year period.

3. The Point of Departure: Adessive Case in Korean Honorifics

This section is divided into three parts. The first introduces the novel notion of "esteemed person" in the Korean honorific system for the theoretical basis of this paper. The second identifies a distinct type of case marker, called the adessive, that is critically involved in subject exaltation. The third argues that the usage of the adessive case markers, i.e., the locative/dative *kkey* and the nominative *kkeyse* may be due to their unique semantic feature, [+obscurity] or [+proximity], which optimally fits the notion of a superior as a *taboo* entity.

3.1. Working Hypothesis

The analysis in this paper is based on the following premise.

(9) An exalted interlocutor, with respect to the speaker, is conceived of as a model of a taboo entity in metaphoric terms.

Under this premise, actions by, and states of, an exalted interlocutor are presented as an instantaneous event. A person's state of affairs (actions and presence) is conceived of as a natural, spontaneous, effortless happenstance or an agentless, emergent event. Furthermore, the site of such a person's actions/states is expressed as a metaphoric sanctuary or a "sacred" vague proximity. Given (9), one can assume what is presented in (10) below.

(10) a. A superior's role of locative is expressed 'vaguely' by the adessive particle *kkey* for dative, which is functionally identical to, and interchangeable with, the unmarked dative *eykey*.

b. The nominative is expressed by the adessive *kkeyse*. Unlike the dative *kkey*, the nominative *kkeyse* cannot be replaced by *ey keyse*, despite their functional compatibility.

c. The adjunct cases ablative and allative are systematically generated by suffixation of *key, se, lo hanthe, puthe*, etc., to the primary base *ey*.

d. The honorific case-marking convention does not apply to the role of theme (Direct Object).

3.2. Adessive Case Particles in Korean

The morpheme *kkey* in Korean falls under the categories of markers of goal and static locations, just as the morpheme *ey* does. Consider the examples from Martin (1992:107) given above in (5). In these examples, *kkey* may be replaced with *ey* without causing problems, except for *mence-kkey*: **mence-ey*.[4] For this special morpheme *kkey*, the term "adessive case particle" is

[4] I have no explanation for this exception.

borrowed, which is commonly found in descriptions of languages of the Fino-Ugric family.[5]

From our observations above, we may say that *kkey* is in essence no different from *ey* in terms of function, as the allative and locative markers. What distinguishes the former from the latter is the quality of the location it denotes, namely, the semantic features of obscurity and nebulous proximity. The next section shows how the *ey* and *kkey* particles correspond to one another, which may lead to clues to the discovery of the elements critically involved in the development of Korean honorific case marking.

3.3. Location-Based Case Marking as a System

Another critical factor that helps us understand the *kkey/kkey.se* markers is the system of postpositional particles in Korean. All case particles and location-related particles (except for the genitive and adjunct cases) share a common morphological form [*ey*-<*x*>], where *x* denotes the subatomic suffixes, *key, se, lo, puthe*, etc. This systematic aspect may be better appreciated by looking at Table 1.[6]

Several regularities can be identified from Table 1. First, Korean case particles seem to be generated regularly in the grammar. Second, all location-related case particles share the morpheme *ey* as the primary base, as in sequences like ((((*ey*)*key*)*se*)*puthe*) or ((((*ey*)*key*)*lo*)*puthe*). Third, the directional morpheme *-lo* 'to/toward' and the dynamic locative *-se* seem to be in complementary distribution. Fourth, the order of sequence seems to be implicational in terms of semantic features, namely, *ey* [+Static Location] ← *key* [+Animate] ← *se* [+Dynamic Location] ← *puthe* [+Direction].[7] A static or existential event will take a static locative (allative) Z-*ey*, while an event like 'X went to Y' or 'X gives Y to Z' must take the dative Z-*eykey*, which has the [+Static Location] feature.

---

5 The adessive case marker is for a special locative case widely used in the Ugric family. The term *adessive* is composed of two Latin words: *ad-* and *essive* 'to be'. It denotes a general, vague, adjacent location.

6 H.-P. Chwe (1929/1931) classified postpositional particles into two major categories: case particles (*Jari.t'ossi*) and auxiliary particles (*Towum.t'ssi*), with the former further divided into six case categories and fifteen sub-auxiliary categories. Chwe's exhaustive enumeration of the postpositional particles is instrumental in identifying regularity in terms of the feature typology involved in the location-based positional particle sequences, which are presented in Table 1. H.-M. Sohn's analysis (1999: 213–214) improves on Chwe's by introducing two sets of semantic distinctions in terms of (in)animacy and the static/dynamic opposition. However, there is no further scrutiny of the interrelationship among these semantic features, with which this section is specifically concerned.

7 As alluded to in the second point just above, such an implicational expansion shows some irregularities with the directional *-lo* 'to/toward'. This may have to do with the complementary distribution of the two case markers *-se* and *-lo*. I will leave this issue for future inquiry.

Table 1. Distribution of Atomic Morphemes in Location-Related Cases

Case	EY [Location]	KEY [+Amimate] KKEY [+Proximity]	SE [+Dynamic]	Remarks: Adessive Shifting to
1. Allative (direction)	ey			
2. Locative (static)	ey			
3. Locative (dynamic)	ey	(key) kkey	se	Nominative [+Honorific]
4. Dative	ey	key kkey		Dative [+Honorific]
5. Allative (purposive)	ey	key kkey		Allative [+Honorific]
6. Ablative	ey	key kkey	se-(puthe) lo-puthe	Ablative [+Honorific]

Thus, *John-i **party-ey** ka-ss-ta* 'John **went** to the party' or *Mary-ka **party-ey** iss-ess-ta* 'Mary **was** at the party' is well formed, whereas *John-i Mary-lul* ****party-ey** manna-ss*-ta 'John met Mary at the party' is ungrammatical because of the incongruence of the static-locative case NP *party-ey* and the action verb 'meet'. The same sentence can be made grammatical by replacing NP-*ey* with the dynamic locative NP-*eyse*. Fifth, the table shows that every *ey-key* sequence has an adessive version *kkey* (i.e., honorific dative, honorific allative, and honorific ablative), except for the nominative case. Markers of the *ey*-based cases and the *kkey*-cases go hand-in-hand and are even interchangeable with each other. From this, one might suggest that the honorific nominative may be formed in exploiting a dynamic locative case marker *kkeyse* (< *-skueysye* < *-s kueysye*), which was already accessible in the lexicon. Sixth, the honorific nominative *kkeyse* seems to resist substitution by *ey-key-se*. Such a restriction may have been developed to ascertain the function of the adessive *kkeyse* only for highlighting the exclusive nature of a nebulous proximity associated with a superior. Seventh, the lack of an honorific accusative case particle is an unexpected disconformity. Examples will show that these are not isolated instances but are natural consequences of a systematic call to the higher order.

4. Resetting an Honorific Sentence as an "Emerging" Event

In this section, we demonstrate how a basic premise of discourse, namely, a superior as a taboo entity, works in Korean honorifics. First, we establish the notion of event emergence and then demonstrate how the adessive dynamic locative case system interacts with such an honorific event grammatically. Some residual problems from our earlier discussion will also be dealt with in this section.

4.1. A Figurative Notion of Statement Submission

The premise, then, is that a superior becomes a subject of isolation. Such an entity is prohibited from being touched, being seen, or being imposed upon by any kind of manipulation by others. Such an entity must be kept at a distance; in short, the entity is taboo.

How can such an overall taboo be achieved in a practical sense? One possible measure is by avoidance of "direct talk to" a superior, since such a speech act constitutes a "linguistic" offense, namely, the trespassing taboo of "don't touch it." (Talking can be analogized as a mode of linguistic touching.) In Korean honorifics, statements addressed to a superior must be "submitted" in presentable "gift-wrapping," so to speak. How? One way of achieving this requirement is to "envelop" an utterance (proposition) as a whole with a special wrapping material—in this case, the morpheme *-supni* attached to the sentence-final predicate. (Korean is a typical verb-final language.) This morpheme is commonly referred to as a marker of Addressee Honorifics, and it allows the paraphrase '**I humbly report** such-and-such, i.e., the message to you, my esteemed', as in [[*Nalssi-ka coh*]-***supni****-ta*], the polite form of the plain, "unwrapped" [*Nalssi-ka coh-****Ø****-ta*] 'The weather is good'. The Japanese sentence-terminal polite forms *-masu* and *-desu* work in exactly the same way as Korean *-(s)upni-ta*, as in [[*Tenki-ga ii*]-***desu***] 'It's a nice day' or [*Hana-ga sak-u*] versus [[*Hana-ga saki*]-***masu***] 'Flowers bloom.'

4.2. Metaphorizing a Superior's Action/State as an Effortless Event

Another way of exalting a superior is to exaggerate a superior's doing something (or being somewhere) as a magical happenstance. Thus, 'the emperor eats' is figuratively presented as a self-realizing event: 'an event [the emperor eats] takes place effortlessly'. Consider the Korean example (11).

(11) a. Kyoswu.nim-i secey-eyse chayk-ul ssu-si-n-ta
professor-NOM study-in book-ACC write-SHS-PRES-DEC
'Professor writes a book in his study.'

b. $[\text{kyoswu.nim-kkeyse}]_{\kappa}$[8]
[*kyoswu.nim-i* secey-eyse chayk-ul ssu-si-n-ta$]_{e}$
professor-NOM study-in book-ACC write-SHS-PRES-DEC
$[\text{ile.na-n-ta}]_{\text{emerge}}$

8 In the metaphoric conversion suggested above, it must be emphasized that the professor's workplace, namely, 'in his study', is a part of the event itself, and therefore it must be distinguished from the location (κ) of the metaphorized event. This special location where the event takes place may be anywhere the superior in question (the subject of the sentence) is present. That is, the place represented by κ is the superior's inviolable proximity.

c. Paraphrase: 'An event that [Professor writes a book in his study] emerges *right there* where Professor is found.'

Schematically, then, the state of affairs in (11) may be represented for the sake of convenience in a version of Davidsonian notation, as in (12).

(12) a. $\exists e[\text{BECOME}(\text{STATE}(e)), \exists \kappa[\text{AT}(e, \kappa)]$
b. $\lambda e[(\text{become}' (\text{state}, e)) \,\&\, \lambda \kappa[\text{at}' (e, k)]](\text{emp eat})$ (at emp's place)
c. $\lambda e[(\text{become}' (\text{state}, e)) \,\&\, \lambda \kappa[\text{at}'(e, k)]]$(Prof. writes . . . in his study) (at his place)

The suggested strategy linguistically ensures the taboo by making use of a locative marker: not a regular locative marker but an adessive locative marker *kkeyse*, which bears complex semantic features ([+location], [+Animate], [+Dynamic], and [+Proximity]) suitable for expressing a superior's "obscure" taboo proximity.

4.3. Functional Shift of Oblique Subject Marker to Nominative

In a construction like (11b), the italicized [*kyoswu.nim-i*] in the nominative case may have become superfluous and may have eventually disappeared, leaving the adessive locative *kkeyse* behind. As noted in Lee and Im (1983: 136), the plain dynamic locative *ey-se*, as the counterpart of *kkeyse*, may serve as a functional substitute for nominative when the subject represents public authorities, such as schools, government administrations, churches, and the like. In Korean, as well as in Japanese, there is some tendency for the locative case (marked with *eyse* in Korean) to serve as nominative, particularly when the subject is involved with governing authorities or public institutions.[9] Note that a public institution as such may generally represent itself as a powerful entity comparable to a discourse superior's figurative attributes, and because of this analogical parallel, it might have been the case that the adessive case particle was extended to exalting a discourse superior's actions and presence.

---

[9] Martin (1992: 504) calls this function of *eyse* 'impersonal oblique subject' and lists examples like the following.

(1) Seoul Kyohyangaktan-eyse Pichang Kyohyangak-ul hanta-n-ta
'The Seoul Symphony Orchestra is playing the Symphony *Pathetique*, you know.'

(3) Wuli hakkyo-eyse ikye-ss-ta
'Our school won (the game).'

(4) Wuli tosekwand-**ey/i** kose-ka manh-ta
'There are many old books in our library.'

(5) Wuli sensayngnim-**eykey/kkey** kose-ka manhu-si-ta.
'There are many books with my teacher.'

4.4. Residual Questions

This section deals with remaining questions raised in reviewing Sohn (2002) and other studies on *kkey*(*se*) in the literature.

4.4.1. Exclusion of Accusative from Honorific Case Marking

As noted in reviewing Table 1 in Section 3.3, the accusative case is left out despite its prominent theme role in the thematic structure. This seems to reflect an important aspect of the Korean honorific system. Exalting a superior is performed in three modes: treating a superior (a) as an <agent>, (b) as a <recipient>, and (c) as an <addressee>. Honorification strategies via (a) and (c) were already discussed in the previous section. Here the superior's role as <recipient> or <indirect object> is particularly significant because the taboo entity is the receiver of the speaker's (selfless) service. (Imagine a bee colony, where the queen never works and is simply served by worker bees. The queen is characteristically a "recipient" of servitude in the colony.) In this line of metaphorically inclined thinking, the assignment of the grammatical role <theme> to a superior may be considered a potential source of taboo violation, since a superior is put in the role of <direct object>, which the speaker operates on or manipulates. Deprioritization of the direct object (DO) role is desired, and hence there is no accusative marking in the Korean honorific system. In many cases, a superior's DO role is converted pragmatically to an indirect object (IO). Thus, [I called her] → [I gave her a call], [I met her there] → [I went to see her there], [I fed her soup] → [I gave her a service of feeding her soup], and so forth. The lack of an accusative honorific case particle is then a natural consequence of the pragmatic constraints we have developed in this paper. For a detailed discussion of the parallelism in Japanese, the reader is referred to Kim (2006a, 2006b, 2011).

4.4.2. The Delayed Appearance of *kkeyse* in Contrast to Dative *kkey*

As noted in previous studies, the appearance of nominative *kkeyse* in the 17th century lagged behind that of dative *kkey* by some 200 years. Noting the interesting coincidence of the appearance of the *kkeyse* marker with the height of the doctrinal tyranny of Neo-Confucianism in the 17th-century Kingdom, Sohn (2002:322) remarks, "The honorific vs. plain distinction in subject case particles seems to have risen inevitably from such a social pressure to denote deference, and . . . [w]hat is significant in this study is the role of language external factors for a grammaticalization process." However, we have strong reservations about such a notion of language-external social factors in language changes, grammatical changes in particular. Indeed, the lexicon of Korean had been overwhelmed by Chinese loans. In contrast, the core grammar in the oldest records of Korean is virtually identical to today's internet Korean. In Japan, on the other hand, the Neo-Confucian Philosophy had virtually no impact until the very end of the 17th century, and yet, as we will see in the next subsection, the honorific nominative case particle *-ni okaseraretewa* emerged in pre-modern Japanese. Moreover, while Korean has had the single subject honorification suffix *-si* since the Shilla period (57 BCE – 935 CE), one finds in Japanese four different productive subject honorification suffixes (besides the now-extinct Old Japanese *-si*), including passive-based *-rareru*, inchoative-verb-based *-ni naru*, and one based on the passive 'do' verb *nasaru*. In short, social pressure may be one contributing factor, but it can hardly be a critical factor in introducing the honorific nominative case marker into Korean, and it may well be irrelevant. A language-external social factor does not "invent" a new mechanical device such as the honorific nominative *kkeyse*. There must be a grammatical trigger that compels the introduction of the dative *kkey* as well as the nominative *kkeyse* into the system. Alternatively, one might suggest a notion like "inception" or "cultivation" that requires a prolonged period of time. Suppose speakers of a language conceive an idea that turns a superior's actions/states into a self-emerging event and then search for a way to implement such a notion. Then they happen to realize that their language has a device like adessive case that has semantic qualities ideally suited to materialization of the idea of "event-emergence." Such a process of cultivation would require a longer time compared to a grammaticalization like allative-to-dative conversion. We leave this suggestion open for future scrutiny.

4.4.3. Japanese Honorific Nominative *okaseraremasitewa*

It might be worth noting that a special honorific subject case particle is also found in Japanese. Unlike in Korean, the usage of Japanese *okaseraremasitewa* is reserved strictly for an emperor and the members of his royal family. One other difference from the Korean counterpart is that it must cooccur with the locative marker *ni* 'at/in/on', as seen in example (13) below.

Despite these minor differences, the phrase *-ni okaseraretewa* highly resembles Korean *kkeyse* in conceptual terms. Consider the following example, quoted from Ikegami (1981:199).

(13) Tennô-heika-**ni okaseraremasitewa** o-mesiagari-ni nari-masi-ta
Emperor-at *okaseraremasitewa* HON-eat-at become-HON-PST
'Emperor, [ ] becomes to eating'

As Ikegami rightly points out, the subject 'Emperor' is "locativized," so to speak. The linguistic rendition of a simple expression 'Emperor ate' is thus presented as an emergence of the event of Emperor's eating at the location expressed by the postpositional locative *-ni okaseraremasitewa*. This state of affairs shows a remarkable parallelism with the Korean adessive *kkeyse* expressions examined in this paper and suggests that the speakers of the two languages seem to share a certain conceptual disposition toward their superiors. They seem to "translate" their discourse superiors by means of a linguistic code for a taboo entity. Ikegami's notion of "locativization" of a superior's actions or states in Japanese honorifics is regarded as being in the same line of thinking as the notion of "event emergence" pursued in this paper. Etymologically, *okaseraremasitewa* may be decomposed into six parts: (1) the base form *ok-* ('to place X to a location'), (2) *-ase* (subject honorific), (3) *-rare* (subject honorific as hypercorrection), (4) *-masi* (continuative form of addressee honorific marker *-masu*), (5) *-te* (gerundive marker), and (6) contrastive marker *-wa*. According to some etymological sources, the alleged base verb *ok-u* was artificially devised in Middle Japanese for the Chinese locative etymon written 於. In contrast to traditional views, *okase*, equivalent to (1) and (2) above, may rather be contrasted with the Korean honorific nominative adessive case marker *kkeyse*. Readers will find a detailed discussion of this issue in Kim (2013).

5. Conclusion

What has been clarified in this paper may be summarized as follows. Previous analyses are largely concerned with the etymological composition of the honorific dative *kkey* and the honorific nominative *kkeyse*. In this effort, three or four components are isolated. However, the analyses in these studies are largely confined to local morphological constructions independent of the more general rule system readily available for formation of postpositions and case marking, or they rely on localist hypotheses or cross-linguistic grammaticalization with little information on how these general linguistic dispositions work in the formation of *kkey* and *kkeyse* in Korean. As an alternative to such analyses that are locally confined or that vaguely rely on certain cross-linguistic notions of grammaticalization, this paper adopts a radically different approach. The notion of a person subject to the target of the speaker's deference is reexamined and redefined as a taboo entity in the metaphorical sense. A superior's action (e.g., *King visits the Expo*) may be paraphrased metaphorically as 'The event [King visits the Expo] takes place spontaneously and effortlessly at his vague sanctuary-like location'. The event site 'at King's proximity' is expressed in Korean as *King-**kkeyse***. The morpheme *kkey* is defined as an adessive case marker denoting a location of vague proximity that is appropriate for expressing the locus of a metaphorized superior's presence. Like the locative and dative *eykey*, its adessive counterpart *kkey* serves as a locative/allative/dative case marker in Korean honorifics. Likewise, the adessive *kkeyse*, a combination of adessive dative *kkey* + *se* (the dynamic locative indicator) serves as an honorific dynamic locative (and allative), eventually replacing the nominative *i/ka*. The present approach, based on the notion of a superior as a metaphoric entity of taboo, makes it possible to explain in a principled and systematic way a number of issues, including not only phenomena such as the lack of accusative case marking in the Korean honorific system but also the delayed appearance of the honorific nominative marker in Korean.

References

Anderson, J. M. 1971. *The Grammar of Case: Toward a Localist Theory*. London: Cambridge University Press.

Chwe, H.-P. 1929/1931. *Uri Malpon* (Our Grammar). Seoul: Chŏngŭm.sa.

Chwe, S.-H. 1964. Chyŏkyŏk-ŭy Byŏnchŏn (Historical Changes in Locatives). *Tongdae Kukŏ Munhakhwe Nonmunjip*.

Heine, B., Claudi, U., and Huennemeyer, F. 1991. *Grammaticalization: A Conceptual Framework*. Chicago: University of Chicago Press.

Hŏ, U. 1975. *Uri Yes.malpo: 15 seki kukŏ.hyŏngt'ae.ron* (The Theory of 15th-century Middle Korean Morphology). Seoul: Ŭlyu.munhwa.sa.

Ikegami, Y. 1981. *Suru to naru no gengogaku* (The Linguistics of *suru* and *naru*). Tokyo: Taishūkan.

Kim, A. H.-O. 2004. Nihongo no keigo taikei no gensoku to meta-gengo-teki bunpōka (Principles in the Japanese Honorific System and Meta-linguistic Grammaticalization). *Nihongo no bunseki to gengo ruikei*, ed. T. Kageyama and H. Kishimoto, 25–46. Tokyo: Kurosio.

Kim, A. H.-O. 2006a. Grammaticalization in Sentence-final Politeness Marking in Korean and Japanese. *Harvard Studies in Korean Linguistics XI*, ed. S. Kuno, I.-H. Lee, J. Whitman, J. Maling, Y.-S. Kang, P. Sells, H.-S. Sohn, and Y. Jang, 72–85. Seoul: Hanshin.

Kim, A. H.-O. 2006b. On Origins of Korean *supni-ta* and Japanese *desu/masu*: Deriving Addressee Honorific Markers from 'Reporting' Verbs. *Inquiries into Korean Linguistics II*, ed. W. O'Grady, J.-Y. Yoon, J.-Y. Han, P. Lee, H.-Y. Kim, S.-H. Hong, S. Chung, and F. Torres, 15–26. Seoul: Hanshin.

Kim, A. H.-O. 2008. Japanese Honorifics as a System of Metaphors. Paper presented at the 4th International Symposium on Politeness: "East Meets West." Budapest.

Kim, A. H.-O. 2010a. Ilponŏ Kongson.pŏp <*desu/masu*>-ŭi Hankukŏ Kiwŏn-e Taehayŏ: Saeroun ŭnyu.iron-ŭi Sikak-esŏ (On Korean connections of Japanese *desu/masu* forms). *Hankuk.ŏ Yŏku-ŭi sae jipyŏng* (*New Horizons in Korean Language Studies*), ed. C. Sŏng-Yŏ and C Lee, 227-283. Seoul: T'aehak.sa.

Kim, A. H.-O. 2010b. Keitaiso kara kōbun kōzō e: Nara-chō kogo ni okeru sonkei no setubigo <si> no shōmetsu o megutte (From a Morpheme to a Syntactic Construction: On the Demise of the Subject Honorific Morpheme *si* in Old Nara Japanese). Paper presented in the NINJAL Salon series, Tokyo.

Kim, A. H.-O. 2011. Chapter 8: Korean Politeness. *Politeness in East Asia: Theory and Practice*, ed. S. Mills and D. Kadar, 176-207. Cambridge, UK: Cambridge University Press.

Kim, A. H.-O. 2013. On the Honorific Adessive Nominative Markers in Korean and Japanese. (ms.) Southern Illinois University-Carbondale.

Kim, S.-K. 1992. *Kukŏ T'ossi Yŏnku* (Studies on Korean Particles). Seoul: Sŏ-kang. haksul.jaryo.sa.

Kim, T.-S. 2003. *Kankokugo Hensenshi* (A History of the Korean Language), trans. Eiji Kurita. Tokyo: Akeshi Shoten.

Lee, I.-S. and Im, H.-P. 1983. *Kukŏ.Mun.Pŏp.Ron* (Korean Grammar). Seoul: Hakyŏn.sa.

Lee, I. and Ramsey, S. R. 2000. *The Korean Language*. Albany: SUNY Press.

Lee, K.-C. 1992. *Kukŏ.Jondae.Pŏp.Ron* (A Study of Korean Subject Honorification) Seoul: Jipmun.dang.

Lee, S. N. 1979. *Jungse.Kukŏ.Munpŏp* (A Study of Middle Korean Grammar). Seoul: Ulyu.munhwasa.

Lyons, J. 1977. *Semantics*, vol. 2. Cambridge: Cambridge University Press.

Martin, S. E. 1992. *A Reference Grammar of Korean*. Rutland: Charles E. Tuttle.

Nam, K.-W. 1997. *Kyohak Koŏ Sajyŏn* (Kyohak Dictionary of Middle ['Old'] Korean). Seoul: Kyohak.sa.

Rhee, S. 1979. *The Semantics of Verbs and Grammaticalization: The Development in Korean from a Cross-linguistic Perspective*. Seoul: Hankuk.

Rhee, S. 2006. Grammaticalization of Postpositional Particles from Spatial Terms in Korean. *Japanese/Korean Lingusitics 14*, ed. T. J. Vance and K. Jones, 139–150. Stanford: CSLI Publications.

Paek, T.-S. 2003. *Ilponŏ-ŭi Tae'u P'yohyŏnYŏnku* (A Study of Japanese Addressee Honorifics). Seoul: Poko.sa.

Sŏ, J.-S. 1984. *Jondae.Pŏp-uy Yŏn'gu* (A Study on Honorifics). Seoul: Hanshin. Munhwa.sa.

Sohn, H.-M. 1999. *The Korean Language*. Cambridge: Cambridge University Press.

Sohn, S.-O. and Strauss, S. 1998. The Intersection of Diachronic Syntax and Current Morphology: Analysis of *-ey* and *-eyse* in Korean. *Proceedings of the 11th International Conference on Korean Linguistics*, ed. B.-S. Park and J. H. S. Yoon, 881–890. Seoul: Hankwuk.munhwa.sa.

Sohn, S.-O. 2002. The Grammaticalization of Honorific Particles in Korean. *New Reflections on Grammaticalization*, ed. I. Wischer and G. Diewald, 309–326. Amsterdam: John Benjamins.

Song, J. J. 2005. *The Korean Language: Structure, Use and Context*. London: Routledge.

Yu, K.-S. 1984. Jukyŏk <kkeysŏ> ko (A Study of the Subject Honorific Case Particle *kkeysŏ*). *Kuk'ŏ Kyŏngŏ.pŏp Yŏnku*, ed. J. Kim, 95–114. Seoul: Jipmun.tang.

A Discrepancy in the Degree of Grammaticalization of Korean and Japanese Negative Sensitive Items: A Corpus-Based Study

KANGHUN PARK*
Jeonju University

1. Introduction

Negative Sensitive Items (NSIs hereafter) show several patterns that correspond with each other in Korean and Japanese. Among them, it has been said that *pakkey* 'only' in Korean and *sika* 'only' in Japanese correspond with each other in terms of their syntactic and semantic properties (Martin 1975; Nam 1994; Kim 2001; Lee 2002; inter alia). The two words appear only in negative contexts (i.e, they are NSIs) and form constructions with the meaning of 'only' in combination with negations such as *-anh-ta* in Korean or *-nai* in Japanese, as seen in (1).

* Section 3 of this paper was partly presented at NRG 5 (Park 2012). In this paper, I particularly focus on the discrepancy in the degree of grammaticalization of Korean and Japanese NSIs. I would like to thank John Whitman, SeongHa Rhee, Akira Watanabe, Asako Miyachi, Koichi Takezawa, JinHo Park, Peter Sells, and the J/K22 editors for their constructive comments and suggestions. Needless to say, all remaining errors are mine.
Japanese/Korean Linguistics 22.
Edited by Mikio Giriko, Naonori Nagaya, Akiko Takemura, and Timothy J. Vance.

(1) a. (K) Chelswu-nun sakwa-*pakkey* mek-ci anh-ass-ta
-TOP apple-*PAKKEY* eat-COMP NEG-PAST-DECL
(*mek-ess-ta).
eat-PAST-DECL
'Chelswu ate only an apple.'

b. (J) Taroo-wa ringo-*sika* tabe-na-katta (*tabe-ta).
-TOP apple-*SIKA* eat-NEG-PAST eat-PAST

Moreover, they have similar distributional properties. Specifically, they can be attached not only to a subject or an object (i.e., an argument), but also to non-arguments, as shown in (2).

(2) a. (K) chenchenhi-*pakkey* yeki-eyse-*pakkey* han pen-*pakkey*
slowly-*PAKKEY* here-from-*PAKKEY* 1 CL-*PAKKEY*
'only slowly' 'only from here' 'only once'
hepi-han-ta-ko *pakkey*
waste-PRES-DECL-QUO *PAKKEY*
'(that) just waste'

b. (J) yukkuri-*sika* koko-kara-*sika* ik-kai-*sika*
slowly-*SIKA* here-from-*SIKA* 1-CL-*SIKA*
tubusi-te iru-to *sika*
waste-ASP-QUO *SIKA*

It seems that *pakkey* and *sika* are exactly the same, as proposed by past studies. However, this study will suggest that the two words should not be treated as exactly the same in certain respects, following Park (2012).

This paper aims to clarify the discrepancy in the degree of grammaticalization of the NSIs *pakkey* and *sika*. To achieve this goal, the study examines grammaticalization as a panchronic process.

2. Puzzles

Elucidating the relationship between *pakkey* and *sika* is, however, not a simple task, because we face a number of puzzles. This study focuses on so-called Multiple NSI Constructions (MNCs hereafter), in which multiple occurrences of NSIs express a single negative proposition. The Korean and Japanese items behave differently in these constructions.

First, *pakkey* can co-occur with other NSIs when it is attached to a subject or an object, whereas *sika* cannot, as seen in (3) and (4).

[Puzzle 1: arguments (subject/object) + *pakkey/sika* in MNCs]

(3) a. (K) Talo-*pakkey* *amwu-to* o-ci anh-ass-ta.
-*PAKKEY* *anyone* come-COMP NEG-PAST-DECL
'Except for Taro, no one came.'

b. (J) *Taroo-*sika* *dare-mo* ko-na-katta.
-*SIKA* *anyone* come-NEG-PAST
(Kuno and Whitman 2004)

(4) a. (K) Swuni-*pakkey* *amwukes-to* mek-ci anh-ass-ta.
-*PAKKEY* *anything* eat-COMP NEG-PAST-DECL
'Except for Swuni, no one ate anything.'
(Sells 2001)

b. (J) *Taroo-*sika* *nani-mo* tabe-na-katta.
-*SIKA* *anything* eat-NEG-PAST
(Aoyagi and Ishii 1994)

Second, both *pakkey* and *sika* are allowed in MNCs when they are attached to non-arguments, such as primary postpositions, as demonstrated in (5) and (6).

[Puzzle 2: non-arguments (primary postpositions) + *pakkey/sika* in MNCs]

(5) a. (K) Wuli-nun ku pwun-eykey nolae-**lo**-*pakkey* *amuwkes-to*
we-TOP the person-to song-with-*PAKKEY* *anything*
kapul swu ep-ta.[1]
pay.back POSS NEG-DECL
'We can pay him back only with songs.'

b. (J) Watasi-tati-wa sono kata-ni uta-**de**-*sika* *nani-mo*
we-PL-TOP the person-to song-with-*SIKA* *anything*
kaes-e-nai.
pay.back-POSS-NEG

(6) a. (K) I pilting-un ciha 10-chung-kkaci issci-man,
this building-TOP basement 10th-floor-up.to exist-but
ciha 5-chung-**kkaci**-*pakkey* *awmu-to* ka pon cek-i
basement 5th-floor-up.to-*PAKKEY* *anyone* go experience-NOM
eps-ta.
NEG-DECL
'This building has 10 floors underground, but no one has been down below the 5th floor.'

[1] In this study, the Korean and Japanese data of the modern period are based primarily on judgments received from twenty Korean and fifty Japanese native linguists.

b. (J) Kono biru-wa tika 10-kai-made aru-ga,
this building-TOP basement 10th-floor-up.to exist-but
tika 5-kai-**made**-*sika* *dare-mo* itta koto-ga nai.
basement 5th-floor-up.to-*SIKA* *anyone* go experience-NOM NEG

Third, *pakkey* is not allowed in MNCs when it is attached to more complicated types of non-arguments, such as secondary postpositions, while *sika* is allowed, as illustrated in (7) and (8).

[Puzzle 3: non-arguments (secondary postpositions) + *pakkey/sika* in MNCs]

(7) a. (K) *Ipen-ey-nun nongep-**ey** **kwanhayse**-*pakkey*
this-time-TOP agriculture-with regard.to-*PAKKEY*
amwukes-to enkup-ha-ci anh-ass-ta.
anything mention-COMP NEG-PAST-DECL
'They will mention only with regard to agriculture this time.'

b. (J) Konkai-wa noogyoo-**ni** **kansite**-*sika* *nani-mo*
this.time-TOP agriculture-with regard to-*SIKA* *anything*
genkyuusi-nai.
mention-NEG

(8) a. (K) *Ikes-un sako-wenil-ul ceytaylo haymyeyngha-**ko**
this-TOP accident-cause-ACC surely figure out-and
nase-*pakkey* *amwukes-to* hal swu ep-ta.
then-*PAKKEY* *anything* can-NEG
'We can do it only after we definitely figure out the cause of the accident.'

b. (J) Kore-wa ziko-gen'in-o tyanto kaimeisi-**te** **kara**-*sika*
this-TOP accident-cause-ACC surely figure.out-and then-*SIKA*
nani-mo deki-nai.
anything can-NEG

The syntactic environments observed so far of *pakkey* and *sika* appearing in MNCs are summarized in Table 1.

Table 1. Syntactic Environments of *pakkey* and *sika* Appearing in MNCs

May appear in MNCs when attached to:	*pakkey*	*sika*
a. arguments (subject/object)	✓	*
b. non-arguments (primary postposition)	✓	✓
c. non-arguments (secondary postposition)	*	✓

3. A Grammaticalization Approach

3.1. *Hoka-nai* in Japanese

In Japanese, there is an expression which is syntactically and semantically similar to *sika*: *hoka* (for more details see Yamada 1922; Konosima 1966; Yamaguchi 1991; Miyachi 2007). Similar to *sika*, *hoka* forms a construction with the meaning of 'only' with negation, and it also has to appear in a negative context, as shown in (9).

(9) a. Taroo-**no**-*hoka* (dare-mo) ko-na-katta *(ki-ta).
-GEN-*HOKA* anyone come-NEG-PAST come-PAST
'Only Taro came.'

b. Singaku-o akirameru-*hoka* na-katta *(at-ta).
going.to.school-ACC give.up-*HOKA* NEG-PAST be-PAST
'I have only one choice, which is to give up going to school.'

3.1.1. *Hoka* vs. *sika* in the Late Edo, Meiji, Taishō, and Shōwa (Modern) Periods

There are, however, some differences between *hoka* and *sika*. First, *hoka* can only be attached to nouns or verbs, as seen in (9). It cannot be attached to other elements, such as postpositions, classifiers, adverbs, and quotative markers, as shown in (10).

(10) *koko-kara-*hoka* *ik-kai-*hoka* *yukkuri-*hoka*
here-from-*HOKA* 1-CL-*HOKA* slowly-*HOKA*
'only from here' 'only once' 'only slowly'
*tubusi-te iru-to *hoka*
waste-ASP-QUO *HOKA*
'(that) just waste'

Second, *hoka* requires a genitive marker *no* when it is attached to a noun, as shown in (9a). Third, most Japanese speakers use *sika* as an NSI more frequently than *hoka*. In fact, this difference is clear in our corpus data, as shown in Table 2.[2]

[2] The data of this study come primarily from diachronic and synchronic corpora. For Japanese, data was collected from 78 literary works, primarily from (i) the *Shin Nihon Koten Bungaku Taikei* (Collection of Classical Japanese Literature) corpus, (ii) the *Aozora Bunko*, (iii) the NINJAL-LWP for BCCWJ, (iv) the Asahi newspaper corpus, and (v) six dictionaries. The Korean data was collected from 69 books, mainly from the (vi) Korean National Corpus of the 21st Century Sejong Project and (vii) five dictionaries. In addition, the data in section 3 is primarily based on Park (2012).

Table 2. Frequency of *sika* and *hoka* in Modern Japanese (3 of 20 samples)

	sika	*hoka*
a. *1Q84: book 1* (347,261 words, 2009)	108	12
b. *Kokushikan satujin jiken* (295,234 words, 1977)	47	23
c. *Gokuchū e no tegami* (67,371 words, 1943)	15	4

According to Bybee (2001, 2003), frequency of use affects the degree of grammaticalization. Such a "frequency effect" (cf. Park 2012) implies that an item with higher frequency has undergone more advanced grammaticalization.

Interestingly, however, according to Park (2012), from the Late Edo period (mid-18th century) to the Taishō period (1920s), *hoka* behaved quite differently from *hoka* in Modern Japanese. First, *hoka* between the Late Edo period and Taishō period could be attached not only to nouns/verbs, but also to various elements, such as adverbs, classifiers, primary postpositions, and quotative markers, as shown in (11).

(11) a. Tubu **hodo**-*hoka* gozanse-nu.
grain about-*HOKA* exist-NEG
'There is only a little left.' (*Hotoke gozen ōgiguruma*, 1722)

b. Tomodati-ga **hitori**-*hoka*-ni-wa dare-mo i-masen.
friend-NOM 1.CL-*HOKA*-LOC-TOP anyone exist-POL-NEG
'I have only one friend, that is, him.' (*Marumaru shinbun*: 525, 1886)

c. Kyōto-**made**-*hoka* ika-nai.
Kyoto-until-*HOKA* go-NEG
'They go only up to Kyoto.' (Yamada 1922)

d. Dandan raku-ni nari-yasu **to** *hoka* itta
gradually comfortably become-POL QUO *HOKA* said
koto-ga na-katta.
experience-NOM NEG-PAST
'He had only said that it would gradually get comfortable.' (*Mazushiki hitobito no mure*, 1916)

Second, during this earlier period, *hoka* did not require a genitive marker, even when it was attached to a noun, as seen in (12).

(12) a. Omae-no **na**-*hoka* demase-nu.
you-GEN name-*HOKA* appear-NEG
'Only your name appeared.' (*Shinjū yoi gōshin*, 1722)

b. **Watasi**-*hoka* sira-nu.
I-*HOKA* know-NEG
'(lit.) Only I know it.' (Yamada 1922)

We can see in (11) and (12) that *hoka* was grammaticalized as a postposition or an NSI, unlike *hoka* in Modern Japanese. In particular, *hoka* behaved quite similarly to *sika* in the Taishō period. Therefore, Yamada (1922:193) treats *sika* and *hoka* as the same kind of expression, calling them *kakari-musubi* 'bound forms'. Third, more interestingly, it seems that the use frequency of *hoka* was higher than that of *sika* during the Taishō period, as shown in Table 3.

Table 3. Frequency of *hoka* and *sika* in the Taishō period (3 of 16 samples)

	sika	*hoka*
a. *Mazushiki hitobito no mure* (58,634 words, 1916)	1	18
b. *Sōsaku no shinri ni tsuite* (3,800 words, 1912)	0	4
c. *Gogo* (1,320 words, 1917)	0	2

To sum up this section:

(i) Both *hoka* and *sika* were similarly grammaticalized as a postposition or an NSI between the late Edo and Taishō periods.
(ii) However, *sika* has been more grammaticalized as a postposition and an NSI since the Showa period, whereas *hoka* has been degrammaticalized to a noun and a quasi-NSI for certain reasons (synonymic collision by 'dialect contact'; see Park 2012 for details).

(13) Grammaticalization Processes of *hoka* and *sika* (based on Park 2012)[3]

a. [*hoka*]

(Stage I, II)	Stage III-a	Stage III-b	Stage IV
(Noun > Adverb) >	1st p stage (NSI) >	2nd p stage (NSI) >	Noun (quasi-NSI)
9th C	early 17th C	end of 19th C	mid 20th C (1930s)
(*hoka* >*hoka*[*ni*]) >	*hoka* (*ni*) >	*hoka* >	*hoka*

[3] The "1st p(ostposition) stage" refers to the stage at which *hoka* and *sika* attaches to nouns or verbs, and the "2nd p(ostposition) stage" refers to the stage at which they are accompanied by various primary postpositions, such as *de* 'with', *made* 'until', etc. The "3rd p(ostposition) stage" refers to the stage at which *sika* attaches to secondary postpositions, such as *-ni kansite* 'with regard to' or *-te kara* 'and then', etc.

b. [*sika*]

Stage III-a[4]		Stage III-b		Stage IV
1st p stage (NSI)	>	2nd p stage (NSI)	>	3rd p stage (NSI)
mid-18th C		19th C		mid 20th C (1930s)
sika	>	*sika*	>	*sika*

3.1.2. Specialization of *sika* and *hoka* in Modern Japanese

According to Park (2012), there is a division of labor between *sika* and *hoka* in Modern Japanese. More specifically, it may be plausible to argue that they have shared functions with the division of labor due to different "specialization" (Hopper 1991). For example, they share their functions in (i) distributional properties, (ii) rhetorical questions, and (iii) MNCs. We can see the differences between them in MNCs in (14) and (15).

(14) a. Taroo-no-*hoka* *dare-mo* ko-na-katta.
-GEN-*HOKA* *anyone* come-NEG-PAST
'Except for Taro, no one came.'
Cf. (3b): *Taroo-*sika* *dare-mo* ko-na-katta.
-*SIKA* *anyone* come-NEG-PAST

b. Taroo-no-*hoka* (dare-mo) *nani-mo* tabe-na-katta.
-GEN-*HOKA* anyone *anything* eat-NEG-PAST
'Only Taro ate everything.'
Cf. (4b): *Taroo-*sika* (dare-mo) *nani-mo* tabe-na-katta.
-*SIKA* anyone *anything* eat-NEG-PAST

(15) a. Watasi-tati-wa sono kata-ni uta-**de**-**hoka*/*sika* *nani-mo*
I-PL-TOP the person-to song-with-*HOKA*/*SIKA* *anything*
kaes-e-nai.
pay.back-POSS-NEG
'We can pay him back only with songs.'

b. Konkai-wa noogyoo-**ni** **kansite**-**hoka*/*sika* *nani-mo*
this.time-TOP agriculture-with regard.to-*HOKA*/*SIKA* *anything*
genkyuusi-nai.
mention-NEG
'They will mention only with regard to agriculture this time.'

In (14) *hoka* and *sika* are attached to arguments (subject or object), and *hoka* is possible, whereas *sika* is not. In contrast, in (15) they are attached to non-arguments (primary or secondary postpositions), and *hoka* is not possible, whereas *sika* is. Interestingly, although examples are not given here,

[4] Unfortunately, there is no way to investigate the previous stages of *sika* due to insufficient data. See Yamaguchi (1991) and Miyachi (2007) for more details.

sika attached to other non-arguments, such as adverbs, quantifiers, or quotative markers, is allowed in MNCs as well. This study proposes that *hoka* and *sika* share their functions in MNCs for certain reasons.[5]

3.2. *Pakkey* vs. *hoka*

3.2.1. Similarities between *pakkey* and *hoka*

Pakkey in Modern Korean corresponds not only to *sika* but also to *hoka*. Moreover, the grammaticalization processes of *pakkey* are intriguingly similar to those of *hoka* and *sika*. In particular, *pakkey* and *hoka* show the same grammaticalization processes from Stage I to Stage III-b (Park 2012):

(16) Grammaticalization processes of *pakkey* and *hoka* (Stages I to III-b)

a. [*pakkey*]

Stage I, II		Stage III-a		Stage III-b
mid-15th C		early 20th C		early to mid-20th C
pas > *paskuy*	>	*paskey*	>	*pakkey*

Categorical change: noun > adverb > 1st p stage (NSI) > 2nd p stage (NSI)
Semantic change: physical space > non-physical space > exception
> delimitation

b. [*hoka*]

Stage I, II		Stage III-a		Stage III-b
9th C		early 17th C		end of 19th C
hoka > *hoka* (*ni*)	>	*hoka* (*ni*)	>	*hoka*

Categorical change: noun > adverb > 1st p stage (NSI) > 2nd p stage (NSI)
Semantic change: physical space > non-physical space > exception
> delimitation

In fact, *pakkey* and *hoka* have morphological similarities (Park 2012), as shown in (17).

(17) a. *pakk* (noun 'outside') + *ey* (locative marker 'at') = *pakkey*
b. *hoka* (noun 'outside') + *ni* (locative marker 'at') = *hoka* (*ni*)

This morphological similarity has a close relationship with the similar etymological roots of the words.

3.2.2. Differences between *pakkey* and *hoka*

There are, however, two significant differences between *pakkey* and *hoka*. First, *pakkey* has never collided with any synonymous expressions, unlike Japanese *hoka* and *sika*. Therefore, *pakkey* has been more grammaticalized as a postposition/NSI on its own. More specifically, *pakkey* does not need to share its function with any other elements. In contrast, Japanese *hoka* has been degrammaticalized to a noun/quasi-NSI since the early Shōwa period

[5] See Park (2012) for more details, including two other differences.

because it has been defeated by *sika*, which is similar to *hoka*. This is Stage IV in (13). Finally, *hoka* and *sika* have come to share their functions in the modern age, as already discussed in section 3.1.2. The differences between *pakkey* and *hoka* at Stage IV are summarized in Table 4.

Table 4. Differences between *pakkey* and *hoka* at Stage IV

	pakkey	*hoka*
a. Period	mid-20th c. –	Shōwa (1930s) –
b. Categorical change	3rd p stage (NSI)	noun (quasi-NSI)
c. Semantic change	delimitation	exception/delimitation
d. (Status)	(still ongoing)	(still ongoing)

Second, there is one more difference between *pakkey* and *hoka*, namely, the period of grammaticalization as an NSI. Based on the periods shown in (16) and Table 4, *pakkey* as an NSI appeared in literature in the early 20th century, whereas *hoka* emerged in literature in the early 17th century. That is, *hoka* had undergone grammaticalization to an NSI three centuries earlier than *pakkey*. The difference could be due to the time period of their first appearance in literature. Whereas *pakkey* first appeared in the middle of the 15th century, *hoka* first developed in the late 9th century, as shown in (16).

3.3. *Pakkey* vs. *sika*

3.3.1. Similarities between *pakkey* and *sika*

The grammaticalization processes, as an NSI/postposition (Stage III-a > Stage III-b > Stage IV) are similar, as seen in (18).

(18) a. [*pakkey*]

Stage III-a		Stage III-b		Stage IV
early 20th C		early to mid-20th C		since mid-20th C
paskey	>	*pakkey*	>	*pakkey*

Categorical change: 1st p stage (NSI) > 2nd p stage (NSI) > 3rd p stage (NSI)
Semantic change: delimitation > delimitation > delimitation

b. [*sika*]

Stage III-a		Stage III-b		Stage IV
mid-18th C		19th C		since Shōwa (1930s)
sika	>	*sika*	>	*sika*

Categorical change: 1st p stage (NSI) > 2nd p stage (NSI) > 3rd p stage (NSI)
Semantic change: delimitation > delimitation > delimitation

Examples of StageIII-b are shown in (19) (see Park 2012 for more details).

(19) a. Anhay-ga ssunun ton-un nay-gey-nun taman
wife-NOM spend money-TOP me-for-TOP just
silepnun salam tul-**lo**-*pakkey* poi-ci-anhnun.
silly person-PL-as-*PAKKEY* see-COMP-NEG
'It seems just silly to me that my wife spends her money.'
(*Nalkay*, 1925)

b. Ce ilsin-uy ancen-ul tomohanunte-**kkaci**-*pakkey*-nun
that own safety-ACC consult-until-*PAKKEY*-TOP
kungli-ka ttulhli-ci moshan kesun.
plan-NOM approach-COMP can-NEG thing
'The reason why he tries to consult only his own convenience.'
(*Mincokuy coyin*, 1948)

(20) a. Dooka mukoo-wa oira-ga tukaikonde-demo iru-**to**-*sika*
likely they-TOP we-NOM use.all-though-ASP-QUO-*SIKA*
omowa-ne-wana.
think-NEG-MODAL
'It seems that they only think that we all carelessly use.'
(*Sharebon: Kakutamago*, 1784)

b. Yuugata-**kara**-*sika* dekakere-nu.
evening-from-*SIKA* go.out-NEG
'I can go out only after the evening.' (Yamada 1922)

3.3.2. Differences between *pakkey* and *sika*

Let us now look at the differences in the grammaticalization processes of *pakkey* and *sika*. These differences are summarized in Table 5 (see Park 2012 for more details).

Table 5. Differences between *pakkey* and *sika* at Stage IV

	pakkey	*sika*
a. Status	incomplete (still ongoing)	more highly grammaticalized
b. Period	mid 20th c. –	Shōwa (1930s) –

4. Discrepancy in the Degree of Grammaticalization of *pakkey* and *sika*

Table 5 shows that the degree of grammaticalization of *sika* as an NSI/ postposition is higher than that of *pakkey*. This line of reasoning is supported by the following four pieces of evidence.

First, it seems that it is difficult to attach *pakkey* to secondary postpositions, unlike *sika*, as shown in (21) and (22). In (21), the attachment is to *-ni* *oite*/*-ul tonghayse* 'in regard to', and in (22), the attachment is to *-te kara*/ *-ko nase* 'and then'. In contrast to *sika*, the attachment of *pakkey* is not possible in these cases.

[Evidence 1: discrepancy in attachment to secondary postpositions]

(21) a. (J) Donna riron-mo gakusetu-mo kizyoo-**ni oite**-*sika*
any theory-even theory-even desk-on -*SIKA*
tuuyoosi-nai.
work-NEG
'All theories can work only on the desk.' (*Enshutsu ni tsuite*, 1938)

b. (K) *Wuli-nun nam-uy cwukum-**ul tonghayse**-*pakkey*
we-TOP other.people-GEN death-ACC through-*PAKKEY*
casin-uy cwukum-ul sayngkakhal swu ep-ta.
oneself-GEN death-ACC think POSS NEG-DECL
'We can think about our death only through the other's death.'

(22) a. (J) Kore-wa ziko-gen'in-o tyanto
this-TOP accident-reason-ACC surely
kaimeisi-**te kara**-*sika* deki-nai.
figure.out-and then-*SIKA* can-NEG
'We can do it only after we definitely figure the out the cause of the accident.'
(*Asahi Shinbun* 2011/4/20)

b. (K) *Ikes-un sako-wenil-ul ceytaylo haymyeyngha-**ko**
this-TOP accident-reason-ACC surely figure.out-and
nase-*pakkey* hal swu ep-ta.
then-*PAKKEY* do POSS NEG-DECL

Second, this study investigated the frequency of *pakkey* and *sika* in eight different types of texts: (i) Japanese and Korean translations of the same English novels, (ii) Japanese novels and their Korean translations, (iii) Korean short stories and their Japanese translations, (iv) Korean novels, and (v) Japanese novels. The results obtained, shown in Table 6 (a–d) below, are quite interesting. In parts (a), (b), and (d) of Table 6, we see that *sika* greatly outnumbers *pakkey*. This means that Japanese *sika* is more widely used than Korean *pakkey* in these texts. Furthermore, around 40% of the occurrences of *pakkey* in part (a) and about 35% in part (b) do not correspond to *sika*. The question that arises is, What items in Korean correspond to *sika* in these translated books? The answer is that Korean *-man* 'only' or *-ppwun* 'only' are often used instead of *pakkey* to translate of *sika*.

[Evidence 2: discrepancy in frequency of use]

Table 6. Frequency of *sika* and *pakkey* (J=Japanese, K=Korean, E=English)

a. J and K Translations of E Novels (2 of 20 samples: *Harry Potter and the Sorcerer's Stone*)

sika	*pakkey*
54	22

b. J Novels and K Translations (2 of 20 samples: *Noruwei no mori*)

sika	*pakkey*
91	68

c. K Short Stories and J Translations (2 of 6 samples: *Ppong*)

sika	*pakkey*
3	2

d. J Novels and K Novels (2 of 20 samples)

Byakuyakō 466,732 words	*Chakhan yecha* 449,793 words
sika	*pakkey*
70	41

Consider the following examples.

(23) a. (J) Watasi-no sundẹ iru ryoo-nante tenzyoo-to
I-GEN live-ASP dormitory-though roof-and
mado-*sika* nai-mono.
window-*SIKA* NEG-MODAL
'The dormitory where I live has only a roof and window.'
(*Noruwei no mori*)

b. (K) Ce-ka sal-ko issnun-kiswuksa-nun chencang-kwa
I-NOM live-ASP dormitory-TOP roof-and
changmwun *ppwun*-in kelyo.
window *PWUN*-MODAL
(*Noruweyi-uy swup*)

It has been said that Korean *-man* and *-ppwun* are semantically quite similar to *-pakkey* (Kim 1997; Sells 2001; inter alia). However, many studies, such as Kuno and Kim (1999), argue that *-pakkey* is not exactly the same as *-man* or *-ppwun*. Similar expressions also exist in Japanese, such as *dake* and *bakari* 'only', and it is reported that these are not exactly the same as *sika*, although they are semantically similar to *sika* (see Kuno 1999 for more details). In contrast to the situation in Japanese, it appears that many Korean speakers still use *-man* or *-ppwun* instead of *pakkey*.

The third piece of evidence is the discrepancy in distributional properties. Specifically, Japanese *sika* occurs more freely than *pakkey* and tends to be attached to a variety of elements, as shown below in Tables 7 and 8. Table 7 shows that *sika* typically attaches to a major or intermediate category, such as a noun or a classifier. Table 8 shows that the same is true of *pakkey*, but it is clear that *sika* attaches more freely to a variety of elements than *pakkey*. This result implies that *sika* as a postposition is more highly grammaticalized than *pakkey*.

[Evidence 3: discrepancy in distributional properties]

Table 7. Distribution of Japanese *sika* (3 of 30 samples)

attached to / book type[6]	major/intermediate category (e.g., noun, classifier, etc.)	minor category (e.g., primary/secondary postposition)
i. J novel	70%	30%
ii. J trans. of E novel	76%	24%
iii. J novel	77%	23%

Table 8. Distribution of Korean *pakkey* (3 of 30 samples)

attached to / book type[7]	major/intermediate) category (e.g., noun, classifier, etc.)	minor category (e.g., primary postposition)
i. K trans. of J novel	93%	7%
ii. K trans. of E novel	98%	2%
iii. K novel	95%	5%

The final piece of evidence is the discrepancy in the periods of grammaticalization to NSIs, as shown in (24).

[Evidence 4: discrepancy in the period of grammaticalization to NSI]

(24) a. [*sika*]

	Stage III-a		Stage III-b		Stage IV
	mid-18th C		19th C		mid-20th C (1930s)
	1st p stage (NSI)	>	2nd p stage (NSI)	>	3rd p stage (NSI)

b. [*pakkey*]

(Stage I, II)		Stage III-a		Stage III-b		Stage IV
(mid 15th C –)		early 20th C		mid-20th C		still ongoing
(noun > adv.)	>	1st p stage (NSI)	>	2nd p stage (NSI)	>	3rd p stage (NSI)

---

[6] The books are: (i) *Noruwei no mori*, (ii) *Harry Potter and the Half-Blood Prince*, and (iii) *Byakuyakō*.

[7] The books are: (i) *Noruweyi-uy swup*, (ii) *Harry Potter and the Half-Blood Prince*, and (iii) *Chakhan yecha*.

Notice that *sika* was grammaticalized to an NSI (StageIII-a) approximately 1.5 centuries earlier than *pakkey*.

Based on the discussion thus far, the evidence that the degree of grammaticalization of *sika* is higher than that of *pakkey* can be summarized as follows:

(i) *Sika* can be attached to secondary postpositions, whereas *pakkey* cannot.
(ii) The frequency of use of *sika* is higher than that of *pakkey*.
(iii) *Sika* tends to be attached to a variety of elements more freely than *pakkey* ("generalization"). In fact, *pakkey*, unlike *sika* almost always attaches to a major category.
(iv) *Sika* was grammaticalized to an NSI (Stage III-a) approximately 1.5 centuries earlier than *pakkey*.

5. Conclusion

This paper has examined the discrepancy in the degree of grammaticalization of Korean and Japanese NSIs, focusing on *pakkey* and *sika*. The conclusions of this paper are as follows. First, the degree of grammaticalization of *sika*, as an NSI and a postposition, is higher than that of *pakkey*. Second, the reason that *sika* and *pakkey* behave differently in MNCs can be explained by the discrepancy in their grammaticalization. There is a division of labor between *sika* and *hoka*: *sika* is allowed to occur with other NSIs when it is attached to non-arguments, while *hoka* is allowed to occur with other NSIs when it is attached to arguments In contrast, *pakkey* is allowed to occur with other NSIs no matter where it is attached because it has never undergone a synonymic collision with any other item (see Park 2012). Nevertheless, unlike *sika*, *pakkey* is not allowed to occur with other NSIs when it is attached to secondary postpositions, because its Stage IV grammaticalization is not yet complete.

References

Aoyagi, H. and Ishii, H. 1994. On NPI Licensing in Japanese. *Japanese/Korean Linguistics 4*, ed. N. Akatsuka, 295–311. Stanford: CSLI.

Bak, S. Y. 1997. *Pakkey*-uy Mwunpephwa Hyensang. *Ene* 22(1): 57–50.

Bybee, J. L. 2001. *Phonology and Language Use.* Cambridge: Cambridge University Press.

Bybee, J. L. 2003. Mechanisms of Change in Grammaticalization: The Role of Frequency. *The Handbook of Historical Linguistics*, ed. R. Janda and B. Joseph, 602–623. Oxford: Blackwell.

Hopper, P. J. 1991. On Some Principles of Grammaticalization. *Approaches to*

Grammaticalization 1, ed. E. C. Traugott and B. Heine: 17–35. Amsterdam: John Benjamins.

Kim, A. H.-O. 1997. The NPI *Pakkey* and Universal Quantifier Negation in Korean. *Harvard Studies in Korean Linguistics 6*, ed. S. Kuno et al., 323–337. Seoul: Hanshin.

Kim, A. H.-O. 2001. Correspondences in Scalar Focus Particles of Japanese and Korean: A Comparative Perspective. *Cognitive-Functional Linguistics in an East Asian Context*, ed. K. Horie and S. Sato, 207–234. Tokyo: Kurosio.

Konoshima, M. 1966. *Kokugo joshi no kenkyū*. Tokyo: Ōfūsha.

Kuno, S. 1999. The Syntax and Semantics of the *Dake* and *Sika* Constructions. *Harvard Working Papers in Linguistics 7*, ed. S. Kuno and B. Vaux, 144–172. Cambridge: Harvard University Department of Linguistics.

Kuno, S. and Kim Y. J. 1999. The Syntax and Semantics of the *Man* and *Pakkey* Constructions. *Harvard Studies in Korean Linguistics* 8: 436–456.

Kuno, S. and Whitman, J. 2004. Licensing of Multiple Negative Polarity Items. *Studies in Korean Syntax and Semantics by Susumu Kuno*, ed. Y.-K. Kim-Renaud and J. Whitman, 207–228. Seoul: International Circle of Korean Linguistics.

Lee, C. M. 2002. Negative Polarity in Korean and Japanese. *Japanese/Korean Linguistics 10*, ed. N. Akatsuka and S. Strauss, 481–494. Stanford: CSLI.

Martin, S. E. 1975. *A Reference Grammar of Japanese*. New Haven: Yale University Press.

Miyachi, A. 2007. *Nihongo joshi shika ni kakawaru kōbun kōzō shiteki kenkyū*. Tokyo: Hitsuji Shobō.

Nam, S. H. 1994. Another Type of Negative Polarity Item. *Dynamics, Polarity, and Quantification*, ed. M. Kanazawa and C. Piñon, 3–15. Stanford: CSLI.

Park, K. H. 2012. Grammaticalization of Negative Sensitive Items *Pakkey* in Korean and *Sika* in Japanese. Paper presented at the 5th New Reflections on Grammaticalization Conference, Edinburgh.

Rhee, S. H. 2004. Grammaticalization of Spatio-temporal Postpositions in Korean. *Journal of Linguistic Science* 31: 169–188.

Sells, P. 2001. Negative Polarity Licensing and Interpretation. *Harvard Studies in Korean Linguistics 9*, ed. S. Kuno et al., 3–22. Cambridge: Harvard University Department of Linguistics.

Yamada, Y. 1922. *Nihon kōgohō kōgi*. Tokyo: Takara Bunkan.

Yamaguchi, G. 1991. Fukujoshi *shika* no genryū. *Gogen Kenkyū* 3: 34–48.

Distributional Patterns of *GA* and *NO* in Four Japonic Varieties

SHOICHI IWASAKI*
University of California, Los Angeles
NORIKO YOSHIMURA
University of Shizuoka

One common grammatical feature found among different varieties within the Japonic language family is the use of case particles. Among them, GA and NO show particularly interesting distributional patterns. They mark attributive and subject noun phrases syntactically on the one hand, and focused constituents pragmatically on the other. The exact match between the form (GA or NO) and the function, however, is not consistent across different varieties. This paper takes the current usage patterns of these particles and puts them into a historical perspective with the aim of understanding the diverse developmental paths that were followed in this language family. It will become clear that the domains of syntax, semantics, and pragmatics are dynamically involved in exhibiting intricate networks among forms and functions.

Through the discussion in this paper we make two specific proposals.

---

* We acknowledge the invaluable assistance that we received from many people while preparing this paper, including Rumiko Shinzato (Naha), Terufusa Yamashita (Kumamoto-Yatsushiro), Hiryoyuki Nakama and members of the Ikema communities (Ikema). We also want to thank Maggie Camp for her editorial work. Any errors are of course ours.
Japanese/Korean Linguistics 22.
Edited by Mikio Giriko, Naonori Nagaya, Akiko Takemura, and Timothy J. Vance.

The first proposal is that the current distributional patterns all began with the distinction in the animacy feature associated with the noun phrase that the particles are attached to. The second proposal is that the current pattern of focus marking in different varieties can be better understood if we take into account the designated focus marker ZO in classical Japanese.

The four varieties of Japonic languages we examine in this paper are Tokyo Japanese (TJ), Kumamoto-Yatsushiro Japanese (KYJ), Naha Ryukyuan (NR), and Ikema Ryukyuan (IR). Tokyo Japanese and Kumamoto-Yatsushiro Japanese belong to the eastern and western (specifically Kyushu) branches of Japanese, respectively. Naha Ryukyuan and Ikema Ryukyuan (a dialect of Miyako Ryukyuan) belong to the northern and southern branches of Ryukyuan, respectively. Japanese and Ryukyuan together constitute an overarching Japonic language family. Section 1 outlines the synchronic distributional patterns of GA and NO in these four varieties. Section 2 brings classical Japanese into the discussion. Section 3 discusses the use of GA as a focus marking particle in TJ and KYJ, the dedicated focus particle ZO in classical Japanese, and DU in NR and IR. Section 4 concludes the paper.

1. Synchronic Distributional Patterns

In the modern varieties of the Japonic languages under discussion, GA and NO are involved in marking 'attributive' and 'subject' noun phrases in different ways. For subject marking, the syntactic environments of the main clause (MC) and the embedded clause (EC) are crucial. The data sets below (Tables 1.a and 1.b) provide a first approximation of the different distributional patterns of GA/NO. The three key structures to be translated into the four varieties are:

1. Attributive: *my father's sandals*
2. Subject (main clause): *My father is wearing sandals.*
3. Subject (embedded clause): *the sandals my father is wearing*

Table 1.a. Data Set (1)

	Tokyo Japanese	Kumamoto-Yatsushiro Japanese
1.	*chichi *ga/**no** zoori*	*toochan *ga/**no** zoori*
2.	*chichi **ga**/*no zoori o haiteiru*	*toochan *ga/**no** zoori ba haitorasu*
3.	*chichi **ga/no** haiteru zoori*	*toochan *ga/**no** haitorasu zoori*

Table 1.b. Data Set (2) (Note that NU is the Ryukyuan cognate of NO.)

	Naha Ryukyuan	Ikema Ryukyuan
1.	*wattaa suu *ga/**nu** saba*	*zza **ga/nu** saba*
2.	*wattaa suu **ga**/*nu saba hachooN*	*zza **ga/nu** saba u hmi-ui*
3.	*wattaa suu **ga/nu** hachooru saba*	*zza **ga/nu** hmi-ui saba*

In Tokyo Japanese and Naha Ryukyuan, GA and NO are distributed between the subject and the attributive, although the distinction is neutralized in the embedded clause environment (i.e., *ga-no* conversion). In Kumamoto-Yatsushiro Japanese and Ikema Ryukyuan, the form-meaning clarity is completely absent; in the former, only NO is used for all markings, while in the latter, both particles mark all functions. Assuming that these language varieties developed from a single mother language (Proto-Japonic), this preliminary comparison of the synchronic patterns of particle use suggests that GA and NO/NU have followed different paths for their semantic and pragmatic developments in different language varieties. To consider this possibility, we need to expand the database to further refine the distributional patterns and to identify steps that were involved in the development of these particles.

1.1. Tokyo Japanese (TJ)

The use of the two particles in Tokyo Japanese is syntactically systematic as stated in the previous paragraph. This is irrespective of the type of noun that is marked by the particles. This is summarized in Table 2. Notice that two horizontal lines clearly demarcate the syntactic division associated with the particle distribution, regardless of the type of the noun phrase.

Table 2. Particle Distribution in Tokyo Japanese (1, 2, 3 = 1st-, 2nd-, 3rd-person pronoun, PN = proper name, H = human, Non-H = non-human, Ina = inanimate)

	1	**2**	**3**	**PN**	**H**	**non-H**	**Ina**
ATT	NO	NO	NO	NO	NO	NO	NO
Sub (EC)	GA/NO	GA/NO	GA/NO	GA/NO	GA/NO	GA/NO	GA/NO
SUB (MC)	GA	GA	GA	GA	GA	GA	GA

1.2. Ikema Ryukyuan (IR)

We saw in Table 1.b that in Ikema both GA and NU appear in all contexts of subject and attributive marking with the human noun meaning 'father'. However, personal pronouns (e.g., *ba* 'I', *vva* 'you') are marked only by GA, and personal names (proper noun) (e.g. *Hiroko*) are usually marked by GA.[1]

[1] The acceptability of NU with a personal name sometimes fluctuates.

Attributive

(1) ba/hiroko ga/*nu sansin
I/(name) GA/*NU sanshin
'my/Hiroko's *sanshin* (a three-string musical instrument)'

Subject (MC)

(2) ba/hiroko ga/*nu sansin nu chufii-ai
I/(name) GA/*NU sanshin ACC make-ASP
'I/Hiroko made a *sanshin.*'

Subject (EC)

(3) ba/hiroko ga/*nu chufii-ai sansin
I/(name) GA/*NU make-ASP sanshin
'the *sanshin* that I/Hiroko made'

In contrast, non-human (e.g., 'dog', 'fish') and inanimate (e.g., 'boat', 'house') nouns allow only NU to code an attributive noun and a subject. In addition, in this language, the noun meaning 'children' is treated as non-human. (DU is a focus particle, which we will return to later.)[2]

Attributive

(4) in *ga/nu zyuu
dog *GA/NU tail
'a dog's tail'

yaa *ga/nu yadu
house *GA/NU door
'a house's door'

Subject (MC)

(5) zzu *ga/nu du uugi-ui
fish *GA/NU FOC swim-ASP
'Fish are swimming.'

funi *ga/nu hari-yui
boat *GA/NU run-ASP
'A boat is sailing.'

Subject (EC)

(6) zzu *ga/nu du uugi-ui in
fish *GA/NU FOC swim-ASP ocean
'the ocean where fish are swimming'

funi *ga/nu hari-yui in
boat *GA/NU run-ASP ocean
'the ocean where a boat is sailing.'

The patterns described so far are presented in Table 3, which has the same basic format as the table used for Tokyo Japanese (Table 2). However, for Ikema, we need two vertical lines to mark the distributional pattern of particles controlled by the animacy feature of the noun in question.

2 Plurality is marked either by *-mmi* or *-ta* in Ikema. The former is invariably followed by NU and the latter by GA, e.g., *midun-mmi nu . . .*; *midun-ta ga . . .* 'children'. Takubo (p.c.) suggests that the selection is semantically motivated in that *-mmi* makes the nominal concept inanimate and *-ta* makes it animate. See Ono and Iwasaki (in preparation) for further discussion.

Table 3. Animacy Hierarchy in Ikema Ryukyuan (1, 2, 3 = 1st-, 2nd-, 3rd-person pronoun, PN = proper name, H = human, Non-H = non-human, Ina = inanimate)

	1	2	3	PN	H	non-H	Ina
ATT	GA	GA	GA	GA	GA/NU	NU	NU
Sub (EC)	GA	GA	GA	GA	GA/NU	NU	NU
SUB (MC)	GA	GA	GA	GA	GA/NU	NU	NU

1.3. Naha Ryukyuan (NR)

Although Naha Ryukyuan shows some similarity to Tokyo Japanese according to Tables 1.a and 1.b, additional data show great differences between the two varieties. For marking an attributive noun, NU is used for all types of nouns except for pronouns.

Attributive

(7) takeshi *ga/nu saba
(name) *GA/NU sandal
'Takeshi's sandals'

taarii *ga/nu saba
father *GA/NU sandal
'my father's sandals'

(8) ʔingwaa *ga/nu zyuu
dog *GA/NU tail
'a dog's tail'

yaa *ga/nu ʔwii
house *GA/NU top
'top of the house > roof'

In contrast to the pattern shown above, the first-person pronoun cannot be marked by either GA or NU. In other words, 'my sandals' is simply *wan saba* or *waa saba* without GA or NU.[3] The second-person pronoun (*naa*) in (9) may be marked by NU, although GA is impossible, while the other second-person pronoun (*ʔyaa*) in (9) must remain unmarked.[4]

(9) naa *ga/(nu) saba
you *GA/(NU) sandal
'your sandals'

ʔyaa *ga/*nu saba
you *GA/*NU sandal
'your sandals'

The third-person pronoun *ʔari* 'he/she' is the only personal pronoun that allows GA marking (NU is only marginally possible), as shown in (10). Therefore, in this language, all personal pronouns are separated from all other types of noun phrases, and, among them, first- and second-person pronouns are distinct from the third-person pronouns.

[3] *Wattaa*, which appears in Table 1.b, is the plural form of *waa/wan*.

[4] *ʔyaa* is used with people the same age or younger, while *naa* is used with close senior relatives such as parents, elder siblings, uncles, and aunts.

(10) ʔari ga/(nu) saba
s/he GA/(NU) sandal
'His/her sandals'

The use of the two particles in the attributive context for NR can be aligned along the animacy hierarchy as follows.

Table 4. Animacy Hierarchy for Attributive Phrases in Naha Ryukyuan

	1/2	>	**3**	>	**PN**	>	**H**	>	**non-H**	>	**Ina**
ATT	(no particle)		GA(NU)		NU		NU		NU		NU

A different hierarchy needs to be constructed for the distribution of the particles as subject markers. Table 1.b shows that the main clause subject (*wattaa suu* 'our father') is marked only by GA. The same pattern can be observed for the first-person pronoun in (11) and for a proper name in (12).

Subject MC

(11) waa ga/*nu du ʔiju tuticharu
I GA/*NU FOC fish catch:PAST
'I went fishing.'

(12) takeshi ga/*nu saba hachooN
(name) GA/*NU sandal wear:ASP
'Takeshi is wearing sandals.'

Further investigation reveals, however, that non-human (13) and inanimate (14) subjects can be marked by either particle. Second- and third-person pronoun subjects may also allow NU, though GA is preferable, as shown in (15).

(13) majaa ga/nu ʔiju kadooN
cat GA/NU fish eat:ASP
'A cat is eating a fish.'

(14) ama Nkai koominkan ga/nu ʔan
there LOC community.center GA/NU exist
'A community center is standing there.'

(15) ʔjaa/ʔari ga/(nu) du ʔiitaru
you/he GA/(NU) FOC say:PAST
'You/He said so.'

The pattern of particle distribution for a main clause subject can be summarized as follows.[5]

Table 5. Animacy Hierarchy for Main Clause Subjects in Naha Ryukyuan

	1	**>**	**2/3**	**>**	**PN**	**>**	**H**	**>**	**non-H**	**>**	**Ina**
SUB (MC)	GA		GA(NU)		GA		GA		GA/NU		GA/NU

The animacy-based distinction is neutralized in the embedded context for a proper name (16), exhibiting a GA/NU conversion just like the GA/NO conversion of Tokyo Japanese. The conversion is also allowed for human, non-human, and inanimate nouns.

Subject EC

(16) takeshi ga/nu hachooru saba
(name) GA/NU wear:ASP sandal
'the sandals that Takeshi is wearing'

However, this GA/NU conversion becomes impossible when the subject is a first- (17) or second-person pronoun (18), which can be marked only by GA. The conversion is marginal with a third-person pronoun (19).

(17) waa/wattaa ga/*nu tuticharu ʔiju
I/we GA/*NU catch:PAST fish
'the fish that I/we caught'

(18) ʔjaa/ʔittaa ga/*nu kadeeru naimun
you(sg.)/you(pl.) GA/*NU ate fruit
'the fruit that you(sg.)/you(pl.) ate'

(19) ʔari ga/(nu) kacheeru tigami
s/he GA/(NU) wrote letter
'the letter that s/he wrote'

Thus, in the embedded clause context, personal pronouns disallow NU (third-person pronouns are marginal), but others allow both GA and NU. The situation can be displayed as follows, which seems to indicate that the embedded context in NR is similar to that in TJ except for personal pronouns.

[5] We will leave the question of why second- and third-person pronouns marginally allow NU for future research.

Table 6. Animacy Hierarchy for Embedded Subjects in Naha Ryukyuan

	1/2	>	3	>	PN	>	H	>	non-H	>	Ina
SUB (EC)	GA		GA(NU)		GA/NU		GA/NU		GA/NU		GA/NU

We summarize the distributional patterns of the two particles in the three different syntactic environments for NR in Table 7 below.

Table 7. Animacy Hierarchy in Naha Ryukyuan in Three Syntactic Environments

	1	2	3	PN	H	non-H	Ina
ATT	(no marking)		GA(NU)	NU	NU	NU	NU
SUB (EC)	GA		GA(NU)	GA/NU	GA/NU	GA/NU	GA/NU
SUB (MC)	GA	GA(NU)		GA	GA	GA/NU	GA/NU

The pattern shown in Table 7 indicates that NR's system of marking is a mixed system of the syntax-based TJ type and the animacy-based IR type. The attributive noun is marked only by NU (NO in TJ) when the noun is a personal name or anything below on the hierarchy. The embedded subject is marked by GA/NU (cf. the GA/NO conversion in TJ) for these same noun types. The main clause subject is marked solely by GA except for non-human and inanimate nouns, which can be marked by either. (Second- and third-person pronouns allow NU marginally.) In other words, GA seems to be gaining the position of subject marking exclusively. However, the pattern also retains the animacy-based distribution, as the marking for pronouns are clearly distinguished from the non-pronoun categories in the attributive and the embedded clause context.

1.4. Kumamoto-Yatsushiro Japanese (KYJ)

A distinct characteristic of KYJ is the non-use of GA for both attributive and subject marking (Yoshimura 1994; Yoshimura and Nishina 2004). Observe Table 8 for the GA/NO distribution in the attributive context in this language.

Table 8. Particle Distribution for an Attributive Phrase in KYJ

	1	>	2/3	>	PN	>	H	>	non-H	>	Ina
ATT	n/a		NO		NO		NO		NO		NO

Below, first note that proper names and human, non-human, and inanimate nouns all take NO but not GA.[6]

Attributive (proper name/human noun)

(20) haruko/toochan/inu/teeburu *ga/n(o) ashi
(name)/father/dog/table *GA/NO leg
'Haruko's / my father's / the dog's / the table's legs'

Second- and third-person pronouns are also similar to these cases. In this language, however, there is no pure third-person pronoun, and the noun phrase *ayatsu* 'that person' is used instead.[7]

Attributive (2nd- and 3rd-person pronouns)

(21)	ata *ga/n kutsu	ayatsu *ga/n kutsu
	you *GA/NO shoes	s/he (=that person) *GA/NO shoes
	'your shoes'	'his/her shoes'

First-person pronouns (e.g., *odon*) are distinct from all other categories. They are usually unspecified due to their pragmatic saliency in conversation, although grammatically NO should be available. However, *odon* 'I' can take GA when contrast or focus needs to be encoded, i.e., 'not his, but MY shoes' (see Section 3).[8] Thus, the animacy concern is minimally relevant in the attributive context to the extent that a first-person pronoun behaves differently from the rest for attributive marking in KYJ.

For subject marking also, pragmatic contexts define both first- and second-person pronouns, and they are thus not realized unless they are focused on (Section 3).[9] Other noun phrases are all marked by NO. A few examples follow.

---

[6] NO is realized as *no* after a nasal consonant, but as *n* elsewhere.

[7] Second-person plural pronouns also take *n*: *atatachi-**n**-imoto* 'your (female pl.) sister'; *nushidon-tachi-**n**-imoto* 'your (male pl.) sister'

[8] Note also that kinship terms (e.g. *toochan* 'father') and proper names (*Haruko*) can be used as first- and second-person pronouns. A male speaker, for example, can refer to himself as *toochan* 'father' when he talks, e.g., to his son. In this case, *toochan ga kustsu* means 'my shoes' with a contrast/focus interpretation on 'my.'

[9] It is probably true that also in TJ a first-person pronoun is not coded unless it is in focus. Thus, *boku ga katta kuruma* 'the car that I bought' or *boku ga kuruma o katta* 'I bought a car' with the overt first-person pronoun is marked. However, KYJ being a strictly spoken language, KYJ speakers seem to be more strongly aware of this pragmatic constraint than TJ speakers. In other words, TJ is more 'standardized' to the extent that a non-existent form may be considered as legitimate through logical reasoning, and the examples above are just more readily accepted.

Subject (MC)

(22) haruko *ga/n ie ba tsugashita
(name) *GA/NO house ACC inherit
'Haruko inherited the house.'

(23) neko *ga/n sakana ba kutoru
cat *GA/NO fish ACC eat:ASP
'The cat is eating a fish.'

Subject (EC)

(24) an ojisan *ga/no kawashita kuruma
that uncle *GA/NO bought car
'the car that uncle bought'

(25) fune *ga/n hasshitoru umi
boat *GA/NO run:ASP ocean
'the ocean on which a boat is sailing'

The particle distribution for subject markings in KYJ is summarized below.

Table 9. Particle Distribution for Subjects in KYJ

	1/2	>	**3**	>	**PN**	>	**H**	>	**non-H**	>	**Ina**
SUB (MC/EC)	n/a		NO		NO		NO		NO		NO

2. From the Animacy-Based Distinction to the Socio-Pragmatic-Based Distinction

As shown in the previous section, the animacy concern is evident at least in three languages with various degrees of strength. Tokyo Japanese is exceptional in that it does not show any concern for animacy. We should note, however, that its earlier form (classical Japanese) does exhibit a split of particle uses.[10] In this section, we provide essential information about the GA/NO distribution in classical Japanese and propose that the current distribution of particles should be understood as a consequence of the earlier animacy-based distinction.

---

[10] Since the time of Nara Japanese (8th century CE) both particles have had attributive and subject marking functions. However, while GA's use was restricted to these two functions, NO had the additional functions of marking appositive, metaphorical and general descriptive phrases (Nomura 1993b: 49; Kobayashi 1938: 202; Kinsui et al. 2011). Note also that GA has gone through a complex chain of changes. In Nara Japanese, the two particles marked a subject only in nominalized clauses, but by the Kamakura period (13th century), GA (but not NO) gradually came to also be used in finite clauses. GA also developed the function of concessive conjunction ('but'). See, for example, Nomura (2011:106–117) and Umebayashi (1989) among others.

The split use of GA and NO in classical Japanese has been characterized in different ways by specialists: (i) GA follows pronouns and proper nouns while NO follows everything else, including common human and inanimate nouns; (ii) GA follows a noun whose referent is definite (Nomura 2011:78), and NO follows indefinite or generic nouns (Tōgō 1968:33–35); (iii) GA follows a concept bearing a closer relationship to the speaker (e.g., *imo* 'wife, lover', *haha* 'mother') and NO one which is far from the speaker (e.g., *ohokimi, sumerogi* 'emperor', *kami* 'god'); (iv) GA follows lower status persons (e.g., *kaizoku* 'pirates') while NO follows higher status persons and gods (Aoki 1952).

Although specialists have been debating the most appropriate characterization of the split, these proposals do not have to compete with each other, and as shown here, they actually complement each other. We will show this point by bringing in the 'extended animacy hierarchy' proposed by Croft (1990:130,167). The different proposals above partially overlap with the components of Croft's hierarchy, which breaks down the traditional animacy hierarchy into four sub-domains, as shown below in Table 10. The numbers (i) and (ii) refer to the proposals listed in the preceding paragraph and show the correspondences between those analyses and Croft's.

Table 10. Extended Animacy Hierarchy (Croft 1990)

Person:	first, second $<$ third
Referentiality:	pronoun $<$ proper name $<$ common noun (i)
Definiteness:	definite $<$ referential $<$ non-ref. (nonspecific) (ii)
Animacy proper:	human $<$ animate $<$ inanimate

The 'referentiality' domain and (i) provide a unified account for the consistent GA marking on pronouns (first-person *a, wa, ono*, second-person *na*, third-person *shi* 'he/she/it', and *ta* 'who') and proper nouns (*Hitomaro*) as opposed to common nouns. The 'definiteness' domain and (ii) also explain the GA marking for (non-interrogative) pronouns and proper names, but, at the same time, they explain NO marking for new information (e.g., X *to ifu hito* 'person named X') and generic noun phrases (e.g., *hito* 'other people') (Tōgō 1968:33–35). The 'animacy proper' domain distinguishes human (GA) and inanimate (NO).

Proposals (iii) and (iv) listed above are explained as socio-pragmatic distinctions based on the in-group/out-group distinction in the case of (iii) and on the derogatory/honorific evaluation of the referent in the case of (iv) (e.g., Jugaku 1963): GA indexes humans close to the speaker (iii) or lower-status humans (iv), and NO indexes humans distant from the speaker (iii) or a high-status entity as a non- (i.e., super-) human. These distinctions cannot find an equivalent in Croft's extended animacy hierarchy because they are not intrinsic properties of the noun phrase. Here we propose that these socio-pragmatic distinctions are a consequence of a cognitive shift from the animacy-based distinction. The distance between the human and non-human categories on the animacy hierarchy is projected onto the distinction either between close and distant relations or between ordinary humans and high-status persons, such as emperors and gods. The strategy of marking a high-status person with NO, a marker for non-humans, essentially works to eliminate agency from such an entity. (This is similar to the use of the passive form for high-status person as a means of honorification.) One obvious reason why the socio-pragmatic distinctions may not be primary is that they disregard non-human referents and cannot explain why non-human nouns are often, though definitely not exclusively, marked by NO (e.g., *take NO hayashi* 'bamboo grove', *kamo NO ha* 'feathers of ducks', *yoshino NO kawa* 'river in Yoshino', etc.).

We have some evidence that the animacy effect was still present in the earliest stage of classical Japanese. Yanagida (2007:160) and Yanagida and Whitman (2009:112) note that in Nara Japanese, NO marked both transitive and intransitive subjects, while GA marked an agentive subject of both transitive and intransitive verbs but not non-agentive subjects of intransitive verbs. Based on this distributional pattern, they conclude that GA was a marker of active case and NO a marker of nominative case. However, what this implies is that GA is associated with an agentive subject, e.g., a human subject. Yanagida herself acknowledges that in some cases GA is controlled by the animacy feature of the noun phrase it marks rather than the predicate type, referring to a poem in which a non-agentive human experiencer is coded with GA (Yanagida 2007:177–178). This supports our claim that GA is associated with human nouns, whether agentive or non-agentive. Furthermore, our proposal can go beyond GA and NO used as subject markers and can cover them as attributive markers as well, which does not concern predicate type. Finally, if we assume the animacy hierarchy as the basis for the socio-pragmatic distinction, we can easily make a link between the Ryukyuan branch (Ikema and Naha) and the Japanese branch (classical Japanese). That is, while the Ryukyuan branch, especially Ikema, strongly maintained an animacy distinction, the classical Japanese branch reinterpreted it as a socio-pragmatic distinction. The socio-pragmatic distinction that was clearly operative in Muromachi Japanese, however, came to be unfashionable when GA started to perform its subject marking function in main clauses, and this distinction completely disappeared in Edo Japanese. In other words, the GA/NO distinction which started as an animacy distinction came to code exclusively the syntactic distinction between subject marking and attributive phrase marking that we see in Modern Japanese.

3. Focus Marking Function of GA

In Section 1.4, we noted that, except for very limited cases, Kumamoto-Yatsushiro Japanese does not use GA to code either the attributive or subject nouns. However, as mentioned in passing and as the next examples show, this language uses GA to code a subject which is in focus, while it uses NO to mark a non-focused subject.

(26) yamada shenshee ga/n ie ba taterashita (KYJ)
(name) teacher GA/NO house ACC built
'It's Teacher Yamada who built a house.' (with GA)
'Teacher Yamada built a house.' (with NO)

The two sentences in (26) above are identical except for the choice of particle for the subject noun phrase. With GA, the subject is in focus, and with NO it is not. Modern Tokyo Japanese uses GA to mark both a regular and a focused subject, so the two sentences in (26) come out as identical: *yamada sensee ga ie o tateta* (TJ) 'Teacher Yamada built a house' or 'It is Teacher Yamada who built a house'.[11] The functional distinction in Tokyo Japanese can be marked only prosodically with prominence added to *yamada sensee ga*. In the embedded context as well, GA can add a focus to the noun it attaches to in KYJ.

(27) yamada shenshee ga/n taterashita ie (KYJ)
(name) teacher GA/NO built house
'the house that none other than Teacher Yamada built' (with GA)
'a house that Teacher Yamada built' (with NO)

Both sentences in (27) are translated into Tokyo Japanese as *yamada sensee ga/no tateta ie*, but GA and NO do not distinguish two types of subjects. The focus can be signaled only prosodically. The GA of classical Japanese also had the function of focus marking (Konoshima 1983:102–103; Kobayashi 1938:1469). Kumamoto-Yatsushiro picked up this function of GA, leaving the marking of a non-focused constituent to NO, whereas classical Japanese and Tokyo Japanese picked up the 'subject marking' function (both focused and non-focused) for GA, leaving attributive marking to NO.

At this point, an interesting question emerges. Are there any Japonic languages that use GA solely as a marker of a non-focused subject? The answer seems to be yes. Ryukyuan languages are known to have a designated focus marker DU. Yamada (1954) suggests that the Ryukyuan DU is related to ZO in classical Japanese (see also Uchima 1994, Nohara 1998, and Shinzato 1998). Yamada (2001) further shows that, in the Heian period, ZO

[11] Kuno (1973) refers to the focus marking function associated with GA in (standard) Japanese as 'exhaustive listing'.

was used as a focus marker while GA was used as a pure subject marker. However, as the use of ZO started to decline, GA began to acquire the focus marking function as well. Modern Tokyo Japanese is an end point of this development. Since Ryukyuan languages still retain DU (the cognate of ZO), it is possible that they may still preserve the division between the two types of subject. In Ikema DU can be attached to different sentence constituents as shown below. Hyphens are inserted to clarify morphological structure.

(28) haru-ga-**du** zzu-u yaki-ui
(name)GA-DU fish-ACC cook-ASP
'*Haru* is cooking a fish.'

haru-u zzu-u-**du** yaki-ui
(name)-TOP fish-ACC-DU cook-ASP
'Haru is cooking a *fish.*'

This data suggests the division between subject and focus marking is clearly demarcated in Ikema. This is also the case for Naha. Based on these observations, we propose three distinct types of language with respect to subject and focus marking, as shown in Table 11.

Table 11. Three Types of Language with Respect to Focus Marking

	Subject Marking	Focus Marking
Tokyo	GA	GA (only on subject)
Kumamoto-Yatsushiro	NO	GA (only on subject)
Ikema/Naha	GA/NU	DU (on any constituent)

4. Summary and Conclusion

By surveying the uses of GA and NO (and its variant forms) in one classical and four modern varieties of the Japonic language family, we came away with two proposals. The first was that the distinction between GA and NO/NU was originally made according to the animacy hierarchy. This proposal provides logical explanations for several issues: (i) the two seemingly different systems found in the Ryukyuan (animacy-based distribution) and Japanese branches (i.e., no such distinction in Tokyo Japanese) are linked naturally; (ii) the well-known derogatory/honorific distinction for GA and NO found in classical Japanese has a better foundation, as the animacy-based distinction can explain all types of noun phrases along the hierarchy, not only human referents; and (iii) the animacy features can be naturally linked to the predicate types that GA and NO take in classical Japanese. The second proposal concerns the focus function associated with GA. Although the distinction is not made morphologically in Tokyo Japanese, it is clearly shown by the use of GA (focused subject) and NO (regular subject) in Kumamoto-Yatsushiro Japanese. This distinction is clearly made through the use of the focus particle DU in the Ryukyuan branch. Since DU is believed to be a cognate with ZO in classical Japanese, we support Yamada's (2001) claim that the GA's double function is the result of ZO's decline. We further maintain that the Ryukyuan languages (at least Ikema and Naha) use GA as a pure subject marker. This in turn contrasts with Kumamoto-Yatsushiro Japanese, which uses GA exclusively as a focus subject marker.

In this paper we have shown that cross-linguistic comparison among related languages provides insight hitherto unavailable in research focusing on one single language.

References

Aoki, R. 1952. *Nara jidai ni okeru rentai-joshi 'ga' 'no' no sai ni tsuite* (On the Difference between 'ga' and 'no' as an Attributive Marking Particle in the Nara Period). *Kokugo to Kokubungaku* 29(7): 49–56.

Croft, W. 1990. *Typology and Universals*. Cambridge: Cambridge University Press.

Jugaku, A. 1963. *Muromachi jidai no 'no/ga'* (GA and NO in the Muromachi Period). *Kokugo Kokubun* 27(7): 44–57.

Kinsui, S., Takayama, Y., Kinuhata T. and Okazaki, T. 2011. *Bunpō-shi* (History of Grammar). Tokyo: Iwanami Shoten.

Kobayashi, Y. 1938. *Joshi 'ga' no hyōgen-teki kachi* (Expressive Values of the Particle 'ga'). *Kokugo to Kokubungaku* 15(10):198–213.

Konoshima, M. 1983. *Jodōshi joshi gaisetsu* (General Descriptions of Particles and Auxiliary Verbs). Tokyo: Ōfūsha.

Kuno, S. 1973. *The Structure of the Japanese Language*. Cambridge: MIT Press.

Nohara, M. 1998. *Shinpen Ryūkyū hōgen joshi no kenkyū.* (A New Perspective on the Study of Particles in Ryukyuan). Okinawa: Okinawagaku Kenkyūjo.

Nomura, T. 1993. *Jōdaigo no NO to GA ni tsuite (jō, ge)* (On 'no' and 'ga' in Old Japanese [part 1, part 2]). *Kokugo Kobubun* 62(2): 1–17, 62(3): 30–49.

Nomura, T. 2011. *Hanashi kotoba no Nihon shi* (A History of Spoken Japanese). Tokyo: Yoshikawa Kōbunkan.

Ono, T. and Iwasaki, S. In preparation. Differential Subject Marking in the Ikema Dialect of Miyako.

Shinzato, R. 1998. *Kakari musubi* Revisited: Its Functions and Development. *Japanese Korean Linguistics 18*, ed. David Silva, 203–216. Stanford: CSLI.

Tōgō, Y. 1968. *Heian jidai no 'no' 'ga' ni tsuite: Jinbutsu o ukeru baai* (On 'no' and 'ga' in the Heian Period: When they Follow Person Nouns). *Kokugogaku* 75: 27–44.

Uchima, C. 1994. *Ryūkyū hōgen joshi to hyōgen no kenkyū.* (A Study of Particles and Expressions in Ryukyuan). Tokyo: Musashino Shoin.

Umebayashi, H. 1989. *Nara jidai ni okeru shukaku joshi 'ga' no hōga* (Emergence of the Nominative Marker 'ga' in the Nara Period). *Gobun Ronsō* 17: 64–73.

Yamada, M. 2001. *Shugo hyōji 'ga' no kyōchō hyōgen ni okeru seiryoku kakudai no yōsō: 'zo' to no kanren-sei ni oite*. (Aspects of the Expansion of Subject Marking 'ga' into the Domain of Emphatic Expression with Respect to 'zo'). *Kokugo Kokubun* 70(8):32–48.

Yamada Y. 1954. *Nara-chō bunpō-shi* (History of Grammar in the Nara Period). Tokyo: Hōbunkan.

Yanagida, Y. 2007. *Jodaigo no nōkaku-sei ni tsuite* (On Ergativity in Old Japanese). *Nihongo no shubun genshō* (Main Clause Phenomena in Japanese), ed. Nobuko Hasegawa, 147–188. Tokyo: Hitsuji Shobō.

Yanagida, Y. and J. Whitman. 2009. Alignment and Word Order in Old Japenese. *Journal of East Asian Linguistics* 18:101–144.

Yoshimura, N. 1994. *'GA' no mondai* (A Problem with GA). *Hen'yō suru gengo bunka kenkyū*, ed. Shizuoka Kenritsu Daigaku Ei-Bei Bunka Kenkyū-shitsu, 13–28. Shizuoka: Shizuoka Kenritsu Daigaku.

Yoshimura, N. and A. Nishina. 2004. *Bunretsu-bun no imi to kōzō: Kodai-go to Kyūshū hōgen no setten* (The Meaning and Structure of Cleft Sentences: A Link between Classical Japanese and Kyushu Dialects). *Kotoba to Bunka* 7:55–72.

A Quantitative Approach to Mimetic Diachrony

KIMI AKITA*
Osaka University

SATOSHI NAKAMURA
Meiji University

TAKANORI KOMATSU
Meiji University

SACHIKO HIRATA-MOGI
University of Tokyo

1. Introduction

This paper is the first report of our interdisciplinary project on the diachrony of sound-symbolic, mimetic words (also known as ideophones) in Japanese. The project involves three major neighboring disciplines: linguistics, psychology, and information science. We adopt a quantitative method using the Minutes of the Diet of Japan (1947–2011) as a diachronic corpus. The purpose of this study is not just to investigate the recent change in the semantic and morphosyntactic variations of Japanese mimetics, but also to demonstrate how extensive and efficient a study an interdisciplinary collaboration makes possible in language sciences.

* Earlier versions of this paper were presented at J/K22 and the Sound Symbolism Workshop at Keio University (August 2012). Our special gratitude goes to Mark Dingemanse, Hiroki Fujii, Mutsumi Imai, and Daiki Sawai. This project was originally inspired by Kenjiro Matsuda's comment on Akita (2011; presented in June 2010). Remaining inadequacies are our own. The study was partly supported by JSPS Grants-in-Aid for Young Scientists to Akita (no. 24720179), Nakamura (no. 23680006), and Komatsu (no. 23700248), and by a Spanish Ministry of Science and Innovation grant for Proyectos de Investigación Fundamental no Orientada to Akita (no. FEI2010-14903; PI: Iraide Ibarretxe-Antuñano).
Japanese/Korean Linguistics 22.
Edited by Mikio Giriko, Naonori Nagaya, Akiko Takemura, and Timothy J. Vance.

Based on the quantitative data, we make two major observations about the little explored issue of mimetic diachrony. First, we point out the recent "replacement" of nonmimetic adverbials by certain types of mimetics. Next, we report the increase of quotative marking on mimetics and the decrease of their verbal uses. These lexical and morphosyntactic changes, which partly go against the trends in the earlier history of mimetics, suggest the gradual "reforegrounding" of mimetics over the last century.

The organization of this paper is as follows. Section 2 summarizes three related studies on diachronic change in mimetics. Section 3 describes the methodological details of the present study. Section 4 presents two sets of results. One compares mimetic and nonmimetic adverbials, and the other compares adverbial and verbal mimetics. These results will be discussed from a general perspective in Section 5, where we consider mimetic diachrony in relation to (de)iconization in crosscategorial derivations. Section 6 concludes the paper.

2. Previous Studies

Diachrony is one of the least studied areas in the research on mimetics. In this section, we briefly summarize three exceptional studies on this topic. Their findings will help us arrive at a general story on the basis of the rich data presented in the following sections.

First, Shibasaki (2009) investigates the history of reduplicated words in Japanese. As shown in Figure 1, which is based on the token frequency of words in literary works, he points out the decrease in reduplication of adverbs (e.g., *yokuyoku* 'extremely' [< *yoku* 'sufficiently']) and the increase of mimetic reduplicatives (e.g., *niyaniya* 'grinning') after the 15th and 16th centuries. Although the data are limited in both variety (reduplicated forms only) and size (161 adverbial instances, 182 mimetic instances), the negative correlation between the two types of reduplicative adverbs suggests a gradual lexical shift from nonmimetic to mimetic adverbs, which one might call "iconization" (or "mimeticization") of the adverbial lexicon. In fact, when we go through a list of Japanese adverbs, such as Nitta's (2002), we find many items that are no longer used or are at least highly marked in normal discourse (e.g., *amaneku* 'widely', *iwan'ya* 'let alone', *kanasiikana* 'regrettably', *orisimo* 'just then', *osinabete* 'all'). This idea will be further developed in Section 4.1.

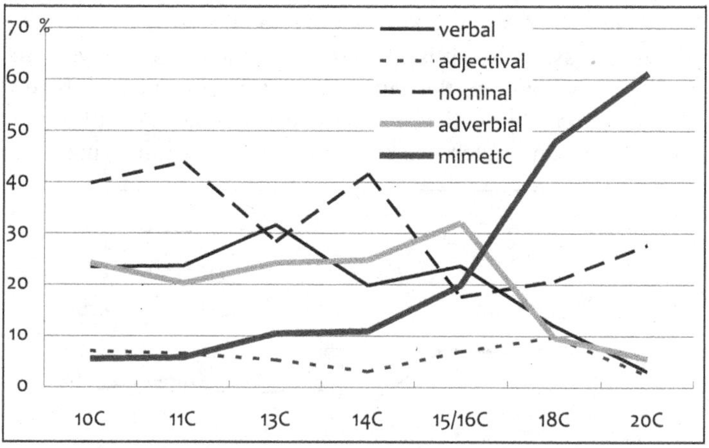

Figure 1. The Vicissitudes of Japanese Reduplication (adapted from Shibasaki 2009:12)

Second, Yamaguchi (2002) is the best-known study in mimetic diachrony. She observes the emergence and disappearance of typical mimetic shapes. According to her chronological table (pp. 34–35), the three currently most productive morphological templates appeared in the following order: reduplicative ($C_1V_1C_2V_2$-$C_1V_1C_2V_2$; e.g., *huwahuwa* 'fluffy') > suffixal ($C_1V_1C_2V_2$-Aff; e.g. *huwaQ/N/ri* 'fluffy') > "emphatic" ($C_1V_1CC_2V_2$*ri*; e.g., *huNwari* 'fluffy').[1] Interestingly, reduplicatives appear to be the most prevalent mimetic type not only in Japanese but across languages (Hinton et al. 1994; Nuckolls 2004). In contrast, emphatic mimetics are unique to Japanese and, even in Japanese, less prototypical due to their low iconicity (Akita 2009:144–147, 2011). In Section 4.1, we will argue that the latter type has made an important contribution to the recent growth of mimetics in the Diet record.

Third, Kawase (2005, 2006) provides token frequency data from collections of humorous stories that have direct relevance to the present study. He focuses on two important features of mimetic morphosyntax in Japanese: the presence and absence of the quotative *-to* (e.g., *burabura-to* [*aruk-*] vs. *burabura* [*aruk-*] '[walk] ramblingly') and incorporation into the dummy verb *su-* 'do' to form a "mimetic verb" (e.g., *burabura-su-* 'ramble'). Figure 2 is based on our recalculation of Kawase's (2005) raw data. A correlation analysis for the percentages and the years revealed a significant decrease of *-to*-marked mimetic adverbs ($r = -.87$, $p < .01$) and a significant increase of

[1] The abbreviations used in this paper are as follows: ACC = accusative; MIM = mimetic; N = moraic nasal; Q = the first half of a geminate cluster; QUOT = quotative.

bare mimetic adverbs ($r = .76$, $p < .05$) and mimetic verbs ($r = .85$, $p < .01$). Therefore, as Kawase notes, it is likely that the three morphosyntactic constructions have developed in the following order: *-to*-marked > bare > verbal (cf. Suzuki 1965). In Section 4.2, these earlier changes will be found to contrast with the recent preference shifts in mimetic morphosyntax.

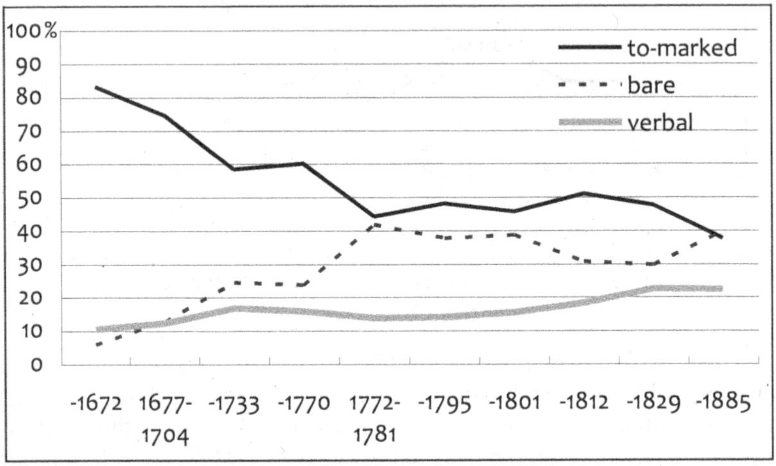

Figure 2. The Diachronic Change of Mimetic Morphosyntax in Japanese (based on Kawase 2005)

3. Method

This study took a quantitative approach to the Minutes of the Diet of Japan (henceforth MDJ), which consist of sixty-five years (1947–2011) of meeting records and are available online (http://kokkai.ndl.go.jp/). See Akita et al. (2012) and Nakamura et al. (2012) for MDJ-based quantitative studies of the pragmatics and dialectology of Japanese mimetics, respectively. It must be admitted that this corpus represents a special type of spoken discourse (i.e., political speeches and debates). More importantly, however, it is the largest diachronic corpus of spoken Japanese currently available (consisting of 48,512,596 sentences, according to the number of punctuation marks and paragraphs), and it has made some noteworthy linguistic studies possible during the first decade of this century (Matsuda 2000, 2004, 2008; Nambu 2007). See Matsuda (2008) for detailed descriptions of the MDJ as a linguistic corpus.[2]

[2] One important feature of the MDJ is its apparent convention of reducing emphatic prolonged vowels, which are especially common in mimetics. For instance, the intensified mimetic form *huwaari* 'very fluffy' appears to be transcribed as *huwari*. This is a favorable convention for our study, which uses a closed list of conventional (i.e., nonintensified) mimetics.

The database was searched for items on two word lists. One list consists of 694 four-mora mimetics mainly taken from Kakehi et al. (1996), and the other consists of 477 nonmimetic manner adverbials taken from Nitta's (2002) index (e.g., *asibaya-ni* 'with quick steps', *iyaiya* 'unwillingly'). The searches used their typical orthographic representations: both hiragana and katakana for mimetics, and the most typical representation for each nonmimetic adverbial. The mimetics were classified both semantically and morphologically. To avoid many cases of semantic ambiguity/vagueness (e.g., *batabata* 'fluttering hastily' [phono-/phenomimic]), only 526 monosemous mimetics were taken and classified into the four semantic types in (1) (for semantic classification, see Martin 1975; Asano 1978; among others). Many members of the fourth category, which has been recognized by several researchers (Tamori and Schourup 1999: 53–55, among others), show exceptional avoidance of quotative marking (e.g., ??*sukkari-to* 'completely', ??*tyokutyoku-to* 'often') (Tamori and Schourup 1999: 68–69). They are characterized not only by this formal feature but also by their abstract meaning and low iconicity, which make them sound like nonmimetic adverbs (see Nitta 2002).

(1) A four-way classification of mimetics (with the numbers of items):

a.	Phonomimic (auditory):	128	e.g., *gataN* 'clunk'
b.	Phenomimic (visual/textural):	315	e.g., *huNwari* 'fluffy'
c.	Psychomimic (internal):	65	e.g., *dokiQ* 'startled'
d.	Semimimetic (degree/frequency):	18	e.g., *tyokutyoku* 'often'

As for forms, we paid special attention to reduplicative ($C_1V_1C_2V_2$-$C_1V_1C_2V_2$) and emphatic ($C_1V_1CC_2V_2ri$) mimetics, which are the first and third most productive morphological types of mimetics in Japanese (Akita 2009: 110).[3] Both types in principle show optional *-to*-marking (e.g., *huwa-huwa*/*huNwari*[-*to*] [*ukab-*] '[float] fluffily'; cf. *huwaQ*/*N*/*ri**[-*to*] [*ukab-*]) (Nasu 2002). These mimetics allow us to make a fair observation of the diachronic variation of mimetic *-to*-marking. As mentioned in Section 2, many emphatic mimetics are low in iconicity, some being classified as semimimetic adverbs (e.g., *meQkiri* 'remarkably', *suQkari* 'completely').

4. Results

4.1. Observation 1: Lexical Changes

In this section, we observe the overall frequency change of mimetics in comparison with that of nonmimetic adverbials. We obtained 1,333,265 mimetic instances and 43,774,104 nonmimetic adverbial instances in total.

---

[3] Other morphological types of mimetics, such as suffixal ones, yielded a similar set of results in the following examinations.

(We excluded the results for the mimetic *haQkiri* 'clear' from all observations presented in this paper, as it showed great deviance in frequency in the corpus.) First, Figure 3 plots the two trajectories in question. Mimetics were found to have increased significantly (r = .83, p < .001), whereas the decrease of nonmimetic adverbials did not reach statistical significance (r = −.16, p = .20). The same set of analyses for the latter half of the period (1978–2011) emphasized the contrast (mimetic: r=.90, p< .001; nonmimetic: r = −.95, p< .001). A significant negative correlation was obtained between the two trajectories both in the overall data (r= −.43, p< .001) and in the latter half (r = −.89, p < .001). This result supplements Shibasaki's (2009) observation about reduplicatives, suggesting the recent replacement of nonmimetic adverbials by mimetics.

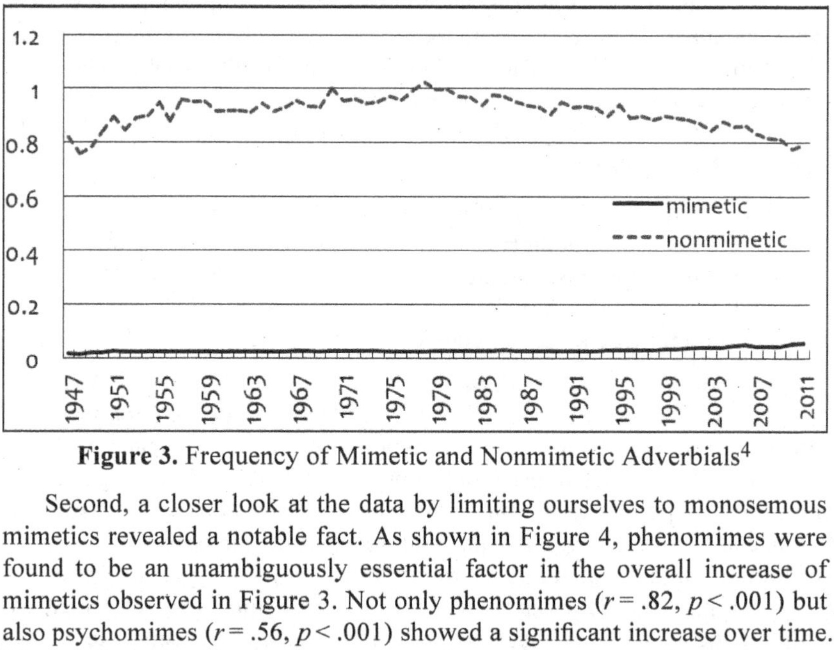

Figure 3. Frequency of Mimetic and Nonmimetic Adverbials[4]

Second, a closer look at the data by limiting ourselves to monosemous mimetics revealed a notable fact. As shown in Figure 4, phenomimes were found to be an unambiguously essential factor in the overall increase of mimetics observed in Figure 3. Not only phenomimes (r= .82, p< .001) but also psychomimes (r= .56, p< .001) showed a significant increase over time. Meanwhile, a significant decrease was observed for phonomimes (r= −.78, p<.001) and semimimetic adverbs (r=−.96, p<.001).

[4] The token frequency was divided by the number of sentences in each year, as the data size differed from year to year. The same is true for Figures 4 and 5.

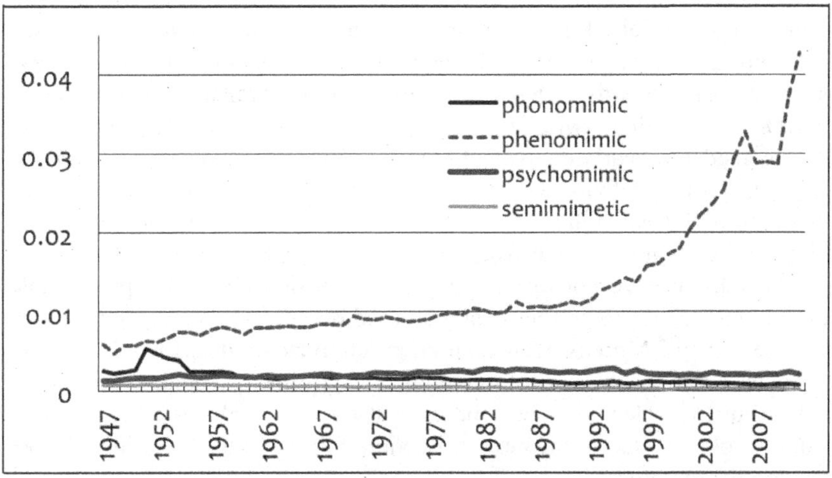

Figure 4. Frequency of the Four Semantic Types of Mimetics

Finally, another striking contribution to the increase of mimetics was found for emphatic forms ($r = .81$, $p < .001$). This result is consistent with Yamaguchi's (2002) chronology, which locates the emphatic template closest to the present. A significant but less remarkable increase was obtained for reduplicative mimetics ($r = .31$, $p < .05$), which replicates Shibasaki's (2009) results.

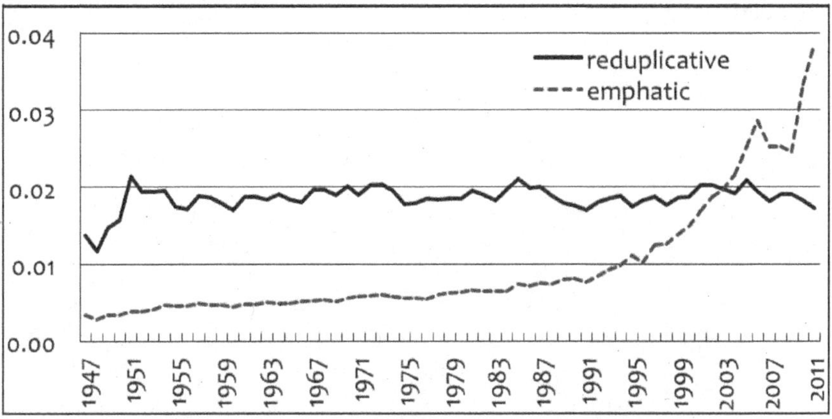

Figure 5. Frequency of the Two Morphological Types of Mimetics

In summary, the observed increase of phenomimic and emphatic adverbials, together with the decrease of semi- and nonmimetic adverbials, reminds us of the idea of lexical substitution accompanied by iconization (Section 2). In fact, we can point out some similarities between these two groups of adverbials. First, the semantic range of phenomimes (i.e., visual and textural eventualities) is relatively similar to nonmimetic manner expressions. This is why, for example, many motion-related mimetics (e.g., *burabura* 'rambling', *nyoronyoro* 'wriggling', *pyonpyon* 'hopping') are often considered nearly equivalent to manner-of-motion verbs (e.g., *ramble, wriggle, hop*) (see Ibarretxe-Antuñano 2006, among others). Second, emphatic mimetics generally lack clear iconicity, which makes them like nonmimetic (i.e., noniconic) adverbials.

Indeed, we have not reached a final conclusion about this presumable lexical change, as the present data are based on token frequency rather than type frequency.[5] Moreover, such an interpretative hypothesis would need an examination of each case of nonmimetic-by-mimetic replacement rather than a holistic calculation like the current one. Nevertheless, the morphosyntactic observation in the next subsection will tempt us to retain and even develop the hypothesis.

4.2. Observation 2: Morphosyntactic Changes

This section focuses on the morphosyntactic variations of mimetics in the MDJ. As shown by the proportional data in Figure 6, we obtained a significant increase of -*to*-marked mimetic adverbs ($r = .84$, $p < .001$) and a significant decrease of bare mimetic adverbs ($r = -.85$, $p < .001$) and mimetic verbs ($r = -.58$, $p < .001$). Interestingly, these results are almost the opposite of the earlier changes in mimetic morphosyntax observed by Kawase (2005, 2006) (see Section 2).

[5] The type frequency of each semantic type of mimetic did not show a significant diachronic change (phonomimes: $r = .15$, $p = .25$; phenomimes: $r = -.09$, $p = .47$; psychomimes: $r = -.03$, $p = .82$).

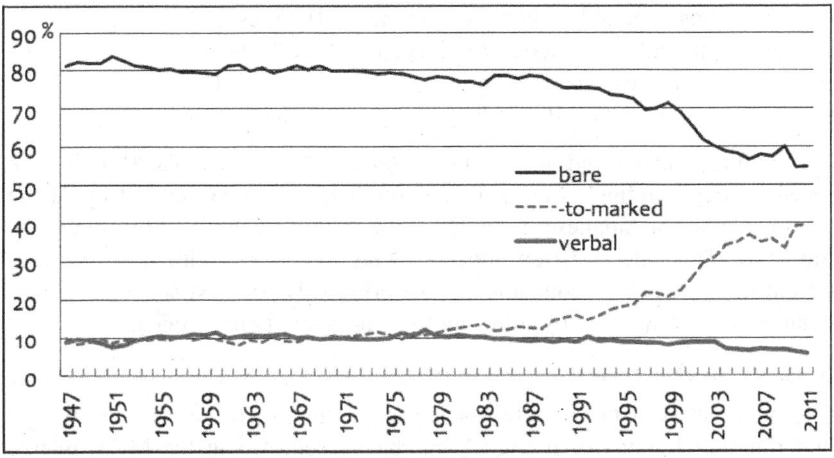

Figure 6. Frequency of the Three Morphosyntactic Types of Mimetics

Akita and Usuki (2012) and Tobishima and Oseki (2012) locate the three morphosyntactic types of mimetics on a cline of syntactic independence from, or integration into, the clause in a continuous fashion. Their proposals can be represented as in (2).

(2) Cline of Syntactic Independence of Japanese Mimetics
-to-marked > bare > verbal

The supporting data they discuss include the (in)divisibility of mimetic-verb sequences in the three realizational types. For example, as Toratani (2006) observes, *-to*-marked mimetics often occur in a position that is not adjacent to the predicate, as in *burabura-to kooen-o aruk-* (MIM-QUOT park-ACC walk) 'walk in the park ramblingly'. This is contrasted with bare mimetics, which tend to immediately precede the verb, as in *kooen-o burabura aruk-* 'walk ramblingly in the park'. Mimetic verbs exhibit a clearer pattern, disallowing an intervening phrase between the mimetic and the verb, as in **burabura kooen-o su-* 'ramble in the park' (intended).

Morphosyntactic variations of this sort have some functional correlates. Following Dingemanse's (2011:147–148) observation regarding Siwu (a Niger-Congo language), Akita (2013) reports that, in Japanese, mimetic verbs are more resistant to expressive morphology (e.g., vowel lengthening, consonantal mora augmentation, partial multiplication) than mimetic adverbs. Thus, the hierarchy in (2) can be functionally enriched by incorporating this positive correlation between syntactic independence and potential expressiveness. The revised cline in (3) is accompanied by frequency information as well.

(3) Morphosyntactic Hierarchy of Japanese Mimetics

syntactic independence:	*to*-marked	>	bare	>	verbal
expressiveness:	high		>		low
frequency in the MDJ:	increasing				decreasing

With all this in mind, we can understand the present data as showing the recent "foregrounding"—or "*re*foregrounding," if the earlier history of the morphosyntax of Japanese mimetics is taken into account—of mimetics in the MDJ. This interpretation appears to be compatible with what we suggested in Section 4.1: iconization of adverbials. In the next section, we will evaluate this conclusion by referring to some related phenomena.

5. General Discussion

The quantitative data in Section 4 led us to the conclusion that the lexical and functional status of mimetics has been promoted in the MDJ. In this section, we discuss how general this presumed diachronic change is, drawing on two sets of phenomena found around the boundary of the mimetic category: (de)mimeticization and lexical innovation.

First, many studies on many languages have reported cases of both mimeticization and demimeticization (Childs 2001:66; Kunene 2001:188; Dingemanse 2011:118; among others). (4) lists demimeticized words in Japanese, divided by their target categories.

(4) Demimeticization in Japanese (Hamano 1998:11–60; Akita 2009:74; Hamano and Sugahara forthcoming):

a. > V:
bura-tuk- 'ramble' (< *burabura* 'rambling'), *hura-tuk-* 'get dizzy' (< *hurahura* 'dizzy'), *zawa-tuk-* 'hum (of a crowd)' (< *zawazawa* 'humming'); *hata-mek-* 'flutter' (< *hatahata/patapata* 'fluttering'), *zawa-mek-* 'hum (of a crowd)' (< *zawazawa* 'humming'); *hikar-* 'shine' (< *pikapika* 'flashing'), *korogar-* 'roll' (< *korokoro* 'rolling'), *sawag-* 'hum (of a crowd)' (< *zawazawa* 'humming'), *soyog-* 'breeze' (< *soyosoyo* 'breezing'), *yurum-* 'get loose' (< *yuruyuru* 'loose')

b. > Adv (= semimimetic):
doNdoN 'rapidly' (< 'stomping'), *dosidosi* 'unreservedly' (< 'thudding'), *sorosoro* 'now, soon' (< 'quietly'), *suQkari* 'completely' (< 'refreshed' [obsolete]), *teQkiri* '(misbelieve) completely' (< 'exactly' [obsolete])

c. > A:
yuru- 'be loose' (< *yuruyuru* 'loose')

d. > N:
boro 'rag' (< *boroboro* 'ragged'), *guzu* 'dullard' (< *guzuguzu* 'peevish'), *koro* 'roller' (< *korokoro* 'rolling'), *putiputi* 'bubble wrap' [unaccented] (< *putiputi* 'popping' [initially accented]), *syabusyabu* 'shabushabu (one-pot dish)' [unaccented] (< *syabu-syabu* 'parboiling a piece of meat' [initially accented]), *waNwaN* 'doggie' [babytalk] (< *waNwaN* 'bowwow')

(5) gives mimeticization examples, classified by their source categories.

(5) Mimeticization in Japanese (Akita 2009:104–105):

a. < V:
hiyahiya/hiyaQ/hiyari/hiNyari 'thrilled, pleasantly cool' (< *hiyas-* 'make cool'), *koNgari* 'cooked lightly brown' (< *kogas-* 'scorch'), *momimomi* 'crumpling' (< *mom-* 'crumple'), *nobinobi/noNbiri* 'relaxed, slow' (< *nob-* 'extend' [archaic]), *simizimi/siNmiri* 'sentimental' (< *sim-* 'soak' [archaic]), *taNmari* 'plentiful' (< *tamar-* 'accumulate'), *ukiuki* 'lighthearted' (< *uk-* 'float'), *wakuwaku* 'excited' (< *wak-* 'spring up')

b. < A:
hoQsori 'slim' (< *hoso-* 'thin')

c. < N:
konagona 'in pieces' (< *kona* 'powder'), *moyamoya* 'hazy' (< *moya* 'haze'), *togetoge* 'prickly' (< *toge* 'prickle'), *tuyatuya* 'glossy' (< *tuya* 'luster')

Notice that it is basically impossible to prove the absence of prehistoric mimeticization preceding demimeticization or vice versa. For example, the mimetic *burabura* 'rambling', which was demimeticized to form the verb *bura-tuk-* 'ramble' in (4a), might have a nonmimetic origin. Nevertheless, it is notable that, contrary to the likely association between conventionality and semiotic arbitrariness, words may not only lose but also gain iconicity.

Second, recent studies on innovative word formation include some instances of demimeticized verbs and adjectives listed in (6a) and (6b), respectively (see also Kubozono 2002). It would be possible to list them in (4), and the distinction between (4c) and (6b), which is solely based on the difference in innovativeness and playfulness, is particularly subtle.

(6) Innovative Words with a Mimetic Root:

a. innovative verbs (Tsujimura and Davis 2011:801; Akita forthcoming):
gudar- 'become tedious' (*gudaguda* 'tedious'), *guzur-* 'be peevish' (< *guzuguzu* 'peevish'), *pakur-* 'steal' (?< *pakupaku* 'gobbling'), *tibir-* 'be stingy' (< *tibiQ/tibitibi* 'sipping')

b. Innovative adjectives (Akita, forthcoming):
boro- 'be ragged' (< *boroboro* 'ragged'), *gotu-* 'be rough' (< *gotugotu* 'rugged'), *hyoro-* 'be lanky' (< *hyorohyoro* 'lanky'), *noro-* 'be sluggish' (< *noronoro* 'sluggish'), *tyara-* 'be flashy' (< *tyaratyara* 'flashy'), *tyoro-* 'slack, easy' (< *tyorotyoro* 'trickling, scuttling')

The striking productivity of these newly grown word classes suggests the essential role of mimetics and iconicity in this innovative facet of present-day Japanese.

The discussion here allows us to conclude that language allows both directions of derivation (mimeticization/iconization and demimeticization/ deiconization), and present-day Japanese may at least partly prefer the former. This conclusion is compatible with the data presented in Section 4, where mimetics, which have a history of backgrounding, have been revitalized in the political center of Japan in the past century.

6. Conclusion

In this paper, we have argued that mimetics have been reforegrounded in the Minutes of the Diet of Japan in two ways. We first observed the slight iconization of adverbials due to the replacement of semi- and nonmimetic adverbials by phenomimic and emphatic ones. This observation was reinforced by the data of morphosyntactic foregrounding of mimetics. The idea of mimetic reforegrounding appears to be consistent with the preference for mimetic-based word creation in present-day Japanese.

There are at least two major remaining issues. First, follow-up investigations using other diachronic corpora of Japanese (and other languages) are necessary in order to see whether the present results are unique to the MDJ or apply more generally to modern Japanese. Second, we have to consider why the reforegrounding has taken place in the MDJ mimetics (or in current Japanese mimetics in general). For example, political speeches in the Diet or spoken Japanese in general may have recently become more informal. If this is true, we will also find other (extra)linguistic features that are associated with the behavioral change (e.g., the use of particular sentence-final particles, interjections, and intonations). We expect recent anthropological and psychological explorations in the pragmatics of mimetics (e.g., Nuckolls 2004, 2010; Dingemanse 2011; Akita et al. 2012) to shed some light on this challenging question.

Interdisciplinary collaborations in language sciences, let alone those in mimetic diachrony, are still in their initial phase. These multiple perspectives will doubtless lead to many fundamental improvements and developments in linguistics and, we hope, in its neighboring disciplines.

References

Akita, K. 2009. A Grammar of Sound-Symbolic Words in Japanese: Theoretical Approaches to Iconic and Lexical Properties of Mimetics. Doctoral dissertation, Kobe University.

Akita, K. 2011. A Constructionist Analysis of Emphatic Mimetics in Japanese. *KLS 31: Proceedings of the 35th Annual Meeting of the Kansai Linguistic Society*, 240–251.

Akita, K. 2013. Expressiveness of Mimetic Syntax: Quantitative Evidence from Japanese and English. Paper presented at the Grammar of Mimetics Workshop, SOAS, University of London, 10 May.

Akita, K. Forthcoming. Register-Specific Morphophonological Constructions in Japanese. *Proceedings of the Thirty-Eighth Annual Meeting of the Berkeley Linguistics Society.*

Akita, K., Nakamura, S., Komatsu, T. and Hirata, S. 2012. Onomatope no Intarakushonsei ni kansuru ryōteki kōsatsu (A Quantitative Study of the Interactional Function of Mimetics). *Proceedings of the 26th Annual Conference of the Japanese Society for Artificial Intelligence, 2012*, 2N1-OS-8c-5.

Akita, K. and Usuki, T. 2012. A Constructional Account of the Morphological Optionality of Japanese Mimetics. Ms., Osaka University and Fukuoka University.

Asano, T. 1978. *Giongo/gitaigo jiten* (A Dictionary of Japanese Mimetics). Tokyo: Kadokawa.

Childs, G. T. 2001. Research on Ideophones, Whither Hence? The Need for a Social Theory of Ideophones. *Ideophones*, ed. F. K. E. Voeltz and C. Kilian-Hatz, 63–74. Amsterdam: John Benjamins.

Dingemanse, M. 2011. The Meaning and Use of Ideophones in Siwu. Doctoral dissertation, Max Planck Institute for Psycholinguistics, Nijmegen, and Radboud University.

Hamano, S. 1998. *The Sound-Symbolic System of Japanese.* Stanford: CSLI.

Hamano, S. and Sugahara, T. Forthcoming. Identifying Mimetic Verbs in Japanese. *Proceedings of the Czuczor-Fogarasi Conference.*

Hinton, L., Nichols, J. and Ohala, J. J., eds. 1994. *Sound Symbolism.* Cambridge: Cambridge University Press.

Ibarretxe-Antuñano, I. 2006. *Sound Symbolism and Motion in Basque.* München: LINCOM Europa.

Kakehi, H., Tamori, I. and Schourup, L. 1996. *Dictionary of Iconic Expressions in Japanese*. Berlin: Mouton de Gruyter.

Kawase, S. 2005. Shōchōshi o dōshika suru keishiki no hensen (The Diachronic Change of Constructions that Verbalize Mimetics). *Gobun Kenkyū* 99:11–24.

Kawase, S. 2006. Shōchōshi no *to*-datsuraku ni tsuite no tsūjiteki kōsatsu (A Diachronic Study of *to*-Drop in Mimetics). *Gobun Kenkyū* 100/101:16–29.

Kubozono, H. 2002. *Shingo wa kōshite tsukurareru* (How to Coin a Word). Tokyo: Iwanami Shoten.

Kunene, D. P. 2001. Speaking the Act: The Ideophone as a Linguistic Rebel. *Ideophones*, ed. F. K. E. Voeltz and C. Kilian-Hatz, 183–192. Amsterdam: John Benjamins.

Martin, S. E. 1975. *A Reference Grammar of Japanese*. New Haven: Yale University Press.

Matsuda, K. 2000. Tōkyō hōgen kakuzyosi *o* no shiyō ni kakawaru gengoteki shoyōin no sūryōteki kenshō (A Quantitative Examination of the Linguistic Factors in the Use of the Case Particle *o* in the Tokyo Dialect). *Studies in the Japanese Language* 201:61–76.

Matsuda, K. 2004. Gengo shiryō to shite no kokkai kaigiroku kensaku shisutemu (The On-Line Full-Text Database of the Minutes of the Diet: Its Potentials and Limitations). *Theoretical and Applied Linguistics at Kobe Shoin* 7:1–28.

Matsuda, K. 2008. *Kokkai kaigiroku o tsukatta Nihongo kenkyū* (Studies in Japanese Linguistics Using the Minutes of the Diet). Tokyo: Hituzi Syobo.

Nakamura, S., Hirata, S. and Akita, K. 2012. Kokkai gijiroku kōpasu o mochiita onomatope no tsūjiteki bunseki (A Diachronic Analysis of Onomatopoeia in the Diet Record). *Proceedings of the 26th Annual Conference of the Japanese Society for Artificial Intelligence, 2012*, 1M1-OS-8a-7.

Nambu, S. 2007. Teiryōteki bunseki ni motozuku *ga/no*-kōtai saikō (Reconsideration of *ga/no* Conversion Based on a Quantitative Analysis). *Gengo Kenkyū* 131:115–149.

Nasu, A. 2002. Nihongo onomatope no gokeisei to inritsu kōzō (Word Formation and Prosodic Structure). Doctoral dissertation, University of Tsukuba.

Nitta, Y. 2002. *Fukushiteki hyōgen no shosō* (Aspects of Adverbial Expressions). Tokyo: Kurosio.

Nuckolls, J. B. 2004. To Be or Not to Be Ideophonically Impoverished. *Texas Linguistic Forum* 47 (*Proceedings of the Eleventh Annual Symposium about Language and Society*): 131–142.

Nuckolls, J. B. 2010. *Lessons from a Quechua Strongwoman: Ideophony, Dialogue and Perspective*. Tucson: University of Arizona Press.

Shibasaki, R. 2009. Semantic Constraints on the Diachronic Productivity of Japanese Reduplication. *Grazer Linguistische Studien* 71:79–98.

Suzuki, M. 1965. Mukashi no giseigo/gitaigo (Mimetics in the Old Days). *Gengo Seikatsu* 171:60–65.

Tamori, I. and Schourup, L. 1999. *Onomatope: Keitai to imi* (Onomatopoeia: Its Form and Meaning). Tokyo: Kurosio.

Tobishima, M. and Oseki, Y. 2012. Onshōchō/ruishōteki imi to tōgo kōzō no intāfeisu (The Interface between Sound-Symbolic/Iconic Meaning and Syntactic Structure). *Handbook of the 144th Semiannual Meeting of the Linguistic Society of Japan*, 80–85.

Toratani, K. 2006. On the Optionality of *to*-Marking on Reduplicated Mimetics in Japanese. *Japanese/Korean Linguistics 14*, ed. T. J. Vance and K. Jones, 415–422. Stanford: CSLI.

Tsujimura, N. and Davis, S. 2011. A Construction Approach to Innovative Verbs in Japanese. *Cognitive Linguistics* 22:799–825.

Yamaguchi, N. 2002. *Inu wa* biyo *to naite ita* (Dogs Used to Cry *biyo*). Tokyo: Kōbunsha.

Part IV

Discourse

Territories of Thought in Korean Conversation

MARY SHIN KIM
University of Hawai'i at Mānoa

1. Introduction

Reported thought, whereby people quote their own thoughts or those of others, has received insufficient attention compared to reported speech. Studies often do not differentiate between reported speech and reported thought, or treat reported thought as a subcategory of reported speech. Studies on these topics in Korean are no different (Yi 1995; Suh 1996; Nam 2001). Moreover, few studies provide interactional accounts of reported thought (exceptions are Barnes and Moss 2007; Couper-Kuhlen 2007; Haakana 2007; Vásquez and Urzúa 2009), in contrast to the large number of studies that examine the interactional role of reported speech in storytelling (Labov 1972; Mayes 1990; Holt 2000), institutional talk (Clayman 2007; Galatolo 2007), and non-narrative contexts (Clift 2007; Couper-Kuhlen 2007; Wu 2012).[1]

[1] Direct reported speech often occurs in the delivery of the climax or punch line of stories to add dramatic effect, thereby allowing the recipients of the stories to assess the stories on their own (Labov 1972; Holt 2000). In addition, direct reported speech often occurs in non-narrative contexts when making assessments (Clift 2007; Couper-Kuhlen 2007), constructing complaints

Japanese/Korean Linguistics 22.
Edited by Mikio Giriko, Naonori Nagaya, Akiko Takemura, and Timothy J. Vance.

Reported thought is similar to, yet still quite distinct from, reported speech. Both reported speech and reported thought provide access to and evidence of a prior event or situation in an effective and economic way (Holt 1996, 2000), reenacting what was said/thought and how it was said/thought at the time. However, reported thought brings another layer of complexity into interaction. According to Haakana (2007), while reported speech represents the surface of the interaction, reported thought shows the process underneath the surface of the interaction—what was thought but not said by the speaker. Hence, a speaker routinely uses reported thought to convey his/her silent criticism of a moment in a past interaction. Couper-Kuhlen's study (2007) reveals that reported thought is frequently deployed when the speaker provides an account for a dispreferred or disaffiliative action that s/he performed. In other words, reported thought justifies why the speaker took or did not take a certain action. A similar observation is made in Barnes and Moss's study (2007), which shows that reported thought serves as a resource for handling rational accountability in explicating actions and events. Vásquez and Urzúa's study (2009) further illustrates how reported speech and reported thought play different roles in constructing identities of novice teachers during mentoring sessions. Using reported speech, teachers represent themselves as competent and resourceful professionals, whereas using reported thought they depict themselves as insecure and unskilled novice teachers. These observations, whether based on naturally occurring conversational data or institutional talk, illustrate the distinct characteristics that separate reported thought from reported speech.

This study will illustrate an additional important use of reported thought observed in Korean conversation, in particular in non-narrative contexts. Reported thought occurs in conversation when the speaker enacts hypothetical thoughts of others. In such cases, the speaker constructs an utterance as reported thought without a framing device. Explicit syntactic framing devices, such as the reporting verb *think*, are not suitable for reporting thoughts of others that have not actually occurred. Instead, the speaker fades in and out of reported thought through different means and resources, such as prosody, interjections, deictics (spatial, referential, temporal), verb tense, certain sentence-enders, gaze, facial expressions (Holt 1996, 2000; Bolden 2004; Sidnell 2006), and more. It will also be shown that, in Korean, the *see* verb *po-ta* plays an essential role in setting up a hypothetical scene where someone's thought emerges. This flexible design of reported thought makes it possible for the speaker to cross over into the territory of others' thoughts

(Holt 2000), or providing accounts for dispreferred actions (Couper-Kuhlen 2007). Direct reported speech is also used by journalists to speak on behalf of the public in news interviews (Clayman 2007).

and enact a hypothetical thought on behalf of another speaker. By enacting a hypothetical thought on behalf of others, the current speaker interweaves his/her own voice with that speaker's and carries out socially and interactionally delicate actions, such as imposing or urging his or her view on another speaker.

Overall, this paper aims to contribute to the study of reported thought, which has been so far mainly focused on English (Barnes and Moss 2007; Couper-Kuhlen 2007; Vásquez and Urzúa 2009), by explicating the additional complexity and diversity of reported thoughts observed in Korean conversations.

2. Data and Methodology

For this study, 21 cases of hypothetical reported thought found in five ordinary telephone conversations and four video-recorded face-to-face Korean conversations were examined. The participants are native speakers of Korean who are friends, family members, or well-known acquaintances. The telephone conversations come from the *Korean Telephone Conversations Speech* corpus data from the Linguistic Data Consortium (Ko et al. 2003). Each conversation lasts 30 minutes. The face-to-face conversational data come from the author's personal collection of recordings of ordinary Korean conversations. Each of these conversations is approximately one hour long. This study focuses on examining the composition and position of reported thought using a conversation analytic approach: how reported thought is designed and in what interactional and sequential environments it occurs.

3. Design Features of Korean Reported Thought

While English is known to have left-side boundaries (Sidnell 2006), so that reporting frame devices occur before the quote (e.g., *She said/I thought* + Quote), Korean is known to have right-side boundaries (Park 2009), with reporting frame devices occurring after the quote. In Korean, reported thought can be grammatically constructed in the same way as reported speech using the following quotative construction (Yi 1995; Suh 1996).

[quoted speaker] + [quoted message] + [*hako/lako* (quotative marker) + quoting verb (*say* or *think*)]

(1) [*na-nun*] *mia-hanthey* [*wa tep-ta*] [*hako/lako malhay-ss-ta.*]
I-TOP NAME-to wow hot-DC QT say-PST-DC
I said to Mia, 'Wow, it's hot.'

(2) [*na-nun*] *honcase* [*wa* *tep-ta*] [*hako/lako sayngkakhay-ss-ta.*]
I-TOP alone wow hot-DC QT think-PST-DC
I thought to myself, 'Wow, it's hot.'

One of the reasons that reported thought has been subsumed under reported speech and has not received much examination as a separate entity is that similar or identical grammatical constructions are used for reported speech and reported thought (Haakana 2007). However, analyses of naturally occurring Korean conversational data show that an explicit reported thought framing device, such as *-hako/lako sayngkakha-ta* (Quotative marker + 'think' verb) 'I thought (that)', is not necessarily required or always used in Korean conversations.

The following segments will show instances of reported thoughts in interactions wherein the speaker first invokes the scene/setting in which the reported thought occurred and then reenacts the thought triggered at that moment. In such cases, reported thought, particularly direct reported thought, is often delivered without any reporting frame; this has been called the *zero quotative* (Romaine and Lange 1991; Mathis and Yule 1994). But how does the speaker design reported thought and mark the boundaries between the current speaker's talk and the reported thought without any syntactic framing devices? Participants can identify the boundaries of reported thought as they do in direct reported speech, with the following cues: changes in prosody, pauses, interjections, deictics (spatial, referential, temporal), verb tense, discourse particles, gaze, and facial expressions (Holt 1996, 2000; Bolden 2004; Sidnell 2006).

(3) Ko 6783
01 B: *tch solcikhi* *tch mwe* *kunyang--* (.) *kulehkey* *kulehkey-kkaci*
tch honestly tch DM just like:that like:that-until
02 *mwe* *celsilhakey-nun* *an* *nukkye-ss-tay-yo*[::?
DM acutely-TOP not feel-PST-HEARSAY-POL
(My husband) said, tch, honestly, tch, he did not fully realize that (I was pregnant).
03 A: [*yey* *yey*
Yeah, yeah.
04 B: *kuntey* *choumpha-lul* <u>*ttak*</u> ***po-nikka,***
but ultrasound-ACC just see-when
But, just when (he) saw the ultrasound,
05 A: [*ung*]
uh huh
06 B: [°*Ha:*°] *cincca ce* *pay* *sok-ey* *ayki-ka* *iss-kwuna::.*
ah really that belly inside-in baby-NOM exist-UNASSIM
(he thought) 'Ah:, there is really a baby inside that belly::.'

07 A: *kuleh-cyo.*
right-COMM:POL
Right.

In this segment, the speaker (B) tells her friend (A) that her husband realized that she was pregnant only after seeing the ultrasound image of the baby. In lines 4 and 6, B replays her husband's thoughts when he saw the baby. Here, although the English translation includes the reporting frame device *he thought* in line 6, 'he thought' was not verbalized in Korean. Instead, various components display that the speaker is enacting her husband's thought in the past moment. The use of the interjection *Ha* 'ah' and the deictic *ce* 'that' authenticate the original reported speaker's inner voice from a there-and-then perspective (Holt 1996; Couper-Kuhlen 2007). The present tense sentence-ending suffix -*kwuna*, which is used in conveying newly perceived information on the speaker's part (Lee 1991), also anchors the utterance to the original reported situation when the husband saw the baby.[2] The retention of the original prosody also demonstrates the speaker's reenacting mode (Holt 1996). The speaker stretches the sound of several words as she replays the husband's inner thoughts, as the transcription shows with colons (:) indicating a prolonged sound.

Furthermore, here the verb *see* in line 4 sets up the scene or context of a prior situation when the husband witnessed the baby, thereby indexing the shift of the speaker's viewpoint from here-and-now to there-and-then when the husband perceived the situation being described. By using the verb *see*, the speaker invokes the whole setting or context in which the thought was triggered in the first place. The verb *see* has a strong tie with reported thought as seeing triggers one's thinking process.[3] Hence, English *see* and Korean *po-ta* 'see' carry the meaning of 'to think' or 'to consider', as shown in (4)–(6).

---

[2] This sentence-ending suffix is frequently observed in reported thought as it conveys the speaker's immediate reaction to an event or situation at the time of his/her perception.

[3] The verb *po-ta* 'see' also has strong ties with reported speech. According to Sohn (2012: 107), the verb *po-ta* initially represented physically looking at someone while speaking, as in (a), but later developed into a particle to mark the goal or indirect object, as in (b) and (c).

(a) *Yongho-nun Mia-lul* ***po-ko*** *papo-la-ko hay-ss-e-yo.*
NAME-TOP NAME-ACC see-and fool-be:DC-QT say-PST-IE-POL
Youngho looked at Mia and said she is a fool.

(b) *Yongho-nun Mia-**poko*** *papo-la-ko hay-ss-e-yo.*
NAME-TOP NAME-to fool-be:DC-QT say-PST-IE-POL
Youngho said to Mia that she is a fool.

(c) *Yongho-nun Mia-**poko/lul*** *papo-la-ko hay-ss-e-yo.*
NAME-TOP NAME-to/ACC fool-be:DC–QT say-PST-IE-POL
Youngho called Mia a fool.

(4) I do not see the matter that way.

(5) *na-nun* *ku* *salam* *chakha-key* *pwa-ss-nuntey.*
I-TOP that person be:good-AD see-PST-CIRCUM
I saw him as a good person.

(6) *nay-ka* *po-ki-ey* *ku* *salam-un* *chakhay.*
I-NOM see-NML-in that person-TOP be:good:IE
In my view, he is a good person.

This function of the verb *see* makes it possible for the speaker to report another speaker's prior thoughts, as seen in (3), and enact the hypothetical thoughts of another speaker in an imaginary context, as shown below in (7). A variant form of the verb *po-ta*, *cikhyepo-ta* 'observe', is used in this segment.

(7) Marriage
08 Y: *ku(liko)* *ttak* ***cikhyepwa-se*** *ssu::* *cokos-i*
and exactly observe-and ah that:thing-NOM
09 *hayngtongha-nun* *kes-i* *ttoltoolha--* *ttolttolha-nci,*
behave-RL thing-NOM smart smart-whether
And, observe (the guy) keenly and (think), 'Ah::, is that one smart-?' whether (he) is smart.

Here, the current speaker provides advice to his female friend on what kind of man she should date. Rather than providing direct advice, he uses reported thought as a means of providing his piece of advice. By using the verb *cikhyepo-ta* 'observe', the current speaker sets up a hypothetical scene where his friend observes a man, and then he enacts certain thoughts on her behalf. As such, the verb *see* makes it possible for the speaker to make his/her thoughts visible to others, and at the same time, make others' thoughts accessible to him/herself.

According to Couper-Kuhlen (2007), an explicit framing device is typically used when the speaker is reporting his/her thoughts in non-narrative contexts in English conversation. However, as shown above, in Korean, sometimes explicit framing devices are not used in non-narrative contexts.

4. Enacting Hypothetical Thoughts on Behalf of Others

This section will discuss the sequential and interactional environments wherein speakers enact hypothetical thoughts on behalf of others for various actions. The following example is from a face-to-face conversation among three interlocutors discussing a documentary on a child genius.

(8) A child genius

01 Y: *ya ne sangwu sangwu: kuke-l* <u>*kkok*</u> *pwa-ya tway.*
wow you NAME NAME that-ACC surely see-NECESS become:IE
Wow, you have to see Sangwoo, Sangwoo's (brilliance).

02 *tch sangwu-nun cincca han pen* [(*pw-aya tway*).
tch NAME-TOP really one time see-NECESS become:IE
Tch, (you) really have to see Sangwoo (at least) once.

03 J: [*po-myen-un chwungkyek pat-ase*
see-then-TOP shock get-because
If (you) see (him), (you) will be shocked,

04 [*kongpwuha-key toy-l ke-yey-yo.*
study-AD become-RL thing-be-POL
it will make you study.

05 Y: [*han pen cincca chwungkyek-ul* <u>*pat*</u>*-aya hay.*
one time really shock-ACC get-NECESS do:IE
(You) really need to <u>be shocked</u> once.

06 J: [*ah cincca chungkyek* <u>*khukey*</u> *pat--*
Ah really shock much get
Ah, it will really shock-.

07 K: [*hh na-poko chwungkyek h pat-ula-ko* [*toy-l il(h)-iey-yo? hh*
I-to shock get-IMP-QT becomes-RL thing-be-POL
Hh Will getting me shocked h change anything? hh

08 J: [*hh hh ani-*
hhhh DM
Hh hh, what (I) mean is, . . .

09 Y: *ANi: chencay-la kule-myen kam-i cal an o-**canh**-a:.*
DM genius-DC say-then feeling-NOM well not come-you:know-IE
What (I) mean is, when (someone) says (the kid is) a genius, (we) don't really get the picture, right.
((Lines omitted. Y explains people's general perception of a genius.))

16 Y: *kunyang kam-i cal an o-**canh**-a:.*
just feeling-NOM well not come-you:know-IE
(We) don't get a good sense, right.

17 >*kunyang kule-nka pota ha-**canh**-a.*<
just be:so-whether appear do-you:know-IE
>(We) just think (he is smart), right.<

18 J: [( )

19 Y: [*kuntey,* <u>*sangwoo*</u> ***po-myen, WA::chencay-ka cincca ilen ke-kwuna***
but NAME see-if wow genius-NOM really this thing-UNASSIM
But, if (you) see Sangwoo, 'WOW::, this is what a genius is like',

20 (.) *a-n-ta-nikka*
know-IMPFV-DC-so
(you) will know.
21 K: *kulem ettehkey hay-ya toy-nun ke-ya wuli?*
then how do-NECESS become-RL thing-be:IE we
Then, what do we do?
22 Y: [*kunikka pwa:.*
so watch:IE
So, (just) watch it.
23 J: [*wuli-nun wulli-uy kil-ul yelsimhi tto hay-ya-cyo.*
we-TOP we-of road-ACC diligently again do-must-COMM:POL
We just have to diligently go about our way.

Y watched a documentary about a child genius named Sangwoo on television and urges K to watch the show (lines 1–2). J, who had also seen the show, indirectly suggests that K watch the show as she describes its possible impact on K (lines 3–4, 6): it will shock him and make him study. Furthermore, Y claims that K needs a shock (line 5). However, K challenges the suggestion by questioning its impact on him (line 7: 'Hhh Will getting me shocked hh change anything? hh'). Although K laughs while delivering his utterance, as the transcript shows with *hh*, this rhetorical question shows that he is somewhat offended by Y and K's suggestion, which implies that K needs to change.[4] Thus, in the following turns (lines 8–9), J and Y both begin their utterances with the discourse particle *ani* (Kim 2013), which serves to treat such a response on K's part as inadequate and to block K's challenge.

Furthermore, note how Y attempts to redirect the focus of the talk to the documentary and persuade K to watch the show by highlighting the special nature of the child. First, Y elicits K's alignment about most people's general perception of geniuses—that people just think they are smart and that's it. The repeated use of the *-canh* suffix, which can be translated as 'you know' or 'right', in lines 9 and 16–17, shows that Y considers this perception to be a shared stance that others easily identify with (Kawanishi and Sohn 1993; Lee 1999). Then, Y contrasts this general perception with a perception of Sangwoo in line 19, which begins with *kuntey* 'but', a contrastive discourse marker. Y first sets up a hypothetical scene where K sees the boy, using the verb *po-ta* 'see' ('if [you] see Sangwoo'), and then, he enacts what and how K will think when he sees the child—that K will un-

[4] Koshik's study (2005) shows that rhetorical questions, which are designed to convey assertions rather than seek new information, are used to perform social actions such as complaints, accusations, and challenges to prior turns. This is also the case in Extract (8) line 7, wherein K's rhetorical question challenges Y and J's suggestion.

derstand what a real genius is truly like ('WOW::, this is what a genius is like.').[5] This reported thought allows Y to think on behalf of K, about something K has yet to witness, and in particular that K has refused to see. This hypothetical thought enables K to have a secondhand experience and indirectly perceive the matter for himself. Note how in response K does not further challenge Y. In line 21, K begins his utterance with *kulem* 'then', granting Y's claim about how special the child is and moving on to ask a different question.

The following segment shows a similar case of a speaker reporting a hypothetical thought on behalf of another speaker in an effort to persuade her.

(9) Ko 6613

01 B: *na-nu::n* (0.5) *ung? na-n banquet-ul manhi haypwase al-ketun?*
I-TOP huh I-TOP -ACC many try know-CORREL
I:: (0.5) huh? I have been to many banquets, you know.

02 A: ° *ung* °
Yeah

03 B: *ne kathun ay-ka wa-ya:,*
you like kid-NOM come-only:if

04 *i phathi pwunwiki-ka cwuk-ketun. HH[hh*
this party ambience-NOM die-CORREL
Someone like you has to come to the party to
spoil the party's ambience HHhh

05 A: *[hhh*
hhh

06 B: *kukey ani-ko sal-ketun::*
that:NOM not:be-and live-CORREL
I mean, to save (the party's ambience).

07 *kulenikka aha: nay-ka ku kuliko elma-- nay-ka tto*
so ah I-NOM that and how I-NOM again

08 *elmana mesisskey ha-ko o-keyss-nya?*
how:much stylish do-and come-must-INTERR
So, ah: imagine how, how stylish I, I would look coming (for the party).

09 *kitay an toy-nya?*
expectation not become-INTERR
Aren't you excited (about it)?

10 (0.5)

---

[5] In line 19, various features, such as an interjection (WA:: 'WOW::'), a spatial deictic (*ilen* 'like this'), and the present tense sentence-ending suffix *-kwuna* suggest that the speaker is directly reporting a thought.

11 B: *emchengnakey mesisskey ha-ko o-keyss-ci.*
tremendously stylish do-and come-must-COMM
(I) will come looking tremendously stylish, you know.

12 A: *ehwu cham*
oh:boy geez
Oh boy, geez

13 B: *kuke-l po-nun ne-nun*
that-ACC see-RL you-TOP

14 ↑*HE:* ((in-breath)) *ni-ka [ilen myen-i iss-ta-ni¿*
you-NOM such side-NOM have-DC-DET
You who see me like that will (think)'↑HE: (I) can't believe there is such a side to you¿'

15 A: *[hhhh*
hhhh

16 B: *i[le-myense tto.*
like:this-while again
(you) will be like.

17 A: *[meli-nun ettehkey tway-ss-nya?*
hair-TOP how become-PST-INTERR
What happened to your hair?

18 B: *mwe?*
What?

19 A: *meli.*
hair.

20 B: *meli mwe. hhh yengkwu meli-ci.*
hair DM NAME hair-COMM
Hair, hhh it's like Youngkoo's hair style.

Prior to this segment, B invited A to his school's festival, but A indicated that it was unlikely she could go because her school is also having a party on the same day. In response, B attempts to persuade A by providing several reasons why A should come to his school party. First, B claims that A's presence will make a vital difference to his school party, thereby indirectly complimenting her (lines 1, 3–4, 6). However, A only responds with laughter (line 5) and delays her response. Next, B indirectly compliments himself as he urges A to imagine how stylish he will look for the party (lines 7–8). B requests A to confirm that she is looking forward to B's party look (line 9), but A does not show any response, and silence occurs in line 10, which projects a dispreferred response (Pomerantz 1984; Schegloff 2007). Then, note how B enacts a hypothetical thought on behalf of A at this critical interactional juncture. He demonstrates how A would feel if she did get to see B at the party (lines 13–14).

Here again the speaker uses the verb *po-ta* 'see' to set up a hypothetical scene where A witnesses B's look (*kuke-l po-nun ne-nun* 'You who see me like that (will),'), and then enacts A's response. B enacts A's surprise not only through her words, but also through an imaginative loud in-breath *HE:* delivered with a sharp rise in pitch (indicated by ↑) which demonstrates A's astonishment at B's look. This hypothetical thought accomplishes important actions. First, through reported thought, B offers A a glimpse of what she will get to see at the party, which may motivate her to attend. Additionally, through enacting another's voice, B indirectly praises himself. A recent study by Wu (2012) shows that in Chinese conversation, two reporting practices, reporting another's words and reporting just the facts, serve as resources for the speaker to tacitly praise him/herself. Here, B praises himself through reporting A's inner voice. This self-praising enactment of B's immediately elicits laughter from A in line 15.

As shown in excerpts (8) and (9), a speaker can enact a hypothetical thought on behalf of others to demonstrate a claim, and thereby persuade others, who display disaffiliation, to accept the speaker's suggestion or invitation. However, it is up to the recipient whether s/he accepts the speaker's action. In extract (9), the recipient continues to avoid providing an answer to the speaker's invitation, and instead diverts attention to a different topic: B's hairstyle (line 17).

The following segment shows a case where the speaker's hypothetical thought receives alignment from the recipient.

(10) Korean church

01 E: *kuntey nay-ka po-nikka: hanin kuke-lul hana talaya-keyss-e.*
but I-NOM see-and Korean that-ACC one hang-should-IE
But, in my view, (they) should hang a Korean (sign board).

02 *keki-se phallosupetisu-ka kakkap-tamyense-yo¿*
there-from Palos Verdes-NOM close-HEARSAY-POL
(The church) is close to Palos Verdes, I hear, isn't it true?

03 S: [*ung.*]
Yeah.

04 E: [*kulikwu*] *hankwuk salam-i manhi sa-n-ta-kwu*[:::]
and Korean people-NOM many live-IMPFV-DC-QT
And, many Koreans live (there).

05 S: [*um*]
mm

06 E: *ka-mye o-mye ilekhey--*
go-and come-and like:this
(You) come and go like this, and
((Eun looks up pretending to see a sign board in front of her.))

07 *hanin mwusun kyohoy* (.) *ile-myen-un,*
Korean what church like:this-then-TOP
if it says that it's some kind of Korean church,
08 *ah:: ceki kapwaya-keyss-ta:. atamha-ko coh-ta::.*
ah there go-should-DC small-and good-DC
'Ah:: (I) should pay a visit there:. It's small and ni::ce.'
09 S: *ku [yayki-l ha-sy-ess-e?]*
that talk-ACC do-SH-PST-IE
Did (you) tell (them) that?
10 E: *[na-n tto kyohoy-ka khu-myen] silh--*
I-TOP again church-NOM big-if dislike
I don't like it if the church is too big.
11 *e ku soli-l hay-ss-ketun:.*
yes that sound-ACC do-PST-CORREL
Yes, (I) told (them) that.
12 S: < *e cal ha-sy-ess-e. ung*
yeah well do-SH-PST-IE yeah
< Yeah, well done, yeah.
13 E: *caki-ney-to ha-llyeko kule-n-[ta-kwu.*
oneself-PL-also do-intend:to like:that-IMPFV-DC-QT
(They) said they themselves are intending to do it.
14 S: *[mac-ass-e cinaka-myense::¿*
correct-PST-IE pass:by-while
(You're) right, while (people are) passing by (they will think so).
15 E: *ku-- ku-chi.*
be:so be:so-COMM
Ri- Right.

This segment comes from a conversation between two female relatives talking about another relative who runs a Korean church in Southern California. Eun, who recently visited the church, tells Soo about her suggestion to have a Korean signboard for the church to attract more Koreans (line 1). After providing an account for her suggestion (lines 2, 4), Eun demonstrates her suggestion in a hypothetical situation where she puts herself in the shoes of a stranger, a third party, who sees the Korean signboard while happening to pass by, and produces the thoughts of this character (lines 6–8 'Ah:: (I) should pay a visit there. It's small and nice.'). Although Eun does not use the verb *see*, she enacts a hypothetical scene where strangers walk by and observe the Korean signboard (lines 6–7). This demonstration is effective in eliciting the recipient's response of putting herself in the same situation and taking the same view. Moreover, this enactment of a third party's thoughts is convincing enough for the recipient to draw the same conclusion as the speaker because the speaker and the recipient, both of whom have personal ties with the church owner, can pretend to be strangers and see the matter from a more objective point of view. Subsequently, Eun's suggestion successfully receives alignment from Soo (lines 9, 12, 14).

Excerpt (11) illustrates an instance where the speaker utilizes reported thought to impose his view of another participant's private matters on that participant.

(11) Marriage (a longer sequence that includes excerpt 7)
01 Y: *yelekaci-ka* *mac-aya* *tway.*
many:things-NOM match-NECESS become:IE
There are many other things that need to match.
02 F: *ku[-chyo?*
be:so-COMM:POL
Right?
03 Y: *[sengkyek-to* *mac-aya* *toy-ko*
personality-also match-NECESS become-and
Personality has to match, and
04 F: *<mal-i* *thonghay-ya* *toy-kwu:,*
word-NOM connect-NECESS become-and
<(One) needs to speak the same language.
05 Y: *mal-i* *thonghay-ya* *toy-kwu* *[ku:* *yelekaci-lo*
word-NOM connect-NECESS become-and that many:things-in
(One) needs to speak the same language, and in many ways,
06 F: *[saynghwalphaytten-to* *pisushay-ya* *toy-ko.*
lifestyle-also similar-NECESS become-and
(one's) lifestyle needs to be similar, and
07 Y: *saynghwalphaythen-to* *kuleh-kwu:,*
lifestyle-also be:so-and
(one's) lifestyle also (needs to be similar), and
((In line 08, Y squints his eyes and tilts his head to the side.))
08 Y: *ku(liko)* *ttak* ***cikhyepwa-se*** *ssu::* *cokos-i*
and exactly observe-and ah that:thing-NOM
09 *hayngtongha-nun* *kes-i* *ttoltoolha--* *ttolttolha-nci,*
behave-RL thing-NOM smart smart-whether
And, observe (the guy) keenly and (think), 'Ah::, is that one smart-?' whether (he) is smart.
10 F: *[HHhh hhh hhh*
HHhh hhh hhh
11 W: *[hhh hh hh*
hhh hh hh

12 F: *WULi emma-ka ha-nun mal-ilang [ttokkath-ay.*
our mom-NOM say-RL word-with same-IE
(Those) are just like MY mom's words.

13 Y: *[kulen key cwungyo-- e. cwungyohay.*
such thing:NOM important yeah important:IE
Those things are important. Yeah, (they are) important.

In this segment, Y provides advice on the kind of man F should meet. Note how Y advises her to judge whether the man is smart or not. In lines 8–9, Y first sets up a scene where F observes a man, using the word *cikhyepo-ta* 'observe' (a variant of the verb *po-ta* 'see'), and makes a 'thinking' face, his head tilted and eyes squinted. Then, Y enacts a thought on behalf of F ('and (think), "Ah::, is that one smart?"'). Y's word choice of *cokos* 'that thing' to refer to a man illustrates how he imposes on F a view of a man as an item that needs detailed examination. Note how this advice from Y, delivered through reported thought, contrasts with his earlier pieces of advice, which were directly explicated in lines 1, 3, 5, 7, on meeting a man who speaks the same language and shares a similar personality and lifestyle. When the speaker imposes a potentially controversial view on F, he manages to have it done through F's inner voice. It is interesting that F validates Y's hypothetical thought, as she identifies it as the same as her mother's words in line 12. As this segment illustrates, reported thought does not simply function to reflect isolated private thoughts of an individual in a past moment, but can also serve as a resource for interweaving the voices of multiple speakers across different time settings.

5. Conclusion

A close examination of Korean reported thought in conversation demonstrates that the speaker's design of reported thought can vary, and that the varied designs correspond to the different functions they accomplish as well as the different sequential positions in which they occur in interactions. This study examined cases wherein speakers enact hypothetical thoughts on behalf of others in interactions. In such cases, instead of using a reporting framing device, the speaker fades in and out of reported thought using various means and resources. With the flexible design of reported thought, the current speaker readily steps into the territory of others' thoughts and subtly carries out socially and interactionally delicate actions, including providing a secondhand experience, praising oneself, and imposing an opinion on another speaker. The findings of this study again confirm the importance of further examining reported thought as a separate entity from reported speech. Various uses of reported thought with different designs remain to be examined further in interaction.

References

Barnes, R. and D. Moss. 2007. Communicating and Feeling: The Social Organization of 'Private Thoughts'. *Discourse Studies* 9:123–148.

Bolden, G. 2004. The Quote and Beyond: Defining Boundaries of Reported Speech in Conversational Russian. *Journal of Pragmatics* 36:1071–1118.

Clayman, S. 2007. Speaking on behalf of the Public in Broadcast News Interviews. *Reporting Talk: Reported Speech in Interaction*, ed. E. Holt and R. Clift, 221–243. Cambridge: Cambridge University Press.

Clift, R. 2007. Getting There First: Non-Narrative Reported Speech in Interaction. *Reporting Talk: Reported Speech in Interaction*, ed. E. Holt and R. Clift, 120–149. Cambridge: Cambridge University Press.

Couper-Kuhlen, E. 2007. Assessing and Accounting. *Reporting Talk: Reported Speech in Interaction*, ed. E. Holt and R. Clift, 81–119. Cambridge: Cambridge University Press.

Galatolo, R. 2007. Active Voicing in Court. *Reporting Talk: Reported Speech in Interaction*, ed. E. Holt and R. Clift, 195–220 Cambridge: Cambridge University Press.

Haakana, M. 2007. Reported Thought in Complaint Stories. *Reporting Talk: Reported Speech in Interaction*, ed. E. Holt and R. Clift, 150–178. Cambridge: Cambridge University Press.

Holt, E. 1996. Reporting on Talk: The Use of Direct Reported Speech in Conversation. *Research on Language and Social Interaction* 29:219–245.

Holt, E. 2000. Reporting and Reacting: Concurrent Responses to Reported Speech. *Research on Language and Social Interaction* 33:425–454.

Kawanishi, Y. and Sohn, S. O. 1993. Grammaticalization of Korean Negation: A Semantic-Pragmatic Analysis of *-canh-a(yo)*. *Harvard Studies in Korean Linguistics* 5:552–561.

Kim, H. R. S. 2013. *Ani* 'No'-Prefaced Response to WH Questions as Challenges in Korean Conversation. In *Japanese/Korean Linguistics 20*, ed. B. Frellesvig and P. Sells, 383–398. Stanford: CSLI.

Ko, E., Han, N., Caravan, A. and Zipperlen, G. 2003. *Korean Telephone Conversations Speech*. Philadelphia: Linguistic Data Consortium.

Koshik, I. 2005. *Beyond Rhetorical Questions: Assertive Questions in Everyday Interaction*. Amsterdam: John Benjamins.

Labov, W. 1972. *Language in the Inner City*. Philadelphia: University of Pennsylvania Press.

Lee, H. S. 1991. Tense, Aspect, and Modality: A Discourse-Pragmatic Analysis of Verbal Affixes in Korean from a Typological Perspective. Doctoral dissertation, University of California, Los Angeles.

Lee, H. S. 1999. A Discourse-Pragmatic Analysis of the Committal *-ci* in Korean: A Synthetic Approach to the Form-Meaning Relation. *Journal of Pragmatics* 31: 243–275.

Mathis, T. and Yule, G. 1994. Zero Quotatives. *Discourse Processes* 18:63–76.

Mayes, P. 1990. Quotation in Spoken English. *Studies in Language* 14:325–363.

Nam, K. S. 2001. *Hyenday Kwuke Thongsalon* [Modern Korean Syntax]. Seoul: Thayhaksa.

Park, Y. J. 2009. Interaction between Grammar and Multimodal Resources: Quoting Different Characters in Korean Multiparty Conversation. *Discourse Studies* 11(1): 79–104.

Pomerantz, A. 1984. Agreeing and Disagreeing with Assessments: Some Features of Preferred/Dispreferred Turn Shapes. *Structures of Social Action*, ed. J. M. Atkinson and J. Heritage, 57–101. Cambridge: Cambridge University Press.

Romaine, S. and Lange, D. 1991. The Use of *Like* as a Marker of Reported Speech and Thought: A Case of Grammaticalization in Progress. *American Speech* 66(3): 227–279.

Schegloff, E. A. 2007. *Sequence Organization in Interaction: A Primer in Conversation Analysis*, vol. 1. Cambridge: Cambridge University Press.

Sidnell, J. 2006. Coordinating Talk, Gaze, and Gesture in Reenactments. *Research on Language and Social Interaction* 39(4):377–409.

Sohn, H. M. 2012. A Grammar of *Po-* 'See' in Korean: A Panchronic Approach. *Language Information* 14:83–117.

Suh, C. S. 1996. *Kwuke Mwunpep* [Korean Grammar]. Seoul: Hanyang University Press.

Wu, R. R. 2012. Self-Praising through Reporting: Strategic Use of Two Reporting Practices in Mandarin Conversation. *Discourse Processes* 49:622–659.

Vásquez, C., and A. Urzúa. 2009. Reported Speech and Reported Mental State in Mentoring Meetings: Exploring Novice Teacher Identities. *Research on Language and Social Interaction* 42(1):1–19.

Yi, P. Y. 1995. *Kwuke-uy Inyong-kwumwun Yenkwu* (A Study on Korean Quotative Constructions). Seoul: Tap.

Japanese Relative Clauses That Stand Alone

YOSHIKO MATSUMOTO*
Stanford University

The forms and functions of relative clauses are predominantly discussed with regard to instances that occur with a main clause. In those instances, the modified head noun is an element of the main clause, and the modifying relative clause takes a clear position of subordination. In contrast to these prototypical cases, instances of a clause that modifies a noun without being embedded in a main clause, i.e., a clause and noun that stand alone, are rarely discussed, although they are not uncommon in Japanese written discourse. Such clausal noun modification without a main clause, especially of a semantically substantial head noun, is the focus of this paper.

Through the examination of naturally-occurring instances, I will illustrate that, despite often being dismissed as a fragment or error, stand-alone clausal noun modification is a sub-type of clausal noun modification, and is a full-fledged construction with a specific function. Naturally-occurring instances suggest that writers use stand-alone clausal noun modification for an

* I am grateful to the audience at the Japanese/Korean Linguistics Conference 22 for their valuable comments. My gratitude is also due to Atsuro Tsubomoto for kindly sending his papers, and to John Whitman for introducing me to Tsubomoto's work.

Japanese/Korean Linguistics 22.
Edited by Mikio Giriko, Naonori Nagaya, Akiko Takemura, and Timothy J. Vance.

invocatory purpose, namely, to introduce to the domain of the discourse referents with the highlighted attributes (described in the clause) in a manner analogous to setting a stage for events and actions to occur.

Although nonprototypcial, stand-alone clausal complex noun phrases are observed frequently in some genres of Japanese writing, such as in essays, fiction, scripts, blogs, advertisements, product names, and in titles of books and articles. These areas, literary or otherwise, demand the reader's involvement in interpreting the material much more prominently than expository writing. In this sense, the context in which stand-alone clausal noun modification is used is emotive and *interactional*, albeit in the sense of a writer reaching out to attract the readers' attention, rather than in a more immediate face-to-face interaction. Proficient users of Japanese would not expect stand-alone clausal complex noun phrases in the main body of academic or other expository writing.

In addition to describing the function of the stand-alone construction, this paper considers implications with respect to interlocutors' knowledge of genres and grammar. Such consideration may be viewed as an effort to explain, within a theory of grammar, variations based on genres and other factors—a position that is advocated by some who work on Construction Grammar (e.g., Östman 2005; Ruppenhofer and Michaelis 2010; Matsumoto 2010).

In the following, I will first briefly discuss prototypical instances of clausal noun modification used with a main clause. Then, in Section 2, I will focus on stand-alone constructions, delineating the target of investigation, and considering the functions of the dependent clause in the stand-alone complex NP, the effects of the construction in discourse, and finally the relation between knowledge of genres and grammar. Section 3 presents a conclusion, based on the current findings.

1. Noun-Modifying Clauses and Their Discourse Functions

Examples (1)–(3) are naturally-occurring spoken and written examples of clausal noun modification within a main clause (examples cited from Matsumoto 1997).

(1) [[suupu no okawari no dekita] **mise**] nado omoidasi . . .
soup GEN second.serving NOM can.do store etc. remember
'(I) was remembering [the **store** [(at which) (we) could have second helpings of soup]] . . .'

(2) konogoro [[toire ni ikenai] **komaasyaru**] ga ookute
lately bathroom GOAL go.cannot commercial NOM many.conj
komaru.
be.in.trouble
'(I'm) in trouble because there are many **commercials**, (because of wanting to watch which) (I) cannot go to the bathroom.'

(3) "sinzyuu-si-sokoneta ato" to, [[nuimono o suru] **te**] mo
love.suicide-do-failed trace QT sewing ACC do hand even
yasume-nai.
rest-not
'(Saying) "(this is) the mark (which was made when) I failed (in a) love-suicide", (she) does not rest even (her) **hand** [(with which she) is sewing].'

In all examples, the meaning of the referent designated by the head noun is restricted by the propositional content expressed in the preceding dependent clause. At the same time, the head noun participates as an argument of the main clause predicate. In contrast to the foregrounded main clause, the content of the dependent clause is backgrounded, as is a typical characteristic of restrictive relative clauses (e.g., Givón 1979; Hopper 1979; Croft 2001). From this functional point of view, the clausal constructions in (1)–(3) are reminiscent of restrictive relative clauses. However, as the translations of (2) and (3) indicate, the relationship between the dependent clause predicate and the head noun is not within the bounds of what is normally expected in relative clauses, since there is no syntactic gap in the subordinate clause predicate that is bound to the head noun. In (2), the referent of the head noun is part of the condition (which can be expressed as an adverbial clause rather than by a noun),[1] and, in (3), the head noun 'hand' represents the focused part of the action done by the whole, namely, the person whose sewing is depicted in the dependent clause.[2] I have proposed a frame-semantics and pragmatics based framework that can account for a wider range of noun-modifying constructions that include instances such as the above (e.g., Matsumoto 1997). Examples that can be labeled as relative clauses are a subset of the more general complex noun constructions modified by (adnominal) clauses—a broad category that includes the stand-alone constructions at issue.

[1] There is no explicit marking or implicit factor present in the discourse that would support the pragmatically (and semantically) untenable interpretation of the head noun 'TV commercials' being the subject of the subordinate clause predicate.

[2] Unlike in English, it would be unnatural in Japanese to say *te ga nuimono o suru* 'a hand sews'. Thus, we cannot treat the head noun as coreferential with the subject of the predicate.

2. Clausal Noun-Modifying Constructions That Stand Alone

The construction at issue may be written as **[[clause] N]**。, where "。" represents the Japanese period, indicating that no other element follows the noun, thus, "standing alone." As was mentioned above, stand-alone clausal noun-modifying constructions are observed relatively frequently in Japanese, mostly in "informal" (as opposed to formal and expository) emotive and interactional writing, such as in blogs, essays, fiction, product names, and advertisements.[3]

Examples (4) and (5) are from an online essay on sushi restaurants; (6) is the first sentence of a blog posting, and (7) is the title of a guidebook.

(4) [taisetu-ni tukaikomareta] tyooriyoo no nabe。
carefully well-used cooking GEN pot
'**cooking pots** [that are and well-used with care]'
(online essay; http://www.1101.com/restaurant/2007-03-22.html)

(5) [syari o tigitte sute-nai] hito。
rice ACC tear.off throw.away-NEG person
'a **person** [who doesn't tear off the rice]'[4]
(online essay; http://www.1101.com/restaurant/2007-03-22.html)

(6) [kintyoo-suru] watasi。
become.tense I
'**I**, [who feel tense]'
(blog; http://blogs.yahoo.co.jp/ozenmix1377/archive/2008/11/12)

(7) [syooboo-kan ni nareru?!] gaido。
firefighting.officer DAT become.can guidebook
'**The guidebook** [(by reading which) you can become a firefighter?!]'
(title of a book shown in a TV program *Bakumon,* October 2012)

I will discuss these and other stand-alone noun modifying constructions in more detail in the following sections, but before doing so, I should note three apparently similar structures, exemplified in (8), that are distinguished from the targets of our investigation.

(8) a. [[clause] N] *da/desu*
COP/COP.POLITE

[3] A cursory survey of the Balanced Corpus of Contemporary Written Japanese shows that instances of the stand-alone construction are found in genres such as magazines, newspapers, online Q&A sites, and online blogs, whereas no or few examples are found in the text of laws, white papers, textbooks, parliament minutes, etc.

[4] In (5), *hito* 'person' refers to a skilled sushi chef who can form a piece of sushi without needing to adjust the amount of rice by taking (tearing) some off in the process.

b. [N Sino-Japanese V(stem)]-(~~*suru/sita*~~)
-(~~do/did~~)

c. [clause] *koto/wake/mono* (*mon*)
matter/reason/thing
(e.g., Teramura 1984; Okamoto 1995; Horie, Kim and Rhee 2012)

The clausal complex noun phrase represented in (8a) differs from the stand-alone construction in that it is followed by a semantically non-vacuous element, a copula, which is used to make the sentence identificational or a definitive statement. Such structures include instances that contain a topic noun phrase, such as *Taroo wa Nagoya ni iku yotei da* ('Taro is planning to go to Nagoya') (e.g., Tsunoda 2011).

The noun-like ending in (8b) reflects the ellipsis of the light verb that normally accompanies a Sino-Japanese verb stem. In other words, the structure is a variation of a verb form rather than a noun phrase. It is, therefore, readily distinguishable from our current concern.

The construction given in (8c) is the closest to the stand-alone noun modification at issue, but is still different in form and function. With regard to the form, the nouns in the (8c) construction (e.g., *mono* 'thing') are semantically bleached and are considered to function as nominalizers, whereas the head nouns in the stand-alone noun modifying constructions (e.g. *gaido* 'guidebook') are semantically more substantial. Functionally, semantically bleached nouns in the (8c) construction, which is referred to as "stand-alone nominalization" by Horie, Kim and Rhee (2012), pragmatically mark the interlocutor's stance, whereas the head nouns in the stand-alone construction at issue express referents and categories. Further, the nominalized construction in (8c) can be understood as an instance of "insubordination," i.e., "the conventionalized main-clause use of what, on *prima facie* grounds, appear to be formally subordinate clauses" (Evans 2007:367), if we see the construction as functioning as "a matrix predicate without any supporting verb (e.g. copula, light verb)" (Horie, Kim and Rhee 2012). In contrast, it is not apparent that the stand-alone noun modifying construction is an example of insubordination. I will claim in this paper that the complex noun phrase does not function as a main clause predicate, but that it is a complex NP with a dependent clause, and that the complex NP as a whole has an invocatory function.

Because the construction at issue stands alone without being embedded in a sentence, various consequences follow. In the next three sections, I will consider (1) functions of the "subordinate clause," (2) the effects in discourse, and (3) implications with respect to the interlocutors' knowledge of genres and grammar.

2.1. Functions of the Clause in the Stand-Alone Complex NPs

The functions of subordinate clauses, including relative clauses, are often contrasted with those of main clauses in terms related to foreground and background (e.g., Hopper 1979; Croft 2001). The proposition expressed in a restrictive relative clause, in particular, has been characterized as "presupposed," "unchallenged," and "taken for granted," reflecting the "backgrounding" in information structure (e.g., Givón 1982; Lambrecht 1994) in contrast to the proposition in the main clause, which is understood to be "asserted" and "foregrounded." These descriptions, which define the function of a subordinate clause in terms of that of the main clause, cannot be directly applied in the case of stand-alone noun modification. Since there is no main clause to depict a state or an event that involves the referent of the complex NP, the subordinate clause must carry the burden of conveying the relevant information about the referent of the noun. Such information may not be presupposed or backgrounded. In this sense, the subordinate clause can be said to take a more assertive responsibility in this context than otherwise.

The assertive (or quasi-assertive) function of subordinate clauses in the stand-alone noun-modifying construction is markedly illustrated by instances in which the dependent clauses contain speech-act elements that normally appear in main clauses, as in (7) above ([*syooboo-kan ni·nareru?!*] *gaido* 'you can become a firefighter?! guidebook', i.e., 'the guidebook by reading which you can become a firefighter?!' or in [*yatte miyoo*] *kenkyuu-zyo* 'let's try research institute', which is the name of a research center (for children), advertised in a newspaper, where children are encouraged to try various ideas and experiments (i.e., the center is the location rather than the object of trying). Example (7) is an unusual case in that the clause presents the illocutionary forces of both an assertive and a directive. The lack of a main predicate may make it more hospitable for the *prima facie* dependent clause to assume a main-clause like role and function. The concept of "dependent main clause," which was introduced by Lambrecht (1994:180) in discussing the function of presentational relative clauses that exhibit main clause phenomena, may well be applicable to these noun-modifying clauses in Japanese.

In a similar vein, while it is usually true that the proposition expressed in a noun-modifying clause that restricts the referent of the head noun (e.g., in restrictive relative clauses) is "unchallengeable" or "presupposed," there are instances that challenge such assumption. The stand-alone complex NP [*yaseru*] *ongaku* 'the music (listening to which) (X) loses weight' in (9), which is a title of a section on an online Q&A site, apparently refers to some type of music that is claimed to help the listener lose weight. The proposition *yaseru* 'lose weight' given in the clause is challenged, however, or at least seriously questioned in the text that follows the title. In that sense, it is not strictly "presupposed" or "unchallengeable," as the excerpt below shows.

(9) [yaseru] ongaku。
become.slim music
'**The music** [(by listening to which) (x) becomes slim]'
. . .
Kiku dake de yaserareru ongaku da soo na n desu ga, sonna no ariemasu ka?
'I hear that it's the music that lets you lose weight by just listening to it (lit.: the music which by just listening you can lose weight), but can that be at all true?
(http://onayamifree.com/threadres/1020855/)

Examples (7) and (9) are not only stand-alone noun phrases without a main predicate, but, being titles or names of entities, they are also used without the context of prior discourse. For that reason, it is less likely that the content of the clause should be taken for granted or presupposed. The categories of background and foreground are not necessarily discrete, and presupposition is found in varying degrees even with regard to prototypical relative clauses with main clauses (e.g., Givón 1987).[5] Similarly, the assertive role of a relative clause in a presentational construction has been recognized (Fox and Thompson 1990; Lambrecht 1994), as exemplified in *Once upon a time there was an old king who lived in a beautiful castle* (Lambrecht 1994:129). In that sense, it is reasonable to suppose that the functional role of noun-modifying clauses in stand-alone complex noun phrases in Japanese can vary along the spectrum of assertiveness or of backgroundedness, depending on multiple contextual and discourse factors.

The fact that modifying clauses exhibit varied degrees of assertiveness and background/foreground effects is related to how closely they resemble main clauses in form and function, a point that was noted earlier with reference to the concept of "dependent main clause." The resemblance between noun-modifying clauses and main clauses in Japanese is rooted in the well-documented historical change whereby the conclusive (finite) form of predicates was almost completely replaced by the attributive form, which originally conveyed "suppressed assertion," or emotive stance in poetry (Iwasaki

[5] Givón (1987:176) mentions that, while the content of the relative clause in the sentence *The man wearing a frilled dress came into the room and . . .* is presupposed, both 'a man' and 'wearing a frilled dress' are not assumed to be known to the hearer in *A man wearing a frilled dress came into the room and . . .* However, intuitively both are backgrounded.

2000). The merged conclusive/attributive form gives rise to the possible ambiguity, especially in written discourse, between the stand-alone complex noun construction and a sentence in which a noun (phrase) is postposed after the main predicate.[6] Examples (10) and (11) below are examples from an "infomercial" on the online site of a cooking utensil company. Example (10) is the first line on the page, originally given in a larger and colored font, and it is followed by example (11), appearing three lines later in the text describing the maker's cookware. The propositional content of the clause and the head noun in each express basically the same information. Example (11) is clearly a stand-alone noun-modifying construction, while (10) is ambiguous. Example (10) contains a comma after the predicate *aru* 'exist', which can be understood to mark a pause. Therefore, it is possible to interpret (10) as a sentence with the postposed subject NP *aiyoo-no ryoori-nabe* 'favorite cooking pot'. On the other hand, it is also plausible to think that a comma was inserted for ease of reading because of the consecutive modification by *aiyoo-no* 'favorite', providing the interpretation of (10) as a stand-alone complex noun phrase, just as (11).

(10) [10-nen saki mo kitto kawar-azu soko ni aru], aiyoo-no
10-years ahead also surely change-NEG there LOC exist favorite
ryoori-nabe。
cooking-pot
'[Even after 10 years will certainly be there without change], (a) **favorite cooking pot**'
OR '(A) **favorite cooking pot**, [which will be certainly there without change even after 10 years]'

(11) [10-nen saki, 20-nen saki mo kitto kawar-azu soko ni
10-years ahead 20-years ahead also surely change-NEG there LOC
aru de-aroo] ryoori-nabe。
exist CONJECTURE cooking-pot
'(A) **cooking pot** [which will certainly be still there without change even after 10, 20 years]'
(online infomercial; http://www.kk-mizuno.com/ryourinabe.html)

It is conceivable that the merger of the conclusive and attributive forms encourages the use of main clause forms in noun-modifying clauses (Horie, n.d.) as we saw in examples such as (7). Such use would increase the possibilities for the noun-modifying dependent clause to convey main-clause like illocutionary force. It may be noted in passing that the observation that the

[6] In spoken instances, the latter often includes main clause pragmatic markers and is more easily distinguished from the former.

head noun is modified by a clause that may convey varying degrees of main-clause-like illocutionary force does not imply that the noun modifying construction is generated by syntactic movement, as evidenced by examples (2)–(3) given earlier.

I now turn to a closer examination of how these stand-alone constructions are used in actual written discourse. The following examples (12a–c) are taken from an online essay written by a food critic on sushi restaurants and sushi chefs. The examples contain a succession of complex NPs, each followed by a period without a main predicate. The examples present typical uses of the stand-alone noun modifying construction. The head nouns of (12a–c) are 'cooking pot' (or 'cooking pots'), 'cookware', and 'hands', respectively.

(12) a. [taisetu-ni tukaikomareta] tyooriyoo no nabe。 = (4)
carefully well-used cooking GEN pot
'**cooking pots** [that are and well-used with care]'

b. [kizu ga tuite bekobeko-no ibitu-na katati ni narihatete,
scratch NOM added bumpy warped shape DAT became
demo sore-koso ga, oisii ryoori o tukuri-tuzukete
but the.very.thing NOM delicious dish ACC make-continue
kita syooko-no yoo-na sonna kibisii] ryoori-kigu。
has.come evidence seems such demanding cook-ware
'[such demanding] **cookware** [which has became bumpy, warped, and scratched, but which is all the more evidence of making delicious food so long].'

c. [sore to onazi-yoo-na susi-syokunin no yawarakakute,
that COMIT similar-seem sushi-artisan GEN soft-and
utukusii te。
beautiful hand
'[soft and beautiful] **hands** [of a sushi chef which are just like it].'
(online essay; http://www.1101.com/restaurant/2007-03-22.html)

The visual format of the essay is reminiscent of a poem in that the paragraphs have the appearance of stanzas. The example (12a) is the first line of the sixteenth paragraph (or stanza). Before this paragraph, the author described the professionalism of sushi chefs and their vinegar-soaked hands, neither of which is obviously related to the content of (12a). The head noun in (12a) designates a new referent in the discourse context, as no cooking pot (*tyooriyoo no nabe*) was introduced in the prior text, although a noun with related meaning, *tyoori-kigu* 'cookware', was mentioned about 50 lines earlier. The content of the modifying clause in (12a), *taisetu-ni tukai-komaereta* 'well-used with care', is not grounded in the prior discourse either, and thus the clause introduces new information. Further, there was no reference to cooking pots in the context that the writer is describing. While the modifying clause in (12a) is an example of a restrictive relative clause, in which the content of the clause functions to describe and characterize what is designated by the head noun, both the clause and the head noun introduce new information. The clause does not describe old information that is "taken for granted," or a referent that has already been introduced. As was argued earlier, since there is no main clause to provide a substantive action or judgment involving the referent of the complex NP, the "subordinate" clause takes a more *assertive* responsibility than otherwise, at least to the extent that it proivdes new information (Lambrecht 1994) about the referent of the head noun.

The second construction given in (12b) can be said to be grounded in the information conveyed by the stand-alone NP in (12a). *Tyoori-kigu* 'cookware' is a more general term for *tyooriyoo no nabe* 'cooking pot' given in (12a), and the content of the clause in (12b) is an elaboration on the use of a cooking pot. It is interesting to note that the modifying clauses in (12b) that precede the head noun 'cookware' form a long sequence of clauses including coordinate structures, and resemble a narrative being developed in sequence, each relying on what is conveyed in the previous clause.

The third construction in the sequence, (12c), is grounded in the description given in the previous stand-alone noun modification in (12a) and (12b), as is indicated by the use of the demonstrative noun *sore* 'that', referring to the cookware and the cooking pot mentioned in earlier NPs. With (12c), the writer draws the readers' attention to the hands of the sushi chef, which were referenced earlier in the essay, while making explicit the analogy between precious cookware and a chef's hands.

After introducing these items, the writer, in the subsequent paragraph, references people who make sushi without knowing the wondrous power that hands can possess, and concludes by expressing his disappointment about such people in the last line: *mottai-nai na . . . , to omoo no desu* 'What a waste . . . I feel'. Until that conclusion, the absence of main clause predicates left it unclear how these elements (props and actors) interact or participate together in a coherent topic. They were merely placed in the domain of discourse in preparation for conveying the writer's insights.

The examples (12a–c) are reminiscent of stage directions used in Japanese scripts, where the relevant aspect of the actors and props are spotlighted through the use of a stand-alone noun modifying clauses, or 'non-restrictive' relative clause, as in (13) and (14) (both from *Tonari no shibafu* [The Neighbor's Grass] by S. Hashida).

(13) [issyun bon'yari tatitukusu] Tomoko。
a.moment blankly keep.standing Tomoko
'**Tomoko**, [who blankly stands for a moment].'

(14) [matte-ita yoo-ni aku] doa。
was.waiting as.if open door
'**The door**, [which opens as if it was waiting].'

Tsubomoto (e.g., 1999, 2009) notes this characteristic, naming the construction exemplified in (12a–c), (13) and (14) *togaki rensa koobun* ('stage direction XP-NP chaining construction'; translation mine), and comparing it with bi-clausal presentational relative clauses (Fox and Thompson 1990; Lambrecht 1994). Although my investigation in this paper shares some theoretical background with Tsubomoto's, my interest lies in the stand-alone noun modifying construction with no copula following the noun (while Tsubomoto includes constructions with copula), and my focus is on the construction as a subtype of the general noun-modifying construction, one that has a particular meaning in discourse (as a rhetorical device used in certain text types).[7] I consider stand-alone noun modifying constructions as presentational only in the sense of being invocatory.

As observed in this section, the content of the modifying clause is used by the writer to invoke an entity in the mind of the reader/interpreter in the domain of the discourse. The information status of the clause may vary, but it describes a crucial attribute of the noun in the context. In the next section, I will illustrate further the invocatory use of the stand-alone noun modifying construction.

2.2. Invocatory Effects of the Stand-Alone Noun-Modifying Construction in Discourse

Props and actors were invoked with the use of stand-alone noun modification in (12a–c), which set up a stage, or a domain of discourse, where the writer expresses his opinion. This format is also observed other places. Example (15) is a shorter blog posting by a different writer (http://blogs.yahoo.co.jp/ozenmix1377/archive/2008/11/12), in which personal referential terms appear as the head nouns of the stand-alone noun-modifying construction. *Watasi* 'I', *kare-si* 'he/my boyfriend', *kare-si no mama* 'his/my boyfriend's mom', and *titi-tati* 'fathers' are each modified by a clause whose content spotlights a certain attribute that is assumed to be particularly pertinent to the scene. In the absence of a main predicate, there is no explicit

[7] I do not consider the construction at issue to be exactly the same as the English existential head RC or bi-clausal presentational construction because (i) there is no introductory clause (*there is* . . .), and (ii) the NP is not established as a topic. For more detailed discussion, see Matsumoto (1991).

indication of how these characters are involved in the scene. The participants and their attributes are simply invoked by the writer, and placed in the discourse scene. Because of the tension of the participants as well as the specific activities that are described in the modifying clauses, the author invokes a scene of the first gathering of a young couple with their parents. While the content of the full sentence in the sixth line (saying that November 9th became an anniversary) does not explicitly specify how that relates to the characters and their actions, a reader can infer the connection from the characters and scene previously described.

(15) [kintyoo-suru] watasi。
become.tense I
'**I**, [who feel tense].'

[mukai-de katamatte-iru] kare-si。
across.from.me being.rigid he/my.boyfriend
'**He** (my boyfriend), [who is being rigid across from me].'

watasi no tonari ni wa doressuappu-sita haha ga
I GEN next LOC TOP dressed.up mother NOM
syaberi-ppanasi。
talk.nonstop
'Next to me, my mother has been talking nonstop.'

[sore ni uke-kotae-suru], kare-si no mama。
that DAT respond my.boyfriend GEN mom
'**My boyfriend's Mom**, [who responds to that].'

[o-sake o nomi-kawasu] titi-tati。
sake ACC drink.exchange fathers
'**Fathers**, who pour *sake* for each other.'

11-gatu kokonoka wa kinen-bi ni narimasita.
11th-month 9th.day TOP commemoration-day DAT became.POL
'November 9th became a commemorative day.'

The above observations suggest that the construction at issue can be used as a rhetorical device to involve readers by making them work harder to understand the described situation. In this sense, while not in a face-to-face situation, it can be described as interactional.

That some examples we have seen are written in the form of stanzas may not be entirely coincidental, since similar stand-alone constructions are found in modern American poetry. The examples (16) and (17) below are not in the form of relative clauses, but of participial clauses. However, they share a similar function to noun-modifying clauses in Japanese. Their occurrence in poetry is not surprising, since poetry is one of the literary forms in which readers are asked to maximally contexualize.

(16) . . .

Truth cantering on a powerful horse,
Chastity, eyes downcast, fluttering with veils.
Each one was marble come to life, a thought in a coat,
. . .

"The Death of Allegory"
by Billy Collins (2001) *Sailing Alone Around the Room*

(17) . . .

pools of water
pools of coal
pools of sand
buried or laid bare
. . .

"Black Mesa Mine #1"
by Gary Snyder (1969) *Turtle Island*

An English example that is even closer to the Japanese stand-alone noun-modifying clause is found in a translation from Polish of a poem by Zbigniew Herbert (translated by Czeslaw Milosz and Peter Dale Scott). The construction at issue is given in the title of the poem, *Nike Who Hesitates*. The poem (which begins, "Nike is most beautiful at the moment when she hesitates . . .") describes the imagined scene in which the goddess Nike hesitates as she sees a young warrior about to face glory and death. As with the Japanese examples, the stand-alone noun-modifying clause in the title invokes both a character (Nike) and an action of the character (hesitation).

The invocatory effect of the stand-alone noun-modifying construction is particular to the construction and is not associated with other uses of noun-modifying constructions embedded in a main clause. For that reason, this form and meaning pair constitutes a specific construction (e.g., Goldberg 1995; Croft 2001) and not simply an unintentional fragment. As was suggested before, the stand-alone noun modifying construction is used more in some genres than in others, i.e., genres that call for the readers' involvement in ascertaining how the invoked referents and category participate in the relevant context (or scene). This brings us to the implications as to how interlocutors' knowledge of genres may be pertinent to the understanding of grammar. That issue is discussed in the next section.

2.3. Knowledge of Genres and Grammar

The naturally-occurring examples of the stand-alone noun-modifying construction in Japanese examined above, together with similar instances in English-language poetry, illustrate the rhetorical purpose of the construction. Through its use, the writer invokes "props" and "actors," along with spotlighted attributes that are described in the modifying clause. Readers are invited to interpret and imagine roles that such invoked entities play in an event or a situation that will unfold. They are expected to be involved in contexualization of the presented materials. That expectation of involvement makes the use of the construction unsuitable in a genre such as scientific expository writing, where little room should be left for the reader's speculation. Genres where the reader's involvement and conscious effort in understanding the unsaid create positive effects are hospitable to this construction. Those genres include essays, blogs, fiction, dramas, advertisements, product names, and titles. We would not expect to find stand-alone noun modification in official government documents. But a competent user of the language would understand the function of the construction when used in a play or in an essay. If an instance of the construction appeared in a government document, it would likely be taken as a mistake (unless used as a heading), while no such inference would arise in a non-academic essay. Conversely, by seeing an instance of the stand-alone construction, competent users of Japanese would be able to imagine the types of text, of genre, and of discourse in which it appeared.

The understanding of the relation between context and the use of a particular form is closely related to the distinction between two types of frames, i.e., "cognitive frame" and "interactional frame," as originally advocated by Fillmore (1982).

> We have both 'cognitive frames' and 'interactional frames', the latter having to do with how we conceptualize what is going on between the speaker and the hearer or between the author and the reader. . . . Further, knowing that a text is, say, an obituary, a proposal of marriage, a business contract, or a folktale, provides knowledge about how to interpret particular passages in it, how to expect the text to develop, and how to know when it is finished. It is frequently the case that such expectations combine with the actual material of the text to lead to the text's correct interpretation. And once again this is accomplished by having in mind an abstract structure of expectations which brings with it roles, purposes, natural or conventionalized sequences of event types, and all the rest of the apparatus that we wish to associate with the notion of 'frame' (Fillmore 1982:117).

The use of stand-alone noun modification invokes a particular interactional frame (Fillmore 1982), or a discourse pattern (Östman 2005), of non-expository writing, which calls for a reader's involvement in contexualization. This understanding is part of grammatical knowledge.

3. Conclusion

Clausal noun modification that is not embedded in a main clause, and therefore stands alone, is often unremarked or excluded from studies of noun modifying constructions. This paper focused on instances of such stand-alone clausal modifications of a noun and suggested that there are ample instances of the construction used in various genres, and that it is a construction in the sense used in construction grammar, with specific pragmatic and discourse functions. Such noun-modifying clauses not only semantically characterize the referent of the noun, but also spotlight the attributes that are most relevant in the context. Because of that dual function, the modifying clause, while in a structurally backgrounded position with respect to the head noun, often contributes new and non-presupposed information and provides an account of the relevant context. It is then not surprising that we find instances of main-clause phenomena in the modifying clause, which, accordingly, can be characterized as a "dependent main clause." The construction as a whole is placed in the discourse world by the writer without an explicit description of how it participates. In other words, the writer invokes the entities and elicits anticipation in the reader's mind by inviting the reader's involvement in interpretation. Pragmatically, it also bears high interactional value, although the writer cannot expect an immediate response from the interactional partners.

Proficient users of Japanese would have acquired, as part of their knowledge of grammar, the understanding that the stand-alone noun-modifying clause, when used in a context or genre that requires interactional attention, is a distinct grammatical construction, rather than a fragment or error. The analysis of the stand-alone clausal noun modifying construction illustrates the advantage of bringing cognitive and interactional aspects of language use into the grammar and the importance of bringing atypical constructions to the fore of investigation.

References

Croft, W. 2001. *Radical Construction Grammar*. Oxford: Oxford University Press.

Evans, N. 2007. Insubordination and Its Uses. *Finiteness: Theoretical and Empirical Foundations*, ed. I. Nikolaeva, 366–431. Oxford: Oxford University Press.

Fillmore, C. J. 1982. Frame Semantics. *Linguistics in the Morning Calm*, ed. Linguistic Society of Korea, 111–138. Seoul: Hanshin.

Fox, B. A. and Thompson, S. A. 1990. A Discourse Explanation of the Grammar of Relative Clauses in English Conversation. *Language* 66:297–316.

Givón, T. 1982. Logic vs. Pragmatics, with Human Language as the Referee: Toward an Empirically Visible Epistemology. *Journal of Pragmatics* 6:81–133.

Givón, T. 1987. Beyond Foreground and Background. *Coherence and Grounding in Discourse*, ed. R. Tomlin, 175–188. Amsterdam: John Benjamins.

Goldberg, A. E. 1995. *Constructions: A Construction Grammar Approach to Argument Structure*. Chicago: University of Chicago Press.

Hopper, P. J. 1979. Aspect and Foregrounding in Discourse. *Syntax and Semantics 12: Discourse and Syntax*, ed. T. Givón, 213–241. New York: Academic Press.

Horie, K., Kim, J. and Rhee, S. 2010. Stand-Alone Nominalizations in Japanese and Korean: Parallelism and Divergences. Paper presented at the Workshop on Epistemicity, Evidentiality and Attitudes in Asian Languages, Hong Kong.

Horie, K. n.d. The Attributive-Final Distinction and the Manifestation of "Main Clause Phenomena" in Japanese and Korean NMCs. Unpublished manuscript.

Iwasaki, S. 2000. Suppressed Assertion and the Functions of the Final-Attributive in Prose and Poetry of Heian Japanese. *Textual Parameters in Older Languages*, ed. S. Herring et al. 237–272. Amsterdam: John Benjamins.

Lambrecht, K. 1994. *Information Structure and Sentence Form: A Theory of Topic, Focus and the Mental Representations of Discourse Referents*. Cambridge: Cambridge University Press.

Matsumoto, Y. 1991. Is It Really a Topic that is Relativized? Arguments from Japanese. *Papers from the 27th Regional Meeting of the Chicago Linguistic Society, Part One: The General Session*, ed. L. M. Dobrin, L. Nichols and R. M. Rodriguez, 388–402. Chicago: Chicago Linguistic Society.

Matsumoto, Y. 1997. *Noun-Modifying Constructions in Japanese: A Frame Semantic Approach*. Amsterdam: John Benjamins.

Matsumoto, Y. 2010. Interactional Frame and Grammatical Descriptions: The Case of Japanese Noun-Modifying Constructions. *Constructions and Frames* 2:136–157.

Östman, J.-O. 2005. Construction Discourse: A Prolegomenon. *Construction Grammars: Cognitive Grounding and Theoretical Extensions*, ed. J.-O. Östman and M. Fried, 121–144. Amsterdam: John Benjamins.

Teramura, H. 1984. *Nihongo no shintakusu to imi II* (Japanese Syntax and Meaning II). Tokyo: Kurosio Publishing.

Tsubomoto, A. 1999. Mono to koto kara mita bunpō (Grammar from the Points of View of Objects and Matters). *Nihongogaku* 18(1):26–40.

Tsubomoto, A. 2009. Sonzai no rensa to bubun/zentai no sukīmā: "Uchi" to "soto" no aida (Chaining of Existence and Part/Whole Schema). *"Uchi" to "soto" no gengogaku* (Linguistics of "Inside" and "Outside"), ed. A. Tsubomoto, N. Hayase, and N. Wada, 299–351. Tokyo: Kaitakusha.

Tsunoda, T. 2011. Ningyo kōbun: Nihongo kara ippan gengo-gaku e no kōken (Mermaid Constructions: Contributions from Japanese Linguistics to General Linguistics). *NINJAL Research Papers* 1:53–75.

Korean Discourse and Identity: Lessons from Heritage Language Research

M. AGNES KANG
University of Hong Kong

1. Introduction

In the last decade, there has been increased awareness that second language learners and heritage language (henceforth HL) learners may bring distinct knowledge and experience to the language classroom. The field of HL learning has focused on who these learners are and how they may differ from other L2 learners. I suggest that a better understanding of these differences will entail attention to the social contexts of HL learning and, specifically, the role of ideologies in mediating between HL and ethnic identity.

The close relationship of heritage language to ethnic identity has been the focus of a great deal of research in HL learning (Cho 2000, Phinney et al. 2001; Tse 2000). Studies show that those with greater proficiency in a heritage language also tended to have a stronger sense of ethnic identity (Phinney et al. 2001; Tse 1997). This was found to be true for Japanese Americans (Chinen and Tucker 2006; Shibata 2000) and Japanese Canadians (Oketani 1997), as well as Korean Americans (You 2005). But other studies report a lack of correlation between ethnic identity and heritage language proficiency (Mah 2005; Smolicz 1992; Jo 2001; Brown 2009), or a

Japanese/Korean Linguistics 22.
Edited by Mikio Giriko, Naonori Nagaya, Akiko Takemura, and Timothy J. Vance.

link between higher proficiency and bicultural identity (Lee 2002), suggesting that fluency in a heritage language cannot always predict stronger ethnic identity ties. These diverse findings are perhaps not surprising to the social constructionist who views identity as discursively constructed rather than an innate property of a person or group. Bucholtz and Hall (2004:376) note that "one of the greatest weaknesses of previous research on identity, in fact, is the assumption that identities are attributes of individuals or groups rather than of situations." The status of "HL learner" cannot bestow on a speaker any particular relationship to ethnic identity. That identity is discursively created, maintained, and varied depending on the situation in which the speaker engages with his or her identity.

In short, the link between HL and identity is one that is mediated by language ideologies, one prominent ideology being that language equals identity in some fundamental way. The ideology linking proficiency in HL to a strong sense of ethnic identity in the studies cited above represents only one of many possible ideologies influencing HL learning. In this article, I focus on recent research in Korean as a Heritage Language from a social perspective. In particular, I discuss specific ideologies reported in recent studies and show how a discourse analytic approach can articulate this complex relationship with some examples from my own research on Korean Americans. I conclude with what I see as important implications of language ideology in HL research, and how this research may impact the Korean heritage language classroom.

Identity research has revealed that multiple identities may be displayed in interaction through relationships of indexicality (Ochs 1992), and this serves as an insightful basis for exploring the links between language use and heritage identities. One productive avenue in identity research has been the study of language ideologies. Silverstein (1979:173) defines language ideologies as "sets of beliefs about language articulated by users as a rationalization or justification of perceived structure and use." Woolard (1998:3) defines language ideology as "representations, whether explicit or implicit, that construe the intersection of language and human beings in a social world." Silverstein's definition emphasizes the beliefs of users and how these serve to guide their use of language, while Woolard highlights the link created between language and the social world. Both of these aspects of language ideology have important implications for HL learners. Through language ideologies, we can explore what beliefs Korean heritage learners have about the Korean language and how this knowledge may translate to constructing a heritage identity.

Research in language ideology has suggested that language ideology mediates between language usage and social organization (Hornberger 2000; Kroskrity 1994:72; Woolard 1998). It provides the necessary link between the way we speak and the way we move within our worlds. Wortham (2001:256) describes how ideologies work in tandem with social positioning:

> Language ideologies mediate social identity, because people rely on their construals of what particular linguistic patterns mean in order to identify speakers as occupying recognizable social positions. Drawing on ideologies that circulate widely in a society, particular speakers position themselves and others in characteristic ways. Consistent positioning over time can establish more enduring identities for individuals and groups.

Wortham explores what speakers do when they speak a language—how ideologies shape not only the language used but also the speakers as social beings. And this is really part of the process of becoming an L2 or HL speaker. In this chapter I explore how these fields can inform one another, focusing on the role of Korean language ideologies in mediating between language and identity.

In reviewing the literature, what we start to see is that heritage language is shaped by language ideologies in manifold ways. I would like to organize these studies in terms of where the ideologies can be located: (1) ideologies held by heritage speakers (or how they value the heritage language), (2) ideologies circulating in the society (either mainstream society or the society of the target language), and (3) ideologies linked to the language itself (what values/beliefs are associated with speaking Korean?).

2. Ideologies Held by Heritage Speakers

For Korean heritage learners, the ideology that language equals identity plays a major role in motivating Korean HL education (Yang 2003; Kim 2002; Jo 2001). Recent studies of Korean HL learners report that the primary reasons for taking Korean language classes were to learn their ethnic language and to reconnect with their Korean roots. Not knowing the language was equated with losing their ethnic identity. Ethnic identity has been talked about in terms of ethnic doing and ethnic being (see Fishman 1982, 1985), and Jeon (2005) offers a nice example to illustrate to what extent Korean language is linked not only to ethnic doing, but to ethnic being. A non-heritage learner in a college-level Korean classroom, Nadia, is known for her love for kimchi, an iconic Korean ethnic food. This endears her to her Korean heritage classmates, but when she suggests that she may one day speak Korean better than her classmates, the tables turn, and she reports that she felt that her statement had threatened her Korean heritage classmates. She says:

> Though my friends never said anything to me about this, I knew that my taking 한국어 (Korean) has in some way threatened them, and any amount of 한국어 that they have learned in the past. I do not think that they felt any anger towards me for wanting to take the language, but anger toward

> themselves for not having taken the initiative to learn their native tongue. Those friends that do know some 한국어 feel that if I surpass their knowledge of the language, they will be proven failures (Jeon 2005:231–232).

It becomes clear in this example that while eating kimchi may make an outsider more of an insider, the act of speaking Korean is closer, if not almost equivalent to, being Korean (which Nadia is not).

And just as an outsider may not be "allowed," in some sense, to speak Korean like a native, or at the very least, may not be considered Korean just by virtue of speaking Korean well, the opposite is true for Korean heritage learners: ethnic Koreans MUST speak Korean. And this is also evident in the reactions of Nadia's heritage learner classmates to her suggestion, that, as she reports, they felt "anger toward themselves for not having taken the initiative to learn their native tongue."

Jeon (2005:207–208) also notes that one Korean heritage learner displayed very different behaviors when learning Spanish as opposed to learning Korean. He was much more reserved in Korean class, fearing making mistakes. This illustrates the observation by Cho et al. (1997) and Jo (2001) that Korean HL learners tend to evaluate their Korean proficiency as much lower than their proficiencies in other foreign languages, and they also evaluate themselves much lower than their non-heritage classmates (Kim 2010). The ideology that ethnic Korean learners should be able to speak Korean, then, appears to color, or diminish, the learners' perceptions of how well they can speak the language. We can see that the ideologies that HL learners hold about themselves as speakers can shape their self-assessments of their language proficiency.

3. Ideologies Circulating in Society

Regarding ideologies circulating in society, there are forces outside the HL learner that exert influence on how heritage languages are perceived and valued. One hotly debated area of late in HL research has been the ideologies associated with standard language and language standardization. For many HL learners who speak a regional or ethnic dialect, the teaching of "standard" language is often imposed by language authorities, as in HL teaching for Arabic, Spanish, Thai, and Russian, to name a few. Blackledge and Creese (2010), for example, examine the oft-contested ways in which standard language is linked to heritage for Bengali students, teachers, and families. Howard (2009) explores how ideologies of respect are taught in the heritage classroom through the teaching of Standard Thai, which is not the native language of the minority students in the classroom. Doerr and Lee (2009) also report in an ethnographic study of a Japanese HL school that administrators, parents, and students struggle to identify what constitutes legitimate Japanese language in light of standardization by the homeland government. In their analysis, while they do not invoke the term, they show how different ideologies about Japanese and the process of HL learning influence the choices made by all parties concerning the HL learner.

For Korean HL learning, Jo (2001:37) discusses the difficulties of Korean HL learners in mastering the use of honorifics in Korean as one example of how "personal versions of Korean language are contextualised and often delegitimated or legitimated against 'standard' Korean." Jo notes that unlike the typical foreign language learner who comes into contact with a completely new language without any prior knowledge or experiences, "the Korean-American language learners' knowledge and habits with informal language expressions were contested and negotiated against the 'standard' Korean language" (ibid.: 39) and often found to be lacking.

In comparing Korean HL learners against standard language practices, language authorities place heritage learners in a position of markedness against the standard language speaker. Bucholtz and Hall (2004) discuss the role of markedness in the social construction of identity to explain how markedness evokes negative evaluations of social groups:

> Because markedness implies hierarchy, differences between groups become socially evaluated as deviations from a norm and, indeed, as failures to measure up to an implied or explicit standard. Hence such differences are used as a justification for social inequality. Those who transgress gender norms in their linguistic and other social practices are often targeted in this way, but members of racialized, ethnicized, or other groups who do not conform to the stereotypical behavior expected of them are also susceptible to accusations of inadequacy or inauthenticity.

The comparison to a standard can be used as a means of constructing an HL learner as an "inadequate" or "inauthentic" speaker of the language. Given that the classroom context promotes standard language learning, HL learners who deviate from the standard through their own experiences (such as the modification of speech levels or honorific markers) run the risk of being seen as less than a proficient speaker of the language.

4. Ideologies Linked to Korean Language

Recent studies have linked Korean language to such ideologies as politeness and relative status. In previous research, I have been interested in the concept of relative status and how it is intimately linked to language practices in both Korean and English. In Kang (2003), I discussed the language practice of code-switching as a mitigating device that is used by Korean-English bilingual speakers as a means of diffusing potential conflict. Other researchers have subsequently taken up similar perspectives in analyses of code-switching between Korean and English that consider the negotiation of social hierarchies in interaction (e.g., Park 2006; Shin 2010).

During the summer of 1996, I conducted ethnographic research among two social service organizations in the northern California Bay Area: a nonprofit agency called the Korean American Center (KAC) and a Korean cultural camp called Camp *Huntulpawui* (HPH). Camp HPH attracted over 30 first-, 1.5-, and second-generation university students who volunteered to work as counselors. Some of their discussions, as they centered around self-categorization and distinct identity affiliations as Korean and Korean American camp counselors, were reported in Kang (2009).

Here I'd like to revisit their interactions in light of language ideologies, in particular, the ideology of relative age and status and how these two factors shape their social interactions. I compare two data excerpts, one a clip from a KAC staff meeting in which a fluent bilingual speaker uses the resources of both Korean and English in negotiating relative status, and another from the camp counselor meetings in which a heritage speaker negotiates relative status by using a Korean kinship term.

First we consider the case of the fluent bilingual speaker. Jin was considered to be the most balanced and fluent bilingual speaker on the staff of KAC. He was equally comfortable speaking English and Korean, and he often shifted between the two very easily. In Excerpt 1, the KAC director, Sam, asks for volunteers. Jin self-selects to counter Sam's suggestion in order to state that what needs to be done next is to divide the work. The activity of disagreeing with Sam is done very delicately through the use of code-switching from English to Korean, which allows Jin to make use of a Korean politeness marker and other interactional cues to mitigate his act of disagreeing with the higher status director:

(1) "Nolet's" (00:21)

SAM: So,
Uh,
Actually,
We need a—
We need a volunteer to handle the food for the reception.

JIN: No no let's—
Yôgi.. iss-ci anh -a-yo ((pointing to paper on table))
Here exist-NOML NEG:do IND-POL
Don't we have to do this?
We have to do—
...We have to divide the work.

SAM: Oh okay.
So- so this is what I think the program is going to look like.

After Sam asks for a volunteer, Jin explicitly disagrees with him in English by saying "No no let's." But he cuts off his utterance and switches to Korean, using code-switching as a mitigating device in accomplishing his disagreement. But he does not disagree while speaking Korean; his Korean utterance is used as a kind of hedge. He switches back to English, contextualizing his disagreement further with another restart ("we have to do—") and a long pause before stating, "we have to divide the work." All of these cues serve to "delay" what conversation analysts call a "dispreferred response," in this case, disagreement. By his careful navigation of the act of disagreement, Jin evokes the ideology of relative status in his interaction with the older and higher status director, Sam.

We can compare this to the interaction in the camp counselor's meeting. Excerpt 2 is from a recreation committee meeting, and immediately we can see that it is a much less formal context. Several conversations are happening at once while the committee leader (and assistant head counselor), Hank, is trying to run the meeting. Hank tries to get the attention of an older counselor, Mike, to ask him what supplies are needed for the last campfire they are planning. Hank first makes an attempt to ask a question indirectly by saying simply, "Last campfire" in a kind of "list intonation." When this does not get any response, he calls out to Mike, addressing him by his name after a false start, and after a brief pause uses the Korean kinship term, *hyeng*, to get his attention.

(2) 'Hyengrec' (00:24)

DUANE:	((SINGING))
JESS:	<X Could you go..down your list again X X>
HANK:	Last campfire. ((Hank makes an implicit request here that no one answers))
DUANE:	Uh=
JILL:	((turning)) Campfire?
HANK:	<VOC Mi- Mike..*hyeng* VOC>,
	What do we need for last campfire? ((Mike and Bill stop their conversation))
MIKE:	Uhm=,
	..Candles.
HANK:	((writing down)) Candles,
JILL:	<VOX Candles.
	Oo= how [shi-shi VOX>].
DUANE:	[X]
DAVE?:	Tissue.
HANK:	((writing))

During the camp itself, all counselors and campers are required to adopt this practice of using Korean kinship terms with one another. Some of the counselors, especially the head counselor and the assistant head counselor (Hank), used the terms while preparing for the camp, although most counselors did not. What is interesting about this particular usage is when it takes place. Several conversations are going on, and Hank needs to get Mike's attention to get an answer to his question. He tries using his name but decides not to pursue this means of addressing him. For the Korean speaker, the use of an older peer's name without the kinship term would be uncomfortable. Adding to this the volume at which he must call out Mike's name would presumably add to this discomfort. I would argue that the use of the kinship term here is highly appropriate for a heritage Korean speaker, and displays a certain sensitivity to the ideology of relative status within the dynamics of social interaction. While the interaction is not as rich in contextualization cues as the first excerpt in how Hank negotiates his relative status in getting an older peer's attention, I would argue that a similar awareness and understanding of social hierarchy is displayed here. While many of the counselors have expressed dislike of the policy of using kinship terms in the camp, attention to ideologies and how they influence our interactions indicate how a practice like using kinship terms can transform the way Koreans relate to one another, which is an explicit goal of Camp HPH (i.e., to learn how Koreans treat and interact with one another). What this suggests about Korean heritage learners is that such ideologies are accessed by speakers and shape how they interact in a way that a non-heritage speaker would have to learn in order to use these terms competently.

5. Discussion

Given the findings from the current research in HL learning, the question of what specific ideologies influence the social interactions of Korean HL learners can lead to a clearer understanding of how these learners construct themselves as legitimate speakers of Korean. If we apply Silverstein's definition of language ideologies as "sets of beliefs about language articulated by users as a rationalization or justification of perceived structure and use," heritage language learners, before even entering the heritage language classroom, may have already created rationalizations for how language is used in social interaction. And this may or may not be in tandem with the acquisition of standard Korean linguistic forms, which is part of the purview of the language classroom.

By looking at situated studies of interaction, we can identify the practices by which language ideologies mediate between heritage language and identity, specifically, the identity of the HL learner. The language ideologies discussed here play a role in the process of HL learning, but a future aim will be to clarify their respective roles not only for HL learners but for non-HL learners as well. The language ideologies discussed here are relevant mainly to the HL learner, and such distinctions between kinds of learners may inform the current debate about whether or not HL and non-HL learners should be taught together. The ideologies of non-HL learners also invite further research and investigation. Any language ideologies that learners bring to the classroom could serve as a potentially valuable resource for enriching the HL learning curriculum. In this way, the further study of language ideologies could play an important role in encouraging a more positive trend in Korean heritage language maintenance.

References

Blackledge, A. and Creese, A. 2010. *Multilingualism: A Critical Perspective*. London/New York: Continuum.

Brown, C. L. 2009. Heritage Language and Ethnic Identity: A Case Study of Korean-American College Students. *International Journal of Multicultural Education* 11(1):1–16.

Bucholtz, M. and Hal, K. 2004. Language and Identity. *A Companion to Linguistic Anthropology*, ed. A. Duranti, 268–294. Oxford: Blackwell.

Chinen, K., and Tucker, G. R. 2006. Heritage Language Development: Understanding the Roles of Ethnic Identity, Schooling and Community. *Heritage Language Development: Focus on East Asian Immigrants*, ed. K. Kondo-Brown, 89–126. Philadelphia: John Benjamins.

Cho, G. 2000. The Role of Heritage Language in Social Interactions and Relationships: Reflections from a Language Minority Group. *Bilingual Research Journal* 24(4):369–384.

Cho, G., Cho, K-S. and Tse, L. 1997. Why Ethnic Minorities Want to Develop Their Heritage Language: The Case of Korean-Americans. *Language, Culture, and Curriculum* 10(1):106–112.

Doerr, N. M. and Lee, K. 2009. Contesting Heritage: Language, Legitimacy, and Schooling at a Weekend Japanese-Language School in the United States. *Language and Education* 23(5):425–441.

Fishman, J. 1982. Sociolinguistic Foundations of Bilingual Education. *Bilingual Review/La Revista Bilingue* 9(1):1–35.

Fishman, J. 1985. *The Rise and Fall of the Ethnic Revival*. Berlin: Mouton.

Hornberger, N. 2000. Educational Linguistics as a Field. *New Perspectives and Issues in Educational Language Policy*, ed. R. Cooper, E. Shohamy, and J. Walters, 271–296. Philadelphia: John Benjamins.

Howard, K. M. 2009. 'When Meeting Khun Teacher, Each Time We Should Pay Respect': Standardizing Respect in a Northern Thai Classroom. *Linguistics and Education* 20(3):254–272.

Jeon, M. 2005. Language Ideology, Ethnicity, and Biliteracy Development: A Korean-American Perspective. Doctoral dissertation, University of Pennsylvania.

Jo, H.-Y. 2001. 'Heritage' Language Learning and Ethnic Identity: Korean Americans' Struggle with Language Authorities. *Language, Culture and Curriculum* 14(1): 26–41.

Kang, M. A. 2003. Negotiating Conflict Within the Constraints of Social Hierarchies in Korean American Discourse. *Journal of Sociolinguistics* 7(3): 299–320.

Kang, M. A. 2009. Constructing Ethnic Identity through Discourse: Self-Categorization among Korean American Camp Counselors. *Beyond Yellow English: Toward a Linguistic Anthropology of Asian Pacific America*, ed. A. Reyes and A. Lo, 131–147. New York: Oxford University Press.

Kim, H. H. 2002. The Language Backgrounds, Motivations, and Attitudes of Heritage Learners in KFL classes at University of Hawaii at Manoa. *Korean Language in America 7: Papers from the Seventh Annual Conference and Professional Development Workshop*, ed. J. J. Ree, 205–222. Tallahassee: American Association of Teachers of Korean.

Kim, H.-Y. 2010. Korean in the USA. *Language Diversity in the USA*, ed. K. Potowski, 164–178. New York: Cambridge University Press.

Lee, J. S. 2002. The Korean Language in America: The Role of Cultural Identity in Heritage Language Learning. *Language, Culture and Curriculum* 15(2):117–133.

Mah, B. 2005. Ethnic Identity and Heritage Language Ability in Second Generation Canadians in Toronto. Master's thesis, Ryerson University.

Ochs, E. 1992. Indexing Gender. *Rethinking Context: Language as an Interactive Phenomenon*, ed. A. Duranti and C. Goodwin, 335–358. Cambridge: Cambridge University Press.

Oketani, H. 1997. Additive Bilinguals: The Case of Post-War Second Generation Japanese Canadian Youths. *Bilingual Research Journal* 21(4): 359–379.

Park, E. 2006. Grandparents, Grandchildren and Heritage Language Use in Korean. *Heritage Language Development: Focus on East Asian Immigrants*, ed. K. Kondo-Brown, 57–88. Amsterdam: John Benjamins.

Phinney, J. S., Romero, I., Nava, M., and Huang, D. 2001. The Role of Language, Parents, and Peers in Ethnic Identity Among Adolescents in Immigrant Families. *Journal of Youth and Adolescence* 30(2):135–153.

Shibata, S. 2000. Opening a Japanese Saturday School in a Small Town in the United States: Community Collaboration to Teach Japanese as a Heritage Language. *Bilingual Research Journal* 24(4): 465–474.

Shin, S.-Y. 2010. The Functions of Code-Switching in a Korean Sunday School. *Heritage Language Journal* 7(1): 91–116.

Silverstein, M. 1979. Language Structure and Linguistic Ideology. *The Elements: A Parasession on Linguistic Units and Levels*, ed. R. Cline, W. Hanks, and C. Hofbauer, 193–247. Chicago: Chicago Linguistic Society.

Smolicz, J. J. 1992. Minority Languages as Core Values of Ethnic Cultures: A Study of Maintenance and Erosion of Polish, Welsh, and Chinese Languages in Australia. *Maintenance and Loss of Minority Languages*, ed. W. Fase, K. Jaspaert, and S. Kroon, 277–305. Philadelphia: John Benjamins.

Tse, L. 1997. Affecting Affect: The Impact of Ethnic Language Programs on Student Attitudes. *The Canadian Modern Language Review* 53(4):705–728.

Tse, L. 2000. The Effects of Ethnic Identity Formation on Bilingual Maintenance and Development: An Analysis of Asian American Narratives. *International Journal of Bilingualism Education and Bilingualism* 3(3):185–200.

Woolard, K. 1998. Language Ideology as a Field of Inquiry. *Language Ideologies: Practice and Theory*, ed. B. Schieffelin, K. Woolard, and P. Kroskrity, 3–47. Oxford: Oxford University Press.

Wortham, S. 2001. Language Ideology and Educational Research. *Linguistics and Education* 12(3):253–260.

Yang, J. S. 2003. Motivational Orientation of Korean Language Learners and Ethnic Identity Development of Heritage Learners. *Korean Language in America 8: Papers from the Eighth Annual Conference and Professional Development Work shop*, ed. C. You, 295–314. Berkeley: American Association of Teachers of Korean.

You, B.-k. 2005. Children Negotiating Korean American Ethnic Identity through Their Heritage Language. *Bilingual Research Journal* 29(3):711–722.

Part V

Syntax and Semantics

1-Deletion: Measure Nouns vs. Classifiers

AKIRA WATANABE*
University of Tokyo

Measure nouns in Japanese exhibit a curious property of being linked directly to a numeral without the mediation of a classifier, as in *yon meetoru* 'four meters', unlike ordinary nouns in the language. This peculiarity goes away once a cross-linguistic perspective is taken. Typological studies observe that measure nouns tend to lack plural marking. Japanese counterparts can be made to fit this pattern if the feature content of measure nouns and classifiers is taken into account. Comparison with numerical bases is particularly illuminating in this respect, since they also tend to be devoid of plural marking cross-linguistically and are combined with a basic numeral without the help of a classifier in Japanese (as in *yon hyaku* 'four hundred'). This comparison leads to the discovery that measure nouns and numerical bases in Japanese share the ability to allow 1-deletion, which has been associated only with numerical bases in cross-linguistic surveys (Hurford 1987, 2003).

* I would like to thank the audience for interesting discussion. I am also grateful to Chizuru Nakao, Uli Saulerland, and Ayaka Sugawara for comments on a longer version. The research reported here was supported by Grant-in-Aid for Scientific Research (C) 22520492 from the Japan Society for the Promotion of Science.
Japanese/Korean Linguistics 22.
Edited by Mikio Giriko, Naonori Nagaya, Akiko Takemura, and Timothy J. Vance.

The overall analysis will highlight the significant role that number features play in this domain.

In the literature on classifiers, measure nouns are often treated as mensural classifiers (Lyons 1977), as opposed to ordinary sortal classifiers, which are strongly tied to particular subcategories of nouns. In Japanese, too, measure nouns give the impression of being classifiers due to the fact, mentioned above, that they directly follow a numeral. Compare (1a) and (1b).

(1) a. yon meetoru
    four meter
    'four meters'

  b. yon satsu (-no hon)
    four classifier (-link book)
    'four (books)'

Allan (1977) claims that measure expressions are classifiers, pointing to a shared word order pattern in Thai. The recent consensus, however, is that they should be treated as distinct in nature from ordinary classifiers, since they find counterparts in classifier-less languages like English (Aikhenvald 2000; Croft 1994; Downing 1996; Grinevald 2004). Commenting on Chinese, Gebhardt (2011) states that mensural "classifiers" are not classifiers but nouns. I will argue that the inability of numeral classifiers in Japanese to allow 1-deletion provides us with another argument that measure words are not classifiers.

The discussion will deal with Japanese expressions that correspond to the following types of standard measuring units and some additional ones.

(2) a. time: year, month, week, day, hour, etc.
  b. length: mile, foot, inch, etc.
  c. weight: ton, pound, etc.
  d. money: dollar, pound, etc.

Among them, expressions of temporal units exhibit very intriguing complexities, which provide important insights into the nature of measure nouns in general. Section 1 lays out background assumptions concerning the role of number features in relation to measure nouns, classifiers, and numerical bases. Section 2 presents an account of 1-deletion on that basis, extending Watanabe's (2010) account of numerical bases to measure nouns.

1. Featural Characterization of Measure Nouns

It is well known that measure nouns tend to lack the plural morphology. In Swedish, where ordinary count nouns make a singular-plural distinction, measure nouns do not display such a distinction (Holmes and Hinchliffe 2000), as shown in (3).

(3) a. en kilometer ~ femtio kilometer
'one kilometer' 'fifty kilometers'
b. en fot ~ två fot
'one foot' 'two feet'

Similarly, some German measure nouns such as *Pfund* 'pound', *Gramm* 'gram', and *Fuss* 'foot' remain singular when the plural form is expected (Acquaviva 2006). The same is true with a minority of measure nouns in Scottish Gaelic such as *là* 'day' and *bliadhna* 'year' (Greene 1992). In Early Modern English, too, measure words tend to be used without plural marking until the end of the 18th century (Lass 1999). The four classes of measure nouns in (2) are indeed the ones that Jespersen (1914/1954) lists under the heading of the unchanged plural.

Given this pervasive characteristic of measure nouns reviewed above, it is quite tempting to connect the absence of classifiers associated with Japanese measure nouns to the absence of number marking. The key to this connection is the theory of number features. Once the conditions for the appearance of classifiers are captured in terms of features, it becomes possible to explain why measure nouns in Japanese are generally used without a classifier.

Let us first lay out the system of number features (Harbour 2011a, 2011b; Noyer 1997) as the background for discussion. Two features are involved in defining the number categories of singular, dual, and plural, as in (4).

(4) a. Singular: [+singular, –augmented]
b. Dual: [–singular, –augmented]
c. Plural: [–singular, +augmented]

The combination [+singular, +augmented] is impossible, given the following definitions of individual features.

(5) a. [+singular] = $\lambda x[\text{atom}(x)]$
b. [+augmented] = $\lambda P.\ \lambda x{:}\ P(x).\ \exists y[P(y) \wedge y \subset x]$

The minus value is given as negation of the plus value. Informally speaking, [+augmented] picks out non-minimal entities in the domain already specified with respect to [±singular]. Since only one numerical value corresponds to [+singular], only [–augmented] is combinable with it. (5b) is the version that uses a subset relation. Harbour (2011b) substitutes a part relation. "λx: P(x)" means that P is a presupposition on x. Harbour opts for the use of the part relation instead of the subset relation in the definition of [+augmented] to capture the link with the aspect domain. The subset relation suffices here because we are dealing with a discrete system when we distinguish among singular, dual, and plural. We will see later on, though, that the part-whole relation entailed by [+augmented] seems to play an important role when we try to extend the empirical coverage.

The next step is to characterize the conditions that enable numeral classifiers to appear in terms of number features. Watanabe (2010) puts forth the following proposals.

(6) Numeral Classifiers and Selection of Numerals in Japanese
   a. A numeral classifier appears only when both [±singular] and [±augmented] are specified.
   b. [±augmented] always selects a numeral in Japanese.

(6a) receives support from the fact that there is a classifier that changes shape according to the number value, as in (7).

(7) a. hito-**ri**
   one-classifier

   b. futa-**ri**
   two-classifier

   c. san-**nin**
   three-classifier

   d. yo-/go-/roku-/nana-/etc. **nin**
   four-/five-/six-/seven- classifier

The classifier for counting human beings has two forms: *ri* for singular and dual and *nin* for plural. Given the number system in (4), one can say that *ri* is the special form for [–augmented].

With (6a) and (6b) combined, it is guaranteed that classifiers in Japanese must be accompanied by a numeral. This is a parametrized property of Japanese classifiers, since Chinese classifiers can be used without a numeral (Cheng and Sybesma 2005).

Now, it is easy to see why measure nouns in Japanese generally occur without a classifier. Suppose they lack the [±singular] specification. On the assumption that classifiers reflect the number specification of the head noun, (6a) prohibits the appearance of a classifier in the case of measure nouns.

The hypothesis that (overt) measure nouns in Japanese lack the [±singular] specification receives interesting support from the suppletion exhibited by the noun meaning 'day'.

(8) a. ichi-**nichi**
   one-day
   'one day'

   b. futsu-**ka**, mik-**ka**, yok-**ka**, . . . , too-**ka**
   two-day three-day four-day ten-day
   'two days' 'three days' 'four days' 'ten days'

c. juu-ichi-**nichi**, juu-ni-**nichi**, . . . , juu-go-**nichi**, . . . , san-juu-**nichi**
ten-one-day ten-two-day ten-five-day three-ten-day
'eleven days' 'twelve days' 'fifteen days' 'thirty days'

The generalization is that a special form *ka* is used from two to ten, putting aside further idiosyncrasies found with *juu-yok-**ka*** 'fourteen days' and *hatsu-**ka*** 'twenty days'. An important point is that the line between (8a) and (8b) can be drawn without using the [±singular] specification. In the absence of [±singular], [–augmented] corresponds to singular, and [+augmented] to plural (Harbour 2011a). One can then say that *ka* is the form for [+augmented]. A complication is that this [+augmented] form is limited to simplex numerals. For complex numerals involving a numerical base plus an additional digit numeral from one to nine, the general form *nichi* must be used as in (8c). This number distinction looks baroque, but it is a general characteristic of the number system in Maltese involving the singular–plural opposition (Watanabe 2010).

Though the noun meaning 'day' is the only measure word in Japanese that exhibits suppletion in a way sensitive to what numeral comes in front of it, it is striking that the division made in the range up to ten is not between two and three, unlike the classifier for counting human beings. This behavior is explained in a principled way by assuming that measure nouns are not specified with respect to [±singular], without which [±augmented] makes a two-way distinction between singular and plural.

Japanese has another set of lexical items that are combined directly with a numeral, namely, numerical bases such as *hyaku* 'hundred' and *sen* 'thousand'.

(9) a. ni-hyaku b. nana-sen
two-hundred seven-thousand
'two hundred' 'seven thousand'

Numerical bases behave like nouns, as can be clearly seen from Hurford's (2003) discussion of languages with active gender agreement. In Welsh, for example, *chant* 'hundred' is masculine, whereas *mil* 'thousand' is feminine. This difference in inherent gender is reflected in lower-valued digit numerals, which agree in gender with head nouns in ordinary nominal projections, when they are put together with a base to form a complex numeral.

(10) a. tri chant b. tair mil
three.m hundred three.f thousand
'three hundred' 'three thousand'

In English, the noun-like nature of these words can be seen in their ability to take the plural form, as in *thousands of books*. At the same time, they remain singular when combined with a basic numeral, as indicated by the English translations given in (9) and (10). The same is true with *dusan* 'dozen', *fichead* 'twenty', *ceud* 'hundred', and *mìle* 'thousand' in Scottish Gaelic (Greene 1992). Thus, numerical bases are quite similar to measure nouns, as remarked by Acquaviva (2006).

Once we recognize this similarity, it becomes possible to apply to numerical bases the account of why measure nouns are directly combined with a numeral without the help of a classifier. Numerical bases in Japanese also lack the [±singular] specification, blocking the appearance of a classifier in accordance with (6a).

Acquaviva (2006) coins the term "unit nouns" to refer to measure nouns and numerical bases as a class and goes so far as to analogize them to classifiers. In the case of numerical bases, however, there is no tradition of classing them together with genuine (sortal) classifiers. The reason is that when a complex numeral consisting of a numerical base and a basic numeral is combined with a noun, the complex numeral itself must be accompanied by a classifier appropriate for the head noun, as in (11).

(11) hon ni-hyaku-satsu
book two-hundred-classifier
'two hundred books'

Since there can be only one classifier per noun, numerical bases cannot be classifiers.

The similarity of measure nouns and numerical bases, then, presents another argument that measure nouns are not classifiers. There is a further respect in which measure nouns and numerical bases go together as against classifiers, to which we turn next.

2. 1-Deletion

A fairly widespread phenomenon associated with numerical bases is so-called 1-deletion (Hurford 1987, 2003), where a numerical base is used alone but multiplication by 1 is implied. The phenomenon, however, is not limited to numerical bases. Measure nouns, too, allow 1-deletion in the context of expressions that indicate a ratio. Close attention to this phenomenon in Japanese is quite revealing with regard to the nature of measure nouns.

2.1. Cross-Linguistic Patterns

There are two major generalizations concerning 1-deletion (Hurford 1987, 2003). First, it is obligatory for smaller bases, while it is impossible for bases with higher numerical values, with intermediate items displaying optionality, as the following German data illustrate.

(12) a. zehn ~ *ein zehn (obligatory for 10)
b. hundert ~ ein hundert (optional for 100)
c. tausend ~ ein tausend (optional for 1,000)
d. *Million ~ eine Million (impossible for 1,000,000)

The same is true in Japanese.

(13) a. juu ~ *ichi-juu (obligatory for 10)
b. hyaku ~ *ip-pyaku (obligatory for 100)
c. sen ~ is-sen (optional for 1,000)
d. *man ~ ichi-man (impossible for 10,000)

At the same time, languages vary as to exactly where 1-deletion becomes optional or impossible.

The other generalization is related to suppletion found with numerical bases. In German, for example, 10 is *zehn*, whereas 40 is *vierzig* and 50 *fünfzig*. In other words, a special form is used only for 10, with *zig* being the regular form of the base 10.[1] The same is true in English, the base for 10 alternating between *ten* and *ty*. Hurford (1987) observes that the special suppletive form invariably uses 1-deletion, pointing to languages like Hawaiian, where there is an additional idiosyncrasy for 20.

(14) Hurford's Generalization
1-deletion is used for the suppletive form of the numerical base.

(15) Hawaiian (Hurford 1987)

		10	umi
3	kolu	30	kana-kolu
4	ha	40	kana-ha
5	lima	50	kana-lima
6	ono	60	kana-ono

It is interesting to observe that the base for 10 is affected by suppletion in English, German, and Hawaiian. The two generalizations combined predict that suppletion should be impossible for higher numerical bases.

In Japanese, numerical bases are free from suppletion. The alternations shown in (13) are due to a semi-regular phonological process, which affects the numeral *ichi*, too. When we turn to units of time, however, suppletion is rampant. Quite interestingly, the pattern of 1-deletion turns out to be consistent with Hurford's generalization (14) in this domain, too.

[1] Uli Sauerland pointed out to me that *zig* can also be used without a digit numeral, as in *zig Bücher*, meaning 'some multiple of ten books'. This use of *zig* should be kept distinct from 1-deletion, since it does not mean exactly 10.

2.2. Measure Nouns in Japanese

Though I am not aware of any systematic treatment of this fact, 1-deletion is not limited to numerical bases. In Japanese, it figures prominently in the structure that expresses ratios with a measure noun, as in (16), where one can omit *ichi* 'one'.

(16) (ichi-)kiro san-zen-en-no kome
one-kilo three-thousand-yen-link rice
'rice that costs three thousand yen per kilo'

In English, too, the noun following *per* appears without an article or a numeral, but the numerical value 1 is understood, as in the translation given for (16). In Japanese, the numeral *ichi* 'one' can appear. In (16), there is no overt item meaning 'per'. Alternatively, one can use *ni-tsuki*, *atari*, or *tan'i*, as in (17).

(17) a. ichi-kiro-ni-tsuki san-zen-en-no kome
one-kilo-dat-attach three-thousand-yen-link rice

b. (ichi-)kiro-atari san-zen-en-no kome
one-kilo-per three-thousand-yen-link rice

c. (ichi-)kiro-tan'i san-zen-en-no kome
one-kilo-unit three-thousand-yen-link rice

The possibility of 1-deletion seems to vary depending on which version is used. It is disallowed in (17a).

Turning to measure nouns corresponding to units of time, we find suppletion correlated with 1-deletion. Consider the following examples:

(18) a. **hi**-ni san-kai-no tooyaku[2]
day-per three-time-link medication

b. ichi-**nichi**-ni san-kai-no tooyaku
one-day-per three-time-link medication
'three medications per day'

(19) a. **shuu**-ni san-kai-no kaigi
week-per three-time-link meeting

---

[2] The proper analysis of *kai*, glossed as 'time' here, is an interesting question left open. It looks like a classifier for event nouns in (18), but it measures the number of verbal events in (i).

(i) Hanako-wa hito-ban-ni san-kai toire-ni okita
Hanako-TOP one-night-per three-time bathroom-to woke.up
'Hanako woke up three times in one night to go to the bathroom.'

b. is-**shuukan**-ni san-kai-no kaigi
one-week-per three-time-link meeting
'three meetings per week'

(18a) and (19a) have the same interpretation as (18b) and (19b), respectively, though there is no numeral for 'one' in (18a) and (19a), to which such a numeral cannot be added. Crucially, the (a) version with 1-deletion and the (b) version without it use different forms of the measure nouns. The allomorph that triggers obligatory 1-deletion is also used together with a demonstrative, as in (20).[3]

(20) a. sono hi
that day
'that day'

b. sono shuu
that week
'that week'

The form *hi* belongs to the native Yamato vocabulary, while *nichi, shuu,* and *shuukan* are all Sino-Japanese. Thus, this difference in vocabulary classification is not related to the way 1-deletion works. It should also be mentioned that the alternation between *shuukan* and *shuu* does not count as an instance of suppletion in the ordinary sense of the term. Rather it has to do with the presence or absence of a morpheme (*kan*). In the featural analysis presented below, it will turn out that what matters is not suppletion but feature content of measure nouns, with *kan* serving as the locus of a particular feature responsible for the appearance of a numeral.

Moving on to months, we find a slightly different pattern.

(21) a. (hito-)**tsuki**-ni san-kai-no kaigi
one-month-per three-time-link meeting

b. ik-**kagetsu**-ni san-kai-no kaigi
one-month-per three-time-link meeting
'three meetings per month

In (21a), which expresses 'one month' with the native lexical items *hito* and *tsuki*, 1-deletion is optional, unlike the case for 'day' and 'week'. For 'year', only a single form is involved, as in (22).

---

3 Temporal units are quite unusual among measure nouns in being able to combine directly with a demonstrative. This property is related to the fact that temporal units form a core part of bare NP adverbs in the sense of Larson (1985). In fact, temporal units seem to be the only class of nouns that can head a bare NP adverb in Japanese.

(22) (ichi-)**nen**-ni san-kai-no kaigi
one-year-per three-time-link meeting
'three meetings per year

Again, 1-deletion is optional. (22) is parallel to (16).

Outside the domain of temporal units, allomorphy seems rare. But when it is found, it is correlated with 1-deletion, as in the following pair:

(23) a. **rittaa** hyaku-go-juu-en-no gasorin
liter hundred-five-ten-yen-link gasoline

b. ichi-**rittoru** hyaku-go-juu-en-no gasorin
one-liter hundred-five-ten-yen-link gasoline
'gasoline that costs a hundred fifty yen per liter'

Although there may be an idiolectal variation, 1-deletion is obligatory for me in the case of *rittaa*, which is intended to mimic the English pronunciation of *liter* more closely. On the other hand, *rittoru* does not allow 1-deletion.

2.3. Licensing of Numerals

A first step to understanding the nature of Hurford's generalization (14) concerning 1-deletion and suppletion, which turns out to hold in the domain of Japanese measure nouns as well, is to remember that morphological alternation is described in terms of number features in the case of the noun meaning 'day'. Watanabe (2010) posits the following universal condition on the appearance of numerals, given that numerical bases are not necessarily equipped with [±singular].

(24) Licensing of Numerals
Numerals are licensed only when [±augmented] is present.

The idea is that once we have a principle governing the distribution of numerals stated in terms of features, it becomes possible to link 1-deletion, which should arise from the failure to license a numeral, to the morphological alternation exhibited by numerical bases and measure nouns, which should receive featural characterization. Notice also that (6b), repeated here, is a stronger version of (24).

(6) b. [±augmented] always selects a numeral in Japanese.

The rest of the task is to explain why (24) can indeed account for 1-deletion.

Recall from section 1 that in the absence of [±singular], [±augmented] marks the singular-plural opposition, as in (25).

(25) a. Singular: [–augmented]
b. Dual/Plural: [+augmented]

Adding [+singular] to (25a) does not affect the number opposition already made. It follows, however, from the combinatorics of [±singular] and [±augmented] that [–augmented] is redundant in the presence of [+singular], as noted by Watanabe (2010). Omission of the redundant [–augmented], then, gives:

(26) a. Singular: [+singular]
b. Dual/Plural: [+augmented]

Interestingly, (24) blocks the use of the numeral for 1 under the feature system in (26). In other words, 1-deletion obligatorily arises when number features are distributed as in (26).

Given this result, we are now in a position to see why numerical base suppletion is correlated with 1-deletion. Under (26), the singular corresponds to the feature not used in the category of the dual/plural. Suppletion is nothing other than the reflection of this featural difference. We can characterize the English base for 10 as follows.

(27) a. ten: [±singular]
b. ty: [+augmented]

The form *ten* is compatible with [–singular] in view of expressions like *tens of thousands of books* (Kayne 2010: ch. 3). Note also that the featural difference in (26) does not have to be reflected in morphological shape, in which case there is no suppletion even when 1-deletion is dictated.

This account carries over to the behavior of measure nouns. The shapes of the noun meaning 'day' are characterized as follows.

(28) 'day'
a. hi: [+singular]
b. nichi: [±augmented]
c. ka: [+augmented] (limited to use with a simplex numeral)

(28b) and (28c) can be combined with a numeral, whereas (28a) cannot. (28b) and (28c) must, in fact, given (6b). The difference between (28b) and (28c) was already taken up in section 1. Note also the [–singular] form *hibi*, created from (28a) through reduplication (and voicing).

Likewise, the noun for 'week' receives the following account, as a first approximation.

(29) 'week' (to be revised)
a. shuu: [+singular]
b. shuukan: [±augmented]

A tricky question is the status of *kan*. The characterization in (29) leads us to suppose that this morpheme is the locus of [±augmented]. Furthermore, we need to make sure that the [+singular] feature carried by *shuu* will not show up in *shuukan*. An easy solution is to posit a null morpheme that hosts [+singular] and competes with *kan*. This null morpheme is used in *shuu* but does not appear in *shuukan*.

This analysis is somewhat reminiscent of the Bantu class markers, which encode number as well as gender information (see Katamba 2003). Unlike a Bantu class marker, however, *kan* does not change shape according to the number value.

The productive usage of *kan*, however, is an expression of duration, as in (30).[4]

(30) a. Hanako-wa mik-ka-kan ie-ni tojikomotta
Hanako-TOP three-day-KAN house-to confined
'Hanako confined herself to her house for three days.'

b. Hanako-wa ichi-nen-kan ie-ni tojikomotta
Hanako-TOP one-year-KAN house-to confined
'Hanako confined herself to her house for a year.'

The fact that the two usages of *kan* are written with the same Chinese character pushes us towards the view that they may be related. Harbour (2011b) associates mass nouns in Kiowa with [+augmented] by pointing to a part-whole relation found in the denotation of these nouns. Likewise, I speculate that the part-whole relation inherent in the notion of duration translates into the interpretation assigned to [+augmented]. The morpheme *kan*, then, is an expression having to do with the presence or absence of the part-whole relation in the temporal domain.[5]

---

[4] The durational *kan* apparently cannot be added on top of the use of *kan* as the carrier of [±augmented], as shown in (i).

(i) Hanako-wa ni-shuu(*-kan)-kan ie-ni tojikomotta
Hanako-TOP two-week-KAN-KAN house-to confined
'Hanako confined herself to her house for two weeks.'

I suspect, though, that the carrier of [±augmented] can sometimes be null, as indicated by the parentheses in (i), in view of the fact, pointed out to me by Taro Kageyama and Chizuru Nakao, that a numeral can be added to *shuu* without the help of *kan* in cases like (ii).

(ii) ni-shuu-renzoku
two-week-in.a.row
'two weeks in a row'

The task for future research is to figure out when the null version of *kan* can be used.

[5] The significance of a part-whole relation for the durational use of *kan* can be seen in the impossibility of *kan* in the following example.

A somewhat different story must be told for 'month', since 1-deletion is not obligatory in this case. In fact, *tsuki* can also be combined with a few other numerals, as in (31).

(31) Tatta go-peeji kaku-no-ni futa-tsuki kakatta
only five-page write-COMP-for two-month took
'It took two months to write up just five pages.'

The contrast between *tsuki* and *kagetsu*, therefore, cannot be attributed to a difference in the number features discussed so far.

A very interesting property of *tsuki* is that it can only be combined with lower numerals, as illustrated in (32).

(32) hito-tsuki, futa-tsuki, mi-tsuki, *?yo-tsuki, *itsu-tsuki, …
one-month two-month three-month four-month five-month

This means that *tsuki* covers singular and paucal numbers. And within this range, it operates with the following feature system.

(33) a. Singular: [+singular] or [–augmented]
b. Dual/Plural: [+augmented]

The choice available for the feature representation of the singular gives rise to the optionality of 1-deletion. The same feature system is used for *nen* 'year' as well as for other items such as *kiro* 'kilo', for which 1-deletion is optional. No suppletion is found in these cases.

The Sino-Japanese version *kagetsu*, which prohibits 1-deletion, is not limited to singular and paucal. One is again tempted to treat *ka* as a separate morpheme, since it is dropped when the proximal demonstrative is added to refer to the span including the speech time, as in (34), where the final vowel /o/ is truncated. Compare (35).

(i) Hanako-wa ichi-nichi(*-kan) ie-ni tojikomotta
Hanako-TOP one-day-KAN house-to confined
'Hanako confined herself to her house for a day.'

The difference from the acceptable examples in (30) is probably due to the fact that one day is not felt to be long enough to allow a part-whole relation, even though we can talk about duration using units shorter than one day, as in (ii).

(ii) Hanako-wa ni-fun-kan me-o tojita
Hanako-TOP two-minute-KAN eye-ACC closed
'Hanako closed her eyes for two minutes.'

Incidentally, there is also a locative postpositional use of *kan*, as in:

(iii) Tookyoo-Shinbashi-kan
'between Tokyo and Shinbashi'

In this case, *kan* indicates a bounded space that is, again, compatible with a part-whole relation.

(34) kon-getsu
this-month
'this month'

(35) kono hon
this book
'this book'

Thus, *getsu* and *shuu* are parallel, as can be seen by putting (34) side by side with (36).

(36) kon-shuu
this-week
'this week

This parallelism leads us to suppose that *ka* is also the locus of [±augmented] for *getsu* just as *kan* is for *shuu*, though the position vis-à-vis the nominal root differs.

(37) Morphemes Carrying [±augmented]
a. *-kan* (week)
b. *ka-* (month)

In view of the structure posited by Watanabe (2010), I am inclined to suppose that the suffixal *kan* stays in the original position in the structure given in (38) and that *ka* is shifted to the left by a morphological operation.

(38) $[_{\#P}$ numeral $[_{NP}$ shuu$]$ $[_{\#^\circ}$ kan$]]$

The morpheme *ka* is also used for *koku* 'country', as in *san-ka-koku* 'three countries'. Among ordinary nouns, *koku* is an isolated exception. One might think that *kasho* 'place' is similar, but *kasho* can be used without a numeral unlike *ka-koku,* as in *ki ni naru kasho* '(a) place that bothers me'. Recall that (6b) forces a numeral to be used when [±augmented] is present. One must therefore conclude that *kasho* is an unanalyzed exceptional non-measure noun that can be directly combined with a numeral as in *san-kasho* 'three places', which means that it has a defective number specification lacking [±singular] but can optionally be supplied with [±augmented].

There is one important difference between *shuu* and *getsu* that needs to be mentioned. Unlike *shuu, getsu* does not allow 1-deletion, as the ungrammaticality of (39) indicates.

(39) ***getsu**-ni san-kai-no kaigi
month-per three-time-link meeting
'three meetings per month'

The limited distribution of *getsu* should be attributed to competition with the native version *tsuki*. It may be the case that *getsu* cannot carry [+singular], unlike *tsuki*, thus being disqualified from appearing in the structure expressing a ratio, which requires an explicit marking of singularity.

2.4. The Prediction for Numeral Classifiers

In contrast to measure nouns, classifiers do not allow 1-deletion. This result is predicted by (6), repeated here.

(6) Numeral Classifiers and Selection of Numerals in Japanese
  a. A numeral classifier appears only when both [±singular] and [±augmented] are specified.
  b. [±augmented] always selects a numeral in Japanese.

It follows from (6a) that when a classifier is used, [±augmented] is specified. (6b) ensures that a numeral must co-occur in such a situation. The point is briefly made in section 1. It gains significance when we compare measure nouns with classifiers in relation to 1-deletion.

The prediction is borne out. Ratios can be expressed with classifiers as in (40), but *ichi* (or its morphophonological variants) can never be omitted. Thus, the examples in (41) are ungrammatical.

(40) a. is-satsu ni-sen-yen-no hon
  one-classifier two-hundred-yen-link book
  'a book that costs two hundred yen per copy'

  b. ichi-dai ni-hyaku-man-yen-no kuruma
  one-classifier two-hundred-ten.thousand-yen-link car
  'a car that costs two million yen apiece'

(41) a. *satsu ni-sen-yen-no hon
  classifier two-hundred-yen-link book

  b. *dai ni-hyaku-man-yen-no kuruma
  classifier two-hundred-ten.thousand-yen-link car

Adding an overt marker of the ratio such as *ni-tsuki*, *atari*, or *tan'i* does not help, either.

Since there are cases where measure nouns disallow 1-deletion (recall (17a) and (39), for example), this may not be a knockout argument against putting measure words in the same category as classifiers. But the incompatibility of classifiers with 1-deletion is quite systematic and robust, reinforcing the conclusion, reached independently on other grounds, that measure words are not classifiers.

References

Acquaviva, P. 2006. Goidelic Inherent Plurals and the Morphosemantics of Number. *Lingua* 116:1860–1887.

Aikhenvald, A. Y. 2000. *Classifiers*. Oxford: Oxford University Press.

Allan, K. 1977. Classifiers. *Language* 53:285–311.

Cheng, L. and Sybesma, R. 2005. Classifiers in Four Varieties of Chinese. *The Oxford Handbook of Comparative Syntax*, ed. G. Cinque and R. Kayne, 259–292. Oxford: Oxford University Press.

Croft, W. 1994. Semantic Universals in Classifier Systems. *Word* 45:145–171.

Downing, P. 1996. *Numeral Classifier Systems: The Case of Japanese*. Amsterdam: John Benjamins.

Gebhardt, L. 2011. Classifiers are Functional. *Linguistic Inquiry* 42:125–130.

Greene, D. 1992. Celtic. *Indo-European Numerals*, ed. J. Gzovdanović, 497–554. Berlin: Mouton de Gruyter.

Grinevald, C. 2004. Classifiers. *Morphologie/Morphology*, vol. 2, ed. G. Booij, C. Lehmann, J. Mugdan, S. Skopeteas, in collaboration with W. Kesselheim, 1016–1031. Berlin: Mouton de Gruyter.

Harbour, D. 2011a. Descriptive and Explanatory Markedness. *Morphology* 21:223–245.

Harbour, D. 2011b. Valence and Atomic Number. *Linguistic Inquiry* 42:561–594.

Holmes, P. and Hinchliffe, I. 2000. *Swedish: A Comprehensive Grammar*, 2nd ed. London: Routledge.

Hurford, J. R. 1987. *Language and Number*. Oxford: Blackwell.

Hurford, J. R. 2003. The Interaction between Numerals and Nouns. *Noun Phrase Structure in the Languages of Europe*, ed. F. Plank, 561–620. Berlin: Mouton de Gruyter.

Jespersen, O. 1914/1954. *A Modern English Grammar on Historical Principles, Part 2: Syntax*. Reprint, London: George Allen & Unwin.

Katamba, F. 2003. Bantu Nominal Morphology. *The Bantu Languages*, ed. D. Nurse and G. Phillipson, 103–120. London: Routledge.

Kayne, R. S. 2010. *Comparisons and Contrasts*. Oxford: Oxford University Press.

Larson, R. K. 1985. Bare-NP Adverbs. *Linguistic Inquiry* 16:595–621.

Lass, R. 1999. Phonology and Morphology. *The Cambridge History of The English Language, vol. 3: 1476–1776*, ed. R. Lass, 56–186. Cambridge: Cambridge University Press.

Lyons, J. 1977. *Semantics*. Cambridge: Cambridge University Press.

Noyer, R. 1997. *Features, Positions, and Affixes in Autonomous Morphological Structure*. New York: Garland.

Watanabe, A. 2010. Vague Quantity, Numerals, and Natural Numbers. *Syntax* 13: 37–77.

Korean Nominative Case-Stacking: A Configurational Account

THEODORE LEVIN*
Massachusetts Institute of Technology

1. Introduction

Variable case morphology and case-stacking are two phenomena that pose difficulties for configurational accounts of case assignment (e.g., Marantz 1991; McFadden 2004; Preminger 2011). Korean, a canonically nominative-accusative language, demonstrates such case-marking variability in possession and psychological verb constructions, as seen in (1).

(1) Cheli-**eykey/-ka/-eykey-ka** ton-**i** iss-ta
Cheli-DAT/-NOM/-DAT-NOM money-NOM exist-DEC
'Cheli has money.'

While the distribution of nominative- and dative-marked nominals is quite free, the distribution of stacked-case is constrained to focused nominals (Yoon 1996; Schütze 2001; inter alia).

In this paper, I argue that a slight modification to Marantz's formulation

* I would like to thank David Pesetsky, Norvin Richards, and the audience at J/K 22 for their insightful comments and criticisms. I would also like to thank Chanyong Pak, Daeyoung Sohn, and Suyeon Yun for their judgements.
Japanese/Korean Linguistics 22.
Edited by Mikio Giriko, Naonori Nagaya, Akiko Takemura, and Timothy J. Vance.

of configurational case assignment allows us to capture such variable case distribution. I posit that in Korean psychological and possession constructions, the experiencer subject is always *underlyingly* assigned both dative and nominative case. Multiple case assignment is achieved by allowing a nominal to be evaluated for case within each phase it occupies.

The paper is organized as follows. Section 2 outlines the relevant empirical facts. Section 3 briefly summarizes the configurational approach to case assignment and illustrates how case-stacking is problematic for this approach. Section 4 provides an emendation to the theory which allows us to account for the data in (1) and related examples. Section 5 concludes with some suggestions as to how the current proposal is preferable to an Agree-based analysis.

2. Empirical Facts

Korean is a nominative-accusative language. The subjects of both transitive and intransitive predicates bear *-i* following a vowel and *-ka* following a consonant. Direct objects bear *-(l)ul*.

(2) a. John-i mek-ess-ta
J.-**NOM** eat-PST-DEC
'John ate.'

b. Mary-ka John-ul t'ayli-ess-ta
M.-**NOM** J.-**ACC** hit-PST-DEC
'Mary hit John.'

However, in some cases subjects can bear unusual case marking. Such case marking most famously occurs with predicates expressing possession and psychological states. In these cases, subject nominals can bear dative, nominative, or stacked (dative and nominative) case. All three possibilities are illustrated in (3).

(3) a. John-eykey Mary-ka mwusep-ta
J.-**DAT** M.-**NOM** be.afraid-DEC

b. John-i Mary-ka mwusep-ta
J.-**NOM** M.-**NOM** be.afraid-DEC

c. John-eykey-ka Mary-ka mwusep-ta
J.-**DAT-NOM** M.-**NOM** be.afraid-DEC
'John is afraid of Mary.'

Notice, too, that the direct object does not bear accusative case as in (2b). Rather, regardless of the case of the subject nominal, *Mary* is marked nominative.

Nominative stacking is not limited to the subjects of psychological and possession predicates. It is also attested on adjuncts (4) and even some nominative marked subjects (5).

(4) ecey-pwut^{h}-(ka) nals'i-ka cohaci-ess-ta
yesterday-since-**NOM** weather-NOM become.good-PST-DEC
'Since yesterday, the weather has been good.'

(5) sengsayngnim-tul(-kkeyse)-man(-i) kulen il-ul ha-sipni-ta
teacher-PL-HON.**NOM**-only-**NOM** that.kind work-ACC do-SH-DEC
'Only teachers do that kind of work.'

It is critical to note that while the distribution of single-case-marked DPs is quite free, the distribution of stacked case is restricted to focus contexts—including *wh*-subject questions and their answers, correction contexts, and co-occurrence with overt focus-markers like *-man* 'only' (Schütze 2001).

The observation that stacked-nominative only occurs in focus contexts has led to some debate regarding whether the stacked case suffix should be treated as a case-marker (e.g., Yoon 1996, 2004) or a homophonous focus-marker (Schütze 2001). Crucially, this debate has been conducted against the background of an Agree-based approach to case-assignment (Chomsky 2000, 2001).

However, a number of recent studies have argued for a *configurational* approach to case-assignment independent of Korean (e.g., Marantz 1991; Bobaljik 2008; Preminger 2011). In its original formulation, the configurational approach to case-assignment faces the same problem faced by an Agree-based approach: nominals are expected to only receive case once. In this paper, I present an alteration to the configurational approach, which allows us to capture stacked-case. This proposal is advantageous in that it improves the configurational theory of case-assignment, and it removes unnecessary ambiguity in positing a focus-marker that is homophonous and in identical distribution with the nominative case marker. Additionally, it accounts for data which cannot be captured under an Agree-based approach.

3. Configurational Case Assignment

3.1. The Theory

Under the configurational proposal, nominals are not licensed by Case. Rather, the θ-criterion, EPP, and rules governing the distribution of PRO suffice. Originally, it was suggested that case was solely a morphological phenomenon and that case assignment was a post-syntactic process (Marantz 1991; Bobaljik 2008). However, recent proposals have argued that configurational case assignment must take place within the syntax (Preminger 2011).

The configurational model assigns case to a nominal based on the interplay of two factors: the identity of the head that (c-)selects it, and the position of the nominal relative to others in the clause. Case is assigned via Marantz's (1991) disjunctive case hierarchy:

(6) *DISJUNCTIVE CASE HIERARCHY*
lexical/oblique case ≫ dependent case ≫ unmarked case

Case assignment proceeds from left to right along (6) as follows. First, all DPs that are selected by lexical items which idiosyncratically specify a case marking for their arguments, including prepositions and verbs that govern so-called "quirky case," are assigned the idiosyncratic case in question. Second, those nominals that did not receive lexical case are evaluated for dependent case. For every pair of as-yet-caseless nominals within a local domain (a phase) that stand in a c-command relation, one will be assigned dependent case. In an ergative language, the *c-commanding* nominal receives dependent case. In an accusative language, the *c-commanded* nominal receives dependent case. Both of these patterns are schematized in (7).

(7) *REALIZATIONS OF DEPENDENT CASE*

a. NP ... NP "ACC" (nominative-accusative alignment)

b. "ERG" NP ... NP (ergative-absolutive alignment)

Finally, every nominal that has not been assigned lexical/oblique or dependent case in the preceding steps will be assigned unmarked case, which we can informally call "nominative" or "absolutive." Within the nominal domain unmarked case is realized as "genitive."

3.2. The Problem

In short, the problem that the configurational model faces is that case-stacking is expressly barred in Marantz's formulation. Once a nominal receives case by means of (6), it is said to exit the disjunctive hierarchy, rendering the nominal in question invisible to further case assignment operations. A case-marked nominal cannot receive case, although, as we have seen, it can affect the case-marking of another nominal. Thus, stacked nominative is completely unexpected. Moreover, as we shall see below, nominative marking on both subject and object, as in (3b), is also unexpected.

The configurational model is capable of capturing the assignment of case in (2b) and (3a). In (2b), the direct object *John* does not receive lexical case from the verb. It is eligible for and receives dependent accusative by virtue of being asymmetrically c-commanded by the subject *Mary*, which itself has not received case.

(8) a. Mary-ka John-ul t'ayli-ess-ta = (2b)
M.-**NOM** J.-**ACC** hit-PST-DEC
'Mary hit John.'

b.
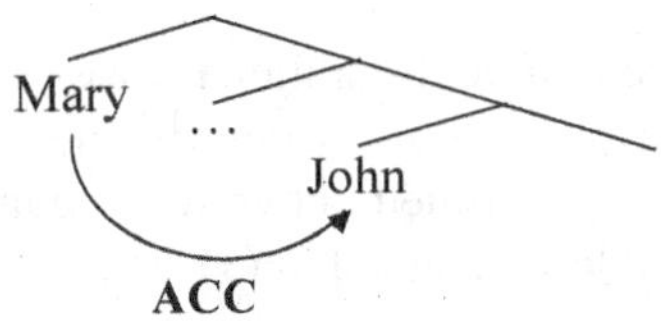

Mary receives unmarked nominative case, because it is unavailable for either lexical or dependent case.

In (3a), we can attribute dative morphology of the subject to lexical case assigned by the verb. Under this approach, nominative morphology on the direct object is expected. While still asymmetrically c-commanded by the subject, dependent accusative is unavailable, as the subject already bears lexical case.

(9) a. John-eykey Mary-ka mwusep-ta = (3a)
J.-**DAT** M.-**NOM** be.afraid-DEC
'John is afraid of Mary.'

b.
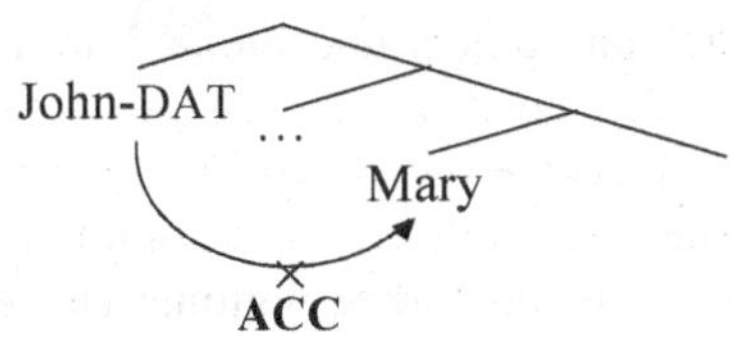

As the direct object is not eligible for dependent case assignment given the implementation of (6) sketched above, the only option is for it to receive unmarked nominative case.

Unfortunately, the patterns in (3b, c) and those in (4) and (5) cannot be captured by the configurational model in its current state. The nominative-subject nominative-object pattern in (3b) is unexpected, because the object should receive accusative case if no lexical case is realized on the subject, just as it is in (8).[1] When dependent case is evaluated, the asymmetrically c-commading subject will still be caseless. Similarly, stacked case of the kind seen in (3c), (4), and (5) is unexpected, because each nominal is assigned case only once. Thus if a nominal receives lexically-specified case or nomi-

[1] One possibility of capturing (3b) under the current formulation would be to treat the nominative case of the subject as lexical case just like dative in (3a). This requires assuming, however, that a predicate would assign multiple quirky cases.

native case by means of the appropriate step in (6), it cannot receive any other case morphology.

4. A Solution

Following Preminger (2011), I assume that configurational case assignment occurs derivationally within the narrow syntax. I propose the following emendation to the configurational model outlined above to account for the case-stacking and case-variation examples presented in (3)–(5).

(10) *CASE-STACKING IN A CONFIGURATIONAL MODEL*
A nominal receives case, via the Disjunctive Case Hierarchy, in each phase it occupies.

This modification immediately allows us to capture stacked-case examples seen in (3c), (4), and (5). Given the current proposal, there are now three instances of case assignment: the subject receives case in *both* Spec-vP and Spec-TP. Consider (11), which is quite similar to (3c).

(11) Cheli-eykey-ka ton-i iss-ta
C.-DAT-NOM money-NOM have-DEC
'Cheli has money.'

Within the vP, both the subject *Cheli* and object *ton* 'money' are evaluated for lexical case. As mentioned above, I posit that subjects of Korean psychological and possession predicates receive dative case in Spec-vP. With the subject assigned lexical case, the direct object is not eligible to receive dependent case. Thus, the object receives unmarked nominative. After undergoing movement to Spec-TP, the subject, which already bears lexical case, is evaluated for case again as in (6). As it is the only nominal in the CP phase, the subject will be marked with nominative case.

The current emendation can now capture (5), repeated below as (12).

(12) sengsayngnim-tul(-kkeyse)-man(-i) kulen il-ul ha-sipni-ta
teacher-PL-HON.**NOM**-only-**NOM** that.kind work-ACC do-SH-DEC
'Only teachers do that kind of work.'

Given (10), we expect the subject to receive unmarked nominative twice: once in Spec-vP and once in Spec-TP. The direct object is assigned dependent accusative, because it is c-commanded by the as-yet caseless subject within the vP phase.

Examples like (4) require slightly more exposition.

(13) cip-aneyse(-ka) Swunhi-eykey namp^{h}yen-i mwusep-ta
house-in-NOM S.-DAT husband-NOM fear-DEC
'In the house, Swunhi fears her husband.'

The locative adjunct *cip* 'house' receives lexical case within the vP, and unmarked nominative after undergoing movement to some position above the subject in Spec-TP.[2] The adjunct will not generate accusative marking on the subject, because it has already been case-marked within the vP phase, and thus does not meet the requirements of dependent case assignment when it moves to asymmetrically c-command the subject.

The current proposal amounts to suggesting that every moved nominal in Korean (and maybe every language) underlyingly carries stacked case morphemes. If this is true, we must answer three key questions. (1) Why are non-case-stacked subjects permitted in both focus and non-focus contexts? (2) Why are stacked-case subjects only permitted in focus contexts? (3) Why can't more combinations of case be realized overtly?

4.1. Obscuring Stacked-Case

Under the proposed analysis, dative-marked subjects, nominative-marked subjects, and stacked-case subjects are *all* stacked-case nominals at Spell-Out. If this is the case, something must intervene at PF to (at times) render one of the two assigned case-markers inaudible.

In this regard, Korean behaves like other case-stacking languages. Such languages often do not pronounce all the case morphology a nominal receives. Richards (2007) observes that Lardil (Tangkic, Australia) displays unpronounced case-stacking. Direct objects usually bear accusative case (14a), but this case is not realized in the future tense, where future morphology spreads to the direct object (14b).

(14) a. Ngada ngthungu warnawu dulnhuka-n̈
I slowly cook monkfish-**ACC**
'I slowly cooked the monkfish.'

b. Ngada ngthunguthu-r warnawu-thur dulnhuka-thur
I slowly-**FUT** cook-**FUT** monkfish-**FUT**
'I will slowly cook the monkfish.'

Given (14a), we could explain the lack of accusative case in (14b) in one of two ways: either accusative case is never assigned, or accusative case is assigned as in (14a) but is obscured by future tense concord. Evidence from

---

[2] Under common assumptions temporal adjuncts like *ecey* 'yesterday' (4) and locative ones like *cip* 'house' (13) are generated within a PP. The lexical case they receive is then either analyzed as idiosyncratic case assigned by a null P° or the over realization of P⁰ itself. Under this analysis, one might wonder why a PP should receive case just as a DP does. I suggest that the PP layer may be invisible to the configurational case assignment algorithm. Similar invisibility of PP layers can be seen in binding facts. Sentences like *John talked to Mary about herself* demonstrate that PP layers to do not seem to affect the ability for a DP contained within one *Mary* to bind a reflexive which it technically does not c-command.

relative clauses shows that the latter hypothesis is correct. In Lardil, relative clauses agree with the head noun in case.

(15) Kara nyingki kurri kiin-i thungal-i kirdi-thuru-Ø
Q you see that-ACC tree-ACC cut-FUT-ACC
'Do you see that tree which I am going to cut down?'

Relative clauses which modify direct objects of future verbs also bear ACC, even though ACC is no longer visible on the direct object itself.

(16) Ngada kurri-thur karnjin-kur
I see-FUT wallaby-FUT
[ngithun thabuji-kan-i la tharrba-Ø]
my brother-GEN-ACC spear-ACC
'I want to see the wallaby that my older brother speared.'

This suggests that, although not audible, accusative case was assigned to the direct object and later obscured by tense concord.

Similarly in Russian, case and number mismatches occur between a noun and its modifiers when the noun is modified by a paucal numeral. Compare (17a) and (17b).

(17) a. posledn-ie krasiv-ye stol-y
last-NOM.PL beautiful-NOM.PL table-NOM.PL
'the last beautiful tables'

b. posledn-ie dva krasiv-yx stol-a
last-NOM.PL two-NOM beautiful-GEN.PL table-GEN.SG
'the last two beautiful tables'

In oblique environments such mismatches disappear and dative plural is realized throughout.

(18) a. (k) posledn-im krasiv-ym stol-am
(to) last-DAT.PL beautiful-DAT.PL table-DAT.PL
'to the last beautiful tables'

b. (k) posledn-im dvu-m krasiv-ym stol-am
(to) last-DAT.PL two-DAT.PL beautiful-DAT.PL table-DAT.PL
'to the last two beautiful tables'

Pesetsky (2010) suggests that nouns enter the derivation valued with genitive case. Furthermore, D^0 assigns nominative and P^0 assigns oblique case—including dative. In (17a), D^0 merges and assigns nominative on top of the "primordial" genitive case of the noun, forming a stack. However numerals like those in (17b) have the ability to block assignment of nominative on nouns preserving the original genitive morphology. In (18), the P^0 *k* 'to' assigns dative on top of the nominative case of D^0 and genitive case of the noun.

Pesetsky's analysis of Russian requires that not all cases assigned to a nominal be pronounced. To account for this, Pesetsky, following Richards, proposes the *One Suffix Rule*.

(19) *ONE SUFFIX RULE* (Pesetsky 2010)
Delete all but the outermost case suffix.

We can account for the behavior of Korean by adopting a version of the One Suffix Rule. Such a rule would need to be less rigid than (19), because, as we have seen, either of two stacked case morphemes can be pronounced. Thus, I propose (20).

(20) *KOREAN ONE SUFFIX RULE*
Delete all but one case suffix.

Employing (20) allows us to capture the optionality of stacked *-ka*, which Schütze attributes to it being a focus-marker.

If the proposed analysis is on the right track, evidence from Icelandic independently suggests that Pesetsky's One Suffix Rule must be a parameterization of a more basic rule such as (20). In Icelandic quirky case is preserved during passivization.

(21) a. skipstjórinn sökkti skipinu
the.captain.NOM sank the.ship.**DAT**
'The captain sank the ship.'

b. skipinu var sökkt af skipstjóranum
the.ship.**DAT** was sunk by the.captain
'The ship was sunk by the captain.'

If (19) were universal, we would always expect quirky case to be replaced, because the raised subject would receive nominative in the CP phase. Instead, Icelandic appears to follow another instantiation of the One Suffix Rule—one in which all but the innermost case morpheme is deleted.

Combining (20) and (10) allows us to accurately capture dative-subjects and nominative-subjects in (3). As discussed above, dative is assigned to the subject in Spec-vP and nominative is assigned in Spec-TP forming a stack. After the stack is formed, (20) applies requiring either case marker to be deleted. Unfortunately, employing (20) as an inviolable constraint categorically blocks the realization of stacked case morphology.

4.2. Pronouncing Stacked-Case

If (20) is correct, case variability can be captured, but case-stacking in unexpected in any context. However, I posit that while correct, (20) is *not* inviolable. As we have seen, under certain circumstances (focus) both case morphemes assigned to a nominal can be pronounced.

It is interesting to note that the behavior of Korean case-stacking with regards to focus is also not entirely unexpected when considering related phenomena. In general, items which receive focus are undeletable. In English, pseudo-gapping constructions have been argued to be a special instance of VP-Ellipsis in which the direct object of the elided VP remains overt and requires focus prosody (e.g., Johnson 2009).

(22) a. John will select me more happily than Bill will YOU.
b. Bill ate the peaches more quickly than Harry did the GRAPES.

More closely related to the phenomenon at hand, Yatabe (1999) observes that in colloquial Japanese nominative case on subjects cannot be deleted if the subject has a focus interpretation. In neutral contexts, the Japanese nominative marker *-ga* varies with no (overt) case morphology. However, *-ga* is required when the nominal it suffixes too is focused. To account for these and related facts, Yatabe proposed the Antifocus Constraint:

(23) *ANTIFOCUS CONSTRAINT* (Yatabe 1999)
A nominative case particle cannot be dropped when a string immediately preceding it is focused.

As with the One Suffix Rule (19), a less rigid version of (23) is required for Korean—confirmed by native speakers. Consider the examples in (24), which illustrate preservation of accusative case in colloquial Korean under focus.

(24) a. Cinmi computer-ul/Ø sa-ss-e
C. computer-ACC/Ø buy-PST-IND
'Cinmi bought a computer.'

b. aniya, hywutep^{h}on-ul/*Ø sa-ss-e
no cell.phone-ACC buy-PST-IND
'No, (she) bought a cell phone.'

Much like nominative preservation in Japanese, (24a) illustrates that accusative case is optional in Korean except in focus-contexts like the correction in (24b). In such contexts overt case morphology is required.

In light of (24), I emend (23), as follows, to capture the case-stacking data.

(25) *KOREAN ANTIFOCUS CONSTRAINT*
A case particle cannot be deleted when a nominal immediately preceding it is focused.

If (20) and (25) both hold of Korean, then they compete against one another. (20) looks to delete case morphemes while (25) looks to preserve them. Through employing these rules simultaneously, we can capture the case-stacking and variation in (3)–(5). After Spell-Out, (20) will mark one case morpheme of a stack accrued by a nominal for deletion. Similarly, in focus-contexts (25) marks one case morpheme with focal prominence. When both (20) and (25) are applied to a stack of two morphemes, four logical possibilities arise, as illustrated in (26). I mark a case marker targeted for deletion (via [20]) by underlining it and one marked for preservation (via [25]) by bolding it.

(26) *PF OPERATIONS ON STACKED CASE*

a. Cheli-**eykey**-ka → Cheli-eykey
b. Cheli-eykey-**ka** → Cheli-ka
c. Cheli-eykey-**ka** → Cheli-eykey-ka
d. Cheli-**eykey**-ka → Cheli-eykey-ka

In (26a) and (26b), (20) and (25) operate on different morphemes, marking one for deletion and one for preservation. In (26a), *-ka* is deleted and *-eykey* preserved, resulting in a dative-marked subject. In (26b), *-eykey* is deleted and *-ka* is preserved, resulting in a nominative-marked subject. In (26c) and (26d), both (20) and (25) operate on the same morpheme. In (26c), *-ka* is marked both for deletion and for preservation. In (26d), it is *-eykey* that is marked both for deletion and for preservation. In these scenarios, I suggest that (25) overrides (20), resulting in the marked morpheme remaining overt. Moreover, as neither (20) nor (25) has applied to the other morpheme, it too will be pronounced. It is in these environments stacked-case morphology is pronounced.

The inability to realize stacked-case morphology in non-focus contexts falls out from this analysis. As (25) does not apply in non-focus contexts, we never expect stacked morphology, because one case morpheme will always be deleted and none will ever be marked for preservation. Thus, we can capture the behavior of stacked nominative case while treating it as a true instance of unmarked case assigned in the same fashion as unstacked nominative case, contra Schütze, who used the observation that stacked-nominative only occurs in focus contexts to suggest that it must be a focus-marker.

5. Conclusion

The proposed analysis accounts for case-stacking within a configurational model of case-assignment by allowing a nominal to receive case in every phase it occupies. Thus, all moved nominals bear underlying stacked case. Case-stacking is obscured in non-focus contexts by the *One Suffix Rule*, which requires all but one case morpheme to be deleted. Stacked case can be realized in focus contexts because the *Antifocus Constraint* can intervene, blocking the deletion of case morphology.

5.1. Limits to Case-Stacking?

Up until now I have avoided a crucial question: Why aren't other combinations of stacked case attested? Given that all moved nominals received case within each phase they occupy, we might expect a subject to bear stacked (non-honorific) nominative-nominative or a raised possessor to bear stacked genitive-accusative. Both of these (and many other possible combinations) are ungrammatical:

(27) a. *John-ga-ga Mary-lul sarangha-ta
J.-**NOM-NOM** M.-ACC love-DEC
('John loves Mary.')

b. *Mary-ga John-uy-lul tali-lul cap-ass-ta
Mary-NOM John-**GEN-ACC** leg-ACC grab-PST-DEC
('Mary grabbed John's leg.')

I follow a number of authors in suggesting that such combinations are impossible due to morphological cooccurrence restrictions (e.g., Cho and Sells 1995; Schütze 2001).

There are four post-nominal particle slots, as schematized in (28): each particle is confined to a particular slot, and each slot can contain at most one particle at a time.

(28) *NOMINAL TEMPLATE*

N_{root}	Postposition		Conjunctive		X-lim		Z-lim	
	eykey	DAT	(k)wa	'and'	man	'only'	ka	NOM
	hant^{h}ey	DAT	pwut^{h}e	'from'	k'aci	'even'	i	NOM
	k'ey	HON.DAT	*etc.*		*etc.*		(l)ul	ACC
	ey	DAT/LOC					(n)un	TOP
	eyse	LOC					uy	GEN
	(u)lo	DIR						
	k'aci	GOAL						
	k'eyse	HON.NOM						

While nominals which receive two cases that must occupy the same slot cannot bear stacked case, we expect them to exhibit case variation, due to the One Suffix Rule. Such variation is attested in Possessor Raising Constructions (29) and ECM (30).

(29) a. John-**uy** tali-ka ap^{h}u-ta
J.-GEN leg-NOM be.hurt-DEC

b. John-**ka** tali-ka ap^{h}u-ta
J.-NOM leg-NOM be.hurt-DEC
'John's leg hurts.'

(30) a. Tom-un Swunhi-**lul** yeyp'u-ta-ko sayngkakha-ess-ta
T.-TOP S.-ACC be.pretty-DEC-COMP think-PST-DEC

b. Tom-un Swunhi-**ka** yeyp'u-ta-ko sayngkakha-ess-ta
T.-TOP S.-NOM be.pretty-DEC-COMP think-PST-DEC
'Tom thought Swunhi to be pretty.'

Case variation of this kind provides additional evidence that a stack of case morphology is acquired by a moved nominal in the syntax. As we have seen above, either of the stacked cases can be pronounced in all contexts. Moreover, both morphemes of the stack can be overtly realized if the appropriate conditions are met.

5.2. Arguments Against an Agree-Based Approach

As mentioned at the outset, commonly held Agree-based accounts (Chomsky 2000, 2001) face a similar problem in accounting for the case-stacking in examples like (3)–(5). Much like the original configurational proposal, these accounts forbid multiple case assignment outright. However, even if we were to permit multiple case assignment, an Agree-based account lacks the explanatory capabilities of the current proposal.

In an Agree-based framework, case is assigned to an as-yet caseless nominal by virtue of structural proximity to a designated functional head. Given a designated case-assigning functional head F^0, and a nominal α that is non-immediately c-commanded by F^0, the case marking associated with F^0 (e.g., nominative for T^0, accusative for v^0, and so forth) will be assigned to α. The realization of nominative case is taken to be a by-product of φ-agreement with T^0. As such, to account for examples like (3b) where both the subject an object bear nominative case, we would need to permit Mutiple Agree (Hiraiwa 2001), whereby the φ-probe on T^0 can simultaneously agree with both the subject in Spec-vP and the object in Compl-V and thereby assign nominative case to both of them. Furthermore, we would need to permit psychological and possession verbs to assign lexical dative case to their subjects, just as in the current proposal. By allowing both case assignment operations to occur, two cases could be assigned to a single nominal underlyingly. At this point the Agree-based approach and the configurational approach appear to be quite similar, and we can further restrict the overt realization of case (in both systems) using the *One Suffix Rule* and

Antifocus Constraint. Thus, the canonical case-stacking examples in (3) appear to be captured in either approach.

However, examples like (5), repeated below as (31), pose a more difficult challenge to the Agree-based approach which we have briefly sketched here.

(31) sengsayngnim-tul(-kkeyse)-man(-i) kulen il-ul ha-sipni-ta
teacher-PL-HON.**NOM**-only-**NOM** that.kind work-ACC do-SH-DEC
'Only teachers do that kind of work.'

Unlike the previous examples, in which nominative case was realized on two distinct nominals, (31) provides a situation in which nominative case is realized twice on a single nominal. Under the configurational approach, such examples show that unmarked nominative case can be assigned twice to the same nominal—once within the vP phase and once in the CP phase. However, such a scenario cannot be accounted for under an Agree-based analysis that utilizes Multiple Agree, because even though Multiple Agree can permit a probe to seek out more than one goal of the same type, it is not possible for a single token to be agreed with twice. Thus T^0 cannot be responsible for assigning both instances of nominative case to the subject in (31). Such examples provide Schütze with further evidence that stacked nominative case cannot be true case in an Agree-based system, but as we have seen above, in a configurational system multiple case assignment of the same case to the same nominal can be captured.

References

Baker, M. C. and Vinokurova, N. 2010. Two Modalities of Case Assignment: Case in Sakha. *Natural Language and Linguistic Theory* 28:593–642.

Bobaljik, J. D. 2008. Where's phi? Agreement as a Post-syntactic Operation. *Phi Theory: Phi-Features across Interfaces and Modules*, ed. D. Harbour, D. Adger, and S. Béjar, 295–328. Oxford: Oxford University Press.

Cho, Y. Y. and Sells, P. 1995. A Lexical Account of Inflectional Suffixes in Korean. *Journal of East Asian Linguistics* 4:119–174.

Chomsky, N. 2000. Minimalist Inquiries: The Framework. *Step by Step: Essays on Minimalist Syntax in Honor of Howard Lasnik*, ed. R. Martin, D. Michaels, and J. Uriagereka, 89–155. Cambridge: MIT Press.

Chomsky, N. 2001. Derivation by Phase. *Ken Hale: A Life in Language*, ed. M. Kenstowicz, 1–52. Cambridge: MIT Press.

Gerdts, D. B. and Youn, C. 1988. Non-Nominative Subjects in Korean. *Harvard Studies in Korean Linguistics III: Proceedings of the 1989 Workshop on Korean Linguistics*, ed. S. Kuno et al., 235–248. Seoul: Hanshin.

Gerdts, D. B. and Youn, C. 1999. Case Stacking and Focus in Korean. *Harvard Studies in Korean Linguistics VIII*, ed. S. Kuno et al., 325–339. Seoul: Hanshin.

Hiraiwa, K. 2001. Multiple Agree and the Defective Intervention Constraint in Japanese. *The Proceedings of the MIT-Harvard Joint Conference (HUMIT 2000)*, ed. O. Matsushansky et al., 67–80. Cambridge: MIT.

Johnson, K. 2009. Gapping is Not (VP) Ellipsis. *Linguistic Inquiry* 40:289–328.

Levin, T. and Preminger, O. 2012. Case in Sakha: Are Two Modalities Really Necessary? Unpublished manuscript.

McFadden, T. 2004. The Position of Morphological Case in the Derivation: A Study on the Syntax–Morphology Interface. Doctoral dissertation, University of Pennsylvania.

Marantz, A. 1991. Case and Licensing. *Proceedings of the 8th Eastern States Conference on Linguistics*, ed. G. Westphal, B. Ao, and H. R. Chae, 234–253. Ithaca: CLC Publications.

Pesetsky, D. 2010. Russian Case Morphology and the Syntactic Categories. http://ling.auf.net/lingBuzz/001120.

Preminger, O. 2011. Agreement as a Fallible Operation. Doctoral dissertation, MIT.

Richards, N. 2007. Lardil "Case Stacking" and the Structural/Inherent Case Distinction. http://ling.auf.net/lingbuzz/000405.

Schütze, C. T. 2001. On Korean "Case Stacking": The Varied Functions of the Particles *-ka* and *-lul*. *The Linguistic Review* 18:193–232.

Yatabe, S. 1999. Particle Ellipsis and Focus Projection in Japanese. *Language, Information, Text* 6:79–104.

Yoon, J. H. S. 1996. Ambiguity of Government and the Chain Condition. *Natural Language and Linguistic Theory* 14:105–162.

Yoon, J. H. S. 2004. Non-Nominative (Major) Subjects and Case Stacking in Korean. *Non-Nominative Subjects*, vol. 2, ed. P. Bhoskaravao and K. V. Subbarao, 265–314. Amsterdam: John Benjamins.

Multiple Accusative Constructions: The Case of V+*tate* in Japanese

MIKA KIZU*

PETER SELLS
University of York

HIDEKAZU TANAKA
University of York

This paper examines multiple accusative constructions in Japanese, focusing on certain sentences containing a nominalized phrase marked by the suffix *tate*, which basically means 'just finished and the resultant state of the action or event is positively recognized'. Unlike Korean, multiple accusatives are not allowed in standard Japanese; this has been the prevalent view in Japanese syntax since Harada (1973). Recently, Hiraiwa (2010) examines the nature of the Double-*o* Constraint and claims that nothing prevents multiple accusatives in a single domain from occurring in narrow syntax. This paper explores this possibility with new kinds of data using Verb+*tate* constructions.

The outline of this paper is as follows. Section 1 illustrates relevant basic facts regarding multiple accusative and V+*tate* constructions and pre-

* A preliminary version of this paper was presented at FAJL 6. We thank Shin-Sook Kim for assistance with the Korean data. For this version of the paper, we would like to thank the participants of the J/K Linguistics 22 conference, in particular, Hiroshi Aoyagi, Kentaro Nakatani, Kunio Nishiyama, Takeo Suzuki, and Noriko Yoshimura, for valuable comments. This research was partially supported by the Japan Foundation Japanese Studies Fellowship Program 2012–13, awarded to Mika Kizu. The authors remain responsible for any errors.

Japanese/Korean Linguistics 22.
Edited by Mikio Giriko, Naonori Nagaya, Akiko Takemura, and Timothy J. Vance.

sents our main claim. Section 2 shows empirical evidence to support part of our main claim: two accusative phrases in V+*tate* constructions do not form a constituent. Then, Section 3 discusses V+*tate* constructions involving raising out of the *tate*-phrase. Section 4 offers an analysis from a Case-theoretic viewpoint. Section 5 points out that *tate* constructions are similar to Korean floating quantifier constructions. Section 6 concludes the paper and addresses other possibilities for further research.

1. Basic Facts

The nominal morpheme *tate* attaches to a transitive or unaccusative verb, to highlight the resultant state of the underlying object of the verb (Yamada 2005). (1a) and (1b) contain transitive verbs; *sibor*(*u*) 'squirt' in (1a) is an activity verb of creation, and *age*(*ru*) 'fry' in (1b) is an activity verb of change-of-state. The suffix, *tate*, can go with an unaccusative verb like *kawak*(*u*) 'dry' in (1c) but not an unergative verb like *wara*(*u*) 'smile, laugh' in (1d).

(1) a. sibori-tate-no gyuunyuu
squirt-*tate*-COP milk
'fresh milk'

b. age-tate-no tenpura
fry-*tate*-COP tempura
'freshly fried tempura'

c. kawaki-tate-no taoru
dry-*tate*-COP towel
'refreshingly dried towel'

d. *warai-tate-no kodomo
smile-*tate*-COP child
'the child who just gave a nice smile'

Interestingly, the order of [V+*tate-no* NP] in (1) above can be switched to [NP-*no* V+*tate*] without causing a difference in meaning, as shown in (2).

(2) a. gyuunyuu-no sibori-tate
milk-GEN squirt-*tate*
'fresh milk'

b. tempura-no age-tate
tempura-GEN fry-*tate*
'freshly fried tempura'

c. taoru-no kawaki-tate
towel-GEN dry-*tate*
'refreshingly dried towel'

More interestingly, examples like (3), which are basically grammatical, show that double accusative phrases are possible in this construction.

(3) a. ?**koora-o tukuri-tate-o** nom-asete kureru basyo-ga atte ne
cola-ACC make-*tate*-ACC drink-CAUS give place-NOM exist SFP
'There are places where you can drink freshly made cola.'

b. ?**musi-mono-nado-o** **tukuri-tate-o** tabete itadaite
steam-thing-and.such-ACC make-*tate*-ACC eat receive
ori-masu
exist.HUMBLE-POLITE
'You can eat freshly made steamed food and the like.'

The examples in (3) are slightly degraded in acceptability due only to the presence of two accusatives; however, they show that changing the genitive case marker of the *tate*-phrases in (2) to an accusative case marker is possible in contexts such as those in (3). In fact, acceptability can be increased by replacing the first accusative phrase with a focus marker, as in (5a), or by clefting or scrambling the two accusative phrases apart, as in (5b–c) (Hiraiwa 2010).

(4) ?Taroo-ga koora-o tukuri-tate-o nom-asete kureta
Taro-NOM cola-ACC make-*tate*-ACC drink-CAUS gave
'Taro let me drink freshly brewed beer.'

(5) a. Taroo-ga koora-mo/sae/wa/dake tukuri-tate-o
Taro-NOM cola-also/even/TOP/only make-*tate*-ACC
nom-asete kureta
drink-CAUS gave

b. [Taroo-ga tukuri-tate-o nom-asete kureta-no]-wa
[Taro-NOM make-*tate*-ACC drink-CAUS gave-NMLZ]-TOP
koora(-o)-da
cola(-ACC)-COP

c. koora-o, Taroo-ga tukuri-tate-o nom-asete kureta
cola-ACC Taro-NOM make-*tate*-ACC drink-CAUS gave

The question arises as to how examples such as (3) and (4), with NP+accusative and V-*tate*+accusative in the same example, are derived, given the existence in Japanese of the Double-*o* Constraint (Harada 1973).

One possible analysis is that the first accusative NP is the object of the verb in the *tate*-clause; the first accusative phrase in (3) and (4), which is the notional object of the predicate, might be internal to the constituent headed by the *tate*-phrase. Then the two accusative cases would technically be assigned in different domains. Under this analysis, the Double-*o* Constraint would not be violated, as illustrated in (6).

(6) **[[koora-o tukuri-tate]-o** nom-asete kureru] basyo . . .
cola-ACC make-*tate*-ACC drink-CAUS give place
'the place you can drink freshly made cola . . .'

However, we argue that this structure does not correctly represent these examples. Rather, the first and the second accusative phrases do not form a constituent, as shown in (7).

(7) **[koora-o [tukuri-tate]-o** nom-asete kureru] basyo . . .
cola-ACC make-*tate*-ACC drink-CAUS give place
'the place you can drink freshly made cola . . .'

Specifically, we adopt the analysis in (8), in which *koora* 'cola' is merged in the complement position of the *tate*-phrase as in (8a) and raises out of the *tate*-phrase as in (8b).

(8) a. **[$_{NP}$ [$_{VP}$ koora tukuri]-tate]-o**
cola make-*tate*-ACC

b. **koora$_i$-o [$_{NP}$ [$_{VP}$ t$_i$ tukuri]-tate]-o**
cola-ACC make-*tate*-ACC

As we will see, (8a) cannot stay as it is, as no Case is licensed for the object of the verb, *tukur*(*i*) 'make'. The NP, *koora*, raises to the matrix clause where it can check its Case.[1]

2. Constituency

2.1. Contrast with Head-Internal Relative Clauses

Our proposal is that the two accusative phrases found in this *tate*-construction do not form a single constituent, as shown in (9a). We show

[1] Although we do not go into details here, there are other possibilities for the first accusative phrase to check its Case feature, shown in (i). In (ia), the object is relativized, and hence there is an empty category of some kind; the *tate*-phrase is a kind of relative clause, as in the examples in (1) above. Another possibility is shown in (ib), where the object moves to the edge of its containing NP, which seems to allow genitive Case to be licensed (Hiraiwa 2012).

(i) a. **[$_{NP}$ [$_{RC}$ [$_{VP}$ [e]$_i$ tukuri]-tate-no] koora$_i$]-o V-*tate*-no NP**
make-*tate*-COP cola-ACC

b. **[$_{NP}$ koora$_i$-no [$_{VP}$ t$_i$ tukuri]-tate]-o Genitive argument**
cola-GEN make-*tate*-ACC

here that it is not possible to analyze the construction as a kind of head-internal relative clause (HIRC), which we assume to have the structure in (9b).

(9) a. koora$_i$-o [$_{NP}$ [$_{VP}$ t$_i$ tukuri]-tate]-o
cola-ACC make-*tate*-ACC

b. [$_{NP}$ [$_{TP}$ *pro* koora-**o** tukuri]-tate]-**o**
cola-ACC make-*tate*-ACC

There are many empirical differences between *tate*-constructions and HIRCs. First, the internal head cannot be accusative if the predicate is unaccusative, but this is fine in *tate*-constructions, as shown in (10).

(10) a. ?tenpura-o agari-tate-o tabe-sasete kureru
tempura-ACC fry-*tate*-ACC eat-CAUS give
'(They serve) freshly fried tempura for you.'

b. *[tenpura-o agatta-no]-o tabe-sasete kureru
tempura-ACC fried-NMLZ-ACC eat-CAUS give

Second, an adverb modifying the embedded predicate, such as *hukkura* 'with/into fluffiness', cannot precede the first accusative phrase (the notional object of the predicate) in *tate*-constructions, whereas this is possible in an HIRC, as shown in (11).

(11) a. *hukkura mame-o taki-tate-o tabeta
fluffy beans-ACC cook-*tate*-ACC ate
'(I) ate freshly cooked beans boiled into fluffiness.'

b. [hukkura mame-o taita-no]-o tabeta
fluffy beans-ACC cooked-NMLZ-ACC ate

Similarly, when a PP intervenes between the first accusative phrase and the following *tate*-phrase, the PP can modify either verb, as shown in (12a), but such a reading is not possible in the HIRC in (12b).

(12) a. ?Taroo-wa koora-o koozyoo-de tukuri-tate-o nonda
Taro-TOP cola-ACC factory-in make-*tate*-ACC drank
'Taro drank cola [freshly made in the factory].'
'Taro drank [freshly made cola] in the factory.'

b. Taroo-wa [koora-o koozyoo-de tukutta-no]-o nonda
Taro-TOP cola-ACC factory-in make-NMLZ-ACC drank
'Taro drank cola [freshly made in the factory].'
*'Taro drank [freshly made cola] in the factory.'

(9)–(12) clearly show that the two accusative phrases in *tate*-constructions do not form a constituent (one inside the other), unlike in HIRCs.

2.2. Further Evidence for Constituency

Further evidence for the above view can be found in the following examples. As with (12a) above, the examples in (13) clearly allow a matrix interpretation for the adverbs.

(13) a. ?[gohan-o] **yuttarito** [taki-tate]-o tabeta
[rice-ACC] comfortably [steam-*tate*]-ACC ate
'(I) ate freshly steamed rice comfortably.'

b. ?John-ga [biiru-o] **isoide** [tukuri-tate]-o nonda
John-NOM beer-ACC hurriedly [make-*tate*]-ACC drank
'John hurriedly drank freshly made beer.'

The interpretations in (13) cannot be easily derived if the first accusative and the *tate*-phrase form a constituent.

As expected, a PP associated with the *tate*-phrase, as in (14), cannot precede the raised phrase.

(14) ?John-ga **koozyoo-de** biiru-o tukuri-tate-o nonda
John-NOM factory-at beer-ACC make-*tate*-ACC drank
'John drank [freshly brewed beer] **at the factory**.'
*'John drank [beer freshly brewed at the factory].'

Furthermore, two *tate*-phrases containing a genitive argument can be coordinated, as shown in (15), but coordinating *tate*-phrases containing NP-*o* is impossible, as shown in (16).

(15) John-ga [biiru-no tukuri-tate]-to [koohii-no ire-tate]-o
John-NOM [beer-GEN make-*tate*]-and [coffee-GEN brew-*tate*]-ACC
nonda
drank
'John drank freshly brewed beer and freshly made coffee.'

(16) *John-ga [biiru-o tukuri-tate]-to [koohii-o ire-tate]-o
John-NOM [beer-ACC make-*tate*]-and [coffee-ACC brew-*tate*]-ACC
nonda
drank

Finally, the distribution of Negative Polarity Items (NPIs) in (17) also shows that the *o*-phrase is not inside the *tate*-phrase. The sequence [*nani* . . . *mo*] forming the NPI must be within the same constituent.

(17) John-ga [nan(i)-no tukuri-tate-mo] nom-anai
John-NOM [what-GEN make-*tate*-also] drink-NEG.PRES
'John does not drink anything freshly made.'

(18) *John-ga [nani-o] [tukuri-tate-mo] nom-anai
John-NOM what-ACC make-*tate*-also drink-NEG.PRES

The facts here all show that the two accusative phrases in *tate*-constructions do not form a constituent, and hence (7), but not (6), correctly represents the structure of the two *tate*-phrases.

3. Our Analysis

The preceding section has shown that the first accusative phrase (*koora-o* 'cola-ACC' in (8)) and the second accusative phrase (*tukuri-tate-o* 'make-*tate*-ACC' in (8)) do not form a constituent. This section demonstrates that the first phrase is externally merged as the object of the V(+*tate*) but moves out of the *tate*-clause. Our proposed structures are repeated below.

(8) a. **[$_{NP}$ [$_{VP}$ koora tukuri]-tate]-o** ⇒
cola make-*tate*-ACC

b. **koora$_i$-o [$_{NP}$ [$_{VP}$ t$_i$ tukuri]-tate]-o**
cola-ACC make-*tate*-ACC

The base structure in (8a) contains *koora* 'cola' as a complement of *tukuri* (-*tate*) 'make-*tate*'. The examples below show that *koora* is merged as a complement in the *tate*-clause and then raises to the main clause as in (8b).

First, the *tate* examples in (19) contain a numeral quantifier (NQ) associated with the notional object NP. Crucially, (19) shows that there must be a position inside the V-*tate* phrase associated with the raised accusative NP; otherwise, the floating quantifier could not be a modifier for the accusative phrase due to the locality conditions on floating quantifiers (i.e., the need for mutual c-command).

(19) a. ?ranborugiini$_i$-<u>o</u> [koozyoo-de t$_i$ zyuu-dai tukuri-tate]-<u>o</u>
Lamborghini-ACC factory-in ten-CL make-*tate*-ACC
yunyuusita
imported
'(I) imported ten Lamborghini just produced in the factory.'

b. ?gohan$_i$-<u>o</u> [nabe-de t$_i$ san-goo taki-tate]-<u>o</u> tabeta
rice-ACC pot-by three-CL cook-*tate*-ACC ate
'(I) ate three *go* cups of rice just cooked in a pot.'

The interpretations in (19) receive a straightforward explanation under (8) if the numeral quantifier can be associated with the accusative NP ('Lamborghini' in (a) and *gohan* 'rice' in (b)) through a trace within the *tate*-clause.

We have also proposed that in double accusative *tate*-constructions, the complement NP of V+*tate* is moved out of the *tate*-clause, as in (8b). This is confirmed by the fact that the order of double accusatives is restricted; the *tate*-phrase cannot precede the associated NP-*o*.

(20) a. *Taroo-ga [t_j tukuri-tate]-o_k $koora_j$-o t_k nom-asete kureta
Taro-NOM make-*tate*-ACC cola-ACC drink-CAUS gave
'(lit.) Freshly made, Taro gave me cola.'

b. *[t_j tukuri-tate]-o_k Taroo-ga $koora_j$-o t_k nom-asete kureta
make-*tate*-ACC Taro-NOM cola-ACC drink-CAUS gave
'(lit.) Freshly made, Taro gave me cola.'

That is, the accusative NP in (20) starts out internal to the *tate*-phrase, and then raises out. Consequently, the ungrammaticality of these examples is accounted for as a violation of the Proper Binding Condition (Fiengo 1977).

4. Case Marking

4.1. Unaccusative + *tate*

The raising analysis outlined above requires that the verb internal to the *tate*-phrase is not responsible for the accusative on the object NP (on *koora* in *koora-o̲ tukuri-tate-o̲* 'cola-ACC make-*tate*-ACC'). Rather, the higher verb is responsible for this case. The following examples (cf. (14)), in which *tate* is attached to an unaccusative verb, confirm this prediction, since unaccusative verbs do not license accusative case.

(21) a. *siitu-o kawaita
sheet-ACC dried
'The sheets dried.'

b. ?siitu-**o̲** kawaki-tate-**o̲** tatanda
sheet-ACC dry-*tate*-ACC folded
'(I) folded sheets just dried.'

(22) a. *akatyan-o umareta
baby-ACC was.born
'The baby was born.'

b. ?neko-no akatyan-**o̲** umare-tate-**o̲** dakkosita
cat-GEN baby-ACC be.born-*tate*-ACC cuddled
'(I) cuddled kittens just born.'

The verbs, *kawak(u)* 'dry' in (21) and *umare(ru)* 'be born' in (22), are both unaccusatives, and hence (21a) and (22a) are ungrammatical, which is explained under the general assumption that unaccusatives do not license accusative case. However, the initial accusative clearly is licensed in (21b) and (22b), and this must be done by the main verb.

Now the examples of transitive verbs suffixed with *tate* that we have seen so far need to be explained under this analysis. The predicates in question are transitive verbs of creation or change-of-state, such as *tukuru* 'make', *ageru* 'fry', *taku* 'cook', and *ireru* 'pour'. As they are not unaccusative, they should be able to license NP-*o* internally, but when suffixed with *tate*, they do not. The next subsection addresses this.

4.2. Transitive + *tate*

We assume with Saito (2012) that Case is required and valued through Merge, and that accusative Case is valued through merge with the phase head, *v*. That is, accusative Case is actually licensed by V-*v*. This explains the examples with unaccusatives in (21b) and (22b); since they are VP only, there is no V-*v* to license accusative Case.

As for the transitive verbs of creation or change-of-state, we argue that when they are suffixed with *tate*, the whole predicate, V-*tate*(-*no*/*da*), turns into an unaccusative due to its semantics of delimitedness or telicity. Specifically, verbs of creation and change-of-state semantically imply an end point of the event, which is highlighted by adding *tate*. Then V+*tate* indicates the resultant state of the event, and the whole predicate acts like an unaccusative. Similar observations have been made in previous literature (see, for example, Levin and Rappaport Hovav 1995 and Tsujimura 1994 among many others); when some element which must delimit an event appears with a non-unaccusative predicate, the overall phrase behaves like an unaccusative. An unaccusative is VP only, and does not license accusative Case. Thus, accusative Case must be licensed externally, as shown in (23b) (empty categories omitted here).

(23) a. John-ga gohan-o taita
John-NOM rice-ACC cooked
'John cooked rice.'

b. ?gohan-<u>o</u> [$_{VP}$ taki]-tate-<u>o</u> tabeta
rice-ACC cook-*tate*-ACC ate

The proposed analysis makes a predication: if *tate* attaching to a verb of creation or change-of-state does not allow projections above VP, then there is no way to have a subject of the *tate*-phrase. This is indeed the case, as the following examples show.

(24) a. *John-ga gohan-o taki-tate-da
John-NOM rice-ACC cook-*tate*-COP
'John has just cooked rice.'

b. *[(gohan-o) taki-tate-no] John
rice-ACC cook-*tate*-COP John
'John, who just cooked (rice)'

c. *[John-ga taki-tate-no] gohan
John-NOM cook-*tate*-COP rice
'rice freshly cooked by John'

Note especially for (24c) that there is no reason a priori why it should be ungrammatical.

There are some apparent counterexamples to our claim, however. Examples like (25) with accusative objects are in fact possible (Martin 1975: 420; Sugioka 1986:212).

(25) a. [daigaku-o sotugyoo si-tate-no] hito
college-ACC graduate do-*tate*-COP person
'a person who just graduated from college'

b. are-wa [[piano-o narai-tate-no] kodomo]-mo
that-TOP piano-ACC learn-*tate*-COP child-even
hike-soo-na kyoku da
play.can-seem-COP song is
'That is a song that can be played by even a child who just learned the piano.'

In (25), the *tate*-phrases such as *narai-tate-no* 'learn-*tate*-COP' seem to retain their full clausal characteristics. Unlike (24), they are fine with subjects, as in (26)–(27).

(26) a. sono hito-ga daigaku-o sotugyoo si-tate-da
that person-NOM college-ACC graduate do-*tate*-COP
'That person has just graduated from college.'

b. [sono hito-ga sotugyoosi-tate-no] daigaku
that person-NOM graduate-*tate*-COP college
'the college from which that person graduated'

(27) a. kodomo-ga piano-o narai-tate-da
child-NOM piano-ACC learn-*tate*-COP
'The child has just learned piano.'

b. [kodomo-ga narai-tate-no] piano
child-NOM learn-*tate*-COP piano
'piano, which the child has just learned'

The difference between (24) and (25) comes from the type of verb. *Sotugyoo-suru* 'to graduate' is an instantaneous verb, which does not indicate an activity but only a state. *Narau* 'to learn', on the other hand, is a pure activity verb, which do not imply any endpoint of a process. For such verbs, *tate* does not provide the whole predicate with the property of delimitedness or telicity; it does not highlight the resultant state of the end result after the action/event. Thus, the *tate* in (25)–(27) does not change the aspectual property or argument structure of the predicate, which is able to project a full clause.

4.3. Some Consequences

Saito's (2012) theory of Case predicts that Japanese allows multiple accusatives (as well as multiple nominatives) in syntax, which falls in line with our analysis. Indeed, not only double accusatives but also triple accusatives are possible, as shown in (28).[2]

(28) a. ?John-ga gohan-**o** hokahoka-**o** taki-tate-**o** tabeta
John-NOM rice-ACC warm-ACC cook-*tate*-ACC ate
'John ate freshly cooked hot rice.'

b. ?Mary-ga korokke-**o** atuatu-**o** age-tate-**o** dasita
Mary-NOM croquette-ACC hot-ACC fry-*tate*-ACC served
'Mary served freshly fried hot croquettes.'

Also as expected, multiple nominatives are possible for *tate* constructions. This is exemplified in (29).

(29) a. gohan-**ga** hokahoka-**ga** taki-tate-**ga** oisii
rice-NOM warm-NOM cook-*tate*-NOM be.delicious
'Freshly cooked hot rice is delicious.'

b. korokke-**ga** atuatu-**ga** age-tate-**ga** ninki-da
croquette-NOM hot-NOM fry-*tate*-NOM be.popular-COP
'Freshly fried hot croquettes are popular.'

What this very brief data presentation shows is that, just like Korean, Japanese allows potentially multiple accusatives and multiple nominatives in narrow syntax.

---

2 Here, the order of the mimetic NP and the *tate* NP can be switched, but the initial NP, the thematic argument of the predicate, must precede the other two.

5. *Tate* and Floating Quantifiers

5.1. Japanese FQ

A related issue that we address here is how *tate* constructions are positioned within the language and across languages.

Some of the syntactic behaviour in *tate*-constructions seem quite parallel to floating quantifier (FQ) constructions in that an FQ is similar to a *tate*-phrase in terms of the relation to the preceding NP, which we refer to as the "host." For instance, the host NP, but not an FQ or *tate*-phrase, can be clefted. Examples with *tate* are shown in (30) and those with an FQ in (31).

(30) a. John-ga tukuri-tate-o nonda-no-wa biiru(-o)-da
John-NOM make-*tate*-ACC drank-NMLZ-TOP beer(-ACC)-is
'(lit.) What John drank (something) freshly made is beer.'

b. *John-ga biiru-o nonda-no-wa tukuri-tate(-o)-da
John-NOM beer-ACC drank-NMLZ-TOP make-*tate*(-ACC)-is
'(lit.) What John drank beer is (the one) freshly made.'

(31) a. John-ga sanbon nonda-no-wa biiru(-o)-da
John-NOM three.bottles drank-NMLZ-TOP beer(-ACC)-is
'(lit.) What John drank three bottles is beer.'

b. *John-ga biiru-o nonda-no-wa sanbon(-o)-da
John-NOM beer-ACC drank-NMLZ-TOP three.bottles(-ACC)-is
'(lit.) What John drank beer is three bottles.'

In contrast, postposing the host NP is possible, but so is postposing the *tate*-phrase and FQ, as follows.

(32) a. John-ga tukuri-tate-o nonda-yo, biiru-o
John-NOM make-*tate*-ACC drank-SFP beer-ACC
'(lit.) John drank freshly brewed one, beer.'

b. John-ga biiru-o nonda-yo, tukuri-tate-o
John-NOM beer-ACC drank-SFP make-*tate*-ACC
'(lit.) John drank beer, freshly brewed one.'

(33) a. John-ga sanbon nonda-yo, biiru-o
John-NOM three.bottles drank-SFP beer-ACC
'(lit.) John drank three bottles, beer.'

b. John-ga biiru-o nonda-yo, sanbon
John-NOM beer-ACC drank-SFP three.bottles
'(lit.) John drank beer, three bottles.'

However, there are also distinct behavioural properties in *tate* and FQ constructions, as shown in (34); although the sequence of NP-*o* followed by V+*tate* cannot be coordinated with another (see (16)), such coordination is possible with an FQ.

(34) [biiru-o/ga sanbon] to [koora-o/ga nihon]
[beer-ACC/NOM three.bottles] and [cola-ACC/NOM two.bottles]
'three bottles of beer and two bottles of cola'

Another difference between -*tate* and an FQ is that an FQ can precede its associated NP whereas this is impossible in *tate* constructions (see (20)):

(35) John-ga sanbon biiru-o nonda
John-NOM three.bottles beer-ACC drank
'John drank three bottles of beer.'

If, however, the *tate*-phrase is marked by *sika* (followed by -*nai*) or *dake*, both meaning 'only', the ordering restriction seems to be lifted:

(36) a. taki-tate-sika Tanaka-san-wa gohan-o tabe-nai
cook-*tate*-only Mr. Tanaka-TOP rice-ACC eat-NEG
'Mr Tanaka eats only freshly cooked rice.'

b. age-tate-dake okaasan-wa tenpura-o katta
fry-*tate*-only mother-TOP tempura-ACC bought
'My mother bought only freshly fried tempura.'

In this sense, it actually seems that -*tate* is more similar to Korean FQs than Japanese ones, so we end with a brief discussion of Korean.

5.2. Korean FQ

We conclude with some comparative observations on Korean, putting an exact analysis aside for our future research. The closest Korean examples to our *tate*-phrases are like (37a), which look like HIRCs in Japanese and which are nominalized by *kes*. Some speakers allow the object *bread* to be scrambled out of this clause, even though the clause is nominalized, as shown in (37b).

(37) a. [ppang-ul kumpang mantu-n kes-ul] keki-eyse
[bread-ACC just make-PAST NMLZ-ACC] there-at
sa-l swu iss-ta
buy can
'You can buy freshly made bread there.'

b. [ppang-ul] ahop-si-pwuthe [kumpang mantu-n kes-ul]
[bread-ACC] nine-hour-from [just make-PAST NMLZ-ACC]
sa-l swu iss-ta
buy can
'You can buy freshly made bread from 9 o'clock.' (the buying starts at 9)

However, as with FQs, reversing the order of the two accusative phrases leads to complete ungrammaticality, as shown in (38).

(38) a. *ahop-si-pwuthe [kumpang mantu-n kes-ul] [ppang-ul]
nine-hour-from [just make-PAST NMLZ-ACC] [bread-ACC]
sa-l swu iss-ta
buy can

b. *[kumpang mantu-n kes-ul] ahop-si-pwuthe [ppang-ul]
[just make-PAST NMLZ-ACC] nine-hour-from [bread-ACC]
sa-l swu iss-ta
buy can

The order of the FQ and its host NP shows the same pattern as for *tate* constructions (Cho 2003, 25, with some modification):

(39) a. Mary-ka haksayng-tul-ul twul-ul pwullessta
Mary-NOM student-PL-ACC two-ACC called
'Mary called two students.'

b. *Mary-ka twul-ul haksayng-tul-ul pwullessta
Mary-NOM two-ACC student-PL-ACC called

Kang (2002), however, notes that this restriction does not hold for FQs with some discourse markers such as the one in (40), for some speakers.

(40) sey-pyeng-ina haksayng-i photocwu-lul masiessta
3-CL-as many as student-NOM wine-ACC drank
'Students drank (surprisingly) as many as three bottles of wine.'

However, examples like (39b) seem to be considered ungrammatical by all speakers of Korean, while some speakers do accept examples like (40).[3]

Thus, Korean seems to be more restrictive than Japanese in disallowing a predicate or predicate-like constituent from preceding a referential argument. We hope to investigate this in future studies.

[3] The focused phrase should be scrambled directly to the initial position from its base position.

6. Summary and Prospects

In this paper, we have shown that the initial accusative NP and following *tate*-phrase do not form a constituent; the NP is raised out of the *tate*-phrase. Verbs of creation or change-of-state attached to *tate* take a VP only, and hence, accusative Case for a complement NP is not licensed internally. Case marking for the accusative NP is due to the higher predicate, which can license more than one accusative in Japanese.

Here we have argued that because of the raising out of the *tate*-phrase, the NP-*o* and V-*tate-o* observe an ordering restriction, due to the Proper Binding Condition. However, there are other possible analyses. Yoshimura (2011), for instance, claims that Japanese double-*o* phenomena involve "major object" constructions, in which the initial, major object is base-generated in Spec, VP. In this analysis, the ordering between the two accusative phrases is restricted by so-called 'aboutness' relations. Together with this possibility, we need to explore the overall picture of multiple accusative constructions in Japanese and Korean with respect to the grammar of predication relations, considering also multiple nominative/accusative, floating quantifiers, and secondary predicates.

References

Cho, S. 2003. Quantifier Agreement in Korean. *The Role of Agreement in Natural Language: TLS 5 Proceedings*, ed. W. E. Griffin, 25–34. Texas Linguistics Forum.

Fiengo, R. 1977. On Trace Theory. *Linguistic Inquiry* 8:35–62.

Haig, J. H. 1980. Some Observations on Quantifier Floating in Japanese. *Linguistics* 18:1065–1083.

Harada, S. 1973. Counter Equi NP Deletion. *Annual Bulletin, Research Institute of Logopedics and Phoniatrics* 7:113–147.

Hiraiwa, K. 2010. Spelling Out the Double-*o* Constraint. *Natural Language and Linguistic Theory* 28:723–770.

Hiraiwa, K. 2012. The Mechanism of Inverted Relativization in Japanese: A Silent Linker and Inversion. *Journal of Linguistics* 48:345–388.

Levin, B. and Rappaport Hovav, M. 1995. *Unaccusativity: At the Syntax-Lexical Semantics Interface* (Linguistic Inquiry Monograph 26). Cambridge: MIT Press.

Martin, S. E. 1975. *A Reference Grammar of Japanese*. New Haven: Yale University Press.

Saito, M. 2012. Case Valuation without Agree. Paper presented at the 2nd York East Asian Syntax Forum, University of York.

Sugioka, Y. 1986. *Interaction of Derivational Morphology and Syntax in Japanese and English*. New York: Garland.

Tsujimura, N. 1994. Unaccusative Mismaches and Resultatives in Japanese. *Formal Approaches to Japanese Linguistics 1: Proceedings of the First Conference on*

Formal Approaches to Japanese Linguistics (*MIT Working Papers in Linguistics* 24), ed. H. Ura and M. Koizumi, 335–354. Cambridge: MIT.

Yamada, M. 2005. Kekka no shōtenka: 'tate' kōbun no bunseki (Focalizing the Result: Analysis of *tate* Constructions). *Rekishikon Fōramu* 1:267–293.

Yoshimura, N. 2011. New Perspectives on Double *o* Constructions in Japanese. *Proceedings of the 7th Workshop on Altaic Formal Linguistic* (*MIT Working Papers in Linguistics* 62), ed. A. Simpson, 333–348. Cambridge: MIT.

A Corpus-Based Analysis of Adverbial Uses of the Quotative TO Construction: Speech and Thought Representation without Speech or Thought Predicates

SEIKO FUJII*
University of Tokyo

1. Introduction

This paper presents a corpus-based analysis of bi-clausal constructions marked by the quotative particle TO in Japanese, paying particular attention to the clause-external (non-complement) adverbial uses of quotative TO clauses, e.g., (1) and (2), which express speech and/or thought representation without the use of speech or thought predicates.

* The research reported here is part of a larger study supported by a Grant-in-aid from the Japan Society for the Promotion of Science ("An integrated study of lexicon and constructicon" no. 22520391; PI: Seiko Fujii). I am grateful to Makoto Yamazaki and Masaru Inoue for helpful discussions in 1999, to members of FrameNet (Charles J. Fillmore, Collin Baker, and especially Russell Lee-Goldman for his invaluable comments and advice), and to members of Japanese FrameNet (Kyoko Ohara, Hiroaki Saito, and Ryoko Suzuki). I also wish to thank Satoru Uchida, Yoko Suzuki and Hitomi Hirayama for their assistance with the corpus data; their Research Assistantships were supported through the Grant-in-aid Research "Design and compilation of a balanced corpus of written Japanese" (PI: Kikuo Maekawa, National Institute for Japanese Language and Linguistics; the Ministry of Science, Technology and Education, Japan) and "'Pragmaticization' of grammatical function words and constructions in discourse" (no. 18520296; PI: Seiko Fujii, Japan Society for Promotion of Science).
Japanese/Korean Linguistics 22.
Edited by Mikio Giriko, Naonori Nagaya, Akiko Takemura, and Timothy J. Vance.

(1) netu ga deta node
fever NOM turn.out because
inhuruenza no utagai ga atte wa ikenai **to**
influenza GEN doubt NOM have TOP no.good **QUO(tative)**
kurinikku ni iki inhuruenza-kensa o simasita.
clinic DAT go influenza-test ACC do-POL-PAST
'Since I got a fever, I went to a clinic and took a test for influenza, [%thinking] that it would be bad if there was a possibility of having influenza.' [% 'thinking' is not mentioned in Japanese.]

(2) iti ni tubu wa arimasu yaro to
one two pieces TOP exist-POL MOD QUO
danbooru-bako ni tenohira o ireru.
corrugated-carton into palm.of.hand ACC insert
'(He) put (the palm of) his hand into the cardboard box, [%saying] that there should be one or two pieces.' [% 'saying' is not mentioned in Japanese.]

Seminal works on the quotative particle TO in Japanese linguistics (Fujita 1986, 2000; Yamazaki 1993; National Institute for Japanese Language and Linguistics 1951; among others) have noted that it has a variety of uses. A TO-marked clause most typically functions as a syntactic complement of the main verb, and is typically headed by a communication, cogitation, or emotion verb. TO-clauses, however, are often *not syntactic* complements, but are *semantically* motivated by the main-clause frame-evoking elements, including nouns (Fujii 2009).

As has been widely recognized (Yamazaki 1996; Okamoto 1996; Suzuki 2000; Kato 2008; among others), TO-clauses are also often used without a main verb, showing the phenomenon of insubordination. This paper examines yet another (intermediate-type) use, illustrated in (1) and (2), where the TO-marked clause appears *not* as an element of the main clause but as a clause-external adverbial. Compared to other uses, this last clause-external adverbial use has received little attention (with the exception of Fujita 2000), and has yet to be investigated empirically or subjected to corpus analysis.

The primary purpose of this paper is thus to examine the clause-external adverbial use of the quotative TO construction, based on a large-scale corpus, and explicate its major semantic and pragmatic characteristics and corresponding syntactic properties.

The outline of this paper is as follows. Section 2 briefly overviews various uses of TO quotative bi-clausal constructions, including clause-internal uses (whose analyses are not the focus of the present paper). It will show how internal and external uses are conceptualized in my study in analyzing the corpus data summarized in Section 3. Sections 4 and 5 will then examine the clause-external adverbial uses, followed by concluding remarks in Section 6.

2. Types of TO Quotative Constructions

The target construction can be generally described as a bi-clausal construction marked by the quotative particle TO (more briefly, the quotative TO construction), but the ways in which the TO-marked clause relates to the main predicate vary.

In its most typical use, as in (3a–c), the TO-marked clause (or phrase) functions as a complement of the main verb syntactically as well as semantically. In this straightforward case, the governing main verb is typically either a **communication verb** (*yuu* 'say', *hanasu* 'tell', *kaku* 'write', etc.) or a **cogitation verb** (*kangaeru, omou* 'think', etc.). The main verb can also be an **emotion verb** (*yorokobu* 'feel happy', *odoroku* 'get surprised', *kuyamu* 'regret', etc.).

(3) a. Itiroo wa [wakarimasita] to itta.
Ichiro TOP [(he) has understood (it)] QUO say-PAST
'Ichiro said that (he) has understood (it).'

b. Itiroo wa [wakatta] to kangaeta.
Ichiro TOP [(he) has understood (it)] QUO think-PAST
'Ichiro thought that (he) has understood (it).'

c. Itiroo wa [wakatta] to yorokonda.
Ichiro TOP [(he) has understood (it)] QUO get.happy-PAST
'Ichiro got happy (feeling/saying) that (he) has understood (it).'

The TO-marked clause (or phrase), however, is often *not* the *syntactic* complement of the main-clause, but still remains *semantically* motivated by the main-clause predicate, as in (4a–b) ('cry', 'bow'), or motivated by the frame-evoking noun, as in (5a) 'send a <u>letter</u>'.[1]

(4) a. Itiroo wa [wakatta] to namida o nagasita.
Ichiro TOP [(he) has understood (it)] QUO tear ACC shed-PAST
'Ichiro cried (feeling/saying) that (he) has understood (it).'

b. Itiroo wa [wakarimasita] to atama o sageta.
Ichiro TOP [(he) has understood (it)] QUO head ACC lower-PAST
'Ichiro bowed (saying/feeling) that (he) has understood (it).'

[1] As part of its broad polysemy, the construction marked with the so-called quotative particle TO also has non-quotative uses (Yamazaki 1993; Fujii 2009), which are not included in the overview in this paper.

(5) a. Itiroo wa [wakatta] to tegami o okutta.
Ichiro TOP [(he) has understood (it)] QUO letter ACC send-PAST
'Ichiro sent a letter (saying) that (he) has understood (it).'

b. Itiroo wa [wakatta] to yuu tegami o
Ichiro TOP [(he) has understood (it)] QUO COMP letter ACC
okutta.
send-PAST
'Ichiro sent a letter that says that (he) has understood (it).'

Compare (5a) with (5b). The clause marked with *to yuu* in (5b) can be regarded as a straightforward syntactic complement of the head noun (*tegami* 'letter'), whereas this explanation does not apply to (5a).

Finally, as illustrated in (6a–b), a TO-marked clause is often not directly evoked by the main-clause predicate (whether it is a verb, verbal noun, noun, or adjective), but rather serves as a clause-external adverbial clause.

(6) a. Itiroo wa [wakatta] to tobi-dete itta.
Ichiro TOP [(he) has understood (it)] QUO jump-out-PAST
'Ichiro jumped out (of the room) (saying) that (he) has understood (it).'

b. Itiroo wa [wakatta] to banana o
Ichiro TOP [(he) has understood (it)] QUO banana ACC
te-watasita.
hand-give-PAST
'Ichiro handed bananas (to somebody) (saying) that (he) has understood (it).'

This latter type of use is the focus of the present paper.

In the past decades, these complex phenomena involving the versatile functions of quotative TO have sparked debates over whether TO-clauses should be considered complements of particular predicates. Fujita (2000) takes the position that all quotative TO clauses are adverbial in nature, whereas many others have taken for granted that they are complements of the main predicate. This study attends to the insights put forward by Fujita (2000, etc.) but seeks to capture the whole family of constructions and the relations among them (i.e., constructional polysemy) by (1) conducting a corpus-based *lexical* analysis of the constructions (for example, to describe what lexical items evoke TO constituents), and (2) proposing semantic (in addition to lexical and formal) parameters based on frame semantics (Fillmore 1982, 1985; Fillmore and Atkins 1992, 1994; Fillmore, Johnson, and Petruck 2003; Fillmore and Baker 2010) in order to distinguish the complement uses like (3), intermediate uses like (4) and (5a), and clause-external adverbial uses like (6).

Regarding frame-semantic parameters (the overall framework of analysis), my approach has been to investigate what type of Frame Element the TO-marked constituent serves in the construction, using the taxonomy of Frame Elements (FE) in FrameNet (http://framenet.icsi.berkeley.edu/), where each FE is either core, peripheral (non-core), or extra-thematic. To give a rough overview, my analysis has revealed the following overall tendency: cases like (3) involve core FEs, and the intermediate cases illustrated by (4) mostly involve peripheral (non-core) FEs. The clause-external adverbial uses, by contrast, can be accounted for as cases where the TO-marked clause does not serve as an integral (core or peripheral) frame element of the main-clause predicate's frame, but serves as an extra-thematic Frame Element (*à la* FrameNet; Ruppenhofer et. al. 2006). Extra-thematic Frame Elements are "ones that combine with many other frames, either taking them into their scope and embedding them in a larger context, or elaborating the descriptions of participants or the setting" (Ruppenhofer et. al. 2006: 135–136).

3. The Corpus

This study used the Balanced Corpus of Contemporary Written Japanese (BCCWJ; National Institute for Japanese Language and Linguistics 2008/2009/2010).[2] The BCCWJ sub-corpora (called "genres" in BCCWJ) whose analyses are reported in the present paper are shown in Table 1.[3] The table summarizes the total number of the quotative TO constructions examined as well as the number of clause-external adverbial uses manually extracted from the former. Examining over 180,000 tokens of the quotative TO construction drawn from BCCWJ, we manually extracted 604 tokens of non-complement, clause-external adverbial uses based on human comprehension of the sentences containing the quotative TO construction.[4]

---

[2] For the Balanced Corpus of Contemporary Written Japanese (BCCWJ), see Maekawa (2007a, 2007b) and Maekawa et al. (2010), among others. I wish to thank Kikuo Maekawa and other members of the project "Design and compilation of a balanced corpus of written Japanese" (PI: Kikuo Maekawa, National Institute for Japanese Language and Linguistics).

[3] I have also been analyzing other sub-corpora (genres) of BCCWJ, including journals, newspapers, and textbooks (made available in later years), but these are not included in the results reported in the present paper. The analysis of other genres (yielding slightly different details but conforming to the general tendency) will be reported elsewhere.

[4] For these preliminary processes of morphological analysis and extraction, MeCab (http://mecab.sourceforge.net/; Taku Kudo and Yuji Matsumoto), and ChaKi (http://chasen.naist.jp/hiki/ChaKi/; Yuji Matsumoto, Masayuki Asahara, et al.) have been used. I wish to thank Yuji Matsumoto and Masayuki Asahara for their advice and assistance as well as permissions to use MeCab and ChaKi.

Table 1. Tokens of Quotative TO Constructions Drawn from BCCWJ

Sub-corpus	# of words	quotative *to* constructions	clause-external adverbial uses
Government Reports	4,800,000	17,513	2
Books: Literature	6,324,175	84,149	272
Books: Language	398,497	6,244	27
Books: Technology	1,115,821	11,733	45
Books: Natural sciences	1,074,332	13,684	58
Books: Philosophy	1,403,199	19,623	57
Books: History	2,141,841	27,846	118
Books: General	521,438	6,515	25
Total	17,979,301	187,307	604

4. Characteristics of Clause-External Adverbial Uses

With all 604 tokens of clause-external uses of quotative TO, I tested the following two working hypotheses.

(i) The speaker/cognizer/experiencer of the quotative TO clause corresponds to the (semantic) subject of the main clause.

(ii) a. The quotative TO clause conveys the psychological state of the main clause's semantic subject (or agent) while s/he is participating in the event expressed in the main clause.
b. That psychological state is typically his/her motivation for participating in that action or being in that state.

Hypothesis (i) is supported by 598 of the 604 tokens, in that the quotative TO clause depicts the voice of the main clause's syntactic subject. This property can be illustrated with (1) and (2), repeated below.

(1) netu ga deta node
fever NOM turn.out because
inhuruenza no utagai ga atte wa ikenai **to**
influenza GEN doubt NOM have TOP no.good **QUO(tative)**
kurinikku ni iki inhuruenza-kensa o simasita.
clinic DAT go influenza-test ACC do-POL-PAST
'Since I got a fever, I went to a clinic and took a test for influenza, [%thinking] that it would be bad if there was a possibility of having influenza.' [% 'thinking' is not mentioned in Japanese.]

(2) iti ni tubu wa arimasu yaro to
one two pieces TOP exist-POL MOD QUO
danbooru-bako ni tenohira o ireru.
corrugated-carton into palm.of.hand ACC insert
'(He) put (the palm of) his hand into the cardboard box, [%saying] that there should be one or two pieces.' [% 'saying' is not mentioned in Japanese.]

In (1), the cognizer of the TO-marked constituent is the subject of the main clause, who "went to a clinic and took a test for influenza." The same is true with (2), in which the cognizer and the speaker of the TO-marked constituent is the subject of the main clause—the person who "put his hand into the box." All of the 604 tokens of clause-external adverbial uses (found in the sub-corpora listed in Table 1) have been coded with respect to this hypothesis, and 598 are found to exhibit this property, namely, that the quotative TO constituent depicts the thought or speech of the individual denoted by main clause's syntactic subject.

The remaining 6 tokens can be accounted for by considering the *(non-subject) agent* of the event described in the main clause, typically in a passive, as illustrated in (7).

(7) tedai ni "ozyoosama oku ni oidenasai-masi" to
sub-manager by lady (miss) inside DAT come-POL-[request] QUO
katteguti ni ture-modosareru.
back.door GOAL bring-back-PASSIVE
'(I) am (called back, and) brought to the back entrance by the sub-manager (of the store) [%while the sub-manager says] "Miss, please come inside."' [% is not explicitly expressed in Japanese.]

The speaker of the quoted utterance is neither the speaker nor the subject of the main clause, but rather *tedai* (the sub-manager), which is conveyed by the NI-marked agent phrase.

A similar phenomenon can be observed in receiving-verb constructions. As seen in (8), a TO-marked clause can also depict the thought of the unmentioned giver (non-subject agent) in a receiving-verb construction.

(8) sengyo-sentaa de yasukute sendo ga yokatta kara
fresh-fish-center at cheap freshness NOM good-PAST because
to iwasi o hitohako itadaki-masi-ta (gozyuppiki kurai)
QUO sardines ACC one-box receive-POL-PAST 50 approximately
'I received a box of sardines (as a gift) [%while the giver told me that (s)he wants to give the gift] because the sardines were cheap and fresh at a fish market (about 50 sardines).' [% is not explicitly expressed in Japanese.]

Here again the cognizer of the quotative TO clause content is neither the speaker nor the subject of the main clause, but the giver of the present, which is not expressed at all in the sentence. We will come back to the discussion of this sentence in Section 5.

Similarly, hypothesis (ii-a) is well-supported by corpus evidence. The core of this hypothesis can be illustrated and confirmed in all the examples shown above and below, in each of which the quotative TO clause conveys the psychological state of the main clause's semantic subject (or agent) while s/he is participating in the event expressed.[5] Whether the quotative TO clause depicts the psychological state of the main clause's syntactic subject or that of the non-subject agent corresponds to the outcome of coding with respect to hypothesis (i) discussed above. The outcome of this coding determines whether the quotative TO clause pertains to the psychological state of the main clause's syntactic subject or that of the non-subject agent.

As further hypothesized in (ii-b), in most typical uses, as illustrated in (9)–(11) below, the psychological state depicted is the subject's (or agent's) motivation for participating in the expressed event, although various other types of psychological states can be depicted.

(9) Pooru wa "karada no naka o seizyoo-suru" to
Paul TOP body GEN inside ACC clean QUO
guriin-tii o aiin site-iru no da
green-tea ACC love.to.drink do-ASP NOM COP
'Paul loves drinking green-tea [feeling] that it cleans inside the body.'
('Paul loves drinking green-tea [feeling] that it is cleansing for the body.')

(10) Nihon no syoogyoo-gakkoo ni nyuugaku siyoo to
Japan GEN commercial-school DAT enter.school do-VOL QUO
benkyoo-tyuu datta
study-in.the.middle.of COP-PAST
'(He/she) was studying, intending to enter a commercial school in Japan.'

5 The corpus of written Japanese texts whose analysis is reported in the present paper shows that it is the psychological state of the protagonist while s/he is participating in the event expressed in the main clause. With spoken Japanese data that I have also been analyzing elsewhere (not included in the present paper), however, I have found new emergent phenomena that do not conform to this basic characterization. Such genre-sensitive emergent uses (mainly found in spoken discourse) will be discussed in another paper.

(11) yononaka no koto o motto siri-tai to
the.world GEN matters ACC more know-want QUO
ozi o tayotte zyookyoo suru
uncle ACC count.on go.to.Tokyo do
'With help from an uncle, (he/she) goes to Tokyo, hoping to get to learn more about the world.'

This characteristic is most clearly exhibited in those uses in which the predicate in the TO quotative clause contains the volitional form of a verb -(*y*)*oo*, as in (10) or is accompanied by the desiderative morpheme -*tai*, as in (11). These morphemes, -(*y*)*oo* and -*tai*, explicitly convey the motivation of the protagonist for participating in the action or state in question, and in fact they frequently collocate with the adverbial uses of quoative TO in the corpus.

5. The Logophoric Nature of TO-Marked Clauses

This section further shows that one of the crucial functions of the clause-external adverbial use is logophoric: the TO quotative clause (or phrase) depicts a perspective distinct from that of the speaker or writer. The constructional properties (i) and (ii), explicated in the preceding section, yield this logophoric effect when the subject or agent of the main clause is different from the speaker/writer, as in (8) above and in (12) and (13) below.

As seen in (13), adding *kara* 'because' makes quotative TO syntactically optional, but with TO it indicates that the feeling/thought/speech expressed in the TO quotative clause is not that of the speaker.

(12) moo dame da **to** akirame-nai-de
already no.good COP **QUO** give.up-NEG-GER
'Don't give up, [thinking that] it's too late.'

(13) moo dame da **kara** (**to**) akirame-nai-de
already no.good COP **because** **QUO** give.up-NEG-GER
'Don't give up, [thinking that you should] because it's too late.'

(14) # moo dame da kara akirame-nai-de
already no.good COP because give.up-NEG-GER
#'Don't give up, because it's too late.

Without quotative TO, as shown in (14), the reasoning of the cause/motivation expressed in the *kara* clause must be attributed to the speaker and thus sounds anomalous. The addition of TO to the *kara* clause ensures a logophoric interpretation: the reasoning of the cause/motivation expressed in the clause is *not* the speaker's perspective but somebody else's.

The same observation can be made with (8), which we looked at earlier.

(8) sengyo-sentaa de yasukute sendo ga yokatta kara
fresh-fish-center at cheap freshness NOM good-PAST because
to iwasi o hitohako itadaki-masi-ta (gozyuppiki kurai)
QUO sardines ACC one-box receive-POL-PAST 50 approximately
'I received a box of sardines (as a gift) [%while the giver told me that (s)he wants to give the gift] because the sardines were cheap and fresh at a fish market (about 50 sardines).' [% is not explicitly expressed in Japanese.]

Consider who the cognizer of the reason clause is. The cognizer of the TO-marked reason clause is neither the speaker/writer of the sentence nor the subject of the main clause. By virtue of the marker TO in the causal clause, we must look for a cognizer different from the speaker. Thus, even though the giver is not expressed in the sentence, we can interpret the unexpressed giver as the cognizer of the reason clause.

A further interesting example, (15), comes from an advertisement for an English language school found on a train. Consider the cognizer of the TO-marked reason clause in (15a) (that is, who thinks it is possible to speak without restraint at business lunches in English). In (15a), the customer rather than the speaker is the subject of the main clause and the experiencer of the quoted comment, and the customer is the one who thinks it is possible to speak without restraint at business lunches in English. This interpretation is ensured by the addition of TO to the *kara* clause.

(15) a. Eigo de no business lunch
English in GEN
kigane naku hanaseru kara to okyaku wa konomu
constraint without speak-POT because QUO customers TOP like (it)
'My customers love having business lunches in English [% feeling that (business lunches in English are great)] because (they) can speak without restraint.' [% is not explicitly expressed in Japanese.]

b. [continuation of (15a) above]
kigane naku Eigo ga hanasenai watasi wa
restraint without English NOM speak-POT-NEG I TOP
komaru
be.in.trouble
'I, who cannot speak English without restraint, am in trouble.'

c. Eigo de no business lunch
English in GEN
kigane naku hanaseru kara okyaku wa konomu
constraint without speak-POT because customers TOP like (it)
'My customers love holding business lunches in English because (they) can speak without restraint.'

The speaker, in fact, thinks the opposite, and feels that s/he herself/himself cannot speak English without restraint, as is made explicit in the follow-up line of the advertisement, (15b). Even without the follow-up comment, this speaker's attitude is still clearly detached and differentiated from the customer's attitude, as conveyed in (15a). What makes this possible is the quotative marker TO on the causal *kara* clause.

The above point can be clarified by comparing (15a) with (15c), the latter of which has no quotative marker TO. In English, the statement *My customers love holding business lunches in English because (they) can speak without restraint*, could have two different interpretations, analogous to (15a) and (15c), depending on the intonation (as well as the scope relation of the clauses). In Japanese, the difference is marked by the use or non-use of the quotative TO, as seen in (15a) and (15c). The same unambiguous interpretations in Japanese hold for (13) and (14) above, whereas the English statement *Don't give it up because it's too late* could be ambiguous, depending on the intonation.

6. Conclusion

This paper has examined the clause-external adverbial use of the quotative TO construction in order to explicate its major syntactic, semantic, and pragmatic properties. My analysis of the Balanced Corpus of Contemporary Written Japanese has shown that the speaker/cognizer/experiencer of the TO quotative clause corresponds to the subject or (non-subject) agent of the main clause. The TO-marked constituent in the construction conveys the psychological state felt by the main-clause agent while being involved in the event, which is typically but not always his/her motivation for the action or state expressed in the main clause.

This paper has further shown that the above constructional properties yield a logophoric effect when the subject or agent of the main-clause is different from the speaker/writer: the TO quotative clause (or phrase) depicts a perspective distinct from that of the speaker or writer.

Note that although this construction *can* often be paraphrased with an explicit verb of saying or thinking, for instance, by adding *itte* 'saying (that)' or *omotte* 'feeling/thinking (that)', such a paraphrase (using *te*-linkage) does not apply naturally to cases like (7) and (8) (where the cognizer of the TO-marked constituent is neither the speaker nor the subject of the main clause).[6] Based upon evidence gathered from examining these cases, taken alongside a separate analysis of spoken discourse (reported elsewhere), this paper argues that the construction is not mere ellipsis of a verb of speech or thought, but rather an adverbial which has grammaticalized the function of speech/thought representation without the use of such predicates.

References

Fillmore, C. 1982. Frame Semantics. *Linguistics in the Morning Calm*, ed. Linguistic Society of Korea, 111–138. Seoul: Hanshin.

Fillmore, C. 1985. Frames and the Semantics of Understanding. *Quaderni di Semantica* 6:222–253.

Fillmore, C. and Atkins, B. 1992. Toward a Frame-Based Lexicon: The Semantics of RISK and Its Neighbors. *Frames, Fields, and Contrasts: New Essays in Semantic and Lexical Organization*, ed. A. Lehrer and E. Kittay, 75–102. Hillsdale: Lawrence Erlbaum.

Fillmore, C. and Atkins, B. 1994. Starting Where the Dictionaries Stop: The Challenge for Computational Lexicography. *Computational Approaches to the Lexicon*, ed. B. Atkins and A. Zampolli, 349–393. Oxford: Oxford University Press.

Fillmore, C. and Baker, C. 2010. A Frames Approach to Semantic Analysis. *The Oxford Handbook of Linguistic Analysis*, ed. B. Heine and H. Narrog, 313–340. Oxford: Oxford University Press.

Fillmore, C., Johnson, C. and Petruck, M. 2003. Background to FrameNet. *International Journal of Lexicography* 16:235–250.

Fujii, S. 2009. Capturing Constructional Polysemy via Frames and Frame-to-Frame Relations: A Lexical Analysis of Quotative TO Constructions. *PACLING* 11. *The proceedings of the 11th Conference of the Pacific Association for Computational Linguistics.*

Fujita, Y. 1986. Bunchū in'yōku '–to' ni yoru 'in'yō' o seiri suru (Notes on 'Quotation' via Sentence-Medial Quotative Phrases). *Ronshū Nihongo kenkyū (1): Gendaihen.* (Studies on the Japanese Language, vol. 1: Modern Japanese), ed. Y. Miyaji, 206–230. Tokyo: Meiji Shoin.

Fujita, Y. 2000. *Kokugo in'yō kōbun no kenkyū* (A Study of Japanese Quotative Constructions). Osaka: Izumi Shuppan.

Katō, Y. 2008. *Hanashi-kotoba ni okeru in'yō no kenkyū* (A Study of Quoative Expressions in Spoken Japanese.) Doctoral dissertation, University of Tokyo.

Maekawa, K. 2007a. KOTONOHA and BCCWJ: Development of a Balanced Corpus of Contemporary Written Japanese. *Corpora and Language Research: Pro-*

[6] E.g., a possible paraphrase of (1): *inhuruenza no utagai ga atte wa ikenai* ***to*** ***omotte*** *kurinikku ni iki inhuruenza-kensa o simasita.*

ceedings of the First International Conference on Korean Language, Literature, and Culture, 158–177. Seoul, Yonsei University.

Maekawa, K. 2007b. Design of a Balanced Corpus of Contemporary Written Japanese. *Proceedings of Symposium on Large-Scale Knowledge Resources (LKR2007)*, 55–58.

Maekawa, K., Yamazaki, M., Maruyama, T., Yamaguchi, M., Ogura, H., Kashino, W., Ogiso, T., Koiso, H. and Den, Y. 2010. Design, Compilation, and Preliminary Analyses of Balanced Corpus of Contemporary Written Japanese. *Proceedings of LREC 2010*, Malta, 1483–1486.

Kokuritsu Kokugo Kenkyūjo. 1951. *Gendaigo no joshi, jodōshi: Yōhō to jitsurei* (Bound Forms ['zyosi' and 'zyodōsi'] in Modern Japanese: Uses and Examples). Tokyo: Shūei Shuppan.

Okamoto, S. 1996. Pragmaticization of Meaning in Some Sentence-final Particles in Japanese. *Topics in Semantics and Pragmatics*, ed. M. Shibatani and S. Thompson, 219–246. Amsterdam: John Benjamins.

Ruppenhofer, J., Ellsworth, M., Petruck, M. R. L., Johnson, C. R. and Scheffczyk, J. 2006. FrameNet II: Extended Theory and Practice. http://framenet.icsi.berkeley.edu/book/book.pdf.

Suzuki, S. 2000. Surprise and Animosity: The Case of the Copula *da* in Quotative Sentences. *Pragmatic Markers and Propositional Attitude*, ed. F. Thorstein and G. Andersen, 239–253. Amsterdam: John Benjamins.

Yamazaki, M. 1993. In'yōku no joshi 'to' no yōhō o saiseiri suru (Reconsidering the Usages of the Quotative Particle *to*). *Kokuritsu Kokugo Kenkyūjo Hōkokushū* 14: 1–29. Tokyo: Shūei Shuppan.

Japanese Passives with Verbal Nouns

YUTAKA SATO
International Christian University

1. Introduction

Japanese has a set of vocabulary items called verbal nouns (VNs, Martin 1975; Kageyama 1993), which when followed by the light verb *suru* 'do' (or *sita* 'did') realize their arguments in verbal cases (Iida 1987), as shown in (1). (VNs will hereafter be highlighted in small capitals for ease of reference.)

(1) Keisatu ga hannin o TAIHO sita.
police NOM offender ACC arrest did[1]
'The police arrested the offender.'

The VN in (1) is an instance of a transitive VN, which in this paper refers to a VN that has to cooccur with both a nominative NP (subject) and an accusative NP (possibly along with some other cases, e.g. dative) when followed by *suru*. The theme argument of the transitive VN *TAIHO* cannot appear in

[1] ACC: accusative case, COP: copula, GEN: genitive case, NOM: nominative case, PASS: passive, PAST: past, Q: question marker, and QUO: quotative marker.

Japanese/Korean Linguistics 22.
Edited by Mikio Giriko, Naonori Nagaya, Akiko Takemura, and Timothy J. Vance.

any overt morphological case other than accusative, unless, for example, the passive morpheme *rare* attaches to the light verb, as in (2).

(2) Hannin ga (keisatu ni-yotte) TAIHO s-are-ta.
offender NOM police by arrest do-PASS-PAST
'The offender was arrested (by the police).'

The sentence in (3) with *hannin* 'offender' in the nominative and a transitive VN followed by *sita* 'did' can only be interpreted as the English given there. It is ungrammatical for the reading 'The offender was arrested'.

(3) Hannin ga TAIHO sita.
offender NOM arrest did
'The offender arrested (someone).'

Interestingly, when a transitive VN is followed by a copula, both a transitive construction, as in (4), and a passive construction, as in (5), are possible.

(4) Keisatu ga hannin o TAIHO da.
police NOM offender ACC arrest COP
'The police arrested the offender.'[2]

(5) Hannin ga (keisatu ni-yotte) TAIHO da.
offender NOM police by arrest COP
'The offender was arrested by the police.'

Passive examples like (5), where the theme of a transitive VN appears in the nominative rather than in the accusative, without the passive morpheme, are unexpected in light of examples like (3). Hence, they deserve further investigation. This paper focuses on this phenomenon.

Kageyama (1993) and Ono (1997) have also noted transitive VNs co-occurring with nominatively marked themes as well as accusatively marked ones when they are followed by an aspectual element, as in (6b) and (7b).

(6) a. Purozyekutotiimu ga iseki o SYUUHUKU tyuu da.
project-team NOM ruins ACC restoration during COP
'The project team is restoring the ruins.' (Ono's [24a], 1997:160)

b. Iseki ga SYUUHUKU tyuu da.
ruins NOM restoration during COP
'The ruins are being restored.' (Ono's [24b], 1997:160)

---

[2] More than one interpretation of tense is possible for a VN-*da* sentence like (4) or (5), but only one of them is given for each example in this paper. The kinds of tense available for this construction are similar to those available for honorific sentences with a copula (see Niwa 2008).

(7) a. Sizuoka-kenkei ga satuzinhan o TAIHO no
Shizuoka-Pref.-police NOM murderer ACC arrest GEN
sai, . . .
occasion
'When the Shizuoka Prefectural Police arrested the murderer, . . .'

b. ?Sizuoka-kenkei ni-yotte renzoku-satuzinhan ga TAIHO
Shizuoka-Pref.-police by serial-murderer NOM arrest
no sai, hutari no keikan ga nagaredama de sinda.
GEN occasion two GEN officer NOM stray-bullet with died
'When the serial murderer was arrested by the Shizuoka Prefectural Police, two officers were killed by stray bullets.'
(Kageyama's [126c], 1993:238; the judgment is his.)

Kageyama (1993:238) calls (7b) passive, but the passivehood of examples like (7b) has not been fully investigated by him, or in the literature.

Moreover, the status of VNs followed by a copula as in (4) or (5) is not well established in the literature, compared, for example, to VN constructions like (6) and (7). One reason may be that VN-*da* constructions, like (4) and (5), sound rather marginal and stylistically skewed. There have been only sporadic and cursory discussions of VN-*da* constructions in the literature, and their exact nature is far from clear (Okutsu 1978; Nitta 1980; Masuoka and Takubo 1982; Takahashi 1984; Matsumoto 1996; Sells 1996; Iwasaki 1999; Masuoka 2000; Sato 2008, 2012; Oshima 2010; Suzuki 2010; Kubota 2010).

The purpose of this paper is to (i) characterize VN-*da* constructions, particularly of the passive type, based on a survey of their actual use on the internet, (ii) demonstrate that passive-like VN-*da* constructions such as those in (5) and (7b) are indeed passives, and (iii) present a syntactic analysis of the observed phenomena. The organization of this paper is as follows. Section 2 reports on a survey conducted with the Google search engine on the actual use of VN-*da* sentences and characterizes the type of VNs that can occur in passive VN-*da* constructions. Section 3 argues that they are passives based on the results of tests of passivization and postulates syntactic structures for their passive and active constructions. This will be followed by a conclusion in section 4.

2. The Actual Use of *da*-Constructions

In the literature, VN-*da* constructions have been noted as denoting actions rather than states, unlike other nominal predicates (Takahashi 1984:20–21; Masuoka 2000:47). VN-*da* sentences with a goal argument (with *e* 'to' or *ni* 'to'; Okutsu 1978:26; Matsumoto 1996:81; Sells 1996:617; Iwasaki 1999:175; Oshima 2010:91) and a locative adjunct (with *de* 'at'; Nitta 1980:168) were given as examples. VN-*da* sentences with an accusative object, like (4), were presented as actually observed data by Suzuki (2010) and Sato (2008). Suzuki (2010) characterized VN-*da* sentences (including those with an accusative object) as bearing a special discourse function to highlight an event that has taken on a new aspect and typically (although not exclusively) used as a "headline" by newscasters introducing a new news item in their news reports. Passive VN-*da* sentences were referred to by Kubota (2010) and Sato (2008). This section will show the results of the survey I conducted on the use of VN-*da* constructions and characterize them based on its results.

I conducted a survey between September 8 and October 11, 2011, on the use of transitive VNs on the internet with Google's Advanced Search, confining my search to exactly matching, to see whether, and how frequently, they occur in the following patterns.

(8)	a.	*o* ACC	VN	*da* COP
	b.	*o* ACC	VN	*tyuu* during
	c.	*ga* NOM	VN	*da* COP

The *o*-VN-*da* pattern in (8a) was designed to search for sentences like (4), the *o*-VN-*tyuu* pattern in (8b) for sentences like (6a), and the *ga*-VN-*da* pattern in (8c) for sentences like (5). A VN was confirmed as used for one of the patterns in (8) if all of the following conditions were met: (i) if one or more instances of the VN pattern in question were found within the first 20 results, (ii) the theta role of the accusative or nominative NP preceding the VN was confirmed as corresponding to its direct internal argument, and (iii) each of the VN-*da* sentences in question was judged as acceptable Japanese.[3] The transitive VNs were chosen from the list of VNs selected by Aizawa (1993) (see Sato 2012 for details).[4]

Of the sample of 461 transitive VNs, 386 (84%) were found used in the

---

[3] In addition, for the pattern in (8c), to exclude VNs used referentially or adjectivally, only those which passed all of the following tests were counted as occurring in the pattern (8c): (i) if changing the VN-*da* portion to VN-*sareru* 'is done', VN-*sarete iru* 'is being done', or VN-*sareta* 'was done' results in a natural sentence; (ii) if inserting the demonstrative *sono* 'that' before VN results in anomaly; and (iii) if inserting the degree adverb *totemo* 'very' results in anomaly.

[4] This paper examines 461 transitive VNs, seven less than the 468 transitive VNs examined in Sato 2012. This is because those seven VNs were later judged to be alternating between transitive and intransitive, rather than strictly transitive.

o-VN-*da* pattern (8a), 403 (87%) in the *o*-VN-*tyuu* pattern (8b), and 68 (15%) in the *ga*-VN-*da* pattern (8c). These figures show that *o*-VN-*da* sentences like (4) are as frequently occurring as *o*-VN-*tyuu* sentences like (6a). The breakdowns of the frequencies of telic and atelic VNs and of agentive and nonagentive VNs occurring in each pattern are shown in Table 1.

Table 1. Number of VNs Found Used for Each Category

	Total		*o*-VN-*da*		*o*-VN-*tyuu*		*ga*-VN-*da*	
telic	292	63.3%	238	61.7%	244	60.5%	59	86.8%
atelic	169	36.7%	148	38.3%	159	39.5%	9	13.2%
agentive	410	88.9%	347	89.9%	362	89.8%	67	98.5%
nonagentive	51	11.1%	39	10.1%	41	10.2%	1	1.5%
total	461		386		403		68	

VNs were classified as atelic if they passed at least two of the following tests: if (i) they appear in the phrase TIME *no aida* VN *suru* 'do VN for TIME', (ii) they appear in the phrase VN *si-tuzukeru* 'continue doing VN', and (iii) they do not occur in the phrase TIME *inai-ni* VN-*suru* 'get VN done within TIME'. As can be seen from Table 1, there is no specific tendency for either type to occur in *o*-VN-*da* or *o*-VN-*tyuu* sentences. The proportion of the telic VNs is more or less constant (about 60%) across the total sample, the *o*-VN-*da* sentences, and the *o*-VN-*tyuu* sentences. In contrast, those that appeared in the *ga*-VN-*da* pattern were mostly telic (86.8%).

The proportion of the agentive VNs (about 90%) also does not vary much among the total sample, the *o*-VN-*da* pattern, and the *o*-VN-*tyuu* pattern. In contrast, almost all the VNs (except for one) that appeared in the passive pattern were agentive (98.5%).

Ono (1997) argued regarding examples like (6) that causative VNs with a complex Event Structure consisting of a process and a resultant state undergo the externalization of internal arguments in the VN-*tyuu* construction due to special aspectual properties of -*tyuu* 'during'. The fact that VN-*da* sentences without such an aspectual element sometimes allow externalization, as in (5), shows that it is not the aspectual element that permits this process. Ono's (1997) characterization of VNs, however, seems to be hitting pretty close to the mark. VNs that have a complex event structure with a process (presumably an action) and a resultant affected state can be characterized as agentive and telic. A problem with his characterization, however, is that although the majority of VNs that occurred in the *ga*-VN-*da* construction were both agentive and telic, there were some which deviated from this description. There were nine VNs classified as atelic and one nonagentive VN that occurred in this pattern. The delineation of those VNs that can appear in the passive probably can be achieved not in absolute formal terms like Ono's (1997) but rather in relative or implicational functional terms.

In this paper I adopt the notion of Transitivity proposed by Hopper and Thompson (1980) to describe transitive VNs that can appear passivized as in (5) and (7b).[5] That is, the more characteristics a transitive VN has that match those in (9), the easier it is to occur passivized when followed by a copula or an aspectual element. An example is given in (10).

(9) An event in which some agent volitionally does some action which has an end point such that the patient is totally affected (Hopper and Thompson 1980).

(10)
Huzi-san	no	sekai-isan-tooroku	ga	ENKI	da
Mt-Fuji	GEN	world-heritage-listing	NOM	postponing	COP

to	ka.
QUO	Q

'(I) heard that the listing of Mt. Fuji as a World Heritage site was postponed.' (orz.fujiblog.jp/?eid=1054098, accessed September 15, 2011)

It is difficult for transitive VNs with fewer or none of the characteristics in (9) to occur in a passive pattern. Thus, for example, the transitive VN *ANKI* 'memorizing', which possibly denotes a telic event but takes a nonagentive (or experiencer) subject and a non-affected object in the active voice, cannot occur with its theme in the nominative, as shown in (11). Similarly, the transitive VN *BENKYOO* 'study', which takes an agentive subject but denotes an atelic event with a non-affected object in the active voice, cannot occur in the passive pattern either, as shown in (12).

(11)
*Koosiki	ga	ANKI	da/no	ori
formula	NOM	memorizing	COP/GEN	occasion

'The formula is (to be) memorized.'/'when the formula is memorized, . . .'

(12)
*Huransugo	ga	BENKYOO	da/no	sai
French	NOM	study	COP/GEN	occasion

'French is being studied.'/'when French is being studied, . . .'

In addition to having the high Transitivity properties underlined in (9),

---

5 The criteria in (9) may be too strict for sentences like (6b) because an atelic VN like *KENKYUU* 'research' can occur in the passive pattern in (8c), as in (i).

(i)
. . . tiryoo-hoo	ga	kenkyuu	tyuu	de-aru
treatment	NOM	research	during	COP

'. . . treatment is being studied'

those 68 transitive VNs that appeared in the passive seem to denote that their themes end up in some noticeable resultant states, as in (13).

(13) The theme/patient comes to be in one of the following states: (a) existing (from non-existing) or available, (b) selected or designated as having some property, (c) positioned at or moved to some place, (d) sought or forced to be carried out, or (e) some other salient resultant state.

The addition in (13) explains the ungrammaticality of the passive VN-*da* sentence in (14) with the VN *HAISUI* 'drain', which is both agentive and telic. This sentence normally does not describe what resultant state the theme is in after the event has been completed. The state of the drained rainwater is usually unknown, i.e., it is gone, unless a special context is given as to the final state of the drained water.

(14) *Tamatta amamizu ga HAISUI da/no sai-ni
accumulated rainwater NOM drain COP/GEN occasion-on
'(when) the accumulated rainwater was drained.'

Having the properties in (13) facilitates the passivization of VNs slightly lower in Transitivity. One of the 68 VNs which appeared passivized despite its nonagentive and nonvolitional orientation was *HAKKEN* 'discovery'. The VN *HAKKEN* can occur in the passive because the sentence can depict a salient state (i.e., now found existing) that the theme is in.

(15) Kodaisyu no unagi ga HAKKEN da to ka.
ancient-species GEN eel NOM discovery COP QUO Q
'I heard that an ancient species of eel was discovered.'
(http://b.hatena.ne.jp/entry/www.afpbb.com/article/environment-science-it/science-technology/2820822/7651182, accessed September 22, 2011)

Of the 68 VNs that appeared in the passive pattern, there were nine VNs that were judged to denote atelic events according to the results of the telicity tests mentioned above. Those atelic VNs, however, seem to describe in the examples found that some change has happened to the theme so that it is now in one of the resultant states in (13). The VNs *KOOEN* 'performing (a play)' and *ZYOOEN* 'playing', labeled as atelic, were used to mean 'presenting a play', and the play is now available for watching. The VN *HOGO* 'protection' was used to mean '(dogs and cats) were taken under protection', and *SIYOO* 'use' was used to mean '(some pieces of alloy) were put to use or welded onto a ring'. The VN *SYUUGEKI* 'attack' was used to mean 'the headquarters have come under attack', and *KOOZI* 'construction' to mean 'the street is now under construction', *BOOGAI* 'disturbing' to mean 'sleep has disrupted'. The VNs *SEIKYUU* 'requesting' and *KYOOSEI* 'forcing' were used to mean that the theme is now 'under request or coercion'. All of these VNs usually denote a process, but they can also mean a transition into some resultant state.

This section has shown that VN-*da* sentences in the active are as commonly occurring as VN-*tyuu* sentences, and that transitive VNs very high on the Transitivity scale—and of the type described in (13)—may appear in passivelike VN-*da* sentences.

3. Passive Tests

The "passive" constructions with a transitive VN, like those in (5), (6b), and (7b), can take a nominative NP bearing a theme role as well as an adjunct agent phrase. In contrast, a corresponding sentence with the same VN followed by *sita* (the past tense of *suru*) does not permit its theme to occur in the nominative, as in (3), let alone an adjunct agent phrase. Moreover, inserting a reflexive after the nominative NP, as in (16), allows coreference between the reflexive and the nominative NP, whereas such coreference between the reflexive and an implied agent, the arrester, is unavailable.

(16) hannin$_i$ ga [zibun$_i$ no heya] de TAIHO da/no sai
offender NOM self GEN room in arrest COP/GEN occasion
'(when) the offender was arrested in self's room'

The above evidence from case realization and reflexive binding supports the view that the nominative NP in question is a subject.

There is one non-passivelike behavior of "passive" VN constructions that needs to be noted, before looking into their passivehood by applying passive tests. That is, unlike the construction with a VN followed by *sareru* 'is done' (the passivized form of *suru*), the acceptability of those passive constructions containing a VN without the passive morpheme degrades when *ni* 'by' appears instead of *ni-yotte* 'by' in the agent phrase, as shown below in the contrast between (17), one the one hand, and (18)–(20), on the other.

(17) Kokuoo ga sinka ni / ni-yotte ANSATU-s-are-ta.
king NOM retainer by by assassination-do-PASS-PAST
'The king was assassinated by his retainer.'

(18) Kokuoo ga sinka ni*? / ni-yotte ANSATU da (COP)
'The king was assassinated by his retainers.'

(19) Kokuoo ga sinka ni*? / ni-yotte ANSATU tyuu-ni ('during')
'While the king was assassinated by his retainers, . . .'

(20) Kokuoo ga sinka ni*? / ni-yotte ANSATU no ori ('on the occasion of')
'When the king was assassinated by his retainers, . . .'

This, however, cannot be taken as evidence against the passivehood of the constructions in question. The lower acceptability of the agent phrase with *ni* likely comes from the absence of the passive morpheme *rare* in those constructions in (18)–(20). This contrast, although subtle, indicates that marking an agent phrase with *ni* is not necessarily intrinsic to passives per se in Japanese; rather its occurrence is induced by the passive morpheme *rare*. It follows from this that dichotomizing the *ni* agent phrase in *ni* direct and *ni* indirect passives into two different categories, adjuncts and arguments (e.g., Hoshi 1999, contra Kitagawa and Kuroda 1992), needs some revision, i.e., there needs to be a mechanism to somehow license the occurrence of a *ni* agent phrase by *rare* in both types of passives. As shown above, the three types of VN constructions in (18)–(20) are subject to the same constraint, but I will focus in the rest of this paper on VNs followed by a copula or, as in (20) and (7), by *no*, which I will assume is an adnominal form of the copula.

In the following, we will investigate if these passivelike constructions with transitive VNs are really passives by running three passive tests.

3.1. Controllability of a Rationale Clause

The implied agents of passives with VNs, just like those of other bona fide passives, can control a rationale clause. The PRO subject of the rationale clause (the preventer) in (21a), when followed by (21b) or (21c), can be construed as being controlled by the entity referred to by the adjunct agent phrase in (21b) or (21c), i.e., the suppressed subject.

(21) a. [PRO Syooko-inmetsu o husegu tame-ni],
evidence-destruction ACC prevent in-order-to

b. (keisatu ni-yotte) yoogisya ga TAIHO da nante
police by suspect NOM arrest COP surprising-that
interpretation of (21a) + (21b): '(It's surprising that) the suspect was arrested (by the police) to prevent destruction of evidence.'

c. (keisatu ni-yotte) yoogisya ga TAIHO no ori-ni
police by suspect NOM arrest GEN occasion-on
media ni wa nani-mo sirasarete inakatta.
media to TOP anything informed was-not
interpretation of (21a) + (21c): 'When the suspect was arrested (by the police) to prevent destruction of evidence, nothing was released to the media.'

In contrast, the PRO subject of the rationale clause in (22) can only be construed as someone referred to by the matrix clause subject, the self-surrenderer. The example in (22) sounds a little unnatural because it is rather difficult to interpret the sentence in such a way that a suspect deliberately surrendered himself to prevent the destruction of evidence, say, by the police, but I believe it is possible.

(22) [PRO Syooko-inmetsu o husegu tame-ni],
evidence-destruction ACC prevent in-order-to
yoogisya ga ZISYU da nante / no ori-ni
suspect NOM surrender COP (surprising-that) / GEN occasion-on
'(It's surprising that/when) the suspect surrendered himself to prevent destruction of evidence.'

The contrast, i.e., the control of the rationale clause subject by the suppressed agent, rather than by the matrix subject in (21) vs. its control by the matrix subject in (22), is due to the difference in transitivity: *TAIHO* 'arrest' is transitive, whereas *ZISYU* 'self-surrender' is intransitive. Replacing the unergative VN *ZISYU* 'self-surrender' in (22) with the unaccusative VN *SISSOO* 'disappearing' still does not allow an outside agent to control the rationale clause.

3.2. Floated Numeral Quantifier

The nominative subject in passives with a transitive VN can be associated with a numeral quantifier "floated away" from it. The transitive VN *SYOOTAI* 'inviting' in (23) allows its theme to occur in the nominative with its numeral quantifier (NQ) floated away from it; the NQ 3-*nin* immediately to the left of the VN in (23) can be construed as modifying sentence-initial *seizika* 'politicians'. This suggests that there is a trace of *seizika* to the left of the VN whereby the trace and the NQ can mutually c-command each other (Miyagawa and Arikawa 2007; Miyagawa 1989).

(23) Seizika$_i$ ga syusaisya ni-yotte sono paatii ni t$_i$
politician NOM organizer by that party to
3-nin$_i$ SYOOTAI da soo-desu / no ori-ni
3-people inviting COP I-heard / GEN occasion-on
'(I heard that/when) three politicians were invited to the party by the organizer.'

On the other hand, *syusaisya* 'organizer' in the nominative in (24), which bears an agent role and occurs away from the NQ, cannot be associated with it.

(24) Seizika$_i$ o syusaisya$_j$ ga sono paatii ni t$_i$ 3-nin$_{i/*j}$
politician ACC organizer NOM that party to 3-people
SYOOTAI da soo-desu / no ori-ni
inviting COP I-heard GEN occasion-on
'(I heard that/when) the organizer invited three politicians to the party.'

Thus, a contrast obtains between (23), where the nominative NP can be modified by a distant NQ, suggesting movement from the object to the subject position, and (24), where the nominative NP cannot be modified by a distant NQ.

The posited empty category coreferential with *seizika* in (23) cannot be pro, because substituting *karera* 'them' or *zibuntati* 'themselves' for the empty category in (23) renders the sentence ungrammatical, as shown in (25).

(25) *Seizika$_i$ ga syusaisya ni-yotte sono paatii ni karera$_i$ /
politician NOM organizer by that party to them
zibuntati$_i$ o 3-nin$_i$ SYOOTAI da soo-desu / no ori-ni
themselves ACC 3-people inviting COP I-heard / GEN occasion-on
*'(I heard that/when) three politicians$_i$ were invited them$_i$/themselves$_i$ to the party by the organizer.'

3.3. Scope Ambiguity

Fukuda (2006), following Hoji (2008) and Kitagawa and Kuroda (1992), has pointed out a contrast in scope ambiguity, which obtains in case of the *ni-yotte* passive in (26a), but not in case of the *ni* direct passive in (26b), due to some type of movement from an object to a subject position in the former (*ni-yotte* passive) and lack thereof in the latter (*ni* direct passive).[6]

(26) 3-nin no gakusei ga Itoo-sensei ni-yotte / ni maikai
3-people GEN student NOM Ito-prof. by / by every-time
sas-are-ta.
call-PASS-PAST
'Three students were called on by Prof. Ito every time.'
(Fukuda's [2006:91] examples [10a] and [10b])
(a) *ni-yotte* passive {3 > every, every > 3}
(b) *ni* direct passive {3 > every, *every > 3}

The same scope ambiguity as in (26a) obtains with a VN followed by a copula in (27), which suggests that (27) also involves a similar type of

---

[6] See Fukuda 2006 for an analysis using a special movement operation.

movement. (Because a *ni* agent phrase lowers the acceptability of (27), only the example with *ni-yotte* is given.)

(27) 3-nin no gakusei ga gakutyoo ni-yotte mai-gakki
3-people GEN student NOM president by every-semester
syootai da soo desu / no ori-ni
inviting COP I-heard / GEN occasion-on
'(I heard that/when) three students are invited by the president every semester.' {3 > every, every > 3}

Based on the results of the three tests of passivization shown in subsections 3.1 to 3.3, it is not unreasonable to say that VN constructions followed by a copula, as in (5) and (7b), are indeed instances of passivization.

3.4. Structure of Light Verb Constructions

To account for *su*(*ru*) or a copula cooccurring with different types of VNs, i.e., the transitive type and the unaccusative type, as in (28), I postulate that *su*(*ru*) and a copula are light verbs in the sense of Chomsky (2001).[7] The idea is that these light verbs have a transitive and an unaccustive variant and that both merge with a VN in the configurations shown in (29a) and (29b), following Ivana and Sakai (2007), Folli, Harley and Karimi (2005), and Karimi-Doostan (2005).

(28) Unaccusative VN

a. Inseki ga RAKKA sita.
meteorite NOM fall did
'A meteorite fell.'

b. Inseki ga RAKKA da.
meteorite NOM fall COP
'A meteorite has fallen.'

(29) a. Transitive Light Verb

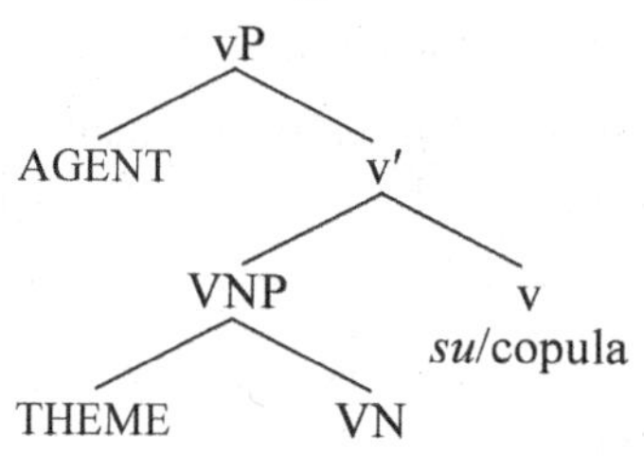

b. Unaccusative Light Verb

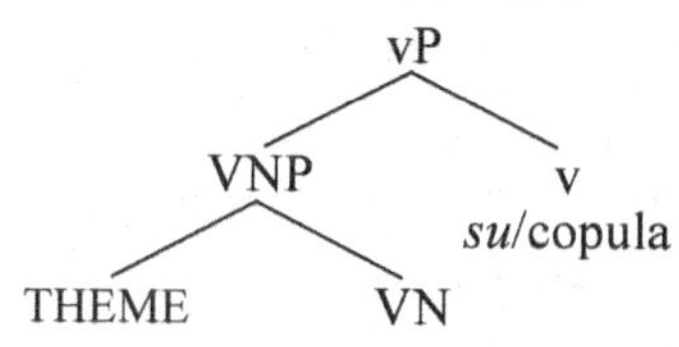

A transitive variant of the light verb *su*(*ru*) or copula occurs in the configuration in (29a) and undergoes the operation in (30a), resulting in transitive sentences with VNs like (1) and (4). I assume that VNs, like verbs (Harley and Noyer 2000), are specified for their [cause] value, as shown in

[7] The light verb *suru*, which hitherto has been mostly treated as unanalyzed, can be analyzed into the verb root *su* and the inflectional suffix *-ru* (nonpast tense).

(31). An unaccusative variant of the light verb *su(ru)* or copula appears in the configuration in (29b) and undergoes the operation in (30b), resulting in unaccusative sentences with VNs like (28a) and (28b).[8]

(30) How a light verb merges with a VN

a. A transitive variant of *su(ru)* or copula merges with a VN with a [+cause] feature; it licenses the external argument of the VN and assigns accusative case to the direct internal argument of the VN.

b. An unaccusative variant of *su(ru)* or copula merges with a VN with a [−cause] feature; it neither licenses an external argument nor assigns accusative case to the direct internal argument of the VN.

c. An unaccusative variant of copula can merge with a VN with a [+cause] feature (resulting in a passive); it neither licenses an external argument nor assigns accusative case to the direct internal argument of the VN.

(31) a. *TAIHO*, 'arrest', [+cause], . . .

b. *RAKKA*, 'falling', [−cause], . . .

c. *KAITOO*, 'thawing', [±cause], . . .

The transitive VN *TAIHO*, for example, which has a [+cause] feature, is merged with either transitive *su(ru)* to derive (1) or a transitive copula to derive (4). The transitive light verb (*su* or copula) licenses the external argument *keisatu* 'police' and assigns accusative case to the direct internal argument *hannin* 'offender' in the specifier of the VNP (i.e., Verbal Noun Phrase). On the other hand, the unaccusative VN *RAKKA* 'falling', which has a [−cause] feature, is merged with either unaccusative *su(ru)* to derive (28a) or an unaccusative copula to derive (28b). In either case, the unaccusative light verb does not license an external argument (which does not cause any problem because this VN does not have one), nor does it assign accusative case to the direct internal argument of the VN. The direct internal argument *inseki* 'meteorite' thus left caseless moves to the specifier of a tense projection to get nominative case.

An unaccusative copula is given another option in (30c) to derive a passive VN-*da* sentence like (5). I assume that this option of an unaccusative copula merging with a [+cause] VN is possible because (i) being nominal, VNs can merge with a copula, whereas verbs cannot do so, and (ii) due to another nominal property of VNs, namely, that the external argument of a

[8] VNs alternating between transitive and intransitive, like *KAITOO* 'thawing' in (31c), are marked [±cause]. This alternating type follows the option for unaccusative VNs in (30b) to be realized as intransitive, and follows the option for transitive VNs in (30a) to be realized as transitive.

VN or a complex event nouns is suppressed, i.e., it does not have to be syntactically realized (Grimshaw 1999). Consequently, the transitive VN *TAIHO* with a [+cause] feature is merged with an unaccusative copula. Being unaccusative, the light verb can neither license an external argument nor assign accusative case. The direct internal argument of the VN thus left caseless raises to the specifier of a tense projection to receive nominative case. The external argument of the VN is left suppressed.

4. Conclusion

In this paper, I have illustrated the syntactic behavior of a transitive VN followed by a copula. First, I have shown the results of a survey of 461 transitive VNs with a copula. The results show that, although stylistically skewed, VN-*da* sentences with an accusative object occur as frequently as VN-*tyuu* sentences with an accusative object. The results also show that those transitive VNs high on the Transitivity scale and denoting an event where the theme ends up in some salient resultant state can appear in the passive when followed by a copula. Second, I have run three tests of passivization to see if those passive VN-*da* sentences are really passive. The controllability of a rationale clause by the suppressed agent of a passive VN-*da* sentence, the ability of the nominatively marked theme subject of a passive VN-*da* sentence to be modified by its numeral quantifier at distance, and the scope ambiguity that the subject of a passive VN-*da* sentence exhibits with regard to a *v*P-peripheral element all support the view that those VN sentences in question are indeed passive. Lastly, I proposed a syntactic analysis of VN-*da* sentences, where *su*(*ru*) or a copula functioning as a light verb (in the sense of Chomsky 2001) merges with a VN to derive transitive, unaccusative, or passive constructions.

References

Aizawa, M. 1993. Nihongo kyōiku no tame no kihongo chosa to fukugō sa-hen dōsi (A Survey on Basic Vocabulary and Compound Verbs with *Suru* for Japanese Language Education). *Kokuritsu Kokugo Kenkyūjo Hōkoku* (National Language Research Institute Report) *105: Kenkyū Hōkokushū* (Research Report) 14:281–332.

Chomsky, N. 2001. Derivation by Phase. *Ken Hale: A Life in Language,* ed. M. Kenstowicz, 1–52. Cambridge: MIT Press.

Folli, R., Harley, H., and Karimi, S. 2005. Determinants of Event Type in Persian Complex Predicates. *Lingua* 115:1365–1401.

Fukuda, S. 2006. Japanese Passives, External Arguments, and Structural Case. *San Diego Linguistic Papers* 2:86–133.

Grimshaw, J. 1990. *Argument Structure*. Cambridge: MIT Press.

Grimshaw, J. and Mester, A. 1988. Light Verbs and θ-Marking. *Linguistic Inquiry* 19:205–232.

Harley, H. and Noyer, R. 2000. Formal Versus Encyclopedic Properties of Vocabulary: Evidence from Nominalisations. *The Lexicon-Encyclopedia Interface*, ed. B. Peeters, 349–374. Amsterdam: Elsevier.

Harley, H. 1995. Subjects, Events and Licensing. Doctoral dissertation, MIT.

Hoji, H. 2008. Reconstruction Effects in Passive and Scrambling in Japanese. *Japanese/Korean Linguistics 13*, ed. M. Endo Hudson, S.-A. Jun, P. Sells, P. Clancy, S. Iwasaki, and S.-O. Sohn, 152–166. Stanford: CSLI.

Hopper, P. and Thompson, S. 1980. Transitivity in Grammar and Discourse. *Language* 56:251–299.

Hoshi, H. 1999. Passives. *The Handbook of Japanese Linguistics*, ed. N. Tsujimura, 191–235. Oxford: Blackwell.

Iida, M. 1987. Case Assignment by Nominals in Japanese. *Working Papers in Grammatical Theory and Discourse Structure: Interactions of Morphology, Syntax, and Discourse*, ed. M. Iida, S. Wechsler, and D. Zec, 93–138. Stanford: CSLI.

Ivana, A. and Sakai, H. 2007. Honorification and Light Verbs in Japanese. *Journal of East Asian Linguistics* 16:171–191.

Iwasaki, Y. 1999. Three Subcategories of Nouns in Japanese. Doctoral dissertation, University of Illinois at Urbana-Champaign.

Kageyama, T. 1993. *Bunpō to gokeisei* (Grammar and Word Formation). Tokyo: Hituzi Syobo.

Karimi-Doostan, G. 2005. Light Verbs and Structural Case. *Lingua* 115:1737–1756.

Kitagawa, Y. and Kuroda, S.-Y. 1992. Passive in Japanese, v. 5.3. Ms., Indiana University and UCSD.

Kubota, K. 2010. VN-da bun no kinō (The Function of VN-*da* Sentences). *Proceedings of the 141st Conference of the Linguistic Society of Japan*, 104–109.

Martin, S. 1975. *A Reference Grammar of Japanese*. New Haven: Yale University Press.

Masuoka, T. 2000. *Nihongo bunpō no Shosō* (Aspects of the Japanese Grammar). Tokyo: Kurosio Publishers.

Masuoka, T. and Takubo, Y. 1992. *Kiso Nihongo bunpō, kaitei-ban* (A Basic Grammar of Japanese, Revised Edition). Tokyo: Kurosio Publishers.

Matsumoto, Y. 1996. *Complex Predicates in Japanese: A Syntactic and Semantic Study of the Notion 'Word'*. Stanford: CSLI.

Miyagawa, S. and Arikawa, K. 2007. Locality in Syntax and Floated Numeral Quantifiers. *Linguistic Inquiry* 38:645–670.

Miyagawa, S. 1989. *Syntax and Semantics 22: Structure and Case Marking in Japanese*. New York: Academic Press.

Nitta, Y. 1980. *Goironteki tōgoron* (Lexical Syntax). Tokyo: Meiji Shoten.

Niwa, T. 2008. Dōshi no Keigokei *o/go . . . da* no tensu-asupekuto (The Tense and Aspect of the Verbal Honorific Form *o/go . . . da*). (Osaka City University) *Bungaku Kenkyū* 48:67–76.

Okutsu, K. 1978. *"Boku wa unagi da" no bunpō* (The Grammar of "I am the eel"). Tokyo: Kurosio Publishers.

Ono, N. 1997. Externalization and Event Structure. *Verb Semantics and Syntactic Structure,* ed. T. Kageyama, 149–176. Tokyo: Kurosio Publishers.

Oshima, T. 2010. *Nihongo rentai shūshoku-setsu kōzō no kenkyū* (A Study on Japanese Adnominal Clause Constructions). Tokyo: Hituzi Syobo.

Sato, Y. 2008. A Phonologically Null Copula Functioning as a Light Verb in Japanese. *Japanese/Korean Linguistics 13*, ed. M. Endo Hudson, S.-A. Jun, P. Sells, P. Clancy, S. Iwasaki, and S.-O. Sohn, 207–217. Stanford: CSLI.

Sato, Y. 2012. O-VN-da kōbun no shutsugen hindo (The Actual Frequency of the *o*-VN-*da* Construction). *ICU Studies in Japanese Language Education* 8:35–48.

Sells, P. 1996. Case, Categories and Projection. *Morphosyntax in Generative Grammar: Proceedings of 1996 Seoul International Conference on Generative Grammar*, ed. H.-D. Ahn, M.-Y. Kang, Y.-S. Kim, and S. Lee, 47–62. Seoul: Hankwuk Publishing.

Suzuki, T. 2010. Nyūsu hōdō ni okeru "{dōmeishi (VN) / meishi (N)} + desu" bun ni tsuite (On the Use of "{Verbal Noun (VN)/Noun (N)} + *desu*" Sentences in News Reports). (Tokyo University of Foreign Studies) *Bulletin of Japanese Language Center for International Students* 36:57–70.

Takahashi, T. 1984. Meishi-jutsugo-bun ni okeru shugo to jutsugo no imiteki na kankei (The Semantic Relationship between the Subject and the Predicate in Nominal Predicate Sentences). *Nihongogaku* 3(12):18–19.

Dual Selections and Relabeling in Japanese and Korean

TORU ISHII*
Meiji University

1. Introduction

This paper discusses complementizer stacking in Japanese and Korean, exemplified by (1) and (2).

(1) John-wa Bill-ni [dare-ga kita **ka to**] tazuneta
John-TOP Bill-DAT who-NOM came **Q that** asked
Lit. 'John asked Bill *that who* came.'

* This is a revised version of the paper presented at J/K22. I would like to thank the audience at the conference for helpful comments and suggestions. I would also like to thank Hiroshi Aoyagi, Noam Chomsky, Hidehito Hoshi, Yasuyuki Kitao, Shigeru Miyagawa, Norvin Richards, and Mamoru Saito for helpful comments on earlier versions of this paper. I am grateful to Sun-Hee Bae and DaeYoung Sohn for the Korean data. Remaining errors and omissions are, of course, the sole responsibility of the author. This work is supported in part by the Japan Society for the Promotion of Science under grant Scientific Research C 22420511.
Japanese/Korean Linguistics 22.
Edited by Mikio Giriko, Naonori Nagaya, Akiko Takemura, and Timothy J. Vance.

(2) John-nun Mary-eykey [*pro* ku mwuncey-lul phwul-ess
John-TOP Mary-DAT that problem-ACC solved
nya ko] mulessta
Q that asked
'John asked Mary *that whether* she solved that problem.'

In (1) and (2), two complementizers are stacked at the right edge of the complement clause. In the Japanese example (1), the interrogative complementizer *ka* 'Q' and the declarative complementizer *to* 'that' are stacked. Similarly, *nya* 'Q' and *ko* 'that' are stacked in the Korean example (2). I will argue that there are dual selections involved in (1) and (2), i.e., semantic selection between the matrix predicate *tazuneta/mulessta* 'ask' and the interrogative complementizer *ka/nya* 'Q', and syntactic selection between the matrix predicate and the declarative complementizer *to/ko* 'that'. Given the sisterhood condition on selection, which states that an element can only select its sister, no previous analysis can account for why the matrix predicate *tazuneta/mulessta* 'ask' can semantically select the interrogative complementizer *ka/nya* 'Q' skipping over *to/ko* 'that' in (1) and (2). I propose that when a labeling conflict arises, relabeling may apply as part of LF-Transfer, which accounts for the dual selections in complementizer stacking. Since relabeling is an operation where labeling applies without Merge, the analysis to be proposed presents further evidence for the symmetric-Merge-with-labeling-algorithms approach, which claims that Merge and labeling are independent operations.

The organization of this paper is as follows. Section 2 investigates complementizer stacking in Japanese, showing that complementizer stacking involves dual selections. Section 3 presents evidence against a direct quotation analysis of complementizer stacking. Section 4 investigates complementizer stacking in Korean. Section 5 first explicates the symmetric-Merge-with-labeling-algorithms approach, and then proposes a relabeling analysis of complementizer stacking, which accounts for the dual selections. Section 6 makes concluding remarks.

2. Complementizer Stacking in Japanese

2.1. Semantic Selection

Predicates like *tazuneru* 'ask' semantically select an interrogative clause. They can take a clause headed by the interrogative complementizer *ka* 'Q' but not a clause headed by the declarative complementizer *to* 'that', as shown by the contrast between (3a) and (3b).

(3) a. *John-wa Bill-ni [Mary-ga kita **to**] tazuneta
John-TOP Bill-DAT Mary-NOM came **that** asked
Lit. 'John asked Bill that Mary came.'

b. John-wa Bill-ni [dare-ga kita **ka**] tazuneta
John-TOP Bill-DAT who-NOM came **Q** asked
'John asked Bill who came.'

2.2. Complementizer Stacking

As pointed out by Fukui (1986), Saito (2010), Hoshi (2011), and Miyagawa (2011), these two complementizers, *ka* 'Q' and *to* 'that', can be stacked in the complement clause selected by *tazuneru* 'ask', as shown in (1), repeated here as (4).

(4) John-wa Bill-ni [dare-ga kita **ka to**] tazuneta
John-TOP Bill-DAT who-NOM came **Q that** asked
Lit. 'John asked Bill *that who* came.'

Given that selection is local in that an element can only select its sister, a question arises as to how the matrix predicate *tazuneru* 'ask' can semantically select the interrogative complementizer *ka* 'Q', skipping over the declarative complementizer *to* 'that' in (4).

2.3. Syntactic Selection

We cannot simply assume that the declarative complementizer *to* 'that' is transparent for selection in (4). As pointed out by Saito (2010), not all matrix predicates allow complementizer stacking. Although predicates like *siritagaru* 'want-to-know', *tyoosasuru* 'investigate', and *hakkensuru* 'discover' semantically select an interrogative clause, as shown in (5), they cannot take complementizer stacking clauses, as shown in (6) (Saito 2010: 5).

(5) John-wa [dare-ga kita **ka**] siritagatteiru
John-TOP who-NOM came **Q** want-to-know
Lit. 'John wants to know who came.'

(6) *John-wa [dare-ga kita **ka to**] siritagatteiru
John-TOP who-NOM came **Q that** want-to-know
Lit. 'John wants to know *that who* came.'

The contrast between (4) and (6) shows the difference in syntactic selection between *tazuneru* 'ask' and *siritagaru* 'want-to-know'; predicates like *tazuneru* 'ask' can syntactically select a clause headed by *to* 'that', whereas predicates like *siritagaru* 'want-to-know' cannot.

2.4. Dual Selections

I argue that dual selections are involved in the complementizer stacking clause (4):

(7) Dual Selections
  a. semantic selection between *tazuneru* 'ask' and the interrogative complementizer *ka* 'Q' at LF
  b. syntactic selection between *tazuneru* 'ask' and the declarative complementizer *to* 'that' in overt syntax as a driving force of Merge

In the traditional analysis, there are two possible structures of the complementizer stacking clause (4): the head-complement structure (8a) and the adjunction structure (8b).

(8) a. Head-Complement Structure

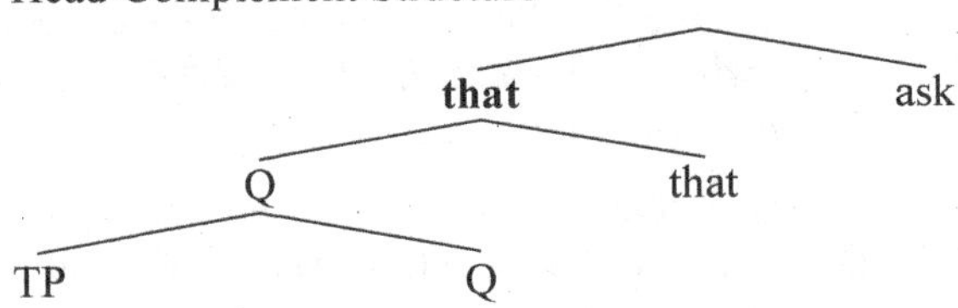

  b. Adjunction Structure

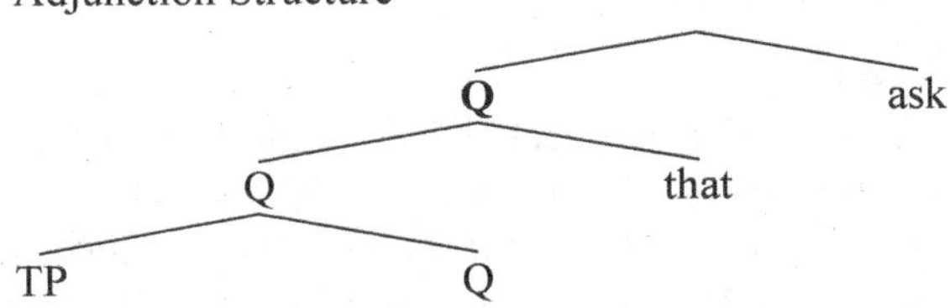

Given the sisterhood condition on selection, the dual selections cannot be captured by either the head-complement structure or the adjunction structure. The head-complement structure (8a) satisfies syntactic selection, but not sematic selection. The adjunction structure (8b), on the other hand, satisfies semantic selection, but not syntactic selection. What we need is a dual structure, where one syntactic object may have more than one structure, i.e., both the head-complement structure and the adjunction structure. One might argue that if we assume the head-complement structure (8a) and allow the Q-feature of the interrogative complementizer *ka* 'Q' to percolate up the *that*-phrase, then the matrix predicate *tazuneru* 'ask' can satisfy the dual selections. The *that*-clause, however, would end up having both an interrogative feature and a non-interrogative feature, which is contradictory, and this would result in an anomalous interpretation at LF. It should also be noted that under the bare phrase structure theory this paper is assuming, such partial percolation is not allowed. Hence, this paper does not adopt a partial percolation analysis.

3. Evidence against a Direct Quotation Analysis

This section presents evidence to show that complementizer stacking clauses are not direct quotations but complement clauses.

3.1. Polite Forms

First, Miyagawa (1987) observes that direct *wh*-questions with *ka* 'Q' are deviant if the verb is in the plain form without the polite suffix *-masu*, as shown by the contrast between (9a) and (9b).

(9) a. *Dare-ga **kita** ka (plain form)
who-NOM came Q
'Who came?'

b. Dare-ga **kimasita** ka (polite form)
who-NOM came Q
'Who came?'

In the complementizer stacking clause (4), repeated here as (10), *ka* 'Q' is used with the plain verb form *kita* 'came'. This shows that the complementizer stacking clause (10) does not involve a quoted direct *wh*-question but a complement clause.

(10) John-wa Bill-ni [dare-ga **kita** ka to] tazuneta (plain form)
John-TOP Bill-DAT who-NOM came Q that asked
Lit. 'John asked Bill *that who* came.'

3.2. Extraction

Second, direct quotations are opaque to extraction, as shown below.

(11) **What** did Mary say, "I am going to buy ***t***?"

(12) ?***Sono situmon-ni** Mary-ga, "Dare-ga ***t*** tadasiku
that question-DAT Mary-NOM who-NOM correctly
kotaeta no kasira" to tazuneta rasii
answered Q PART(ICLE) that asked seem
Lit. '**That question**, it seems that Mary asked, "Who answered ***t*** correctly?"'

Extraction out of a complementizer stacking clause, on the other hand, is possible, as shown in (13). This also shows that complementizer stacking clauses are not direct quotations but complement clauses.

(13) **Sono situmon-ni** Mary-ga [dare-ga ***t*** tadasiku
that question-DAT Mary-NOM who-NOM correctly
kotaeta ka to] tazuneta rasii
answered Q that asked seem
Lit. '**That question**, it seems that Mary asked *that who* answered ***t*** correctly.'

3.3. Pronominal Binding

Third, direct quotations are opaque to pronominal binding, as shown in (14) and (15).

(14) **Mary**$_1$ asked John, "Who cheated **her**$_{*1/2}$?"

(15) **Mary**$_1$-ga John-ni, "Dare-ga **kanozyo**$_{*1/2}$-o damasita
Mary-NOM John-DAT who-NOM **she**-ACC cheated
no kasira," to tazuneta rasii
Q PART that asked seem
'It seems that Mary asked John, "Who cheated her?"'

In (14) and (15), the pronoun within the direct quotation cannot be coreferential with the matrix subject *Mary*. In (16), on the other hand, the pronoun *kanozyo* 'she' within the complementizer stacking clause can be coreferential with *Mary*; complementizer stacking clauses are not opaque to pronominal binding.

(16) **Mary**$_1$-ga John-ni [dare-ga **kanozyo**$_{1/2}$-o damasita ka to]
Mary-NOM John-DAT who-NOM **she**-ACC cheated Q that
tazuneta rasii
asked seem
Lit. 'It seems that Mary asked John *that who* cheated her.'

3.4. *De re* Readings

Fourth, descriptions in direct quotations may not be interpreted as *de re*.

(17) a. Oedipus said, "**My mother** is pretty." (unambiguous)
De dicto: Oedipus knows she is his mother.
**De re*: Oedipus doesn't know she is his mother.
b. Oedipus said **his mother** is pretty. (ambiguous)

(18) Context: Mary saw Jack talking with the man who was a stranger to her. She asked me who Jack was talking with. She doesn't know Jack is a teacher. In the classroom, I say to someone else:

a. #Mary-ga, "**Sensei**-wa dare-to hanasiteita no kasira,"
Mary-NOM **teacher**-NOM who-with was-talking Q PART
to boku-ni tazuneteita yo
that I-DAT asked PART
'Mary asked me who the teacher was talking with.'

b. Mary-ga [**sensei**-ga dare-to hanasiteita ka]
Mary-NOM **teacher**-NOM who-with was-talking Q
boku-ni tazuneteita yo
I-DAT asked PART
'Mary asked me who the teacher was talking with.'

In (17a), *my mother* in the direct quotation can only be interpreted as *de dicto*, not as *de re*. This is in contrast with (17b), where *his mother* in the complement clause can be interpreted as either *de dicto* or *de re*. Similarly, in the Japanese example (18a), *sensei* 'teacher' in the direct quotation cannot be interpreted as *de re*. Hence, (18a) is deviant in the given context. In (18b), on the other hand, *sensei* 'teacher' in the complement clause can be interpreted as *de re*. Hence, (18b) is acceptable. Turning to complementizer stacking clauses, (19) is acceptable in the same context as (18). This shows that *sensei* 'teacher' in the complementizer stacking clause can be interpreted as *de re*. Hence, complementizer stacking clauses are not direct quotations but complement clauses.

(19) In the same context as (18):
Mary-ga [**sensei**-ga dare-to hanasiteita ka to]
Mary-NOM **teacher**-NOM who-with was-talking Q that
boku-ni tazuneteita yo
I-DAT asked PART
'Mary asked me *that who* the teacher was talking with.'

3.5. Temporal Modifiers

Fifth, temporal modifiers in direct quotations are evaluated relative to subjects, whereas those in complement clauses are evaluated relative to utterers.

(20) a. Mary said, "I will come to the party **tomorrow**."

b. Mary-ga John-ni, "Dare-ga **asita** paatii-ni kuru
Mary-NOM John-DAT who-NOM **tomorrow** party-to come
no kasira," to tazuneteita yo
Q PART that asked PART
'Mary asked John, "Who will come to the party tomorrow?"'

(21) a. Mary said she would come to the party **tomorrow**.

b. Mary-ga [dare-ga **asita** paatii-ni kuru ka]
Mary-NOM who-NOM **tomorrow** party-to come Q
John-ni tazuneteita yo
John-DAT asked PART
'Mary asked John who would come to the party the next day.'

In (20), the temporal modifier *tomorrow* in the direct quotation is evaluated relative to the subject *Mary*; *tomorrow* is interpreted as the day after Mary's saying or asking. In (21), on the other hand, *tomorrow* in the complement clause is evaluated relative to the utterer; *tomorrow* is interpreted as the day after speech act. Turning to complementizer stacking clauses, *tomorrow* in a complementizer stacking clause is interpreted as the day after the speech act, as shown in (22). This shows that complementizer stacking clauses are not direct quotations but complement clauses.

(22) Mary-ga [dare-ga **asita** paatii-ni kuru ka to]
Mary-NOM who-NOM **tomorrow** party-to come Q that
John-ni tazuneteita yo
John-DAT asked PART
'Mary asked John *that who* would come to the party the next day.'

3.6. Evaluative Predicates

Sixth, evaluative predicates in direct quotations are evaluated relative to subjects, whereas those in complement clauses are evaluated relative to utterances.

(23) a. Mary said, "I love **that idiot**."

b. Mary-wa John-ni, "Dare-ga **ano orokamono**-ni
Mary-TOP John-DAT who-NOM **that idiot**-DAT
taikin-o watasita no kasira," to tazuneta
a lot of money-ACC gave Q PART that asked
'Mary asked John, "Who gave a lot of money to that idiot?"'

(24) a. Mary said she loves **that idiot**.

b. Mary-wa John-ni [dare-ga **ano orokamono**-ni
Mary-TOP John-DAT who-NOM **that idiot**-DAT
taikin-o watasita ka] tazuneta
a lot of money-ACC gave Q asked
'Mary asked John who gave a lot of money to that idiot.'

In (23), where *that idiot* is within the direct quotation, it is evaluated relative to the subject *Mary*; it is Mary who thinks that he is an idiot. In (24), on the other hand, *that idiot* is in the complement clause, so it is evaluated relative to the utterer; it is the speaker who thinks that he is an idiot. When *that idiot* is in a complementizer stacking clause, it is evaluated relative to the utterer, as shown in (25). This shows that complementizer stacking clauses are complement clauses.

(25) Mary-wa John-ni [dare-ga **ano orokamono**-ni
Mary-TOP John-DAT who-NOM **that idiot**-DAT
taikin-o watasita ka to] tazuneta
a lot of money-ACC gave Q that asked
Lit. 'Mary asked John *that who* gave a lot of money to that idiot.'

3.7. Deictic Terms

Finally, deictic terms within direct quotations are evaluated relative to subjects, whereas those in complement clauses are evaluated relative to utterers.

(26) a. Mary said, "I want **this** picture."

b. Mary-wa John-ni, "Dare-ga **kono** e-o kaita
Mary-TOP John-DAT who-NOM **this** picture-ACC drew
no kasira," to tazuneta
Q PART that asked
'Mary asked John, "Who draw this picture?"'

(27) a. Mary said that she wanted **this** picture.

b. Mary-wa John-ni [dare-ga **kono** e-o kaita ka]
Mary-TOP John-DAT who-NOM **this** picture-ACC draw Q
tazuneta
asked
'Mary asked John who draw this picture.'

In (26), where the deictic term *this* appears within the direct quotation, it is evaluated relative to the subject *Mary*; *this picture* is near *Mary*. In (27), on the other hand, *this* appears within the complement clause, so it is evaluated relative to the utterer; *this picture* is near the speaker. When the deictic term *this* appears in a complementizer stacking clause, it is evaluated relative to the utterer, as shown in (28). Hence, complementizer stacking clauses are complement clauses.

(28) Mary-wa John-ni [dare-ga **kono** e-o kaita ka to]
Mary-TOP John-DAT who-NOM **this** picture-ACC draw Q that
tazuneta
asked
Lit. 'Mary asked John *that who* draw this picture.'

4. Complementizer Stacking in Korean

4.1. Semantic Selection

In Korean complementizer stacking, a matrix verb semantically selects a mood marker within its complement clause, as shown in (29)–(32).

(29) John-nun [Mary-ka ku mwuncey-lul phwul-ess
John-TOP Mary-NOM that problem-ACC solved
ta/*nya/*la/*ca **ko**/*nun] cwucangha-ess-ta
DECL/Q/IMP/EXH that claimed
'John claimed that Mary solved that problem.'

(30) John-nun Mary-eykey [*pro* ku mwuncey-lul phwul-ess
John-TOP Mary-DAT that problem-ACC solved
*ta/**nya**/*la/*ca **ko**/*nun] mul-ess-ta
DECL/**Q**/IMP/EXH that asked
'John asked Mary whether she solved that problem.'

(31) John-nun Mary-eykey [*pro* ku mwuncey-lul phwul
John-TOP Mary-DAT that problem-ACC solve
*ta/*nya/**la**/*ca **ko**/*nun] myengryengha-ess-ta
DECL/Q/**IMP**/EXH that ordered
'John ordered Mary to solve that problem.'

(32) John-nun Mary-eykey [*pro* ku mwuncey-lul phwul
John-TOP Mary-DAT that problem-ACC solve
*ta/*nya/*la/**ca** **ko**/*nun] ceyanha-ess-ta
DECL/Q/IMP/**EXH** that suggested
'John suggested to Mary to solve that problem.'

Verbs like *cwucangha* 'claim' and *mit* 'believe' semantically select the declarative mood marker *ta*, as shown in (29). Verbs like *mul* 'ask' semantically select the interrogative mood marker *nya*, as shown in (30). Verbs like *myengryengha* 'order' semantically select the imperative mood marker *la*, as shown in (31). Verbs like *ceyanha* 'suggest' semantically select the exhortative mood marker *ca*, as shown in (32). Similarly, a matrix noun semantically selects a mood marker in its complement clause, as shown in (33)–(36).

(33) [John-i ku mwuncey-lul phwul-ess **ta**/*nya/*la/*ca
John-NOM that problem-ACC solved **DECL**/Q/IMP/EXH
*ko/**nun**] cwucang
that claim
'the claim that John solved that problem'

(34) [John-i ku mwuncey-lul phwul-ess *ta/**nya**/*la/*ca
John-NOM that problem-ACC solved DECL/**Q**/IMP/EX
*ko/**nun**] cilmwu
that question
'the question whether John solved that problem'

(35) [*pro* ku mwuncey-lul phwul *ta/*nya/**la**/*ca *ko/**nun**]
that problem-ACC solve DECL/Q/**IMP**/EXH that
myenglyeng
order
'the order to solve that problem'

(36) [*pro* ku mwuncey-lul phwul *ta/*nya/*la/**ca** *ko/**nun**]
that problem-ACC solve DECL/Q/IMP/**EXH** that
ceyan
suggestion
'the suggestion to solve that problem'

4.2. Syntactic Selection

A question again arises about how the matrix predicate can semantically select a mood marker skipping over *ko*/*nun* 'that' in (29)–(36). We cannot claim that *ko* and *nun* are transparent for selection. Matrix verbs take *ko* but not *nun*, as shown in (29)–(32). Matrix nouns, on the other hand, take *nun* but not *ko*, as shown in (33)–(36). This shows that matrix verbs syntactically select *ko* 'that', whereas matrix nouns syntactically select *nun* 'that'. Hence, dual selections are also involved in Korean complementizer stacking, with semantic selection between a matrix predicate and a mood marker at LF and syntactic selection between a matrix verb/noun and *ka*/*nun* 'that' in overt syntax as the driving force of Merge.

5. A Proposal

5.1. Merge, Labeling Algorithms, and Labeling Conflicts

Before turning to an analysis of the dual selections in complementizer stacking, I will explicate Merge, labeling algorithms, and labeling conflicts.

In Chomsky's (1995) formulation of Merge (37), labeling is part of Merge, which makes Merge asymmetric.

(37) Asymmetric Merge

Merge is an asymmetric operation; (i) it combines two elements into a set, and (ii) it projects one of the merged elements, providing the set with a label (adapted from Chomsky 1995:243):

$$\text{Merge}(\alpha, \beta) =_{\text{def}} \{\gamma, \{\alpha, \beta\}\}, \text{ where } \gamma \in \{\alpha, \beta\}$$

In the asymmetric formulation of Merge in (37), every node must have a label, but this is a residue of phrase structure grammar. Hence, it is better to separate the labeling part from Merge. Under this view, Chomsky (2004, 2008) formulates Merge as a symmetric operation, as shown in (38). In (38), labels are not created by Merge, but rather determined by the two labeling algorithms in (39).

(38) Symmetric Merge
Merge is a symmetric operation, combining two elements into a set (Chomsky 2004:117; 2008):

$$\text{Merge}(\alpha, \beta) =_{\text{def}} \{\alpha, \beta\}$$

(39) Labeling Algorithms (Chomsky 2008:145)
a. In {H, α}, H an LI, H is the label.
b. If α is internally merged to β, forming {α, β}, then the label of β is the label of {α, β}.

(39a) states that it is always a head that projects. (39b) states that in Internal Merge, it is always the target that projects. The symmetric formulation of Merge is also proposed by Boeckx (2008), Hornstein (2009), and Fukui (2011). This paper assumes the traditional view that labeling is required for both efficient computation and interface conditions.

Under the symmetric-Merge-with-labeling-algorithms approach, Merge and labeling are independent operations, so we should expect that labeling may apply without Merge. I will argue that labeling without Merge applies in complementizer stacking. Specifically, I propose that when a labeling conflict arises, relabeling (i.e., labeling without Merge) may apply as part of LF-Transfer, which accounts for the dual selections in complementizer stacking. If the analysis proposed below is on the right track, therefore, it provides further evidence for the symmetric-Merge-with-labeling-algorithms approach.

The notion of labeling conflict was proposed by Donati (2006), Chomsky (2008), and Cecchetto and Donati (2010, 2011). They argue that a labeling conflict arises in cases like (40), where α is a lexical item (i.e., a head), and β is not a head, and α undergoes Internal Merge with β.

(40) $[\alpha\ [_{\beta}\ \alpha]]$

The labeling algorithms (39) make conflicting predictions. According to (39a), α, which is a head, should become the label. According to (39b), however, β, which is the target of Internal Merge, should become the label. The claim is that a labeling conflict makes the two different labels available, which creates an ambiguous structure.

5.2. Dual Selections and Relabeling

Based on this labeling conflict idea, I argue that a labeling conflict creates not only an ambiguous structure but also a dual structure in the sense that one syntactic object has different structures in overt syntax and LF. Such a dual structure is created by relabeling as part of LF-Transfer. It seems plausible to assume that LF-Transfer can trigger relabeling, where the asymmetric relation between merged elements changes. It should be noted that PF-Transfer alters the (a)symmetric relation between merged elements, converting an unordered set {X, Y} into an ordered pair <X, Y> or <Y, X>. Hence, I claim that Transfer can alter the (a)symmetric relation between merged elements due to linearization in PF-Transfer and relabeling in LF-Transfer.

This paper claims, with Shlonsky (2006), that cartographic structure is created by self-attachment of C, as stated in (41).

(41) a. C is associated with an ordered set of lexical items (or bundles of features if C is null) $<C_1, \ldots C_n>$. These precompiled lexical items (or bundles of features) correspond to Rizzi's (1997) Fin, Foc, Top, etc.

b. The computational system activates these lexical items (or bundles of features) one by one respecting the order of compilation: (i) initial merger of C activates the leftmost lexical item (or bundle of features) in the set; (ii) each time C is internally merged to itself, i.e., self-attachment of C takes place, the leftmost inactive lexical item (or bundle of features) in the set is activated.

c. Once C_m, m > 1, is activated, C_{m-1} is no longer visible to the computational system.

Let us look at how relabeling derives the dual structure property of complementizer stacking, thereby accounting for its dual selections. Let us consider (4), repeated here as (42), as an example. The derivation of (42) proceeds as shown in (43).

(42) John-wa Bill-ni [dare-ga kita **ka to**] tazuneta
John-TOP Bill-DAT who-NOM came **Q that** asked
Lit. 'John asked Bill *that who* came.'

(43)

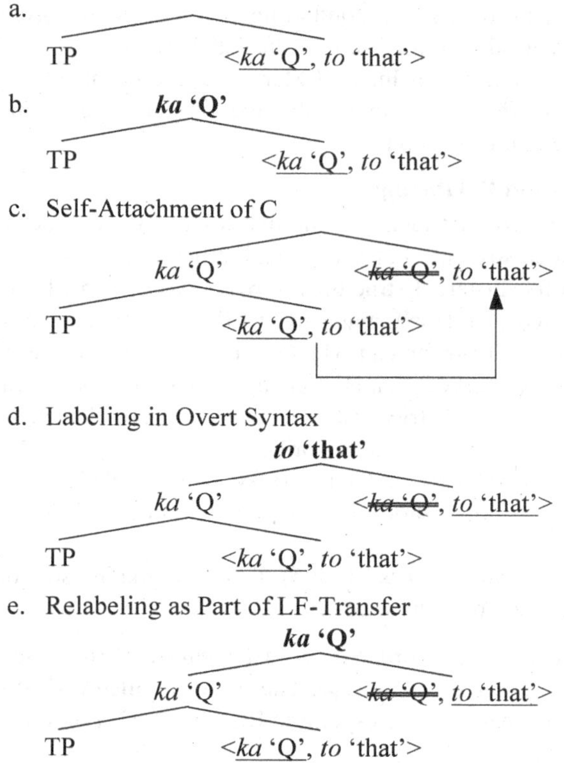

C consists of the ordered set <*ka* 'Q', *to* 'that'>. External Merge applies to TP and C <*ka* 'Q', *to* 'that'>. By this initial merger of C <*ka* 'Q', *to* 'that'>, the leftmost lexical item in the set, i.e., the interrogative complementizer *ka* 'Q', becomes activated. This merger yields {TP, <*ka* 'Q', *to* 'that'>}, as represented in (43a). In (43a) and relevant representations to follow, the activated lexical item (or bundle of features) is underlined. The labeling algorithms in (39) require that <*ka* 'Q', *to* 'that'>, which is a lexical item, should become the label of {TP, <*ka* 'Q', *to* 'that'>} in accordance with the labeling algorithm (39a); (43b) is labeled *ka* 'Q' (= <ka 'Q', *to* 'that'>). Next, we apply self-attachment of C, i.e., attachment (movement) of <*ka* 'Q', *to* 'that'> to itself. In other words, <*ka* 'Q', *to* 'that'> is internally merged into the label *ka* 'Q' (= <*ka* 'Q', *to* 'that'>). When <*ka* 'Q', *to* 'that'> is internally merged into itself, the leftmost inactive lexical item in the set *to* 'that' becomes activated and *ka* 'Q', which was activated in the previous Merge, becomes no longer visible to the computational system, resulting in <~~*ka* 'Q'~~, *to* 'that'>. Hence, self-attachment of C yields {*ka* 'Q' (= <*ka* 'Q', *to* 'that'>), <~~*ka* 'Q'~~, *to* 'that'>}, as represented in (43c). A labeling conflict arises in (43c); the labeling algorithm (39a) requires that <~~*ka* 'Q'~~, *to* 'that'>, which is a lexical item, become the label, whereas the labeling algorithm (39b) requires that the label *ka* 'Q' (= <*ka* 'Q', *to* 'that'>), which is the target of Internal Merge, become the label. I argue that this labeling conflict creates a dual structure. We have two labeling options: either *to* 'that' (= <~~*ka* 'Q'~~, *to* 'that'>) or *ka* 'Q' (= <*ka* 'Q', *to* 'that'>) becomes the label. We take the former option here; *to* 'that' becomes the label in accordance with (39a) in overt syntax, as represented in (43d). This labeling drives Merge with the matrix predicate *tazuneru* 'ask', satisfying the syntactic selection of *tazuneru.* When we come to the stage where LF-Transfer applies, relabeling applies as part of LF-Transfer; *ka* 'Q' (= <*ka* 'Q', *to* 'that'>) becomes the label in accordance with (39b), as represented in (43e). This label satisfies the semantic selection of the matrix predicate *tazuneru* 'ask' at LF. Hence, relabeling due to the labeling conflict creates a dual structure where the complementizer stacking clause (42) is labeled *to* 'that' in overt syntax but *ka* 'Q' at LF, and this accounts for the puzzling dual selections. The dual selections in Korean complementizer stacking can be accounted for in the same way.

Before closing this section, let us consider predicates like *omou* 'think', *yuu* 'say', and *sakebu* 'scream'. These predicates syntactically and semantically select a complement clause headed by the declarative complementizer *to* 'that', as shown in (44).

(44) a. John-wa [Mary-ga kita **to**] omotta/itta/sakenda
John-TOP Mary-NOM came that thought/said/screamed
'John thought/said/screamed that Mary came.'

b. *John-wa [dare-ga kita **ka**] omotta/itta/sakenda
John-TOP who-NOM came Q thought/said/screamed
Lit. 'John thought/said/screamed who came.'

As pointed out by Saito (2010), these predicates can also take a complementizer stacking clause as shown in (45):

(45) John-wa [dare-ga kita **ka to**] omotta/itta/sakenda
John-TOP who-NOM came **Q that** thought/said/screamed
Lit. 'John thought/said/screamed *that who* came.'

Under our analysis, the derivation of (45) proceeds almost in the same way as derivation (43). The only difference between these two derivations is that relabeling due to a labeling conflict, which is optional, does not apply in the derivation of (45). The declarative complementizer *to* 'that', which is the label in overt syntax, remains as the label at LF, and this satisfies the syntactic and semantic selections of these predicates.

6. Conclusion

This paper has investigated complementizer stacking in Japanese and Korean. I showed that complementizer stacking involves dual selections, which cannot be accounted for by either the traditional head-complement or adjunction structure. I then proposed relabeling as part of LF-Transfer due to a labeling conflict, showing that it accounts for the dual selections. This provides further evidence for the symmetric-Merge-with-labeling-algorithms approach.

References

Boeckx, C. 2008. *Bare Syntax*. Oxford: Oxford University Press.

Cecchetto, C. and Donati, C. 2010. On Labeling: Principle C and Head Movement. *Syntax* 13:241–278.

Cecchetto, C. and Donati, C. 2011. Relabeling Heads: A Unified Account for Relativization Structures. *Linguistic Inquiry* 42:519–560.

Chomsky, N. 1995. *The Minimalist Program*. Cambridge: MIT Press.

Chomsky, N. 2004. Beyond Explanatory Adequacy. *Structures and Beyond*, ed. A. Belletti, 104–131. Oxford: Oxford University Press.

Chosmky, N. 2008. On Phases. *Foundational Issues in Linguistic Theory: Essays in Honor of Jean-Roger Vergnaud*, ed. R. Friedin, C. P. Otero, and M. L. Zubizarreta, 133–166. Cambridge: MIT Press.

Donati, C. 2006. On Wh-Head Movement. *Wh-Movement: Moving On*, ed. L. Cheng and N. Corver, 21–46. Cambridge: MIT Press.

Fukui, N. 1986. A Theory of Category Projection and its Application. Doctoral dissertation, MIT.

Fukui, N. 2011. Merge and Bare Phrase Structure. *The Oxford Handbook of Linguistic Minimalism*, ed. C. Boeckx, 73–95. Oxford: Oxford University Press.

Hornstein, N. 2009. *A Theory of Syntax: Minimal Operations and Universal Grammar*. Cambridge: Cambridge University Press.

Hoshi, H. 2011. Merge, Transfer, and Labels. Unpublished manuscript.

Miyagawa, S. 1987. LF Affix Raising in Japanese. *Linguistic Inquiry* 18:362–367.

Miyagawa, S. 2011. Agreements that Occur Mainly in the Main Clause. Unpublished manuscript.

Rizzi, L. 1997. The Fine Structure of the Left Periphery. *Elements of Grammar*, ed. L. Haegeman, 281–337. Dordrecht: Kluwer.

Saito, M. 2010. Sentence Types and the Japanese Right Periphery. Unpublished manuscript.

Shlonsky, U. 2006. Extended Projection and CP Cartography. Unpublished manuscript.

Alternatives Tell You Where You Are

YOSHIYUKI SHIBATA*
University of Connecticut

This article argues that the scope of elements with an alternative-introducing operator (such as focus or exhaustive) reflects their syntactic positions at LF. It shows that, in principle, these elements allow only surface scope, and that this property can be made use of to investigate hierarchical relations among scope bearing elements even in head-final languages like Japanese, where such relations cannot be read off from their surface order.

1. Introduction

In Japanese, normal quantifier phrases (QPs) allow either wide scope or narrow scope readings with respect to sentential negation, as in (1).

* For helpful comments and suggestions, I thank Jonathan Bobaljik, Jon Gajewski, Toru Ishii, Magdalena Kaufmann, Mamoru Saito, Susi Wurmbrand, and especially Željko Bošković. I also thank the participants of J/K22 for their valuable feedback. All remaining errors are mine. This material is based upon work supported by the National Science Foundation under grant BCS-0920888 (PI: Željko Bošković).
Japanese/Korean Linguistics 22.
Edited by Mikio Giriko, Naonori Nagaya, Akiko Takemura, and Timothy J. Vance.

(1) a. Subete-no gakusei-ga ko-nakat-ta.
all-GEN student-NOM come-NEG-PAST
'All students didn't come.' (Subj>¬; ¬>Subj)

b. Go-nin-izyoo-no gakusei-ga ko-nakat-ta.
5-CL-or.more-GEN student-NOM come-NEG-PAST
'5 or more students didn't come.' (Subj>¬; ¬>Subj)

By contrast, focused phrases and disjunctions in subject position allow only wide scope readings over sentential negation, as in (2).

(2) a. Taroo-mo/dake/sae ko-nakat-ta.
Taro-also/only/even come-NEG-PAST
Lit. 'Also/Only/Even Taro didn't come.' (Subj>¬;*¬>Subj)

b. [Taroo-ka Ziroo]-ga ko-nakat-ta.
Taro-or Ziro-NOM come-NEG-PAST
Lit. 'Taro or Ziro didn't come.' (Subj>¬;*¬>Subj)

Interestingly, a similar phenomenon is also observed in English:

(3) All students/A student didn't take the exam. (Subj>¬; ¬>Subj)

(4) Only/John or Tom didn't take the exam. (Subj>¬;*¬>Subj)

Since the subjects in (3) are located in [Spec, TP], that is, outside the scope of the negation, the narrow scope reading of the subject is obtained by some form of a reconstruction process below negation. Thus, focused phrases and disjunctions share the property of "a lack of reconstruction effects."

In this study, I argue that these types of phrases reflect their surface scope and that their scopal properties can be used as a tool to investigate structural relations among scopal elements. The paper is organized as follows. Section 2 gives an account of the lack of reconstruction effects for focused and disjunctive phrases. Section 3 examines several consequences of the scope effects from Section 2. Section 4 is the conclusion.

2. Surface Scope Effects for Alternative-Introducing Elements

In Section 1, we saw that focused phrases and disjunctions lack reconstruction effects in Japanese and English. Why is this the case?

2.1. Focused Phrases and Disjunction Introduce Alternatives

Both focused and disjunctive phrases can be regarded as elements introducing alternatives (Rooth 1985, 1992; Chierchia et al. forthcoming). For instance, in (5), where the focused phrase appears in subject position, there must be a person other than Taro who came in order for the sentence to be true.

(5) Taroo-mo ki-ta.
Taro-also come-PAST
Lit. 'Also Taro came.'

As for disjunction, Chierchia, Fox, and Spector (forthcoming) claim that ordinary scalar items including disjunction are typically interpreted with alternatives. For instance, sentence (6a) only means (6b), not (6c), even though disjunction logically does not exclude the reading in (6c). They argue that this is due to the existence of a silent exhaustive operator similar to English *only*, as in (6d), and that this operator excludes its alternative, (6c).[1]

(6) a. John or Tom will come.
b. John will come or Tom will come.
c. Both John and Tom will come.
d. O_{ALT}(John or Tom) will come.

Thus, the items showing antireconstruction effects can be regarded as elements interpreted with their alternatives.

2.2. Surface Scope Effects

I will now give an account of the antireconstruction property of focused and disjunctive phrases. I adopt two crucial assumptions. First, I assume that A-movement does not reconstruct in the syntax, as argued by, e.g., Chomsky (1995) and Lasnik (1998, 1999).[2]

(7) Assumption I: A-movement does not reconstruct in syntax.

Lechner (1998) notes that the A-scrambled object in German does not reconstruct in the syntax, which accounts for the impossibility of the bound variable reading of the pronoun within the scrambled phrase in (8).

(8) weil sie [ein Bild von $seinem_{*i}$ $Auftritt]_j$ [jedem
since she a picture of his appearance [every
$Kandidaten]_i$ t_j zeigte.
candidate showed
'since she showed a picture of his appearance to every candidate'
(∃>∀; ∀>∃) (Lechner 1998:299)

In (8), the pronoun in the scrambled accusative object cannot be bound by

---

[1] The unavailability of the reading (6c) for (6a) is often treated as a matter of implicature. Chierchia, Fox, and Spector (forthcoming) try to capture the implicatures by grammatical devices like a silent operator, as in (6d).

[2] Chomsky (2001) and Lasnik (2010) adopt different views from the works cited above. Bobaljik and Wurmbrand (2012) also argue that A-scrambling in German and Japanese does not reconstruct in syntax, although they do not exclude the possibility of A-movement syntactic reconstruction in general.

the dative object, which should be possible if the accusative object could reconstruct to the trace position in covert syntax. Yamashita (forthcoming) observes a similar phenomenon in Japanese, giving (9) as an example.

(9) *Taroo-ga otagai-o$_i$ [Mari-to Hanako]$_i$-ni t_i syookaisita.
Taro-NOM each.other-ACC Mari-and Hanako-DAT t introduced
Lit. 'Taro introduced each other to Mari and Hanako.'

In (9), the A-scrambled anaphor cannot be bound by the dative object. If this scrambled phrase could reconstruct in the syntax, (9) should be fine, since the non-scrambled counterpart of the sentence is grammatical:

(10) Taroo-ga [Mari-to Hanako]-ni otagai-o syookaisita.
Taro-NOM Mari-and Hanako-DAT each.other-ACC introduced

These data can be taken to indicate that A-movement does not reconstruct in the syntax (at least in these languages).[3]

Then, one question arises here: If the reconstruction process does not happen in the syntax, how do we get the narrow scope reading of the scrambled accusative object in the German example (8)? In (8), the pronoun contained in the scrambled object cannot be bound by the dative object below, but still the scrambled object shows the scope ambiguity with the dative object. Here, I adopt the approaches in Cresti (1995) and Rullmann (1995) (so-called "Semantic Reconstruction"), as in (11). Schematically, this process is shown in (12).

---

[3] Fox (2000) argues that A-movement can reconstruct in the syntax if the reconstruction creates a new scope reading which is unavailable before reconstruction. Fox (2000:147) gives (i).

(i) a. [Someone from his$_i$ class]$_j$ seems to every professor$_i$ [t_j to be genius].
b. [His$_i$ father]$_j$ seems to every boy$_i$ [t_j to be a genius].

Fox claims that if the subjects do not syntactically reconstruct, there should be a Weak Crossover (WCO) violation in (i), but the sentences are fine, which indicates that the subjects can syntactically reconstruct to a position below the quantifiers and pronouns can be bound without a WCO violation.

I argue in Shibata (2012) that the data above are not decisive, and that (i) is not relevant to the availability of reconstruction. Consider (ii) (Williams 1983:293).

(ii) a. Someone seems to be sick. ($\exists$>seem; seem>$\exists$)
b. Someone seems sick. ($\exists$>seem;*seem>$\exists$)

Williams (1983) points out that if the subject moves from the small clause complement, as in (iib), the reconstructed reading is unavailable, unlike the infinitival complement case in (iia). If the acceptable status of (i) is indeed due to the availability of reconstruction, the change of the complement in (i) into a small clause should make the sentence worse, while if the grammatical status comes from something other than reconstruction, the change should not necessarily make the sentence worse. (iii) below shows that the latter seems correct. Thus, (i) does not necessarily demonstrate the existence of syntactic A-reconstruction.

(iii) a. Someone from his$_i$ class seems to every professor$_i$ very tired.
b. His$_i$ father seems to every boy$_i$ very tired.

(11) Semantic Reconstruction
A moved QP may leave a higher type trace of a generalized quantifier and reconstruct as a consequence of λ-conversion.

(12)

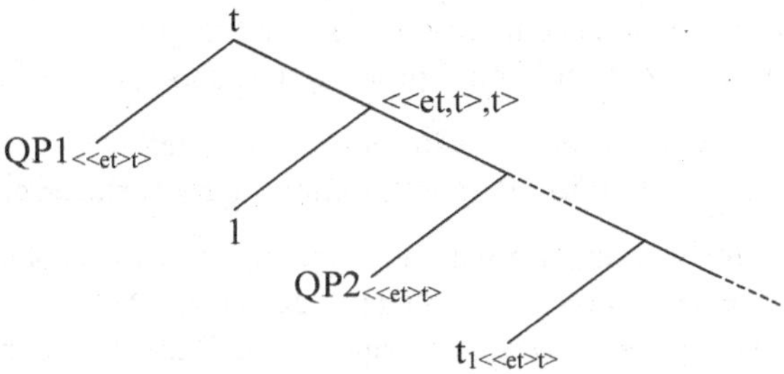

$\mathbf{[QP1]}_{<<et>,t>}$ [$\lambda f \in D_{<<et>,t>}$. [... [QP2 [... $\mathbf{t}_{<<et>,t>}$ ...]]]] (λ-conversion)
= [... [QP2 [...$\mathbf{[QP1]}_{<<et>,t>}$ ...]] = ...

In (12), QP1 leaves a trace of type <<et>,t>, and at the application of λ-conversion, this phrase is plugged into the trace position of t_1, which yields the narrow scope reading of the phrase since the trace position is within the scope of QP2. In this way, A-moved elements can reconstruct to the original position, but crucially this happens in semantics, not in syntax. This accounts for why in (8), the narrow scope reading of the A-scrambled object is still possible even though the pronoun within the A-scrambled object cannot be bound by the dative object.

My second assumption concerns alternatives. I adopt (13).

(13) Assumption II: Alternatives are calculated based on LF structures.

Since LF is the only interface between syntax and semantics under the Minimalist framework, it does not seem so unreasonable to assume (13).

When these two assumptions are combined, we can account for the anti-reconstruction effects observed in (2) and (4). Let us consider (2a) with a particle *-mo* as a sample case, repeated here as (14).

(14) Taroo-mo ko-nakat-ta.
Taro-also come-NEG-PAST
Lit. 'Also Taro didn't come.' (Subj>¬;*¬>Subj)

In (14), assume that the subject position is higher than the negation, namely [Spec, TP] (see Takezawa 1987). Since the subject is outside the scope of the negation at LF, the alternatives are the set of the propositions of the form '[X [didn't come]]' by Assumption II. This yields the presupposition that there is a person other than Taro 'who didn't come' (i.e., the negation is necessarily included in this presupposition), which is compatible only with the wide scope reading of the subject. In order to obtain the presupposition that there is a person other than Taro 'who came' (i.e., the negation not included in the presupposition), which is compatible with the narrow scope reading of the subject, the subject must reconstruct below negation in the syntax, but such a process is excluded by Assumption I. Thus, there is no way for the subject to be interpreted below the negation in (14).

On the basis of the above discussion, I propose the scope effect (15).

(15) Surface Scope Effect of Alternative-Introducing Elements
An element construed with its alternatives allows only surface scope.

This surface scope effect accounts for why the attachment of focus elements suddenly eliminates the reconstructed readings in Japanese (2) and English (4); more importantly, the two cases in Japanese and English can be accounted for uniformly. In the next section, I will discuss several consequences of this scope effect.

3. Consequences

3.1. Implication for Object Phrases in Japanese

The first consequence of the surface scope effects of alternative-introducing elements concerns Japanese object phrases. In Japanese, QP objects allow either wide or narrow scope with respect to sentential negation, as in (16).

(16) Taroo-wa [zen'in/go-nin-izyoo-no gakusei]-o sikar-anakat-ta.
Taro-TOP all/5-CL-or.more-GEN student-ACC scold-NEG-PAST
Lit. 'Taro didn't scold all/five or more students.' (Obj>¬; ¬>Obj)

Then, significantly, when objects are interpreted with their alternatives, the narrow scope reading under the negation becomes impossible:

(17) Taroo-wa pan-mo/dake/sae kaw-anat-ta.
Taro-TOP bread-also/only/even buy-NEG-PAST
Lit. 'Taro didn't buy also/only/even bread.' (Obj>¬;*¬>Obj)

(18) Taroo-wa pan-ka-kome-o kaw-anakat-ta.
Taro-TOP bread-or-rice-ACC buy-NEG-PAST
Lit. 'Taro didn't buy bread or rice.' (Obj>¬;*¬>Obj)

Based on the surface scope effect, these data indicate that object phrases in Japanese are in fact located in a position higher than the negation in the syntax. This contrasts with English examples, where focused or disjunctive object phrases can take scope below the negation:

(19) a. John didn't buy only bread. (ok: ¬>only)
b. John didn't buy bread or rice. (ok: ¬>or)

The English case is not surprising if the objects are located in a position below the negation, and in fact, there is plenty of evidence that this is indeed the case. (E.g., negative polarity items, which need to be within the scope of negation, can appear in object position but not in subject position in simple negative sentences in English). What is significant is that Japanese focused phrases and disjunction in object position behave in the same way as English subject phrases, not object phrases, in this respect. I therefore propose the following for Japanese.[4]

(20) Japanese objects must move to a projection above negation.

Due to this object movement process, Japanese object phrases are located outside the scope of negation in the syntax. Since the attachment of a focus particle traps them scopally in their position at LF, they disallow the narrow scope reading below the negation.

In the literature, however, the obligatory wide scope of focused phrases and disjunction in object position, as in (17) and (18), is treated in different ways. For instance, authors like Hasegawa (1994), Aoyagi (1999), Hoshi (2006), and Miyagawa (2010) argue that focused phrases undergo obligatory movement to some projection above NegP for licensing reasons. This is shown schematically in (21), where the focused phrase moves to FP to check its focus feature and ends up in a position outside of the scope of the negation.[5]

(21) [$_{TP}$ T [$_{FP}$ ▲ F [$_{NegP}$ Neg [$_{vP}$ ... focused.Obj. ...]]]]

A potential problem with this approach is that adding a focus marker normally does not affect scope relations among arguments. For instance, in (22), the focused accusative object does not scope over the dative object.[6]

---

[4] See also Ochi (2009) and Bošković (2011) on Japanese object shift. For a more detailed discussion of the motivation for the movement in question, which is tied to the nature of Japanese particles, see Shibata (2013).

[5] Miyagawa (2010) assumes that focus is in T, hence the focused phrase is assumed to move to [Spec, TP] for focus licensing.

[6] Note that Japanese is known to be a so-called "scope-rigid" language, so in the Dat>Acc order, as in (i), the allowed scope relation is said to be only Dat>Acc, not Acc>Dat.

(i) Taroo-wa [san-nin-no otoko-ni] [yo-nin-no onna-o] syookaisi-ta.
Taro-TOP 3-CL-GEN man-DAT 4-CL-GEN woman-ACC introduce-PAST
'Taro introduced four women to three men.' (Dat>Acc;*?Acc>Dat)

(22) Taroo-ga [san-nin-izyoo-no sensei-ni] [yo-nin-izyoo-no
Taro-NOM 3-CL-or.more-GEN teacher-DAT 4-CL-or.more-GEN
dansi gakusei-mo/sae] syookaisi-ta.
male student-also/even introduce-PAST
Lit. 'Taro introduced also/even four or more male students to three or more teachers.' (Dat>Acc;*?Acc>Dat)

Likewise, the focused dative object does not take scope over the subject:

(23) [San-nin-izyoo-no sensei-ga] [yo-nin-izyoo-no dansi
3-CL-or.more-GEN teacher-NOM 4-CL-or.more-GEN male
gakusei-ni-mo/sae] John-o syookaisi-ta
student-DAT-also/even John-ACC introduce-PAST
Lit. 'Three or more teachers introduced John to also/even four or more male students.' (Subj>Dat;*?Dat>Subj)

This indicates that the alleged focus movement would have to be very short. Furthermore, since a focus particle can also be attached to a subject NP, the focus movement approach in fact requires several distinct licensing heads for those focused phrases, and each movement has to be very local, not crossing a higher argument:

(24) [$_{FP1}$ F [Foc.Subj. [$_{FP2}$ F [Foc.Dat. [$_{FP3}$ F [Foc.Acc. ...

Thus, if one is to argue for this approach, the existence of the type of movements in (24) needs to be proven independently.

As another approach to the obligatory wide scope of focused phrases and disjunctions in object position, Hasegawa (1991) claims that the focus particle *-mo* 'also' is a positive polarity item (PPI).[7] Also, Goro (2007) maintains that Japanese disjunction is a PPI and therefore must move outside the scope of the negation.[8] It is well known that the English PPI *some* cannot take scope below the local negation even though the negation c-commands it in the surface structure (see Szabolcsi 2002, 2004):

(25) John didn't call someone. (*¬>*some*)

Since PPIs cannot appear within the scope of negation, as in (25), it is as-

7 Hasegawa (1994) revises the analysis in Hasegawa (1991) and argues that focus phrases move to [Spec, FocP], which is located between CP and NegP.

8 Goro (2007) also discusses conjunction of the form NP-*mo* NP-*mo* (NP-'also' NP-'also') in Japanese, and claims that this phrase is also a PPI. In fact, this conjunctive form scopally behaves in the same way as a disjunction of the form NP-*ka*-NP. I assume that since this expression involves the focus particle *-mo*, it can be treated on a par with expressions with the focus particle *-mo*.

sumed that they have to move outside the scope of the negation. Thus, Hasegawa (1991) and Goro (2007) analyze the focus particle *-mo* and disjunction as PPIs like *some*. If they are indeed PPIs, it is not surprising at all that they cannot take scope below the negation.

A potential problem for this approach is that focused phrases and disjunctions do not behave in exactly the same way as PPIs. Regarding this point, Goro (2007) himself notes that Japanese disjunction is different from PPIs like English *some* in that the former does not show a so-called "rescuing effect" by another downward entailing (DE) operator. Szabolcsi (2002, 2004) observes that when there is another DE operator above PPIs, those PPIs can take scope under the local negation. Goro (2007:265–266) gives the examples in (26).

(26) a. John didn't call someone. (*¬>some)
b. I don't think that John didn't call someone. (ok: ¬>¬>some)
c. I am surprised that John didn't call someone.
(ok: surprised>¬>some)

By contrast, Japanese focused and disjunctive phrases are still unable to take scope under the local negation even after adding another DE operator:

(27) Taroo-wa [Ziroo-ga ringo-mo tabe-nakat-ta to] omow-anakat-ta.
Taro-TOP Jiro-NOM apple-also eat-NEG-PAST C think-NEG-PAST
'Taro didn't think Jiro didn't eat an apple either.'
(¬>also>¬;*¬>¬>also)

(28) Taroo-wa [Ziroo-ga ringo-dake tabe-nakat-ta to]
Taro-TOP Jiro-NOM apple-only eat-NEG-PAST C
omow-anakat-ta.
think-NEG-PAST
'Taro didn't think that it is only an apple that Jiro didn't eat.'
(¬>only>¬;*¬>¬>only)

(29) John-wa [Taro-ga piza ka pasuta-o tabe-nakat-ta to]
John-TOP Taro-NOM pizza or pasta-ACC eat-NEG-PAST C
omowa-nakat-ta
think-NEG-PAST
Lit. 'John didn't think that Taro didn't eat pizza or pasta'
(*¬>¬>or / ok: ¬>or>¬)
(Goro 2007:267)

In examples (27)–(29), the existence of another DE operator in the matrix clause does not affect the impossibility of the embedded object taking scope below the local negation. Thus, if one is to claim that Japanese focused phrases and disjunctions are PPIs, an account must be provided for why they behave differently from other PPIs like *some*.

The current analysis can unify the two cases in (17) and (18), which have been treated separately in the literature. Object phrases in general undergo movement to a projection above NegP in Japanese, and focused phrases and disjunctions are trapped scopally in the moved position by the surface scope effect of alternative-introducing elements.

Furthermore, this analysis also captures the scope relation between QP objects and negation in Japanese. As shown in (16), normal QP objects can take either wide scope or narrow scope with respect to the sentential negation in Japanese. In fact, according to the experimental study by Han, Storoshenko, and Sakurai (2004), the wide scope reading over the negation is more prominent than the narrow scope reading. This is in contrast to English, where the universal QP object cannot take scope over sentential negation, as in (30).

(30) John didn't scold every student. (*Obj>¬; ¬>Obj)

The availability of the wide scope of Japanese objects would be rather mysterious if object phrases in Japanese were to occupy a position below negation, since Japanese is generally assumed to lack an English-type optional quantifier raising operation. By contrast, under the current analysis, this state of affairs is not surprising at all. Since under the current analysis object phrases in general undergo movement to a position above negation, the 'Obj>Neg' reading is indeed just a surface scope reading. Since it is a surface scope reading, it is not surprising that the 'Obj>Neg' reading is more prominent than the 'Neg>Obj' reading, since a surface scope reading is often stronger than the corresponding inverse scope reading. If one is to argue that Japanese objects stay within the scope of negation at LF, this difference between Japanese and English would be mysterious. On the other hand, under the current analysis, the issue above simply does not arise, since the object is located in a position higher than the negation after object movement. Thus, the current analysis also captures the scope relation between object QPs and negation in Japanese.

3.2. Narrow Scope of Disjunction under Negation

In Section 3.1, I adopted the approach of Chierchia, Fox, and Spector (forthcoming), i.e., that exhaustive implicatures of disjunctive phrases are obtained from a silent operator similar to *only*. The current analysis predicts that when disjunctive phrases are interpreted without a silent exhaustive operator, they should be allowed to take scope below the local negation. (Note that the silent exhaustive operator is a grammatical device proposed by Chierchia, Fox, and Spector to capture the implicature of those phrases.)

Thus, it should be possible for the disjunctive phrase to take narrow scope below the local negation in environments which typically cancel implicatures. This prediction is borne out. Goro (2007) observes that when a disjunctive phrase is in the antecedent of a conditional clause, the narrow scope of the object under the negation becomes available:

(31) John-ga eigo-ka-doitugo-o hanas-ana-i-nara,
John-NOM English-or-German-ACC speak-NEG-PRES-COND
watasi-tachi-wa koma-ru.
I-PL-TOP in.trouble-PRES
'If John doesn't speak English or German, we will be in trouble.'
(ok: ¬>or)

To account for this, Goro (2007) adopts the approach in Kato (1997), where negation in the antecedent of conditional clauses can optionally raise to a position above the subject. Under the current approach, such an additional assumption is not required. Since the *if*-clause cancels the implicature, which means that the disjunctive phrase is interpreted without a silent exhaustive operator, the object is free from the surface scope effect and is predicted to be able to take scope below the local negation, which is indeed the case in (31).

3.3. Lack of Subject-Object Asymmetry with Respect to NPI Licensing

The current analysis accounts for why Japanese seems to lack negative polarity items (NPIs) licensed in object position but not in subject position. Under the current approach, since both subjects and objects are assumed to occupy a position above negation in the syntax, it is predicted that subjects and objects should behave in the same way with respect to NPI licensing.

In English, a subject-object asymmetry in NPI-licensing is recognized:

(32) a. *Anybody didn't hit John.[9]
b. John didn't hit anybody

This suggests that in English, object phrases occupy a position below negation in the syntax. Then, let us look at Japanese.

In this respect, Aihara (2007) reports that expressions of the form 'universal+particle+universal', as in (34), which he calls 'Double Universal Quantifiers (DUQs)', behave in the same way as NPIs but cannot appear in

[9] It is well known that the NPI itself cannot reconstruct below negation, as in (32a), but when the NPI is embedded, the reconstruction of the whole phrase is possible (Linebarger 1980):

(i) Tickets to any of the afternoon concerts weren't available.

This antireconstruction effect of NPIs too is explained with the surface scope effect of alternative-introducing elements if we follow Krifka (1995), where NPIs are assumed to introduce alternatives, and the reconstruction of the subject is blocked by the surface scope effects.

object position in negative sentences. Those expressions pass all of the five criteria for NPIs from Watanabe (2004) in (33). The criteria were originally proposed by Valluduví (1994) and Giannakidou (2000).[10]

(33) NPIs:
  a. can appear in non-negative contexts;
  b. cannot appear in pre-verbal position;[11]
  c. cannot be modified by expressions like *almost*;
  d. cannot be used as an elliptical answer;
  e. can be licensed by superordinate negation.

(34) Double Universal Quantifiers (DUQs)
  a. *minna-ga-minna* 'everyone-NOM-everyone', *minna-o-minna* 'everyone-ACC-everyone', etc.
  b. *zenbu-ga-zenbu* 'all-NOM-all', *zenbu-o-zenbu*, 'all-ACC-all', etc.

First, these expressions cannot appear in positive sentences:[12]

(35) ??Taroo-ga gakkoo-de minna-o-minna mi-ta.
  Taro-NOM school-at everyone-ACC-everyone see-PAST
  'Taro saw everyone at the school.'

These phrases also exhibit the properties listed in (33) (Aihara 2007: 5–7):

(36) a. Minna-ga-minna (mosi) paatii-ni iku-nara, watasi-mo
  everyone-NOM-everyone if party-to go-COND I-also
  iku-daroo.
  go-will
  'If everyone goes to the party, I will go there too.'

  b. *Minna-ga-minna daigaku-e ik-ana-i.
  everyone-NOM-everyone university-to go-NEG-PRES
  'Everyone does not go to a university.'

---

[10] Expressions of the form 'indeterminate+-*mo*' like *dare-mo* ('who-also') have often been regarded as NPIs in the literature, but their NPI status is controversial. In fact, 'indeterminate+ -*mo*' expressions do not pass any of the criteria in (33). As for the status of those expressions, see Watanabe (2004) and Shimoyama (2011).

[11] This holds when a sentence is negative and no DE operator exists higher in the structure.

[12] Aihara (2007) notes that some speakers marginally accept (35) when the phrase is interpreted as emphatic. The same holds for (36d).

c. *[Taroo-ga gakkoo-de *hotondo* minna-o-minna
Taro-NOM school-at almost everyone-ACC-everyone
mi-ta wake] de-wa na-i.
see-PAST reason COP-TOP NEG-PRES
'It is not the case that Taro saw almost everyone at the school.'

d. Q: Dare-ga ki-ta no?
who-NOM come-PAST Q
'Who came?'
A: ??Minna-ga-minna.
everyone-NOM-everyone
'Everyone.'

e. [Taroo-ga gakkoo-de minna-o-minna mi-ta
Taro-NOM school-at everyone-ACC-everyone see-PAST
wake] de-wa na-i.
reason COP-TOP NEG-PRES
'It is not the case that Taro saw everyone at the school.'

These data show that DUQs behave as NPIs. Aihara (2007) notes that DUQs are not licensed in object position in simple negative sentences:

(37) *Taroo-ga gakkoo-de minna-o-minna mi-nakat-ta.
Taro-NOM school-at everyone-ACC-everyone see-NEG-PAST
'Taro didn't see everyone at the school.'

Based on this, Aihara (2007) argues for the structure of negative sentences proposed by Han et al. (2004), where NegP dominates only VP, not *v*P, and object NPs are located in [Spec, *v*P]. That is, negative structure in Japanese is fundamentally different from that in languages like English, where NegP is assumed to be above *v*P. Under the current analysis, there is no need to posit a structural difference between English and Japanese negation; the impossibility of DUQs in object position is not surprising since objects are outside of the scope of negation in the syntax, just like the subject in (36b). The symmetric behavior of subject and object DUQs is then predicted without any special assumptions for negative structure. Thus, the ungrammatical status of (37) can be captured as a natural consequence of the analysis.

4. Conclusion

In this article, I claimed that elements interpreted with their alternatives in principle allow only surface scope readings. Then, using this scope effect as a tool to investigate hierarchical relations among scope bearers, I discussed several consequences of this claim. First, I investigated scope properties of object phrases in Japanese, and argued that Japanese objects always move above the negation in the syntax. This argument was based on the observation that focused phrases and disjunction in object position cannot take scope below the local negation in Japanese. I argued that after object movement above negation, these phrases are unable to reconstruct due to the surface scope effect. This analysis directly accounts for why object QPs in general can take wide scope over sentential negation in Japanese. Since, under the current analysis, object phrases move above negation in Japanese, this availability of wide scope is obtained as a natural consequence of the analysis. Then, I discussed one prediction of the current analysis: when disjunction is free from the exhaustive implicature, it should be able to take narrow scope under local negation. I have shown that this prediction is borne out. Disjunctive phrases can take scope below the local negation when they are in the antecedent of a conditional clause, which is a typical environment in which implicatures are canceled. Finally, I discussed the lack of subject-object asymmetry in NPI-licensing in Japanese. I have shown that the current approach can capture the observation by Aihara (2007) that (true) NPIs cannot appear in object position in Japanese. Since objects are assumed to be outside of the scope of the negation under the current analysis, this is also obtained as a natural consequence of the analysis.

References

Aihara, M. 2007. Double Universal Quantifiers as Negative Polarity Items in Japanese. *Formal Approaches to Japanese Linguistics: Proceedings of FAJL 4*, (*MIT Working Papers in Linguistics* 55), ed. Y. Miyamoto and M. Ochi, 1–12. Cambridge: MIT.

Aoyagi, H. 1999. On Association of Quantifier-like Particles with Focus in Japanese. *Linguistics: In Search of the Human Mind – A Festschrift for Kazuko Inoue*, ed. M. Muraki and E. Iwamoto, 24–56. Tokyo: Kaitakusha.

Bobaljik, J. and Wurmbrand, S. 2012. Word Order and Scope: Transparent Interfaces and the 3/4 Signature. *Linguistic Inquiry* 43:371–421.

Bošković, Ž. 2011. Rescue by PF Deletion, Traces as (Non)interveners, and the *That*-Trace Effect. *Linguistic Inquiry* 42:1–44.

Chierchia, G., Fox, D., and Spector, B. Forthcoming. The Grammatical View of Scalar Implicatures and the Relationship between Semantics and Pragmatics.

Chomsky, N. 1995. *The Minimalist Program*. Cambridge: MIT Press.

Chomsky, N. 2001. Derivation by Phase. *Ken Hale: A Life in Language*, ed. M. Kenstowicz, 1–54. Cambridge: MIT Press.

Cresti, D. 1995. Extraction and Reconstruction. *Natural Language Semantics* 3:79–122.

Fox, D. 2000. *Economy and Semantic Interpretation.* Cambridge: MIT Press.

Giannakidou, A. 2000. Negative... Concord? *Natural Language and Linguistic Theory* 18:457–523.

Goro, T. 2007. Language Specific Constraints on Scope Interpretation in First Language Acquisition. Doctoral dissertation, University of Maryland.

Han, C.-H., Storoshenko, D.R., and Sakurai, Y. 2004. Scope of Negation and Clause Structure in Japanese. *Proceedings of the Annual Meeting of the Berkeley Linguistics Society* 30(1):118–129.

Hasegawa, N. 1991. Affirmative Polarity Items and Negation in Japanese. *Interdisciplinary Approaches to Language: Essays in Honor of S.-Y. Kuroda*, ed. C. Georgopoulos and R. Ishihara, 271–285. Dordrecht: Kluwer.

Hasegawa, N. 1994. Economy of Derivation and A′-Movement in Japanese. *Current Topics in English and Japanese*, ed. M. Nakamura, 1–26. Tokyo: Hituzi Shobo.

Hoshi, K. 2006. Deriving Association with Focus in Japanese within the Single Cycle System. *Language, Culture, and Communication* 37:47–80.

Kato, Y. 1997. Negation, Focus, and Interface Economy. *Sophia Linguistica* 41:29–36.

Krifka, M. 1995. The Semantics and Pragmatics of Polarity Items. *Linguistic Analysis* 25:1–49.

Lasnik, H. 1998. Some Reconstruction Riddles. *University of Pennsylvania Working Papers in Linguistics* 5:83–98.

Lasnik, H. 1999. Chains of Arguments. *Working Minimalism*, ed. S. Epstein and N. Hornstein, 189–215. Cambridge: MIT Press.

Lasnik, H. 2010. Quantifier Lowering? Course material for LING819 Spring 2010 at University of Maryland. Available at: http://ling.umd.edu/~lasnik/LING819%202010/QL%20HO.pdf.

Lechner, W. 1998. Two Kinds of Reconstruction. *Studia Linguistica* 52:276–310.

Linebarger, M. 1980. The Grammar of Negative Polarity. Doctoral dissertation, MIT.

Miyagawa, S. 2010. *Why Agree? Why Move? Unifying Agreement-Based and Discourse-Configurational Languages.* Cambridge: MIT Press.

Ochi, M. 2009. Overt Object Shift in Japanese. *Syntax* 12:324–362.

Rooth, M. 1985. Association with Focus. Doctoral dissertation, University of Massachusetts at Amherst.

Rooth, M. 1992. A Theory of Focus Interpretation. *Natural Language Semantics* 1: 75–116.

Rullmann, H. 1995. Maximality in the Semantics of Wh-Constructions. Doctoral dissertation, University of Massachusetts at Amherst.

Shibata, Y. 2012. A-movement and Reconstruction Effect. Unpublished manuscript.

Shibata, Y. 2013. Negative Structure and Object Movement in Japanese. Unpublished manuscript.

Shimoyama, J. 2011. Japanese Indeterminate Negative Polarity Items and Their Scope. *Journal of Semantics* 28:413–450.

Szabolcsi, A. 2002. Hungarian Disjunctions and Positive Polarity. *Approaches to Hungarian* 8, ed. I. Kenesei and P. Siptar. Budapest: Akademiai Kiado.

Szabolcsi, A. 2004. Positive Polarity–Negative Polarity. *Natural Language and Linguistic Theory* 22:409–452.

Takezawa, K. 1987. A Configurational Approach to Case-Marking in Japanese. Doctoral dissertation, University of Washington.

Vallduví, E. 1994. Polarity Items, N-words and Minimizers in Catalan and Spanish. *Probus* 6:263–294.

Watanabe, A. 2004. The Genesis of Negative Concord: Syntax and Morphology of Negative Doubling. *Linguistic Inquiry* 35:559–612.

Williams, E. 1983. Against Small Clauses. *Linguistic Inquiry* 14:287–308.

Yamashita, H. Forthcoming. Toward a Better Understanding of Japanese Scramblings: On the A- and A′-Properties. *Proceedings of WAFL3*.

Genitive Modifiers: *ga/no* Conversion Revisited

MASAYOSHI SHIBATANI*
Rice University

SUNG YEO CHUNG
Osaka University

BAYAERDULENG
Osaka University

1. Introduction

The phenomenon of *ga/no* conversion in Japanese, where the nominative particle *ga* marking a subject nominal alternates with the genitive particle *no* in certain contexts, has attracted continued attention among Japanese specialists for more than four decades since the publication of S.-I. Harada's (1971) seminal work on this topic. A use of the genitive case in similar contexts is seen across a large number of languages, although different languages impose different restrictions on the distribution of the nominative and the genitive case, ranging from the freer alternation pattern in Japanese

* An earlier version of this article was given as a plenary lecture at the 22nd Japanese/Korean Linguistics Conference on October 13, 2012, at the National Institute for Japanese Language and Linguistics in Tachikawa City, Tokyo. We are indebted to Tooru Hayashi, Duygu Karabağ, Sıdıka Kurtoglu, and Yu Kuribayashi for our understanding of the pertinent Turkish data contained in this paper, to Badema for the data on the Khorchin dialect of Mongolian, and to Alan Hyun-Oak Kim for the useful Korean data and discussions on them. This work was in part supported by a Japan Foundation Japanese Studies Fellowship (2012) to Masayoshi Shibatani and by a Japan Society for the Promotion of Science grant-in-aid (C) 24520426 to Sung Yeo Chung.
Japanese/Korean Linguistics 22.
Edited by Mikio Giriko, Naonori Nagaya, Akiko Takemura, and Timothy J. Vance.

to the obligatory use of the genitive in Turkish and including the intermediate patterns where either the use of the genitive is more restricted, as in Modern Colloquial Korean, or where the use of the nominative is more restricted, as in Mongolian:[1]

(1) Japanese
[hakusi=ga/no aisita] suusiki
doctor=NOM/GEN loved mathematical.formula
'the mathematical formula that the doctor loved'

(2) Turkish
[adam-*Ø/ın bil-diğ-i] dil
man-NOM/GEN know-NMLZ-3SG.POSS language
'(the) language that the man knows'

(3) Korean
[nay-ka/*?uy mantu-n] khephi-lul sensayngnim-kkeyse
I-NOM/GEN make-NMLZR coffee-ACC teacher-NOM.HON
yenkephe twucan-ul tusi-ess-ta.
successively two.cup-ACC drink.HON-PST-IND
Lit. 'The teacher drank two cups successively the coffee that I made.'

(4) Mongolian, Chakhar dialect
a. [*bi/mini mede-h] hʉn
I.NOM/I.GEN know-FUT.PTCP person
'(the) person whom I know'

b. [bi/minii nom ɵgsen] hʉn
I.NOM/I.GEN book give.PRF.PTCP person
'(the) person whom I gave a book'

In English the use of the nominative or the genitive nominal is conditioned by the finiteness of the verb such that a nominative subject occurs with a finite verb, whereas a genitive modifier is permitted with a gerundive nominalization, as in (5b).

(5) a. the trespasser [who John recklessly shot]
b. [John's recklessly shooting the trespasser] outraged the community.

As the appellation "*ga/no* conversion" implies, the phenomenon under

---

[1] Abbreviations: ACC=accusative, ADJVZR=adjectivizer, ADV=adverbializer, CNCL=conclusive, CON=conjunctive, EC=epenthetic consonant, FUT=future, GEN=genitive, HON= honorific, IND=indicative, LOC=locative, NMLZ=nominalization, NMLZR=nominalizer, NMLZM=nominalization marker, NOM=nominative, POSS=possessive, PRF=perfective, PST=past, PTCP=participle, QUOT=quotative, SFP=sentence final particle, SG=singular, TOP=topic, TR=transitivizer, 1=first person, 3=third person

consideration has traditionally been believed to be an instance of simple case alternation that does not affect the grammatical relation of the nominals in question. That is, the genitive nominals in (1)–(4) have generally been considered subjects, whether there is an alternation (as in Modern Japanese, Korean, and Mongolian) or not (as in Turkish, English, and Classical Japanese).[2]

In this paper, we argue that these assumptions are incorrect and offer a much simpler analysis that equates the genitive nominals attributed to *ga/no* alternation, or so-called "genitive subjects" in general, with the genitive modifier of a possessive construction that has the structure NP=GEN NP (e.g., *Taroo=no hon* or its English equivalent *Taro's book*).

A similar proposal has been made by Miyagawa (2011), who recognizes two separate mechanisms for nominative subject constructions and what he calls genitive subject constructions. His approach and ours are, however, fundamentally different in that (i) he and some others believe that it is the D-head of a DP (NP) that licenses the genitives in question, and (ii) Miyagawa and others consider genitive modifiers in possessive constructions to be also subjects.[3] Our analysis offers straightforward answers to the basic questions unanswered in the traditional view, namely why genitive modifiers are found in both relative clause (RC) context and certain non-RC context, or in DP context in Miyagawa's treatment, and why it is genitive rather than any other case that marks the relevant modifiers. Our nominalization-based analysis also obviates such theoretical constructs as D and DP, which are suspect in languages like Japanese that do not have English-style determiners.

We will demonstrate the parallelism between "genitive subjects" and the genitive modifiers of possessive constructions advancing our understanding of both syntax and semantics of genitive modifiers including some longstanding controversial problems such as the placement of adverbs in these constructions. Our analysis makes a strong claim that can be empirically tested. On the basis of expanded data, we attempt verification of the predictions our analysis makes by comparing the patterns of genitive modifiers in Japanese, Korean, Turkish, and Mongolian.

2. Genitives in Possessive Constructions

Our task is made a bit complicated by the recent proposals, like Miyagawa's mentioned above, for analyzing simple possessive constructions as having a

---

2 See, for example, Kinsui (2011) on the "genitive subjects" in Classical Japanese.

3 See Miyagawa (2011) for other works on Japanese in the Generative framework. See also *Lingua* volume 121, which contains papers dealing with "genitive subjects" in other languages.

subject in parallel with clause structure.[4] Such analyses have also been entertained by those working outside the strict Generative tradition such as Payne and Huddleston (2002:325), who offer the following analysis, in which the genitive nominal of a possessive construction is identified as a subject-determiner.

(6)
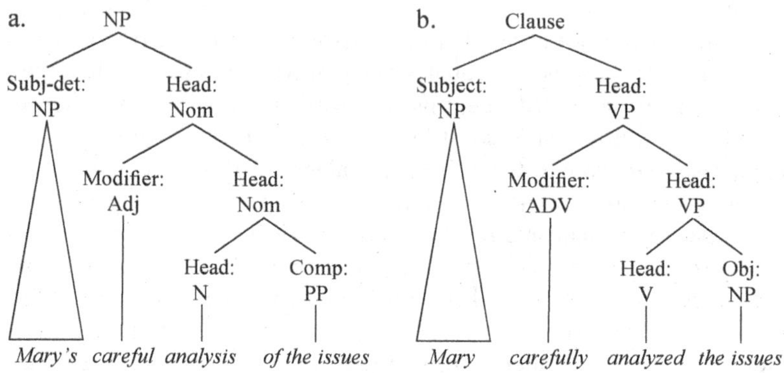

Payne and Huddleston (2002) attempt an empirically-based argument for their analysis, unlike Generative grammarians, whose arguments for the proposed possessor subject analysis tend to be purely theoretical. Accordingly, we will briefly deal with Payne and Huddleston's arguments for their subject-determiner analysis so as to dispose of these proposals.

Payne and Huddleston (2002) actually offer both theoretical and empirical arguments. Their first point is that "[w]e believe . . . that this treatment is justified by significant structural resemblances between these genitives and the subject in clause structure" (472). What they are suggesting obliquely here is a theoretical decision that the notion of subject is structural. Even if the possessive construction and the clause had parallel structures, as assumed in (6) above, there would be no reason to believe that the notion of subject obtains in the former, i.e., in structure (6a), if one did not follow the theoretical decision that grammatical relations are to be defined structurally, e.g., subject as the co-constituent of the head of a maximal projection. There are a variety of theories, e.g., Relational Grammar, Lexical Function-

---

4 In this paper we use the term "possessive construction" in reference to the structure NP_1=GEN NP_2, where NP_1=GEN is a genitive form of various morphological types and where NP_2 contains a lexical head noun. Notice that the term "possessive construction" does not specifically refer to the structure expressing a possessor/owner(NP_1)-possessee(NP_2) relationship. It is simply a label for a specific construction of the above form, which may express other kinds of semantic relationship in addition to its central use for the expression of a possessor-possessee relationship. One of the tasks of this paper is to explicate many other semantic relationships and their grouping as well as the syntactic patterning of genitive modifiers.

al Grammar, and typological frameworks of various sorts, which do not countenance such a structural approach to grammatical relations. Our point in this paper is that Payne and Huddleston's more empirical argument below can be explained without stipulating the structural notion of grammatical subject in possessive constructions.

Payne and Huddleston's (2002) more empirically-based reasoning for their analysis is stated as follows: "We will also see . . . that there are likewise important semantic resemblances between . . . [the genitive nominals of possessive constructions] and subjects of clauses" (472). They demonstrate this by offering sentential paraphrases with a subject for a variety of possessive constructions. For example:

(7) a. Mary's husband — Mary has a husband.
b. Mary's book — Mary writes a book.
c. Mary's obituary — Mary is the topic of an obituary.
d. this year's new fashions — This year is the time of new fashions.

These paraphrases, however, hardly argue for Payne and Huddleston's point, since there is no reason to believe that the paraphrases they offer are the only legitimate ways of paraphrasing the relevant possessive constructions. How about the paraphrases like, *The obituary is about Mary* for *Mary's obituary* and *The new fashions are for this year* for *this year's new fashions*, etc., where the genitive expressions do not correspond to the subjects of the paraphrases?

While English and many other languages permit a fairly narrow range of semantic interpretation of the genitive modifiers in possessive constructions, Japanese permits an incredibly wide range of possibilities, as seen in the small sampling below, which already goes well beyond the notion of the grammatical subject.[5]

(8) a. Taroo=no hon
Taro=GEN book
'Taro's book'

b. Taroo=no kakimono
Taro=GEN writing
'Taro's writing'

c. sin.tairiku=no hakken
new.continent=GEN discovery
'discovery of a new continent'

[5] Nishiyama (2003) is one of the most comprehensive treatments of Japanese possessive constructions. See Section 5 for the phenomena bearing on his classification of them.

d. kinoo=no sinbun
yesterday=GEN newspaper
'yesterday's newspaper'

e. onna=no sensei
woman=GEN teacher
'woman teacher'

f. niwa=no ueki
garden=GEN plant
'garden plants'

g. kinu=no syatu
silk=GEN shirt
'silk shirt'

h. nasu=no karee
eggplant=GEN curry
'curry with eggplants mixed in'

i. kuruma=no kyaku
car=GEN customer
'customer who comes in a car'

j. genkin=no kyaku
cash=GEN customer
'cash-paying customer'

What led Payne and Huddleston to their claim is the fact that some genitives of possessive constructions allow an agentive interpretation just like some sentential subjects, e.g., *Mary's analysis of the issues*, *John's shooting* (*of the trespasser*), *John's drawing* (*of a horse*), etc. But this fact hardly argues for the subject status of these genitive nominals, since the semantic fact can be accounted for by means of pragmatic rules needed in accounting for patterns like (8).[6] We maintain that there is no empirical evidence for the subject status of the genitive nominals of possessive constructions.

3. Why Genitives and Why in RC Context?

The proposals reviewed above are attempts to assimilate simpler possessive

---

[6] See Section 5.4. Payne and Huddleston (2002) also recognize that there are cases even in English where the genitives of possessive constructions do not correspond to clausal subjects. They consider *Persia's conquest by Alexander the Great* to be nonequivalent to *Persia was conquered by Alexander the Great* because there is no passive morphology involved in the former.

constructions to complex clausal structures. We consider these to be wrong-headed. Our attempt below is the opposite, namely, assimilating the more complex genitive versions of *ga/no* conversion, or so-called genitive subjects in general, to simpler possessive constructions, which intuitively makes more sense and which would account for the occurrence of "genitive subjects" in a straightforward manner. That is, the genitive versions seen in (1)–(4) have genitive nominals because they have recruited the genitive modifiers of possessive constructions for the same purpose of modifying the following head constituents. This assertion takes us to the task of explaining why forms like relative clauses permit modification by genitives, which is normally seen in an NP with a lexical nominal head. Our answer to this is that what is known as a relative clause is in fact a nominal element, namely, a nominalization.

3.1. Nominalizations and Their NP-Use and Modification-Use

As discussed extensively in Shibatani (2009) and more briefly in Shibatani (2013), what is known as a relative clause is a modification-use of a nominalization, which, in addition, may head a noun phrase in its NP-use.

(9) Japanese

a. [Hanako=ga nita]=no wa
Hanako=NOM cooked=NMLZM TOP
kono nasu da.
this eggplant COP
'What Hanako cooked is this eggplant.' (NP-use)

a′. $[[[\text{Hanako=ga } Ø^{i} \text{ nita}]^{i}_{NMLZ}]_{N'}]_{NP}$=no

b. [Hanako=ga nita] nasu
Hanako=NOM cooked eggplant
'(the) eggplant that Hanako cooked' (modification-use)

b′. $[[[[\text{Hanako=ga } Ø^{i} \text{ nita}]^{i}_{NMLZ}]_{N'}\ [\text{nasu}]_{N'}]_{N'}]_{NP}$

(10) Korean

a. [Yenghi-ga coli-n] ke-n
Yenghi=NOM cook-NMLZR NMLZM-TOP
i kaci-ta.
this eggplant-COP
'What Yenghi cooked is this eggplant.' (NP-use)

a′. $[[[\text{Yenghi-ka } Ø^{i} \text{ coli-n}]^{i}_{NMLZ}]_{N'}]_{NP}$ kes

b. [Yenghi-ka coli-n] kaci]
Yonghee-NOM cook-NMLZR eggplant
'the eggplant that Yenghi cooked' (modification-use)

b′. [[[[Yenghi-ka $Ø^i$ coli-n]$^i_{NMLZ}$]$_{N'}$ [kaci]$_{N'}$]$_{N'}$]$_{NP}$

There is a recent tradition in the field that considers the NP-use of nominalizations, illustrated in (9a) and (10a), as headless relative clauses or free relatives. We consider this to be a wrongheaded way of viewing nominalizations from the perspective of (headed) relative clauses. Our analysis considers nominalizations as constructions in their own right that have two main uses. One is an NP-use, in which a nominalization heads an NP, as in (9a) and (10a), and where the NP refers to a discourse entity based on the denotation of the nominalization heading it. The other is a modification-use, in which a nominalization (or the N′ it heads) is a co-constituent of a head nominal, as in (9b) and (10b), and where the nominalization restricts the denotation of the head nominal by specifying a subset of the denotation of the head nominal, as described below.[7]

The type of nominalization functioning as so-called relative clauses seen above represents argument nominalizations that denote thing-like entities evoked by nominalization structures that typically lack an argument which the denoted entities represent. For example, in the examples above the nominalizations [*Hanako=ga nita*]$_{NMLZ}$ and [*Yenghi-ka coli-n*]$_{NMLZ}$ have a gap in object position, as shown in the (b′) forms above, which points to the entities denoted by these nominalizations, namely things that Hanako/Yenghi cooked. The indexing notation in (9)–(10) represents this relationship between what is denoted by the nominalization and its role within the nominalization structure. The new nominalization-based analysis of so-called relative clauses proposed here does not recognize coindexing between the gap and the head nominal as in the conventional analysis of RCs. This is because in our analysis the modifying nominalization denotes and specifies a subset of the denotation of the modified head nominal. That is, the denotation of the RC structures in question, the outer N′ in (9b′) and (10b′), is something like 'a subset of the eggplants denoting entities characterized in terms of Hanako's/Yenghi's cooking'.[8]

---

[7] Consider the two parallel uses of the noun *dog* in the sentence *A dog is barking* (NP-use) and in the noun compound *dog food* (modification-use).

[8] Notice that we are distinguishing between denotation and reference. The former refers to a (set of) concept(s) associated with nominals, including nominalizations, whereas the latter is a property of noun phrases and refers to the relationship between an entity in the universe of discourse and the use of an NP in identifying the discourse entity.

The pattern seen above is that of object nominalizations. Subject nominalizations would have a gap in subject position, as in the following Japanese examples.[9]

(11) Japanese

a. [kono nasu=o nita]=no=wa
this eggplant=ACC cooked=NMLZM=TOP
Hanako da.
Hanako COP
'The one who cooked this eggplant is Hanako.' (NP-use)

a′. $[[[\text{Ø}^{i}$ kono nasu=o nita$]^{i}_{\text{NMLZ}}]_{\text{N}'}]_{\text{NP}}$ =no

b. [kono nasu=o nita] Hanako
this eggplant=ACC cooked Hanako
'Hanako who cooked the eggplant' (modification-use)

b′. $[[[\text{Ø}^{i}$ kono nasu=o nita$]^{i}_{\text{NMLZ}}]_{\text{N}'}$ $[\text{Hanako}]_{\text{N}'}]_{\text{NP}}$

So-called subject relativization is a combination of a subject nominalization and a head noun, and so-called object relativization is a combination of an object nominalization and a head noun. The process of relativization itself is juxtaposing of a gap-containing argument nominalization and a head nominal. Notice that the Japanese nominalization particle *no*, known as *juntai-joshi* in the jargon of Japanese grammar, and the Korean counterpart *kes* are not nominalizers. They simply mark an NP-use of what is already nominalized. In Korean the true nominalizer is the so-called adnominal ending *-n*. In Modern Japanese there is no formal difference between nominalized verb forms, known as *rentai-kei,* and finite, indicative verb forms, *shūshi-kei*, due to the merger of the two, which were morphologically distinct for many verbs in the earlier stages of the language. There are also varieties of Japanese that have not developed a marker like *no* and *kes* for the NP-use of nominalizations (see below).

The grammatical nominalizations differ from lexical nominalizations (e.g., *employer*, *employee*), which are lexical units belonging to the noun class, and which have relatively fixed denotations. Grammatical nominalization creates nominal structures for the nonce whose denotation is much more general than those of lexical nouns/nominalizations, for it denotes all kinds of entities evoked by the nominalization structure. For example, the nominalization [*Hanako=ga nita*] (*=no*) 'what Hanako cooked' may denote the eggplants cooked by Hanako, the eggs cooked by Hanako, the meat

[9] Wherever parallel patterns obtain straightforwardly, the Korean counterpart examples will be omitted due to save space.

cooked by Hanako, or anything else evoked by the structure. It is because of this generality in denoted entities that these argument nominalizations are typically used in a specific context that helps the hearer narrow down the range of the denotation.

Besides argument nominalizations used as RCs, there are event nominalizations that denote various entities including events, facts, propositions, times, locations, reasons, etc. These would not have an obligatory gap, as in the case of argument nominalizations, and are typically used as verb complements, as in the following example.

(12) Japanese

a. Teisyu=ga kaet-te kuru=no=o matte iru.
husband=NOM return-CON come=NMLZM=ACC wait be
'(I am) waiting for (my) husband to return (home).'

b. [[[teisyu-ga kaette kuru]$_{NMLZ}$]$_{N'}$]$_{NP}$=no

Our claim about the so-called *ga/no* conversion is that it is not an instance of simple alternation of case forms and that the alternant nominative and genitive structures differ fundamentally such that while the *ga* (nominative) version has a subject, the *no* (genitive) version does not: cf. (16a) and (16a′) and (17a) and (17a′). The latter arises from modification of truncated nominalizations of the following types, where more than a nominalized argument is missing.

(13) Miyasako-kun=wa kuroppoi hurosiki=ni bentoo=o irete
Miyasako-Fellow=TOP blackish wrap.cloth=in lunch=ACC put.in
nanameni seotte tuite kita. Ohiru=ni
diagonally carry follow came lunch.time=at
[[[**aketa**]$_{NMLZ}$]$_{N'}$]$_{NP}$=no=o miruto, . . .
opened=NMLZM=ACC when.see

(Kuniko Mukōda *Chichi no wabijō*)

'My friend Miyasako came following us putting his lunch in the blackish wrap-cloth and carrying it (tied) on his back diagonally. At lunch time, when (I) saw **what (he) opened**, . . .'

(14) Kurai=to ieba, Konno=wa asa ressya=ni
dark=QUOT if.to.say Konno=TOP morning train=on
norikonda=toki=kara ima=made zutto kurai kao=o
get.aboard=time=since now=up.to all.the.way dark face=ACC
site ita=yooni omou. [[[**waratta**]$_{\text{NMLZ}}$]$_{\text{N}'}$]$_{\text{NP}}$=no=wa, ressya=no
do was=like think smiled=NMLZM=TOP train=GEN
naka=de, . . . osikko=no hanasi=o sita=toki=dake=de aru.
inside=in peeing=GEN story=ACC did=time=only=COP be
(Yasushi Inoue *Michite kuru shio*)
'Talking about being dark, I think Konno has been looking dark since we got on board the train in the morning. (Lit.) **Smiling** was only at the time when, in the train, (he) mentioned the story of peeing.'

The nominalization *aketa* (*no*) in (13) is intended by the author as a case of object nominalization denoting the thing Miyasako opened, and the form *waratta* (*no*) in (14) is an event nominalization denoting an event of Konno's smiling. Our claim in this paper is that the genitive nominals that we find together with nominalizations are external to nominalization structures—hence they are not clausal subjects—and are added in order to supply an element with a restricting function. Our point is that the nominalizations in (13) and (14) can be modified by genitives, as in (16a′) and (17a′) below, in exactly the same way as simple nouns can be (optionally) modified by genitives, as in (15a′) below.

(15) a. [[[Tyokin]$_{\text{N}}$]$_{\text{N}'}$]$_{\text{NP}}$=wa sudeni soko=o tukitutu atta=ga,
savings=TOP already bottom=ACC hitting was=but
yatin=ga nakereba mada suukagetu=wa
rent=NOM if.non-existent still several.months=TOP
daizyoobu datta. (Kazufumi Shiraishi *Kaikyo*)
all.right was
'The savings were already hitting the bottom, but if there was no rent to pay, all was still well for several months.'

a′. [[Watasi-tati=no] [[tyokin]$_{\text{N}}$]$_{\text{N}'}$]$_{\text{NP}}$=wa . . .
I-et al.=GEN savings=TOP
'Our savings were . . .'

(16) a. [[[**Miyasako-kun=ga aketa**]$_{\text{NMLZ}}$]]$_{\text{NP}}$=no=o miruto . . .[10]
Miyasako-Fellow=NOM opened=NMLZM=ACC when.see
'When I saw what my friend Miyasako opened . . .' (NP-use)

---

[10] Henceforth the intermediate N′-level may be omitted from the structural representations. See Section 5 for the justification of the analysis for (16a′) and (16b′).

a′. [[Miyasako-kun=no] [[**aketa**]$_{NMLZ}$]$_{N'}$]$_{NP}$=no=o miruto
Miyasako-Fellow=GEN opened=NMLZM=ACC when.see
'When I saw what my friend Miyasako's having opened . . .'

b. [[**Miyasako-kun=ga aketa**]$_{NMLZ}$ [bentoo-bako]$_{N'}$]$_{NP}$
Miyasako-Fellow=NOM opened lunch-box
'the lunch box that my friend Miyasako opened'
(modification-use)

b′. [[[Miyasako-kun=no] [**aketa**]$_{NMLZ}$]]$_{N'}$ [bentoo-bako]$_{N'}$]$_{NP}$
Miyasako-Fellow=GEN opened lunch-box
'the lunch box that my friend Miyasako opened . . .'

(17) a. [[**Konno=ga waratta**]$_{NMLZ}$]$_{NP}$=no=wa . . .
Konno=NOM smiled=NMLZM=TOP
'(when) Konno smiled . . .' (NP-use)

a′. [[[Konno=no] [**waratta**]$_{NMLZ}$]$_{N'}$]$_{NP}$=no=wa . . .
Konno=GEN smiled=NMLZM=TOP
'Konno's smiling was . . .'

The only difference between the two cases of genitive modification is that while the genitive of a simple possessive construction has a noun heading an NP, a so-called "genitive subject" has a nominalization as the head of an NP. Genitive modification in the latter is made possible because of the nominal nature of nominalizations: they are noun-like by virtue of their having entity-denotations (denoting thing-like entities), as opposed to the relational denotations associated with verbs.

3.2. Nominalizers and Nominalization Markers

Notice that there is no direct role played by the relative head or the nominalization markers such as Japanese *no* and Korean *kes* in sanctioning genitive modification. Indeed, genitive modification occurs independently of such a marker in both Classical Japanese and certain modern Japanese dialects that have not developed a nominalization marker corresponding to the *no* of modern central dialects. And these are precisely the constructions that pose a serious problem for positing an element like D or any type of fictitious head element, as in a formal analysis like Miyagawa's (2011).[11]

[11] See Miyagawa's (2011) list of references for various published formal analyses of the relevant constructions.

(18) Late Middle Japanese[12]

maite [kari nado=no [turanetaru]]=ga,
indeed wild.goose and.the.like=GEN line.up.PRF.NMLZR=NOM
ito tiisaku miyuru=wa ito okasi.
very small.ADV visible.NMLZR=TOP very charming
(*Makura no sōshi* 11th C)

Lit. 'What has lined up of wild geese and the like is being visible faintly is indeed very charming.' / 'The line of wild geese and the like's being visible faintly is indeed very charming.'

(19) Izumo dialect[13]

a. Okaka=ga ayu yaita.
mother=NOM *ayu*.fish broiled
'Mother broiled *ayu* fish.'

b. Ayu=wa [okaka=no [yaita]]=ga itiban da.ne.
ayu.fish=TOP mother=GEN broiled=NOM best COP.SFP
'As for *ayu* fish, what mother broiled is the best.'

c. [okaka=no yaita] ayu
mother=GEN broiled *ayu*.fish
'(the) *ayu* fish mother broiled

(20) Hachijō dialect

a. Yamada-san=ga sinbun=o yondaaro-wa.
Yamada-Mr=NOM newspaper=ACC read.be-CNCL
'Mr. Yamada is reading a newspaper.'

b. [Yamada-san=no [yondaaro]]=wa Asahi sinbun dara.
Yamada-Mr=GEN read.be=TOP Asahi Newspaper COP
'What Mr. Yamada is reading is the Asahi Newspaper.'

c. [Yamada-san=no [yondaaro]] sinbun
Yamada-Mr=GEN read.be newspaper
'(the) newspaper that Mr. Yamada is reading'

Our claim in this paper that there is nothing like a genitive subject is

---

[12] Classical Japanese examples are rendered in modern pronunciation in this paper.

[13] *Ga*-versions are also permitted in these dialects, as in (19b,c) and (20b,c), whereas the nominative versions of Late Middle Japanese forms would have no marking on the subject. Notice that while the Izumo dialect, like Standard Japanese, maintains the pattern of merger of the nominalized verb form (*rentai-kei* 'adnominal form') and the conclusive form (*shūshi-k*ei 'conclusive form'), the Hachijō dialect has restored the distinction; *wa*, a likely development of a sentence final particle, in (20a) is now obligatory in ending a sentence. Data from these dialects come from the field notes of the first-named author of this paper.

part of the general claim that the genitive modification of nominalizations is based on the pattern of possessive constructions with a noun head. The general claim, therefore, predicts that the genitive modification of nominalizations is not possible where the semantically parallel possessive constructions do not obtain in the language. We now turn to this prediction.

4. Genitives beyond *ga/no* Conversion

There is a set of data involving genitive modifiers that is difficult to handle by the traditional idea that subjects, normally marked nominative, somehow turn into genitive form under certain circumstances. Compare the pattern in (22a) and (22b) below.

(21) Hanako=ga nasu=o nita.
Hanako=NOM eggplant=ACC cooked
'Hanako cooked an eggplant.'

(22) a. Nasu=wa [Hanako=ga/no nita]=no=ga itiban
eggplant=TOP Hanako=NOM cooked=NMLZM=NOM best
umai.
tasty
As for eggplants, what Hanako cooked is most tasty.'

b. Kono [nasu=no nita]=no=wa totemo umai.
this eggplant=GEN cooked=NMLZM=TOP very tasty
Lit. 'This what is cooked of eggplants is very tasty.'/ 'This cooked eggplant is very tasty.'

(22a) is a standard pattern traditionally dealt with under *ga/no* conversion and is an instance of object nominalization in our analysis. The genitive nominal in (22b) does not alternate with a nominative nominal. The genitive version [Hanako=no nita](=no) 'what Hanako cooked' in (22a) and the possessive construction in (22b) also differ in their modification patterns, as seen below.

(23) a. [Hanako=no nita] nasu
Hanako=GEN cooked eggplant
'(the) eggplants that Hanako cooked'

b. *[nasu=no nita] Hanako[14]
eggplant=GEN cooked Hanako
Intended: 'Hanako who cooked the eggplant'

[14] There are circumstances under which this type of nominalization may modify a noun (see below).

Semantically the genitive in (22b) may seem to correspond to the sentential object in (21). But the nominalization in (22b) cannot be a subject nominalization with a genitive object, since a subject nominalization maintains the accusative case, as in (24a) below. Moreover, a subject nominalization may modify a noun just like an object nominalization. Compare (23b) and (24b).

(24) a. [Nasu=o nita]=no=wa Hanako da.
eggplant=ACC cooked=NMLZM=TOP Hanako COP
Lit. 'Who cooked the eggplant is Hanako.' / 'The one who cooked the eggplant is Hanako.'

b. [nasu=o nita] Hanako
eggplant=ACC cooked Hanako
'Hanako who cooked the eggplant'

The mysterious genitive construction seen in (22b) is integral to the grammar of Japanese nominalization, and examples like (22b) abound in both Classical and Modern Japanese.

(25) Late Middle Japanese
a. syoozin-mono=no [ito asi-ki]=o utikui . . .
vegetarian-thing=GEN very bad-NMLZ=ACC eating
(*Makura no sōshi* 11th C)
Lit. 'eating vegetarian thing's very bad stuff . . .' / 'eating very bad vegetarian-style food . . .'

b. Siroki tori=no [hasi=to asi=to aka-ki], [sigi=no
white bird-GEN beat=and leg=and red-NMLZ sandpiper=GEN
[ookisa naru]] mizu=no ue=ni asobi-tutu io=o kuu.
bigness be water=GEN top=on play-while fish=ACC eat
(*Ise monogatari* 9th–10th C?)
Lit. 'White birds' ones red in the beak and the legs, ones of sandpiper's bigness eat fish while playing on top of the water.' / 'White birds, ones red in the beak and the legs and of the size of a sandpiper, are eating fish while playing in the water.'

c. Hito=no musume=no [kasizuku], ikade kono
person=GEN daughter=GEN raise.cherishingly how this
otoko=ni mono iwan=to omoikeri.
man=DAT thing say=QUOT wonder.PRF (*Ise monogatari*)
Lit. '(the daughter's one that a certain person) raised cherishingly wondered how (she) says a thing to this man.' / 'The daughter, the one a certain person raised cherishingly, wondered how (she) would say a word to this man.'

(26) Modern Japanese

a. onna=no [kusatta]=no mitaini . . .
woman=GEN rotted=NMLZM like
(an old Japanese sexist metaphor)
Lit. 'like a woman's rotten stuff . . .' / 'like a rotten woman . . .'

b. Oimo=no [hukasita]=no=wa, toozi yoku detekuru
sweet.potato=GEN steamed=NMLZM=TOP then often come.out
oyatu=de atta.
treat=COP was (Kuniko Mukōda *Chichi no wabijō*)
Lit. 'Sweet potato's steamed stuff was a treat that frequently came out at the time.'/ 'Steamed sweet potato was a treat that was frequently served at the time.'

c. Takenoko=no [taita]=n
bamboo.shoot=GEN cooked=NMLZM
(a menu in a Kyoto restaurant)
Lit. 'bamboo shoots' cooked ones' / 'cooked bamboo shoots'

That these genitive modifiers are sanctioned by nominalizations themselves is clear from the data from Classical Japanese (25) and from the Izumo and Hachijō dialects, where no nominalization marker corresponding to *no* of Standard Japanese occurs.

(27) a. Izumo dialect
Ora=mo sakana=no [yaita]=o kuitai.
I=also fish=GEN broiled=ACC eat.want
Lit. 'I too want to eat a fish's broiled one.' / 'I too want to eat a broiled fish.'

b. Hachijō dialect
Gakusei=no [wakake]=ga ukuni arodja.
student=GEN young.NMLZ=NOM there exist
Lit. 'A student's young one is there.' / 'A young student is there.'

While the genitives of the intransitive-based nominalizations above, i.e., (25a,b), (26a), and (27b), cannot be replaced by nominatives, some others appear to exhibit *ga/no* alternation. For example:

(28) a. [Kamino-ke=no nagai]=no=ga aruite iru.
head-hair=GEN long=NMLZM=NOM walk.CON be
Lit. 'Hair's long one is walking.' / 'One with long hair is walking.'

b. [Kamino-ke=ga nagai]=no=ga aruite iru.
head-hair=NOM long=NMLZM=NOM walk.CON be
'One whose hair is long is walking.'

(29) a. [Happa=no kareta] ki=o kiritaosita.
leaf=GEN withered tree=ACC chopped.down
Lit. '(I) chopped down the leaves' withered tree.' / 'I chopped down a tree whose leaves had withered.'

b. [Happa=ga kareta] ki=o kiritaosita.
leaf=NOM withered tree=ACC chopped.down
'(I) chopped down a tree whose leaves had withered.'

We do not want to analyze these as cases of *ga/no* alternation for two reasons. First, the (a) and (b) versions above are distinct constructions. The former allow the following, which we consider to be the basic expressions upon which (28a) and (29a) are based. The *ga* versions do not permit the corresponding expressions.

(30) a. [Kamino-ke=no nagai]=no=ga yuka=ni otite iru.
head-hair=GEN long=NMLZM=NOM floor=LOC fall.CON be
Lit. 'Hair's long one is fallen on the floor.' / 'Long hair is fallen on the floor.'

b. [Happa=no kareta]=no=o kaki-atumeta.
leaf-GEN withered=NMLZM=ACC rake-gathered
Lit. '(I) gathered leave's withered ones.' / '(I) gathered withered leaves.'

(31) a. *Kamino-ke=ga nagai=no=ga yuka=ni otite iru.
head-hair=NOM long=NMLZM=NOM floor=LOC fall.CON be
Intended for: 'Long hair is fallen on the floor.'

b. *Happa=ga kareta=no=o kaki-atumeta.[15]
leaf=NOM withered=NMLZM=ACC rake-gathered
Intended for: '(I) gathered withered leaves.'

The second reason that (28) and (29) are not instances of *ga/no* alternation is that we do not find the corresponding genitive versions even in those languages where genitives are obligatory (Turkish) and where genitives are strongly preferred (Mongolian). Compare the genitive versions below with the Japanese genitive forms in (28) and (29).

---

[15] Those who accept this sentence are interpreting it as a so-called internally-headed RC. We will not offer analysis of these two constructions here due to lack of space, but essentially we would analyze (25a) and (26a) as metonymically derived from (27a,b) and (25b) and (26b) as cases of genitive/possessor nominalization.

(32) Korean

a. | [meli-ka/*uy | ki-n] | yeca |
|---|---|---|
| hair-NOM/GEN | long-NMLZ | woman |

'(the) woman whose hair is long'

b. | [ip-i/*uy | malu-n] | namwu |
|---|---|---|
| leaf-NOM/GEN | wither-NMLZ | tree |

'(the) tree whose leaves have withered.'

(33) Mongolian

a. | [gejge-ni/*ni-ne | urt] | uhin |
|---|---|---|
| hair-3POSS.NOM/3POSS-GEN | long | girl |

'(the) girl whose hair is long'

b. | [nawc-ni/*ni-ne | un-san] | mod |
|---|---|---|
| leaves-3POSS.NOM/3POSS-GEN | fall-PRF.PTPC | tree |

'(the) tree whose leaves have withered'

(34) Turkish

a. | [saç-ı/*-ı-nın | uzun] | kız |
|---|---|---|
| hair-3SG.POSS.NOM/-3SG.POSS.GEN | long.PTPC | girl |

'(the) girl whose hair is long'

b. | [yaprağ-ı/*-ın | sol-an] | ağaç |
|---|---|---|
| leaves-3SG.POSS/3SG.POSS.GEN | wither-NMLZ | tree |

'(the) tree whose leaves have withered'

As mentioned earlier, Modern Korean disfavors a genitive modifier with a nominalization, and a form like (3) is felt to be odd in colloquial speech, while such a form is more readily tolerated in written form. However, the genitive versions in (32) are totally unacceptable either in colloquial or written form. Mongolian generally prefers genitive modifiers, though a nominalization with an object permits a nominative version, as in (4b). Forms like (33) should strongly favor genitive modifiers, but they are banned in this context just as they are in Korean. In Turkish, a genitive form is the only possibility in the relevant constructions, as seen in (2); yet the genitive forms in (34) are unacceptable.[16]

---

[16] Kornfilt (2007) blames the possessive suffix on the head noun for the genitive marking in constructions like these. Under this genitive-agreement analysis, we would not expect the forms in (34) to have a genitive modifier, since the head noun is not marked by a possessive suffix. Kornfilt's analysis, however, is problematic in view of the fact there are languages, e.g., Finnish and Yaqui, which allow or require genitive modifiers with a head noun/nominalization unmarked for possession (see Yaqui example (48b) below). The facts in Turkish and these languages render uniform analysis if genitive modifiers are considered sanctioned by noun/nominalization heads rather than by a possessive suffix on the head noun.

4.1. Appositive Possessive Constructions

The key to unraveling the patterns above is found in possessive constructions of the languages in question. As noted earlier, Japanese appears quite unique among the world's languages in permitting an extraordinarily wide range of semantic types in its genitive-marked possessive constructions, as in (8). Indeed, the languages in the vicinity, including Chinese, pale in comparison, although they themselves differ in the range of permitted constructions, with Korean more limited than Chinese, Turkish, and Mongolian. Where Japanese connects a modifier noun and a head noun by way of genitivizing the former, other languages would simply juxtapose the two, forming noun compounds, as in the English glosses in (35) below. Particularly noteworthy are the constructions of the following type, which cannot be easily rendered into genitive-mediated possessive constructions in other languages as far as we know.[17]

(35) Japanese

a. onna=no sensei
woman=GEN teacher
'woman teacher'

b. kami=no gomi
paper=GEN trash
'paper trash'

c. kin=no katamari
gold=GEN nugget
'gold nugget/a nugget of gold'

d. sakana=no hurai
fish=GEN fry
'fish fry'

---

[17] We call the forms below "appositive possessive constructions" or "appositive possessives" for short. These are a subtype of what Nishiyama (2003) identifies as the Type [B] NP_1 *no* NP_2 construction. He analyzes them as deriving from an underlying copular relative clause, deriving *onna no sennsei* 'woman teacher' from [*pro*$_i$*=ga onna de aru*] *sensei*$_i$ 'a teacher who is a woman'. As the English translations for a number of forms in (35) and the corresponding expressions in other languages examined below suggest, these constructions, especially those having generic references, are much closer in meaning to noun compounds. Indeed, many allow both appositive possessive and compound form in Japanese as well. E.g., *onna=no kyoosi: onna-kyoosi* 'woman teacher', *onna no bengosi: onna-bengosi* 'woman lawyer', *ramu=no baabekyuu: ramu-baabekyuu* 'lamb barbecue'. Whatever mechanism is needed in accounting for the meaning pattern of these compounds can be extended to appositive possessives, obviating an abstract, syntax-based derivational analysis like Nishiyama's.

e. nasu=no ni.mono
eggplant=GEN simmer.thing
'simmered eggplant'

The genitive of the kind seen above is sometimes referred to as *dōkaku no no* 'appositive *no*' in the Japanese literature, and it connects two nouns whose denotations are substantially alike. Thus, *onna no sensei* 'woman teacher' denotes a teacher whose denotation is narrowed down by the entities having relevance to the concept of woman. In (35e), *nasu=no ni.mono* essentially denotes food resulting from simmering eggplants, where the simmered food is still recognized as eggplants. The appositive possessive constructions differ from the possessive constructions involving materials and ingredients like *kin=no tokei* 'gold watch' and *tomato=no zyuusu* 'tomato juice'. If you met *onna=no sensei* 'woman teacher', you could say "I met a woman," and if you found *kin=no katamari* 'gold nugget', you could say "I found gold." But you would not say "I found gold" when you found *kin=no tokei* 'a gold watch'. Likewise, while eating *sakana=no hurai* 'fish fry' entails eating fish, drinking *tomato=no zyuusu* 'tomato juice' does not entail drinking or eating tomatoes.

Now, none of the languages we have surveyed can straightforwardly render the Japanese constructions in (35) as possessive constructions. For example, (35a) would be most likely rendered as noun compounds, i.e., as the (b′) forms below.

(36) Korean

a. ku yeca-uy cip
that woman=GEN house
'that woman's house'

b. *yeca-uy sensayng
woman-GEN teacher
'woman teacher'

b′. ye(ca) sensayng
woman teacher
'woman teacher'

(37) Turkish

a. bayan-ın eve-i
lady-GEN house-3POSS
'(the) lady's house'

b. *bayan-ın öğretmen-i[18]
lady-GEN teacher-3POSS
Intended for 'lady teacher'

b′. bayan öğretmen
lady teacher
'lady teacher'

(38) Mongolian

a. ter emegtei-nai ger
that woman-GEN house
'that woman's house'

b. *emegtei-nai bagš
woman-GEN teacher
Intended for 'woman teacher'

b′. emegtei bags
woman teacher
'woman teacher'

4.2. Appositive Possessives in Korean, Turkish, and Mongolian

We now have a straightforward answer for why the Japanese nominalizations in (22) and (24) can be modified by genitives and why their counterparts in Korean, Turkish, and Mongolian are not possible: genitive modification of nominalizations simply follows the pattern of simple possessive constructions permitted in the language. The relevant forms in (22)–(24) all have a grammatical nominalization of either a subject or object nominalization that is modified in the same way as the head nominal in an appositive possessive construction. That is, (25a) and (25c), for example, respectively contain an instance of subject nominalization *ito asiki* 'what is very bad' and of object nominalization *kasizuku* 'one whom (a certain person) raised cherishingly'. These are identified by the genitive modifiers in exactly the same manner as in the appositive constructions in (35). In other words, the modification of nominalizations is done following the pattern of available types of possessive constructions. Where there is no possessive construction model available, a language would not be able to modify nominalizations in the form of the missing model.

Of the three languages we studied closely, Korean is the most straightforward case in that the appositive possessive constructions are totally missing in the language. Accordingly, the appositive-type genitive modification of nominalizations is not permitted. But, significantly from our point of

[18] This example and (38b) are well-formed for the meaning '(the) lady's teacher'.

view, modification of nominalizations does follow the pattern of zero-marked noun compounds in the language.

(39) a. [kaci colim]
eggplant cooked.stuff
'cooked eggplant'

b. [kaci coli-n] ke(s)-l mekko siph-ta.
eggplant cook-NMLZ NMLZM=ACC eat want-IND
Lit. '(I) want to eat eggplant's cooked stuff' / '(I) want to eat cooked eggplants.'

(39a) has the lexical nominalization *colim* 'cooked stuff', similar in meaning and form to the Japanese etymologically compound noun *ni.mono* 'simmer.thing' in (35e). These are nouns just like the English noun *fry* meaning 'fried food'. (39a) shows the same zero-marked noun compound pattern as (36b′). (39b), on the other hand, contains a grammatical nominalization *coli-n*, an object nominalization with the meaning of 'what someone cooked'. And this grammatical nominalization is modified by the non-genitive form *kaci* 'eggplant' in exactly the same way as the zero-marked noun compounds in (36b′) and (39a).

Turkish speakers would generally reject genitive appositive constructions like the (a) and (b) forms below, noting that the zero-marked compound forms, (a′) and (b′), would be used instead.

(40) a. kuzu-nun kebap
lamb-GEN kebab
Lit. 'lamb's kebab'

a′. kuzu kebap
lamb kebab
'lamb kebab'

b. patates-in haşla-ma-sı
potato-GEN boil-NMLZ-3POSS
Lit. 'potato's boiled stuff' / 'boiled potato'

b′. patates haşla-ma-sı
potato boil-NMLZ-3POSS
'potato boiled stuff' (cf. potato fry)

The forms (b) and (b′) contain *haşla-ma* 'boiled stuff (food)', which is a transitive-based lexical nominalization. While the genitive versions in (40) are generally rejected by naïve speakers, perceptive ones would accept them as usable in a specific context. Appositive possessive constructions may be used when, for example, what is denoted by them is contrasted with a different type of denotation, as in the following expressions.

(41) a. Kuzu-nun kebab-ı, haşlama-sı-n-dan daha
lamb-GEN kebab-3POSS boil.thing-3POSS-EC-from more
lezzet-li-dir.
taste-ADJVZR-3SG
Lit. 'Lamb's kebab is tastier than it's boiled thing.'

b. Patates-in haşlama-sı, kızartma-sı-n-dan daha
potato-GEN boil.thing-3POSS fry.thing-3POSS-EC-from more
hafif-tir.
light-3SG
Lit. 'Potato's boiled thing is lighter than it's fried thing.'

This marked pattern of the appositive possessive in Turkish has now partially extended to the modification of grammatical nominalizations such that the appositive genitive modification is possible with subject nominalizations based on intransitive verbs, but not with transitive-based nominalizations.

(42) a. *patates-in haşla-dığ-ı
potato=GEN boil-NMLZ-3POSS
Lit. 'potato's what (they) boil' / 'boiled potato'

b. *kuzu-nun piş-ir-diğ-i
lamb=GEN cook-TR-NMLZ-3POSS
Lit. 'lamb's what (they) cook' / 'cooked lamb'

c. anne-m-in haşla-dığ-ı
mother-1POSS-GEN boil-NMLZ-3POSS
Lit. 'my mother's what (she) boils/my mother's boiled thing' /
'what my mother boils'

The transitive-based nominalizations (42a) and (42b) are similar in form to the Japanese appositive possessive (22b) and to those whose semantics we examine more closely in the next section, but neither of them is well-formed. (42c), on the other hand, is perfectly well-formed, but it is not an intended appositive possessive. The genitive *anne-m-in* 'my mother's' here holds an agentive relation with respect to the head nominalization *haşla-dığ-ı* 'what a third singular person cooked'. Specifically, (42c) cannot mean 'my cooked mother', a reading possible in Japanese (see next section). In order for a transitive verb like *haşla* to head an appositive possessive, it must be intransitivized first, as in (43a), which would align with intransitive-based nominalizations marked by the subject nominalizer/participle-ending -*(y)An* as in (43b,c), instances of appositive possessives.

(43) a. patates-in haşla-n-an-ı
potato-GEN boil-PASS-NMLZR-3POSS
Lit. 'potato's what is boiled' / 'boiled potato'

b. yaprağ-ın sol-an-ı
leaf-GEN wither-NMLZR-POSS
Lit. 'leaf's what has withered' / 'withered leaf'

c. balığ-ın bozul-an-ı
fish-GEN rot-NMLZR-3POSS
Lit. 'fish's what has rotted' / 'rotten fish'

Note again that these appositive possessives are marked constructions typically used in a contrastive context. In particular, they do not have a modification-use, as we saw earlier in (34b), in contrast to Japanese, in which appositive possessives, being fully established, have both a (referential) NP-use and a modification-use.

Mongolian does not have a wide use of the Japanese-style appositive possessive constructions either. What comes closest to them is the partitive-like genitive construction of the following type.

(44) [honi=n[19] maha=ne bolcing] du hamug yehe duratai.
sheep=GEN meat=GEN thigh.meat DAT most big like
Lit. '(I) like best sheep's meat's thigh meat' / '(I) like best thigh meat of sheep's meat.' / '(I) like best thigh meat among various sheep meat.'

In Japanese the relevant noun phrase in (44) above would mean something like 'thigh meat which is sheep meat'. In Mongolian it means something like 'thigh meat among various sheep meat'. And it is this partitive-like reading that obtains when argument nominalizations are modified by genitives.

(45) a. [maha=ne jɵɵlen]=gi ne ide-jei.
meat=GEN soft=ACC ? eat-PRF
Lit. '(I) ate the meat's soft stuff.' / '(I) I ate the soft stuff (meat, part) of the meat.' / 'I ate what was soft among various kinds of meat (available).'

[19] See Qinggeltai (2000) for a treatment of *-n* as a shortened form of the genitive suffix.

b. [jagas=nai yaljir-sen]=i ni ide-cigsen baina.
fish=GEN spoil-PRF.NMLZ=ACC ? eat-PRF be
Lit. 'I ended up eating fish's spoiled stuff (part)' / '(I) ended up eating the spoiled one of several fish (on the plate).'

c. [təbed hasi=in cina-gsan]=i ni ide-jei.
eggplant=GEN cook-PRF.NMLZ=ACC ? eat-PRF
'(I) ate the simmered one among various prepared eggplants.'

We believe that the above discussion confirms our prediction that the genitive modification of nominalizations follows the patterns of possessive constructions available in the language. We shall now turn to the final topic of the syntax and semantics of genitive modifiers, but focusing only on some of the more controversial as well as less explored phenomena that fall within this vast topic in order to demonstrate the viability of the approach advocated in this paper.

5. Syntax and Semantics of Genitive Modifiers

5.1. Internal and External Syntax of Nominalizations

Grammatical nominalizations offer particularly interesting challenges to us because they behave like verbs in certain respects and like nouns in other respects. By using the term *participle*, classical grammarians tried to bring out the dual characteristics of grammatical nominalizations. Nowadays we speak of internal and external syntax of nominalizations in elucidating the noun–verb duality at issue. Namely, nominalizations are internally verbal, while externally they are largely noun-like. This is clearly seen in the following patterns.

(46) Event nominals

a. [Taroo=ga **nessinni** **hon=o** kaku]$_{NMLZ}$=no=**o** mita.
Taro=NOM earnestly book=ACC write=NMLZM=ACC saw
'I saw Taro write a book earnestly.'

b. [Taroo=no **nessinna** **hon=no** [sippitu]$_{N}$]=ni odoroite iru.
Taro=GEN earnest book=GEN writing=at surprised.CON be
'I am surprised at Taro's earnest writing of a book.'

(47) Argument nominals

a. [**Hon=o** yonda]$_{NMLZ}$=no=**ga** kansoo=o nobeta.
book=ACC read=NMLZM=NOM opinion=ACC stated
'The one who read the book stated his opinions.'

b. **[Hon=no** [dokusya]$_N$]=ga kansoo=o nobeta.
book-GEN reader=NOM opinion=ACC stated
'The reader of the book stated his opinions.'

While the phrases head by nouns in (46b) and (47b) have entirely nominal syntax, taking no subject or direct object and permitting genitive and adjectival modifiers, the grammatical nominalizations in (46a) and (47a) display verbal syntax internally, containing a subject and/or a direct object and having an adverbial modifier. Externally, however, grammatical nominalizations are nominal to a large extent, functioning as a subject or a direct object and being case-marked for these functions. Facing us is the task of explicating these internal and external properties of nominalizations. However, the very question of what is internal and what is external to nominalizations is itself a point of contention. Starting with this question, this final section of the paper examines the parallelism in syntax and semantics between the genitives co-occurring with nominalizations and the genitive modifiers of possessive constructions. Due to the subtlety of the phenomena involved, the following discussion focuses exclusively on Japanese.

The traditional understanding of *ga/no* conversion would consider genitive modifiers of nominalizations to be subjects that are internal to nominalizations. And this seems to be the general understanding of genitive modifiers of grammatical nominalizations even in those languages where genitives do not alternate with nominatives. That is, the genitive nominals in the English event nominalization *John's shooting the trespasser* and in the Yaqui object nominalization *jinu-ka-'u* 'what I bought' below are generally analyzed as clausal subjects.

(48) a. [John's shooting the tresspasser] (outraged the community.)

b. Yaqui (Alvarez 2012)
U bisikleeta [in jinu-ka-'u] sikili.
DET bicycle 1SG.GEN buy-PRF-REL red
'The bicycle that I bought is red'

What we are arguing for in this paper is that these genitives are actually outside nominalizations and that they are not subjects. It is easy to show that nominative subjects within nominalizations and genitive modifiers outside nominalizations are syntactically different. Contrary to the generally received view that genitive nominals in Japanese cannot occur followed by an object, actual examples of such forms are sporadically observed in the writings of well-established modern authors, as in the following examples.

(49) a. Watasi=wa soremade **akasia=no** hana=o tukete
I=TOP until.then acacia=GEN flower=ACC put.on.CON
iru=tokoro=o mita=koto=ga nai.
be=NMLZM=ACC saw=NMLZM=NOM non-existent
(Tatsuo Hori *Utsukushii mura*)
Lit. 'To me that I saw acacias' putting on flowers is non-existent until then.' / 'I had not seen acacias having flowers until then.'

b. Sinsuke=wa atama=no naka=de **Tae=no** zibun=o
Shinsuke=TOP head=GEN inside=LOC Tae=GEN self=ACC
miru hyoozyoo=o omoi-egaita.
see expression=ACC visualized
(Hiroshi Itsuki *Seishun no mon*)
'Shinsuke, in his head, visualized the expression of Tae's looking at himself (Shinsuke).'

The nominative versions of the relevant portions of the examples above are also grammatical.

(50) a. [akasia=ga hana=o tukete iru]=tokoro
acacia=NOM flower=ACC put.on.CON be=NMLZM
'where acacias put on flowers'

b. [Tae=ga zibun=o miru] hyoozyoo
Tae=NOM self=ACC see expression
Lit. 'the expression with which Tae looks at himself (Shinsuke)'

Similar to main clause scrambling, objects in these clausal nominalizations may be placed before the subjects, as below.[20]

(51) a. [hana=o akasia=ga tukete iru]=tokoro
flower=ACC acacias=NOM put.on.CON be=where
'where acacias put on flowers'

b. [zibun=o Tae=ga miru] hyoozyoo
self=ACC Tae=NOM see expression
Lit. 'the expression which Tae looks at himself (Shinsuke)'

These may strike one as a bit odd, as is the case with object placement before subjects in main clauses. The forms in (51) improve markedly if modifiers are added to the initial objects, as in *utukusii hana=o* 'beautiful flow-

[20] By "clausal nominalizations," we mean nominalizations containing a clause-size structure, not nominalizations that are clauses. In our view, nominalizations and clauses are two distinct types of structure with different functions; hence there are no nominalizations that are (also) clauses.

ers' and *kurai zibun=o* 'gloomy oneself'. But placing objects before the genitives of the original versions in (49) results in totally ungrammatical forms, even if heavy NPs are used.

(52) a. *(utukusii) hana=o akasia=no tukete iru=tokoro
(beautiful) flower=ACC acacia=GEN put.on be where
'where acacias are having (beautiful) flowers'

b. *(kurai) zibun=o Tae=no miru hyoozyoo
(dark) self=ACC Tae=GEN see expression
'expressions with which Tae looks at his (dark) self'

Those who consider the original forms in (49) slightly odd would find the above forms totally unacceptable. Under our analysis, which treats a genitive nominal as a modifier external to a nominalization, the above data receive a straightforward interpretation. Namely, an element occurring external to a possessive NP (i.e., an NP with a genitive modifier) is not relatable to the head nominal of a possessive construction. That is, while structure (53a) is possible, where scrambling is seen within a nominalization, (53b) for (52a) is not.

(53) a. [(utukusii) hana=o akasia=ga tukete iru]$_{\text{NMLZ}}$=tokoro
b. *[**(utukusii) hana=o**] [[akasia=no] [tukete iru]$_{\text{NMLZ}}$]$_{\text{NP}}$=tokoro

5.2. Adverbial Modification of Nominalizations

The restriction seen above generally holds such that it is difficult for adverbs external to a possessive NP to modify the nominalized verbs.

(54) a. Nasu=wa [Hanako=no [**teineini** nita]$_{\text{NMLZ}}$]$_{\text{NP}}$=no=ga
eggplant=TOP Hanako=GEN carefully cooked=NMLZM=NOM
itiban umai.
most tasty
'As for eggplants, what Hanako carefully cooked is most tasty.'

b. . . . ??**teineini** [Hanako=no [nita]$_{\text{NMLZ}}$]$_{\text{NP}}$=no] . . .
'what Hanako cooked carefully'

(55) a. . . . [Hanako=no [**yawarakaku** nita]$_{\text{NMLZ}}$]$_{\text{NP}}$=no . . .
Hanako=GEN softly cooked=NMLZM
'what Hanako cooked soft'

b. . . . *?**yawarakaku** [Hanako=no [nita]$_{\text{NMLZ}}$]$_{\text{NP}}$=no . . .

There are two types of adverbs that appear to go against the restriction posited above. Compare (54)–(55) with the following, involving a time and a place adverb.

(56) a. Nasu=wa [Hanako=no **[kinoo** nita]$_{NMLZ}$]$_{NP}$=no=ga
eggplant=TOP Hanano=GEN yesterday cooked=NMLZM=NOM
itiban umakatta.
most was.tasty
'As for eggplants, what Hanako cooked yesterday was most tasty.'

b. . . . **kinoo** [Hanako=no [nita]$_{NMLZ}$]$_{NP}$=no . . .

(57) a. [Hanako=no **[Amerika=de** naratte kita]$_{NMLZ}$]$_{NP}$=no=wa hurui
Hanako=GEN America=in study came=NMLZM=TOP old
gengogaku da.
linguistics COP
Lit. 'What Hanako learned in America and came back is old linguistics.'

b. **Amerika=de** [Hanako=no [naratte kita]$_{NMLZ}$]$_{NP}$=no . . .

These are constructions often used in arguing for the subject status of genitive modifiers. That is, if *Hanako=no* were not a subject, why would these structures allow time and place adverbs to scramble out of the nominalizations? Indeed, we demonstrated above that it is generally difficult for adverbs to occur externally to possessive NPs. If, on the other hand, we considered the relevant genitives to be subjects, the pattern in (56) and (57) would be cases of scrambling within clauses, as in (51a,b).

We now offer an alternative account for time and place adverbs that finds support in a larger picture of the modification phenomenon examined below. As indicated by the fact that time and place adverbs typically occur in the periphery of sentences in many languages, these adverbs are not specifically associated with a verb; they modify an entire event. They are, thus, different from the manner and resultative adverbs seen in (54) and (55), which are semantically associated with the actions denoted by the verbs within sentences and nominalizations. In other words, forms like (56b) and (57b) are well-formed because the adverbs in them are not specifically associated with the head of a possessive NP.

5.3. Genitive Modification of Nominalizations

The contrast between manner/resultative adverbs and time/place adverbs is paralleled by two types of genitive modifiers. There are genitive modifiers that are much more intimately related to a head nominal, as manner/resultative adverbs are to a (nominalized) verb. In addition, there are genitive modifiers that contribute less to the characterization of a head nominal, as time/place adverbs have a less direct relation with a (nominalized) verb.

Let us examine these genitive modifiers with a lexical noun head first. Observe the following examples.[21]

(58) a. Hanako=no kakekko
Hanako=GEN running
'Hanako's running'

b. Hanako=no ronbun
Hanako-GEN scholarly.paper
'Hanako's scholarly paper'

c. Hanako=no tuke.mono
Hanako=GEN pickle.thing
'Hanako's pickles'

The genitive in (58a) is interpreted as representing an entity involved in the event of running as an agent. Since running is not a concrete object, the genitive modifier in (58a) does not permit an owner or author interpretation of the sort permitted with other types of noun heads denoting concrete objects. The head noun in (58b) denotes a product of a scholarly endeavor, and its genitive modifier permits only an author interpretation such that Hanako is the author of the scholarly paper in question. Notice that, while a scholarly paper is a concrete object, its modifier does not easily permit a simple owner interpretation. (58b) cannot mean a scholarly paper written by someone else that is owned by Hanako.[22] It cannot mean, for example, Chomsky's paper owned by Hanako. The head noun in (58c), on the other hand, permits both author and owner interpretations such that the whole expression can mean either the pickles made by Hanako or the pickles made by someone else but owned by Hanako.[23] What this distinction suggests is that head nouns show different degrees of nouniness and that the semantics of their genitive modifiers is partly determined by this factor.

The genitives seen above differ from the ones in (59) below.

---

[21] The phenomena discussed below cut across Nishiyama's (2003) classification of Japanese possessive constructions. In his classification, forms like (58a) belong to Type [E], those like (58b,c) and (59a,b) to Type [A], and those like (59c) to Type [B].

[22] This example shows that Nishiyama's Type [A] possessive constructions have an internal structure based on the nature of head nouns and are not pragmatically uniform as his classification has it. Other nouns behaving like *ronbun* include *kakimono* '(a) writing(s)', *sakuhin* 'artistic works', *tyosyo* 'authored books'. Notice that the English nouns *book* and (*scholarly*) *paper* show a similar contrast. *John's paper* normally cannot mean a scholarly paper written by someone else but that is owned by John, whereas *John's book* allows both author- and owner-interpretation with equal ease.

[23] Another interpretation of the genitive here will be discussed below in connection with (59c).

(59) a. hissi=no kakekko
desparate=GEN running
'running of a desperate nature'

b. gengogaku=no ronbun
linguistics=GEN scholarly.paper
'scholarly paper of linguistics'

c. nasu=no tuke.mono
eggplant=GEN pickle.thing
'eggplant pickles'

Compared to those in (58), the genitives in (59), including the appositive type (59c), are descriptive, characterizing the head nouns with a special feature and contributing to the denotations of unique kinds or types of objects with which the entire possessive constructions are associated. Let us call the genitives in (58) "role genitives" and those in (59) "descriptive genitives." Role genitives specify agent (*Mori-sensei=no koogi* 'Prof. Mori's lecture), author (*Hanako=no ronbun* 'Hanako's scholarly paper'), owner (*Hanako=no ie* 'Hanako's house'), patient (*sin.tairiku=no hakken* 'discovery of a new continent), time (*kinoo=no koogi* 'yesterday's lecture'), place (*nikai=no okyakusan* 'customers on the second floor', and many other kinds of relations (e.g., *Hanako=no otoosan* 'Hanako's father', *Hanako=no byooin* 'the hospital that Hanako visits for medical treatment'). Descriptive genitives, on the other hand, are nominal modifiers specifying properties (*nise=no pasupooto* 'false passport') and types (*gengogaku=no koogi* 'linguistics lectures', *gyuudon=no okyakusan* 'customers ordering a beef bowl'), including specification of materials (*kin=no tokei* 'gold watch', *kinu=no syatu* 'silk shirt'). Descriptive genitives can be distinguished from role genitives by their ability to occur in answering a question like *Donna X?* 'What kind of X?'. Thus, *gengogaku=no koogi* 'linguistics lecture' would answer *Donna koogi?* 'What kind of lecture?' felicitously, but *Mori-sensei=no koogi* 'Prof. Mori's lecture' would not. Similarly, *Donna kaban=o osagasi desuka?* 'What kind of bag are you looking for' can be answered felicitously by *Kawa=no kaban desu* 'It's a leather bag' or *Midori-iro=no kaban desu* 'It's a green-colored bag' but not by *Mori-sensei no kaban desu* 'It's Prof. Mori's bag'. In order to elicit this type of answer, one would have to ask *Dare=no kaban/koogi* 'Whose bag/lecture?'.[24]

[24] Notice that many genitives, especially with people's names, may function either as a role genitive (as an owner or author) or a descriptive genitive. For example, the genitive in *Mori Hanae=no kaban* 'Mori Hanae's bag' would be descriptive, as in *a Mori Hanae bag*, if it were intended as a brand name. *Otona=no omotya* 'adult toys' denote a type of toys opposing to *kodomo=no omotya* 'children's toys'. Both these genitives are descriptive.

Now, the semantic difference between role and descriptive genitives is reflected in syntax such that while the former can occur externally to a possessive construction, the latter cannot. Observe:

(60) a. kodomotati=no [hissi=no kakekko]
children.GEN desparate=GEN running
'children's running of a desperate nature'

b. *hissi=no [kodomotati=no kakekko]

(61) a. Hanako=no [gengogaku=no ronbun]
Hanako=GEN linguistics=GEN scholarly.paper
'Hanako's linguistic research paper'

b. *gengogaku=no [Hanako=no ronbun][25]

(62) a. Hanako=no [nasu=no tuke.mono]
Hanako=GEN eggplant=GEN pickle.thing
'Hanako's eggplant pickles'

b. *nasu=no [Hanako=no tuke.mono]

The pattern above is highly analogous to the distinction we drew earlier between manner/resultative and time/place adverbs. Those modifiers that are semantically closer to the head nominal cannot be placed away from the head nominal. Interestingly, time and place nouns parallel time and place adverbs such that they, along with other role genitives, freely occur away from the head nominal.

(63) a. kinoo=no [gyuudon=no okyakusan]
yesterday=GEN beef.bowl=GEN customer
'yesterday's customer of a beef bowl' / 'yesterday's customer ordering a beef bowl'

b. *gyuudon=no [kinoo=no okyakusan]

(64) a. nikai=no [gyuudon=no okyakusan]
second.floor=GEN beef.bowl=GEN customer
'second-floor customer of a beef bowl' / 'second-floor customer ordering a beef bowl'

b. *gyuudon=no [nikai=no okyakusan]

Because of this ordering restriction, change in the order of the two kinds

[25] The grammatical readings of these as [[hissi=no kodomotati]=no kakekko] 'running by desperate children' and [[gengogaku=no Hanako]=no ronbun] 'scholarly paper by the linguistic specialist Hanako' are possible.

of genitive modifiers alters the range of possible readings. (65a) below, for example, is ambiguous in at least three ways. But in (65b), where a role genitive intervenes, the descriptive genitive reading of pickled Hanako disappears.

(65) a. kinoo=no Hanako=no tuke.mono
yesterday=GEN Hanako=GEN pickle.thing
(i) 'pickled Hanako with some relevance to yesterday'
(ii) 'pickles that Hanako made which have some relevance to yesterday'
(iii) 'pickles that Hanako owned which have some relevance to yesterday.'

b. Hanako=no kinoo=no tuke.mono
(i) 'pickles that Hanako made which have some relevance to yesterday'
(ii) 'pickles that Hanako owned which have some relevance to yesterday'

The forms in (65) also show that two role genitives (e.g., time- and owner-genitives as above) may be placed in any order without affecting the grammaticality or meaning. It is only the descriptive genitive interpretation of *Hanako=no* that is affected by shifting the two genitives around. Two descriptive genitives behave similarly; their order does not affect grammaticality or meaning either (but see footnote 28 below).

(66) a. oomori=no sio-azi=no raamen
big.serving=GEN salt-taste=GEN *rāmen*.noodles
'salt-tasting *rāmen* noodles of big serving'

b. sio-azi=no oomori=no raamen
'*rāmen* noodles of big serving of salty taste'

The effect of the difference between a role and a descriptive genitive is clearly seen below.

(67) a. kinoo=no [Hanako=no karaage]
yesterday=GEN Hanako=GEN deep.fried.food
(i) 'deep fried Hanako with some relevance to yesterday'
(ii) 'deep fried food that Hanako made which has some relevance to yesterday'
(iii) 'deep fried food owned by Hanako with some relevance to yesterday'

b. sio-azi=no [Hanako=no karaage]
salt-taste=GEN Hanako=GEN deep.fried.food
'deep fried Hanako of salty taste'

Unlike (67a), (67b) allows only an interpretation of the descriptive appositive possessive, in which the genitive modifier *Hanako=no* specifies a kind of fried food.

The possessive constructions examined above with regard to the two types of genitives all contain lexical nouns as their heads. Our claim that genitive noun phrases cooccurring with nominalizations are not grammatical subjects but are modifiers exactly like the genitive modifiers of possessive constructions predicts that we find similar modification patterns with nominalization heads. Indeed, this is the case. Compare the examples in (68) and (69) below, where the former contain a lexical head and the latter a nominalization head.

(68) a. kinoo=no [Hanako=no [ni.mono]$_{N}$]$_{NP}$ (=wa umakatta.)
yesterday=GEN Hanako=GEN simmer.thing (=TOP was.tasty)
Lit. 'yesterday's simmer.thing of Hanako (was tasty.)'

a′. (Nasu=wa) Hanako=no [kinoo=no
(eggplant=TOP) Hanako=GEN yesterday=GEN
ni.mono]$_{N}$]$_{NP}$ (=ga umakatta.)
simmer.thing (=NOM was.tasty)
Lit. '(As for eggplants,) yesterday's simmer.thing of Hanako's (was tasty.)'

b. kinoo=no [nasu=no [ni.mono]$_{N}$]$_{NP}$ (=wa umakatta.)
yesterday=GEN eggplant=GEN simmer.thing (=TOP was.tasty)
Lit. 'simmer.thing of eggplants of yesterday (was tasty.)'

b′. *nasu=no [kinoo=no [ni.mono]$_{N}$]$_{NP}$ (=wa umakatta.)
eggplant=GEN yesterday=GEN simmer.thing (=TOP was.tasty

(69) a. kinoo=no [Hanako=no [zikkuri
yesterday=GEN Hanako=GEN carefully
nita]$_{NMLZ}$]$_{NP}$=no (=wa umakatta.)
cooked=NMLZM (=TOP was.tasty
Lit. 'yesterday's what (they) cooked carefully of Hanako (was tasty.)'

a′. (Nasu=wa) Hanako=no [kinoo=no
eggplant=TOP Hanako=GEN yesterday=GEN
[zikkuri nita]$_{NMLZ}$]$_{NP}$=no (=ga umakatta.)
carefully cooked=NMLZM (=NOM was.tasty)
Lit. '(As for eggplants) yesterday's what (they) cooked carefully of Hanako (was tasty.)'

b. kinoo=no [nasu=no [zikkuri
yesterday=GEN eggplant=GEN carefully
nita]$_{NMLZ}$]$_{NP}$=no (=wa umakatta.)
cooked=NMLZM (=TOP was.tasty)
Lit. 'what (they) cooked carefully of eggplants of yesterday (was tasty.)'

b′. *nasu=no [kinoo=no [zikkuri
eggplant=GEN yesterday=GEN carefully
nita]$_{NMLZ}$]$_{NP}$=no (=wa umakatta.)
cooked=NMLZM (=TOP was.tasty)

As seen above, whether the head of a possessive construction is a noun or a nominalization, the modification pattern is highly similar.[26] Thus, in both (68a) and (69a) the genitive modifiers allow both a role genitive reading ('simmer.thing/simmered food that Hanako cooked') and a descriptive genitive reading ('Hanako as a simmer.thing/simmered food'). But when *Hanako=no* is moved away from the possessive construction, as in (68a′) and (69a′), the descriptive genitive reading disappears in both constructions, and their best use is as in the context given in the parentheses. This is in line with the fact seen in (68b′) and (69b′), namely, that a descriptive genitive (e.g., *nasu=no* 'eggplant's') cannot be placed beyond a role genitive (e.g., *kinoo=no* 'yesterday's') in either construction. Finally, just as two role genitives may occur in any order, as shown in (68a,a′), two descriptive genitives may occur in any order without affecting the meaning in both noun-headed and nominalization-headed possessive constructions, indicating that the two are the same type of construction. Observe:

[26]There are, however, some important differences between the two cases. Genitive modification is in general much easier with a noun head. Genitive modification of a nominalization gets easier when the degree of nouniness is made higher. For example, *nasu=no nita=no* with a specific denotation is much easier to modify with an owner genitive than simple forms like *nita=no*. On the other hand, a nominalization allows a modification by an external adverb, as in (56b) and (57b), which is not permitted by a noun head. Cf. *kinoo* [*Hanako=no nita*] (*=no*) / *kinoo=no* [*Hanako=no nita*] (*=no*) vs. **kinoo* [*Hanako=no nimono*] / *kinoo=no* [*Hanako=no nimono*]. The former examples show the dual noun–verb character of a nominalization. Masaru Kanetani pointed out to me that while **John's repeatedly shooting of the victim* is ungrammatical, *John's shooting of the victim repeatedly*, with an external adverb, is not nearly as bad.

(70) a. syooyu-azi=no [nasu=no [ni.mono]$_N$]$_{NP}$ (=ga
soy.sauce-taste=GEN eggplant=GEN simmer.thing (=NOM
kuitai.)
want.to.eat)
Lit. '(I want to eat) simmer.thing of soy-sauce tasting eggplants'

b. nasu=no [syooyu-azi=no [ni.mono]$_N$]$_{NP}$ (=ga kuitai.)

(71) a. syooyu-azi=no [nasu=no
soy.sauce-taste=GEN eggplant=GEN
[zikkuri nita]$_{NMLZ}$]$_{NP}$=no (=ga kuitai.)
carefully simmered=NMLZM (=NOM want.to.eat)
Lit. '(I want to eat) what (they) carefully simmered of soy-sauce tasting eggplants.'

b. nasu=no [syooyu-azi=no [zikkuri nita]$_{NMLZ}$]$_{NP}$=no (=ga kuitai.)

Let us now summarize our findings in this section by referring to the pertinent examples in the above discussion. The contrast between (54)–(55) and (56)–(57) shows that manner/resultative adverbs and time/place adverbs differ in their placement pattern. In particular, the former, which are semantically closely related to verbs, must be placed closer to verb-based nominalization heads, while the latter type of adverb has no such restriction. This is consistent with the fact seen in (48), namely, that an object noun phrase cannot be placed external to a nominalization. We have observed that genitive modifiers also divide into two types depending on their semantic relation to the head nominal. What we call descriptive genitives contribute to the semantics of head nominals greatly in distinguishing different kinds or types of objects, while role genitives contribute less in characterizing denoted objects. We found that here too descriptive genitives must be placed closer to the head nominal. In particular, descriptive genitives cannot be placed beyond role genitives (see (68b′), while genitives of the same kind can be placed next to each other without affecting the grammaticality of the possessive constructions; see (68a,a′) and (69a,b). The obvious generalization over the placement of adverbs and genitive modifiers is that the modifiers that have higher semantic relevance to the head nominal show greater physical proximity to the head than those of low relevance—clearly a case of iconicity.[27]

[27]Lack of space prevents us from going into this issue, but even in the combinations of the same type of genitives there is a preferred order. Thus, between (70a) and (70b) and between (71a) and (71b), the (a) versions are better. A similar pattern of preference is seen in the combinations of two role genitives, suggesting that some role genitives (e.g., a patientive genitive) are semantically closer to the head than others (e.g., an agentive genitive), as are some descriptive genitives to others (compare the ordering of the two role genitives in *Taroo=no*

The important point of these observations is that grammatical nominalizations and their genitive modifiers behave parallel to the modification patterns in possessive constructions with a noun head, confirming our claim that the genitive modifiers of grammatical nominalizations are the same type of syntactic objects as those of possessive constructions. The discussion above also makes it clear that the semantic relations of genitive modifiers to the grammatical-nominalization heads parallel those of the genitives of possessive constructions with lexical noun heads.

5.4. Semantics of Genitive Modifiers

The semantics of the genitives of possessive constructions is determined pragmatically in terms of the notion of relevance in conjunction with the nature of the lexical head. The entity most relevant to an action or event is an agent bringing it about. Accordingly, when the head of a possessive construction is an action nominal, the genitive receives an agentive interpretation, as in (72a) below.

(72) a. Hanako=no sippitu
Hanako=GEN writing
'Hanako's writing'

b. Hanako=no kaki.mono
Hanako=GEN write.thing
'Hanako's writings'

c. Hanako=no age.mono
Hanako=GEN fry.thing
'Hanako's fried food'

d. Hanako=no tuke.mono
Hanako=GEN pickle.thing
'Hanako's pickles'

Action nouns like *sippitu* 'writing' in (72a) above differ from those action nouns that may also denote resulting products, such as *kaki.mono* '(a) writing (s)' above. *Kaki.mono=o yomu* 'read a writing' is possible, but not *sippitu=o yomu.* When the head denotes a product, as in (72b–d), the geni-

---

Sooseki=no hon 'Taro's book by Sōseki' and *Sooseki=no Taroo=no hon*; the latter is ungrammatical for the intended meaning conveyed by the former). The iconicity principle also applies to the placement of adverbs in a sentence. In Japanese, time and place adverbs tend to occur in the anterior periphery in this order. A manner adverb occurs before an object noun phrase, while a resultative adverb occurs after an object noun phrase and immediately before a verb. The effect can be seen by trying to reorder the adverbs in *Kinoo daidokoro=de otoosan=ga sinkenni nasu=o yawarakaku nite ita* 'Father was seriously cooking eggplants soft in the kitchen yesterday'.

tive can be interpreted as its author. Depending on the degree of nouniness, these head nouns, in addition, allow an owner interpretation. *Kaki.mono* '(a) writing(s)', for example, is apparently low in nouniness, since (72b) does not allow a pure owner interpretation. (72b) cannot mean a writing done by someone else but that is owned by Hanako. On the other hand, the morphologically parallel expressions *age.mono* 'frying/fried food' and *tuke.mono* 'pickles' can be owned apart from the authors of these products. Semantic congruity permitting, product head nouns also permit appositive possessive interpretations, such that (72c) and (72d) could mean fried and pickled Hanako, respectively.

The nouniness degree of head nouns correlates with their verbal-use, as seen below, where the verbal expressions *X (=o) suru* 'do X' and *X=o tukuru* 'make X' distribute in a near-complementary manner.

(73) a. sippitu (=o) suru/*tukuru
writing (=ACC) do/make
'do/*make writing'

b. kaki.mono (=o) suru/*tukuru
write.thing (=ACC) do/make
'do/*make (a) writing'

c. agemono (=o) suru/tukuru
fry.thing (=ACC) do/make
'do/make (a) frying (food)'

d. tuke.mono (=o) *suru/tukuru
pickle.thing=(ACC) do/make
'*do/make pickles'

Notice that the distinctions and subtlety in the semantic interpretations of these genitives can be accounted for without recourse to the notion of grammatical subject. Indeed, they go well beyond a treatment such as that by Payne and Huddleston (2002), which attempts to describe the semantics of genitive modifiers in terms of the structural parallelism between possessive constructions and sentences (see Section 2).

Finally, the genitive modifiers of nominalizations receive semantic interpretations paralleling those of possessive constructions with a lexical noun head.

(74) a. Hanako=no [aruku]$_{NMLZ}$=no (=o mita.)
Hanako=GEN walk=NMLZM (=ACC saw)
'(I saw) Hanako walk.'

b. Hanako=no [zikkuri ageta/tuketa]$_{\text{NMLZ}}$=no (=o tabeta.)
Hanako=GEN carefully fried/pickled=NMLZM (=ACC ate)
'I ate what Hanako fried/pickled carefully.'

c. boku=no [nasu=no [ageta/tuketa]$_{\text{NMLZ}}$]$_{\text{NP}}$=no
I=GEN eggplant=GEN fried/pickled=NMLZM
(dare=ga tabeta?)
(who=NOM ate)
'(Who ate) my fried/pickled eggplants (?)'

Event nominalization heads, as in (74a), induce an agentive interpretation in the genitive modifier, just as action-noun heads of possessive constructions do; see (72a). Differences in the degree of nouniness are also observed among grammatical nominalizations such that those argument nominalizations that have general denotations, as in (74b), tend to permit only author interpretations, whereas appositive constructions with well-defined denotations, as in the internal possessive construction of (74c), more readily allow an owner interpretation. The former is less nominal than the latter, just as some action nouns are less nominal than others, as we saw above.

6. Conclusion

This paper has offered a simple and empirically testable research program dealing with genitive modifiers co-occurring with nominalizations. In determining the range of possible syntactic patterns and the semantics of these modifiers, one simply needs to examine the syntax and semantics of possessive constructions having the NP=GEN NP structure with a lexical noun head. Whatever mechanism is needed in accounting for these constructions extends to those containing nominalization structures. These constructions both contain nominal heads that denote thing-like entities, and we expect them to show a great deal of similarity in the properties of their external syntax.

Since the approach advocated here does not consider the genitive modifier of a nominalization as a grammatical subject, it opens up a simple and clear, but at the same time challenging, research methodology. Given a nominalization of any size and any kind, one needs to ask what kind of genitive modifier can co-occur with it, and what its semantics is; and then examine if it can be accounted for by the mechanisms needed in accounting for the facts about possessive constructions in the language. Challenges this approach poses are also those encountered in other approaches to nominalizations and include facts like why certain languages, e.g., Western Malayo-Polynesian languages, allow both agent and patient role genitives with grammatical nominalizations (e.g., the equivalent of *the killing of Jiji of Dodong* meaning 'the killing of Jiji by Dodong'), while many others, including Japanese and others examined in this paper, do not. Observe the contrast between *Koronbusu=no sin.tairiku=no hakken* 'the discovery of a new continent by Columbus', which is good with a noun head, and **Koronbusu=no sin.tairiku=no mituketa=no* 'that Columbus discovered a new continent', which is bad with a nominalization head. But challenges like this are brought out in clear form by our claim that the genitive modification of a nominalization is modeled after the modification patterns in simple possessive constructions.

References

Alvarez, A. 2012. Relative Clauses and Nominalizations in Yaqui. *Relative Clauses in Languages of the Americas: A Typological Overview*, ed. B. Comrie and Z. Estrada-Fernandez, 67–96. Amsterdam: John Benjamins.

Harada, S.-I. 1971. Ga-no Conversion and Idiolectal Variations in Japanese. *Gengo Kenkyu* 60:25–38.

Kinsui, S. 2011. *Shirīzu Nihongoshi 3: Bunpōshi*. Tokyo: Iwanami Shoten.

Kornfilt, J. 2007. Verbal and Nominalized Finite Clauses in Turkish. *Finiteness: Theoretical and Empirical Foundations*, ed. I. Nikolaeva, 307–332. Oxford: Oxford University Press.

Miyagawa, S. 2011. Genitive Subjects in Altaic and Specification of Phase. *Lingua* 121:1265–1282.

Nishiyama, Y. 2003. *Nihongo meishiku no imiron to goyōron*. Tokyo: Hitsuji Shobō.

Payne, J. and Huddleston, R. 2002. Nouns and Noun Phrases. *The Cambridge Grammar of the English Language*, ed. R. Huddleston and G. K. Pullum, 323–523. Cambridge: Cambridge University Press.

Qinggeltai. 2000. *Odo ʉye in monggol helen u jʉi*, əbər monggol un arad un heblel un horiya.

Shibatani, M. 2009. Elements of Complex Structures, Where Recursion Isn't: The Case of Relativization. *Syntactic Complexity*, ed. T. Givón and M. Shibatani, 163–198. Amsterdam: John Benjamins.

Shibatani, M. 2013. What Can Japanese Dialects Tell Us about the Function and Development of the Nominalization Particle 'no'. *Japanese/Korean Linguistics 20*, ed. B. Frellesvig and P. Sells, 421–444.

Index